12th Edition

DOLL VALUES

Linda Edward

Reverie

PUBLISHING COMPANY

ACKNOWLEDGMENTS

Thank you to the following collectors and auction houses for sharing their dolls and those of their friends for this edition of *Doll Values*: Alderfer Auctions, Virginia Aris, Carole Barboza, Sidney Bennett, Robin Burgess, Steve Carissimo, Ben Cassara, Ruth Cayton, Lucy DiTerlizzi, Shirley Fisher, Valerie Gomes, Jean Grout, Elaine Holda, Virginia Ann Hyerdahl, William J. Janack Estate Appraisals & Auctioneers, James D. Julia, Inc., Ann Lloyd, Judy Masters, McMasters-Harris Auctions, Ursula Mertz, Morphy Auctions, Dominique Perrin, Louise Scala, Skinner Inc., Patricia Snyder, Sweetbriar Auctions, Turn of the Century Antiques, Patricia Vaillancourt, Suzanne Vlach, Helen Welsh and Richard Withington Inc.

I would also like to thank every doll researcher and collector who has generously shared their dolls and knowledge through the many fine reference books, articles, seminars, special exhibits and doll club programs. Without this constant exchange of information we would all be searching in the dark for answers.

Finally, I must thank my husband, Al Edward, for his encouragement, support and belief in me and the work I pursue.

The values in this book should be used only as a guide. They are not intended to set prices, which vary from one section of the country to another and are affected by condition as well as by demand. Auction prices as well as dealer prices also vary greatly. Neither the author nor the publisher assumes responsibility for any decision or action taken by an individual on the basis of the information presented here, or for any losses that might be incurred as a result of consulting this guide.

First edition/First printing

To purchase additional copies of this book, please contact: Reverie Publishing Company, 414 North Centre Street, Cumberland, Maryland 21502. 888-721-4999.
www.reveriepublishing.com

Library of Congress Control Number: 2012936037
ISBN: 978-1-932485-61-5

On the front cover, clockwise from upper left: 10" Margie, Cameo, composition, $175, photo courtesy of Joan & Lynette Antique Dolls and Accessories • 16" Baby Pebbles toddler, Ideal, all vinyl, circa 1964-1966, $140, photo courtesy of The Museum Doll Shop • 17" Miss Dolly, Schoenhut, wood, decal eyes, $425, photo courtesy of Alderfer Auction Company, Inc. • 15" Chad Valley, designed by Mabel Lucy Atwell, felt, $650, photo courtesy of Richard Withington, Inc. • 20" mold 252 toddler, S.F.B.J., bisque, $7,000, photo courtesy of Richard Withington, Inc. • 23" china, brown eyes, circa 1850s, $1,700, photo courtesy of Richard Withington, Inc. • 16" Princess Elizabeth, Alexander Doll Company, open mouth, $650, photo courtesy of Morphy Auctions • 6" oriental, Simon &Halbig, all bisque, $775, photo courtesy of Morphy Auctions • 15" whistler, mold 8774, Gebruder Heubach, bisque, $1,200, photo courtesy of Richard Withington, Inc.
On the back cover: top, 16" poupeé peau, bisque, unmarked, $4,000, photo courtesy of Morphy Auctions • bottom, 18" Samantha, American Girl, Pleasant Company, vinyl, retired, $125, photo courtesy of Morphy Auctions.

Printed and bound in Korea

INTRODUCTION

This book is a tool for the collector, a place to start on a journey of study that can enrich a lifetime. The best piece of advice I ever received was "buy every doll reference book you can find." Each volume, old or new, contains some piece of information that will be of aid to the collector. Building a reference library of your own will pay you back many times over in the knowledge it will bring you, knowledge that will ultimately allow you to make better decisions when purchasing a doll for your own collection. In addition to building a reference library, I would also suggest that you take every opportunity to look at dolls wherever you go. Nothing beats first-hand examination. Visit every doll museum and special display you can find, go to shows and really look at the dolls that interest you most. Join a doll club to learn more and share your discoveries with others. For help in finding a doll club, contact the United Federation of Doll Clubs (UFDC), an international, charitable and educational organization dedicated to education, research, preservation and enjoyment of dolls. (See page 304 in the Collector's Resources section.) All of these experiences will put you in a better position to understand and evaluate a doll when you are considering a purchase.

The question this book strives to answer is, of course, how much is a doll worth? It is the question we contend with when buying dolls, inheriting dolls, insuring dolls and deciding to sell them. In the doll world there are basically two types of value: historic value and monetary value. Historic value speaks to how important an item is to us and to the world in general. Does an item teach us something about the past, is it significant to some particular event or person, does it have special sentimental value to us personally? This type of value, although important, is not always reflected in an item's monetary value. Monetary value, or market value, reflects how much you would have to pay to purchase a particular item at the present time. Market value is driven by demand for a particular item, combined with the current economic climate. In other words, the market value of any given doll will vary during differing economic conditions. Economic conditions make certain times good "selling times" (also known as a "seller's market") and other times good "buying times" (also known as a "buyer's market"). How can we characterize the current marketplace for dolls?

The Current Marketplace

In compiling the information for this edition some interesting trends emerged. It will be no surprise to anybody involved in the doll market that, while studying the price data collected over the past two years since the publication of the previous edition of this book, I have found that common examples of antique dolls have come down in value. Perhaps more interestingly, though, I have also found that the biggest difference in the sales of antique dolls has not necessarily been price but, rather, in the length of time it takes to sell a doll. While quick sales are being achieved by selling below value, many antique dolls are continuing to sell at fair prices—but it is taking much longer to connect these dolls with buyers. Collectors buying in a difficult economy are not only taking longer between purchases, they are also being more discriminating about the examples of any doll that they add to their collections. Now, more than ever, condition is playing a larger part in determining the monetary value of a doll.

This same trend is evidenced in an interesting phenomenon in the area of vintage dolls. Mint examples of dolls dating from about 1950 onward used to bring almost

Introduction

exactly double that of dolls in good, but not mint, condition. In the past two years this gap has widened; as fewer mint examples of dolls dating from 1930 - 1980 are discovered, the relative value of examples in truly mint condition has risen to as much as three times the value of those in good or played-with condition.

What does this mean to the buyer? It means pay accordingly. If a doll in less-than-perfect condition captures your heart, buy it—but do not pay a premium price for it. By the same token, do not expect to get a premium price when selling a doll in less-than-perfect condition. Buy the best example of a doll that your budget allows and enjoy having it in your collection! I hope this book will serve as a guide to helping collectors make wise purchasing decisions. The first step in making a wise purchase is knowing how to evaluate a doll.

Evaluating Dolls

When evaluating any doll there are several questions to ask. These involve identification, quality, originality, condition, rarity and value. Each component is important to the overall picture of any doll. All dolls should be thoroughly examined before making a purchase.

Identification: What is this doll made of and who made it? A doll is classified by the material from which its head is made, therefore a doll with a composition head and cloth body is considered a composition doll; a doll with a papier-mâché head and leather body is considered a papier-mâché doll, and so on. Markings are key to helping identify who made a doll. Many manufacturers marked their dolls on the back of the head or on the torso. Look for and learn about maker's marks. These are of invaluable aid in identifying a doll. An appendix of maker's initials and an appendix of known mold numbers are included in the Collector's Resources section of this book. To identify an unmarked doll, I can only repeat the advice offered above: to examine as many dolls and photographs of dolls as possible, in order to become as familiar as you can with dolls that interest you. Studying period advertising in old magazines and catalogs is also helpful. Familiarity and a practiced eye can help you recognize unmarked dolls—although some mysteries will undoubtedly always remain in the doll-collecting world.

Quality: As stated by author Patsy Moyer in the first edition of this book, "all dolls are not created equal." The quality of any model of doll made by any particular manufacturer can vary widely, depending on the conditions under which it was made. Remember: most of these dolls were produced in factories which, in many cases, turned out thousands of dolls a year. How worn was the mold when this doll was poured, what weather conditions affected the materials it was made from, how tired was the worker who cleaned or painted a particular doll? If you line up six AM 390s you will be looking at six different degrees of quality of finish. When preparing to make a purchase, consider each example of a doll carefully from the standpoint of quality. A sharply molded, evenly textured, well-painted doll will always be of more value than an example of the same doll with blurry molding, uneven texture or painting of poor quality.

Originality: Does the doll have the eyes, wig, body parts and clothing with which it left the factory? Each of these parts adds value to the doll; a doll on an incorrect body or with replaced clothing or wigs should not bring the same amount in the marketplace as an example in all-original condition.

4

Introduction

Condition: Has the doll been damaged or repaired? Is its finish worn down, or is its clothing tattered or torn? Check carefully for damage, wear and repair. In most cases, a damaged or repaired doll is worth less than a perfect example.

Rarity: How unusual is this doll? How many were made and how many have survived? How difficult would it be to find another example of this doll? Rarity is perhaps one of the most important aspects of doll evaluation. Sometimes rarity can cause us to forgive problems of originality or condition that, in a more common doll, would deter us from adding it to our collection.

Value: As discussed above, value includes monetary and historic value. Value takes into account all of the components already discussed and combines them with somewhat more elusive components such as collector demand and trends. At various points in time collectors favor certain dolls. Every generation of collectors tends to start out collecting the dolls they had or desired as children. A good example of this can be seen in the value of the Bye-lo baby from the 1920s. In the 1950s and 1960s many adult collectors eagerly sought these dolls, and they climbed to command comparatively high prices. Over the past twenty years the value of the Bye-lo has changed very little compared to other antique dolls because collector demand for it has quieted down.

How to Use This Book

The goal of this book is to assist you in figuring out the current market value of a doll you are interested in buying or selling. Unless otherwise noted, the values listed represent dolls in good overall condition with original or appropriate clothing. When looking at the values presented here, gauge the doll you are considering accordingly. Assign lower values to dolls that do not meet the standards described in these pages. This is especially important in judging vintage and contemporary dolls, which must be in perfect, completely original condition with appropriate hang tags to attain the values listed in this guide. For example, an all original #3 Barbie in good condition will bring approximately half to one-third of the price of the same doll mint-in-box.

This book is organized alphabetically by the manufacturer's name or by general type. The general-type headings include dolls made of like materials. Under these headings you will find dolls made by small companies, or ones about which little is known, as well as unmarked, and as yet, un-attributable, dolls. Most dolls are marked, however, in some way that indicates their maker, and wherever possible these markings have been included for reference.

You will notice that this book is not divided into "antique" and "modern" sections as some other books are. The reason for this decision is threefold: first, the line between antique and modern is not as clear cut in doll collecting as it is in other areas. With furniture, for instance, a piece must be at least one hundred years old to be considered antique, whereas with cars, a twenty-five-year-old vehicle is considered antique. In doll collecting the line is blurry, although it generally falls somewhere in the neighborhood of seventy-five years. Dolls thirty to seventy-five years old are most often referred to as "vintage" and dolls produced within the past thirty or so years may be referred to as "collectible" or "contemporary." Second, many manufacturers were in business for such long periods of time that they produced dolls now considered antique as well as dolls that fall into the vintage and contemporary categories. Third, I believe that by not creating divisions between dolls of different ages we can see a more complete picture of

Introduction

the doll world, and promote a better understanding of the history of the dolls we love and of our fellow collectors.

The values listed in this book are compiled from several sources including auction prices, online auction prices, dealer asking prices, dealer prices realized, as well as other sources. (I have also become the nosiest person you will meet, asking everyone I talk dolls with: "what did you pay for that?") I consult with collectors and dealers who specialize in niche areas of doll collecting to get their "take" on how things are moving in their particular specialty. I then use a condition-rating system that allows me to interpret the data at the end of the two-year cycle between editions of this book to average the current market value. Although the collecting world is much more global now than it was even a few years ago, there are still some regional differences in value, which are generated by collector interest and doll availability in certain areas. These differences are also taken into account in ascertaining value.

I cannot emphasize strongly enough that this book is meant as a guide, and not as the "definitive" word on doll value. It is one more tool for a collector to use in the decision-making process of buying or selling a doll. Ultimately a doll is worth whatever a particular collector wishes to pay for it.

In the final analysis, study, evaluation and value, although important, are not the bottom line in doll collecting. The golden rule of collecting applies to dolls as much as to anything else: buy what you love. In other words, we must above all buy dolls that mean something to us, dolls that enrich our collections and our lives.

CODES

GREEN UPPERCASE	**Main Category/Maker's Name or Doll Type** For example: **ADVERTISING DOLLS**
Red	**First subcategory, usually the doll's name or material or type** For example: **Gerber Baby**
Blue Italics	**Second subcategory** For example: *1979 - 1985*
Black	**Third subcategory** For example: Talker

ADVERTISING DOLLS

Dolls of various materials, made by a variety of manufacturers, to promote commercial brands or specific products. Dolls in good condition with original clothing and accessories.

Aunt Jemima, cloth, Aunt Jemima, Uncle Moses, Diana and Wade Davis
16" ....$95 - 105

Blue Bonnet, 1986, for Nabisco, cloth doll by Dakin
10" ....$8 - 12

Babbit Cleanser Boy, composition head, cloth body, compo lower arms and lower legs with molded white boots
15" ....$800 - 900

Bonnie Breck, 1971, made in Hong Kong, vinyl head, plastic body
9" ....$45 - 55

Campbell Kids, 1910 on, based on Grace Drayton's drawings
Composition - painted and molded hair, marked: "EIH © 1910"; cloth label on sleeve reads: "The Campbell Kids// Trademark by //Joseph Campbell// Mfg. by E.I. Horsman Co."
10" - 11" ....$200 - 250
15" - 16" ....300 - 350
Vinyl - painted and molded hair, 1960s - 1970s, unmarked
10" - 11" ....pair $30 - 50

Clicquot Club Eskimo, 1939, Reliable Doll Co, composition, painted eyes, plush snowsuit
14" ....$225 - 275

Colgate Fab Soap Princess Doll, circa 1951
5½" ....$12 - 18

Cream of Wheat, Rastus, printed cloth doll
16" ....$90 - 100

Gerber Baby, 1936 to present. An advertising and trademark doll for Gerber Products, a baby-food manufacturer in Fremont, Michigan. Allow more for black or special sets with accessories
1936, cloth one-piece doll, printed girl or boy, holds can
8" ....$300 - 375
1955 - 1958, Sun Rubber Company, designed by Bernard Lipfert, vinyl
12" - 18" ....$100 - 150
1965, Arrow Rubber and Plastic Co., vinyl
14" ....$125 - 150
1972 - 1973, Amsco, Milton Bradley, vinyl
10" ....$55 - 70
14" - 18" ....$35 - 45
1979 - 1985, Atlanta Novelty, vinyl, flirty eyes, cloth body
17" ....$50 - 65
black version ....$55 - 70
Talker
17" ....$80 - 100
Collector Doll, christening gown, basket
12" ....$75 - 90
Porcelain, limited edition
17" ....$275 - 325
1989 - 1992, Lucky Ltd., vinyl

10½" Campbell Kids Bicentennial dolls, vinyl: $50. **Photo courtesy of Morphy Auctions.**

9" Bonnie Breck for Breck Shampoo, vinyl: $55. **Photo courtesy of Pieces of Old.**

6"..............................$12 - 18
11"..............................$35 - 40
14 - 16" ....$35 - 40
1994 - 1996, Toy Biz, Inc., vinyl
8"..............................$15 - 20
15"..............................$25 - 30
Battery operated
12" - 13" ....$25 - 30
Talker
14"..............................$35 - 40
17"..............................$45 - 50
Green Giant, Sprout, 1973
10½" ....$18 - 25
Hotpoint Devil, 1930s, designed by
Josef Kallus, composition head, wood
segmented body
16"..............................$550 - 600
Kellogg's cereals
Corn Flakes Red Riding Hood, printed cloth
13½" ....$125 - 150
Goldilocks and Three Bears, set of four,
printed cloth
12" - 15"........................$180 - 215
Korn Krisp cereal
Miss Korn-Krisp, circa 1900, cloth
marked body
24"..............................$180 - 205
Little Debbie, 1972, Horsman,
all vinyl with rooted hair
11" ....$20 - 28
Miss Minute Maid, 1950s, hard-plastic
doll, Virga or Fortune, wigged, sleep eyes
10"..............................$30 - 38
Mr. Peanut, 1940s, wood segmented body
9"..............................$225 - 275
Prince Macaroni, mail-in premium
dolls, vinyl, dressed in costumes from
the provinces of Italy
6¼" .... $15 - 20
Sunbeam Bread
Miss Sunbeam, Horsman, all vinyl,
rooted hair
14"..............................$30 - 35
Swiss Miss Hot Chocolate, 1977, cloth
doll, painted features, yarn hair
16"..............................$8 - $10
"The Selling Fool," 1926, Cameo, wood

segmented body, hat represents radio
tube, composition advertising doll for
RCA Radiotrons
16"..............................$600 - 1,000
Too few in database for a reliable range
Uneeda Biscuit Boy, 1914, Ideal
15"..............................$425 - 475
ZuZu, 1916, composition doll, Ideal,
to advertise ginger snaps made by the
National Biscuit Co.
14"..............................$225 - 275

ALABAMA BABY

1900 - 1925, Roanoke, Alabama. Ella Gauntt
Smith, cloth-over-plaster doll, stitched-on
skull cap, painted features. Tab-jointed at
shoulders and hips, painted feet may be
bare with stitched toes or have shoes
painted in pink, blue, black, brown or
yellow.
Earlier model with applied ears
11" - 14"......................$1,800 - 2,400
18" - 24" ....$2,600 - 3,400
Wigged
24" ....$2,800 - 3,300
Black
14" - 18"......................$5,500 - 6,000
20" - 22"......................$6,200 - 6,800
Later model with molded ears, bobbed
hairstyle
14" - 16"......................$1,800 - 1,900
18" - 22"......................$1,900 - 2,100
Wigged
30" $1,000
Black
14" - 18"......................$2,800 - 3,000
20" - 22" ....$3,800 - 5,800

13" Alabama
Baby, Ella Smith,
cloth: $1,800.
**Photo courtesy of
Richard
Withington, Inc.**

ALEXANDER DOLL COMPANY

1923 to present, New York City. In 1923, in New York City, Beatrice Alexander, together with her sisters, began the Alexander Doll Company. They began using the "Madame Alexander" trademark in 1928. Beatrice Alexander Behrman became a legend in the doll world with her long reign as head of the Alexander Doll Company. Alexander made cloth, composition and wooden dolls, and eventually made the transition to hard plastic and vinyl. Dolls are listed by subcategories of the material of which the head is made. With Madame Alexander dolls, especially those made from 1950 on, condition as it relates to value is extremely important. **For the values listed here the doll must be in perfect condition with complete original clothing and tags. Dolls with incomplete or soiled costumes will bring one fourth to one third of the value of perfect examples.** Unusual dolls with presentation cases, trousseaux, or rare costumes may bring much more.

Cloth, 1930 - 1950 on
All-cloth head and body, mohair wig, flat or molded mask face, painted side-glancing eyes
Storybook characters such as Little Women, Dickens characters, Edith and others
16".....................................$400 - 450

18 "Funny, Alexander Doll Company, cloth: $90.
Photo courtesy of Alderfer Auction Company, Inc.

14" Dionne quintuplet, Alexander Doll Company, toddler, worn dress, composition: $325.
Photo courtesy of Morphy Auctions.

Alice in Wonderland
Flat face ....$800 - 900
Mask face
14" - 16"..........................$700 - 800
Animals, such as March Hare, etc.
15" - 16"...........................$300 - 600
Baby
13".................................$475 - 525
17".................................$600 - 650
24".................................$675 - 725
Bobby Q, 1940 - 1942
16"................................$500 - 600
Funny, 1963 - 1977
18".................................$80 - 100
Little Shaver, 1940 - 1944, yarn hair
7"..................................$425 - 500
10"................................$450 - 500
15"................................$575 - 675
22"................................$700 - 800
Muffin, circa 1963 - 1977
14"..................................$65 - 75
So Lite Baby or Toddler, 1930s - 1940s
20"................................$225 - 325
Suzie Q, 1940 - 1942
16"................................$750 - 850
Teeny Twinkle, 1946, disc floating eyes
16" ....$475 - 550
Dionne Quintuplets, various materials
Cloth, 1935 - 1936
16"................................$850 - 950
24"............................$1,600 - 1,800
Composition, 1935 - 1945, all composition, swivel head, jointed toddler or baby body, molded and painted hair or wigged, sleep or painted eyes. Outfit

Alexander Doll Company

13" Alice in Wonderland, Alexander Doll Company, composition: $900.
Photo courtesy of Richard Withington, Inc.

colors: Annette, yellow; Cecile, green; Emilie, lavender; Marie, blue; Yvonne, pink. Allow more for extra accessories or in layette

Baby
    8".....................................$225 - 225
    Complete set,
    dolls only ....$1,400 - 1,500
    Complete set with wooden nursery
    furniture ....$1,600 - 2,000
    Set in ferris wheel ....sold at
                auction for $5,900

Toddler
    8"...................................$225 - 275
    Complete set..............$1,300 - 1,500
    11"..................................$350 - 400
    Complete set ....$2,000 - 2,200
    14"..................................$450 - 500
    Complete set ....$2,700 - 3,000
    16"..................................$600 - 650
    Complete set ....$3,600 - 4,000
    20"..................................$600 - 675
    Complete set ....$3,300 - 4,000
    On cloth body
    22"..................................$650 - 750
    Complete set ....$3,400 - 3,700

Vinyl, 8", in carousel, 1998
    75th anniversary set ....$350 - 400

Dr. Dafoe, 1937 - 1939
    14" ....$1,250 - 1,350

Nurse
    13" - 15" ....$900 - 975

Composition, 1930 - 1950
Babies, cloth body, sleep eyes, dolls such as Baby Genius, Butch, Baby McGuffy, Pinky and others, marked: "Alexander"

10

    10" - 12"..........................$250 - 300
    14" - 16"..........................$200 - 275
    18" - 20" ....$300 - 350

Baby Jane, 1935
    16" ....$900 - 1,100

Child
Alice in Wonderland, 1930s, swivel waist
    7" - 9".............................$375 - 425
    11" - 14"..........................$750 - 900
    18" - 21".....................$1,000 - 1,200

Babs Skater, 1948, clover tag, marked on head: "ALEX"
    18"............................$1,200 - 1,350

Carmen (Miranda), 1942, black hair
    9" - 11"...........................$300 - 425
    14" - 17"..........................$650 - 750
    21" ....$1,400 - 1,800

Fairy Queen, circa 1939 - 1946, clover wrist tag, tagged gown
    15" - 18" ....$500 - 600
    21" - 22"..........................$750 - 800

Flora McFlimsey, 1938, freckles, marked: "Princess Elizabeth"
    14" - 17"..........................$500 - 650
    22"..................................$750 - 800

Jane Withers, 1937 - 1939, green sleep eyes, open mouth, brown mohair wig
    12" - 13½"..................$1,200 - 1,500
    15" - 17" ....$1,100 - 1,300
    18" - 19".....................$1,500 - 1,600
    20" - 22" ....$1,700 - 1,800

Jeannie Walker, tagged dress, closed mouth, mohair wig
    13" - 14"..........................$675 - 750
    18" ....$800 - 1,000

Karen Ballerina, blue sleep eyes, closed mouth, head marked: "Alexander"
    15" ....$950 - 1,000
    18" ....$1,100 - 1,300

Kate Greenaway, yellow wig, marked "Princess Elizabeth"
    13" - 15" ....$750 - 800
    18"..................................$850 - 900
    24" ....$950 - 1,050

Little Betty, 1939 - 1943, side-glancing painted eyes
    9" - 11"...........................$250 - 375

Alexander Doll Company

Little Colonel
  Closed mouth
    11" - 15".............................$625 - 850
  Open mouth
    14" - 17"............................$650 - 700
    23" - 26" ....$850 - 1,000
Little Genius, blue sleep eyes, cloth
body, closed mouth, clover tag
    12" - 14"............................$225 - 250
    16" - 20"............................$275 - 300
Little Women, Meg, Jo, Amy, Beth
    7" $300
    9" $350
    13" - 15"............................$350 - 375
Madelaine DuBain, 1937 - 1944
    14" ....$550 - 600
    17" ....$650 - 700
Marcella, 1936, open mouth, wig,
sleep eyes
    17" - 24"............................$650 - 900
Margaret O'Brien, 1946 - 1948
    14" - 17".............................$650 - 750
    19" - 24" ....$800 - 1,000
McGuffey Ana, 1935 - 1937, sleep eyes,
open mouth, tagged dress
    11" - 13"............................$575 - 650
    14" - 16"............................$675 - 750
    17" - 20"............................$800 - 850
    21" - 25" ....$900 - 1,000
    28" ....$1,100 - 1,400
  Painted eyes
    9"....................................$250 - 300
Marionettes by Tony Sarg
    12"...................................$450 - 550
Portraits, 1941 - 1947, Wendy Ann face
    20" - 22" ....$2,000 - 4,000

14" Sonja Henie,
Alexander Doll
Company,
composition: $700.
**Photo courtesy
of Richard
Withington, Inc.**

16" Princess
Elizabeth,
Alexander Doll
Company,
composition, open
mouth: $650.
**Photo courtesy of
Morphy Auctions.**

Princess Elizabeth, 1937 - 1941
  Closed mouth
    13"...................................$450 - 500
  Open mouth
    13" - 16"............................$600 - 700
    18" - 24"............................$700 - 800
    28" ....$900 - 1,000
Scarlett, 1937 - 1946, add more for rare
costume
    11"...................................$500 - 600
    14"...................................$500 - 700
    18" ....$700 - 1,000
    21"...............................$1,200 - 1,400
Snow White, 1939 - 1942, marked:
"Princess Elizabeth"
    13"...................................$450 - 500
    16" - 18"............................$625 - 700
Sonja Henie, 1939 - 1942, open mouth,
sleep eyes
    13" - 15" ....$800 - 900
    14" with trunk/trousseau set
    sold at auction $1,900
    17" - 18" ....$950 -1,100
    20" - 23"......................$1,100 - 1,500
Three Little Pigs, 1938 - 1939
    12" ....each $750 - 850
    Complete set ....$2,600 - 3,000
Tiny Betty, 1934 - 1943, side-glancing
painted eyes, elaborate or rare costumes
bring high end of range
    7"....................................$200 - 400
W.A.A.C. (Army), W.A.A.F. (Air Force),
W.A.V.E. (Navy), circa 1943 - 1944
    14"...................................$700 - 750
Wendy Ann, 1935 - 1948, allow more
for special outfit

11" - 15"..........................$475 - 600
17" - 21"..........................$600 - 800
Painted eyes
9"....................................$250 - 325
Swivel waist, molded hair or wig
14"...................................$400 - 450
Hard Plastic and Vinyl, 1948 on. Value
can double for MIB
Alexander-kins, 7½" - 8", 1953 on
1953, straight leg nonwalker
   Nude.............................$200 - 275
   Dressed..........................$400 - 550
1954 - 1955, 7½" - 8", straight-leg walker
   Nude..............................$100 - 175
   Dressed..........................$300 - 600
1956 - 1965, bent-knee walker, after
1963 marked: "Alex"
   Nude..............................$125 - 150
   Dressed..........................$250 - 450
1956
1965 - 1972, bent-knee nonwalker, value
depends on costume
   Nude...............................$75 - 95
   Dressed..........................$200 - 450
1973 - 1976, straight leg nonwalker,
value depends on costume, back of torso
marked: "Alex"
   Dressed.............................$40 - 100
1976 - 1994, straight leg nonwalker, back
of torso marked: "Alexander"
   Dressed.............................$20 - 55
Babies
Baby Brother or Sister, 1977 - 1982, vinyl
   14"......................................$65 - 80

11" Three Little Pigs, Alexander Doll Company, composition: set $2,800. **Photo courtesy of Alderfer Auction Company, Inc.**

14" Bride, Alexander Doll Company, composition, Wendy Ann face: $600. **Photo courtesy of Richard Withington, Inc.**

Baby Ellen, 1965 - 1972, vinyl, rigid
vinyl body, marked: "Alexander 1965"
   14"....................................$100 - 125
Baby Genius, 1956 - 1962, hard plastic
and vinyl, value depends on costume
   8"......................................$175 - 250
Baby McGuffy, 1974 - 1976, vinyl, cloth
body
   21"...$100
Bonnie, 1954 - 1955, vinyl
   19"......................................$55 - 65
Fisher Quints, 1964, vinyl
   8" set...............................$200 - 250
Happy, 1970 only, vinyl
   20"......................................$65 - 100
Hello Baby, 1962 only
   22"....................................$150 - 175
Honeybun, 1951, vinyl
   18" - 19"..........................$100 - 125
Huggums
   Big, 1963 - 1979
      25"................................$65 - 85
   Little, rooted hair, 1963 - 1988
      12"................................$40 - 50
Kathy Baby, 1954 - 1956, vinyl
   13" - 15"............................$60 - 75
   20" - 22".............................$80 - 100
Kathy Cry, 1957 - 1958, vinyl, nurser
   11" - 15"............................$65 - 95
   18" - 25"..........................$110 - 130
Kitten, 1961, vinyl, cloth body
   24"....................................$200 - 225
1962 - 1963, vinyl, cloth body
   14" - 18"............................$50 - 75

Alexander Doll Company

Little Angel, 1950 - 1957, vinyl
head, latex body
9".....................................$100 - 125
Little Bitsey, 1967 - 1968, all-vinyl
9".....................................$130 - 150
Littlest Kitten, vinyl
8".....................................$65 - 85
Lively Kitten, 1962, vinyl, cloth body,
knob makes head and limbs move
14"....................................$225 - 275
Mary Cassatt, 1969 - 1970, vinyl
14"....................................$75 - 100
20"....................................$150 - 200
Pussy Cat, 1965 - 1985, vinyl
14"....................................$30 - 50
1989 - 1993, vinyl
18"....................................$65 - 80
Black, 1970 - 1976
14"....................................$60 - 150
Sweet Tears, 1965 - 1974
9"....................................$35 - 50
14"....................................$55 - 60
14" With layette,
1965 - 1973.....................$150 - 175
Victoria, baby, 1967 - 1989
20"....................................$45 - 60
Bible Character Dolls, 1954 only, hard
plastic, original box looks like Bible
8"....................................$8,500+
Cissette, 1957 on 10", hard-plastic head,
synthetic wig, pierced ears, closed
mouth, seven-piece adult body, jointed
elbows and knees, high-heeled feet,
mold later used for other dolls. No

15" Karen Ballerina, Alexander Doll Company, composition, circa 1946: $1,000. **Photo courtesy of Alderfer Auction Company, Inc.**

14" Meg and Amy (Little Women), Alexander Doll Company, hard plastic, circa 1948-1956: each $300. **Photo courtesy of Alderfer Auction Company, Inc.**

marks on body; clothes tagged
"Cissette." Dolls listed are in good
condition with original clothing; value
can double for MIB
Basic doll
In undergarments............$150 - 175
In street dress..................$450 - 550
Beauty Queen in bathing suit
w/sash........sold at auction for $400
In formal wear..............$450 - 1,000
Gibson Girl, 1962 - 1963......$550 - 650
Jacqueline, 1961 - 1962..........$450 - 500
Margot, 1961............................$500 - 600
Portrette, 1968 - 1973............$375 - 450
Queen, 1957 - 1958................$350 - 450
Sleeping Beauty, 1959, authorized
Disney, blue gown..................$275 - 325
Tinkerbelle, 1969.................$150 - 200
Cissy
1955 - 1959, 20", hard plastic, vinyl
arms, jointed elbows and knees, high-
heeled feet.No marks on body; clothes
tagged "Cissy." Dolls listed are in good
condition with original clothing; value
can double for MIB
Basic doll
In undergarments............$400 - 500
In street dress.............$500 - 1,000
In formal wear.............$800 - 2,000
Model 2174, circa 1957, gown,
MIB........sold at auction for $5,660
21" vinyl models made from 1996
on 85th anniversary
Cissy, 2008......................$450 - 500

Alexander Doll Company

8" Wendy Bride, Alexander Doll Company, hard plastic, bent-knee walker, circa 1966-1968: $250. **Photo courtesy of American Beauty Dolls.**

Yardley, 2001 ....$350 - 450
Alice in Wonderland, 1949 - 1952,
hard plastic, Margaret and/or Maggie
    14"...................$350 - 400
    15", 18", 23" ....$400 - 600
    1996, vinyl
    14" ....$35 - 40
American Girl, 1962 - 1963, #388,
seven-piece walker body, became
McGuffey Ana in 1964 - 1965
    8"...................$130 - 160
Annabelle, 1951 - 1952, Maggie head
    14" ....$600 - 700
    20" - 23" ....$800 - 1,000
Anne of Green Gables, 1993, in
Concert Dress
    8"...................$65 - 80
Babs Skater, 1948 - 1950, hard plastic,
Margaret
    15"...................$500 - 800
    17" - 18" ....$700 - 1,000
Bill/Billy, 1960, seven-piece walker body
    8"...................$325 - 375
Binnie Walker, 1954 - 1955, Cissy face,
value varies depending on elaborateness
of costume
    15"...................$300 - 400
    18"...................$500 - 575
    25"...................$550 - 625
Brenda Starr, 1964 only, 12", hard
plastic, vinyl arms, red wig
    In street dress ....$65 - 150
    In formal wear ....$100 - 200
Bunny, 1962 only
    18" ....$175 - 225

Caroline, 1961, #131, vinyl
    15"...................$150 - 200
Chatterbox, 1961, vinyl and plastic,
talker
    24"...................$75 - 100
Cinderella, 1950 - 1951, Mary Ann face,
vinyl
    Ballgown
    14"...................$425 - 500
    18"...................$500 - 600
    Poor Cinderella, gray dress,
    original broom
    14"...................$325 - 400
    1967 - 1992, Mary Ann face,
    plastic and vinyl
    14" ....$20 - 45
Cowgirl and Cowboy, 1967 - 1970,
hard plastic, jointed knees
    8"...................$175 - 225
Cynthia, 1952 only, hard plastic
    15"...................$375 - 450
    18"...................$400 - 500
    23"...................$600 - 700
Easter Doll, 1968, vinyl
    14"...................$200 - 350
Edith, The Lonely Doll, 1958 - 1959,
vinyl head, hard-plastic body
    8"...................$350 - 400
    16"...................$150 - 200
    22"...................$175 - 225
    2003 - 2004, vinyl, with 3" Mr. Bear
    8"...................$75 - 80

7" Fisher Quintuplets, Alexander Doll Company, vinyl: set $250. **Photo courtesy of Alderfer Auction Company, Inc.**

10" Margo, Alexander Doll Company, hard plastic: $550.
Photo courtesy of Richard Withington, Inc.

Elise
1957 - 1964, 16½", hard plastic, vinyl arms, jointed ankles and knees
In street dress ....$200 - 450
Ballerina ....$175 - 225
In formalwear ....$500 - 900
1963 only, 18", hard plastic, vinyl arms, jointed ankles and knees
Bouffant hairstyle ....$150 - 225
1966 - 1972, 17", hard plastic, one-piece
vinyl arms, jointed ankles and knees
Street dress ....$250 - 275
1966 - 1991, Ballerina........$75 - 100
1997, vinyl
16" ....$95 - 125
Fairy Queen, 1948 - 1950, Margaret face
14½" ....$350 - 400
Fashions of a Century, 1954 - 1955, 14" - 18", Margaret face, hard plastic ....$1,200 - 1,600
First Ladies, 1976 - 1990
Set 1
1976 - 1978 ....each $70 - 90
Set 2
1979 - 1981 ....each $50 - 70
Set 3
1982 - 1984..................each $50 - 60
Set 4
1985 - 1987..................each $35 - 45
Set 5
1988 ....each $30 - 40
Set 6
1989 - 1990..................each $40 - 55

Flower Girl, 1954, hard plastic, Margaret
15" ....$375 - 425
Glamour Girl Series, 1953 only, hard plastic, Margaret head, auburn wig, straight-leg walker
18" ....$750 - 900
Godey Bride, 1950 - 1951, Margaret, hard plastic
14" ....$1,000 - 1,200
18" ....$1,300 - 1,500
Godey Lady, 1950 - 1951, Margaret, hard plastic
14" ....$1,400 - 1,600
Godey Groom, 1950 - 1951, Margaret, hard plastic
14" ....$500 - 600
18" ....$600 - 700
Gold Rush, 1963 only, hard plastic, Cissette
10" ....$700 - 800
Grandma Jane, 1970 - 1972, #1420, Mary Ann, vinyl body
14" ....$200 - 225
Groom,
1949 - 1951, Margaret, hard plastic
14" - 16" ....$750 - 850
1953 - 1955, Wendy Ann, hard plastic
7½" ....$525 - 575
Jacqueline, 1961 - 1962, 21", hard plastic, vinyl arms
Street dress ....$700 - 900
Formal wear ....$750 - 950
Riding habit ....$825 - 875
Janie, 1964 - 1966, #1156, toddler, vinyl head, hard-plastic body, rooted hair

21" Cissy, Alexander Doll Company, hard plastic, circa 1955-1956: $2,000.
Photo courtesy of American Beauty Dolls.

12" ....$175 - 225
Jenny Lind and Listening Cat, 1970 - 1971
14" ....$230 - 260
Joanie Nurse, 1960,
36" ....$300 - 350
Kathryn Grayson, early 1950s,
hard plastic
21" ....sold at auction for $2,700
Kelly
1959 only, hard plastic, Lissy face
12" ....$400 - 500
1958 - 1959, hard plastic, Marybel face
15" - 16" ....$225 - 300
1958
18" ....$350 - 375
1958 - 1959
22" ....$300 - 400
Leslie (black Polly), 1965 - 1971, 17",
vinyl head, hard-plastic body, vinyl
limbs, rooted hair
Ballerina ....$375 - 400
In formal..........................$300 - 350
Lissy, hard plastic, wigged
1956 - 1958, 12", elbow and
knee joints
In undies ....$250 - 300
Street dress ....$400 - 500
Formal ....$600 - 700
1959 - 1967, as above but no elbow
or knee joints
Street dress ....$150 - 225
2006, vinyl
12" ....$60 - 100
Little Shaver, 1963 - 1965, painted eyes,
vinyl body

14" Babs skater, Alexander Doll Company, hard plastic: $700. **Photo courtesy of Richard Withington, Inc.**

12" Brenda Starr, Alexander Doll Company, vinyl, MIB: $300. **Photo courtesy of American Beauty Dolls.**

12" ....$200 - 250
Little Women,
1947 - 1956, Meg, Jo, Amy, Beth,
plus Marmee—Margaret and
Maggie faces
14" - 15" .... each $300 - 450
1955, Meg, Jo, Amy, Beth, plus
Marmee—Wendy Ann, straight-leg
walker
8" ....each $175 - 200
1956 - 1959, Wendy Ann, bent-knee
walker
8" ....each $125 - 150
1974 - 1992, straight leg, #411 - #415
8" ....each $45 - 55
1957 - 1958, Lissy, jointed elbows
and knees
12" ....$300 - 400
1959 - 1968, Lissy, one-piece arms
and legs
12" ....$75 - 120
1983 - 1989, Nancy Drew face
12" ....each $40 - 50
Madeline, 1961, vinyl, multiple joints
18" ....$450 - 600
Maggie Mixup, 1960 - 1961, hard plastic,
freckles, value depends on costume
8" ....$190 - 500
Maggie Teenager, 1951 - 1953, hard
plastic, value depends on costume
15" - 18" ....$300 - 350
Maggie, hard plastic
1948 - 1954
20" - 21"..........................$350 - 400
1949 - 1952
22" - 23" ....$400 - 450

Alexander Doll Company

1949 - 1953
17" - 18" ....$450 - 550
1949 - 1953, walker
15" - 18"...........................$325 - 375
Margaret O'Brien, 1949 - 1951,
hard plastic
14" ....$750 - 1,000
18" - 21" ....$600 - 1,100
Margot Ballerina, 1951 - 1953,
Margaret and Maggie, dressed in
various colored outfits
15" - 18" ....$650 - 850
Marlo Thomas as "That Girl," 1967
only, Polly face, vinyl
17"...................................$300 - 400
Mary Ellen, 1954 only, rigid vinyl walker
31"...................................$625 - 675
Mary Ellen Playmate, 1965 only,
bendable vinyl body
17"...................................$300 - 350
Mary Martin, 1948 - 1952, South Pacific
character Nell, two-piece sailor outfit,
hard plastic
14" - 17" ....$900 - 1,000
Marybel, "The Doll That Gets Well,"
1959 - 1965, rigid vinyl, in case with
accessories
16"...................................$120 - 150
1998
75th anniversary re-issue....$90 - 100
McGuffey Ana

1948 - 1950, hard plastic, Margaret
14"...........................$1,000 - 1,200
18" ....$950 - 1,050
21"...........................$1,200 - 1,400
1956 only, hard plastic, #616,
Wendy Ann face
8" ....$675 - 750
1963 only, hard plastic, Lissy face,
rare
1977 - 1986, vinyl, Mary Ann face
14" ....$35 - 45
Melanie, 1979 - 1980, dotted-swiss
gown with pink trim
21" ....$130 - 150
Melinda, 1962 - 1963, plastic/vinyl,
cotton dress
14" - 22"...........................$250 - 275
Miss Flora McFlimsey, 1953 only,
vinyl head, inset eyes
15"...................................$725 - 800
Muffin, 1989 - 1990, Janie face, vinyl
12".......................................$25 - 35
Nancy Drew, 1967 only, vinyl body,
Literature Series
12"...................................$250 - 300
Nina Ballerina, 1949 - 1951, Margaret
head, clover wrist tag
15"...................................$300 - 400
19"...................................$450 - 700
21" - 23" ....$700 - 900
Pamela, 1962 - 1863, Lissy face,
changeable wigs
12" in box with
wardrobe ....$900 - 1,100
Peter Pan, 1953 - 1954, Margaret

Alexander Doll Company

17" Polly, Alexander Doll Company, vinyl, circa 1965: $350.
Photo courtesy of American Beauty Dolls.

15" ....$600 - 800
1969, 14" Wendy (Mary Ann head)
12" Peter, Michael (Jamie head)
10" Tinkerbelle (Cissette head)
Peter, Wendy ....$200 - 225
Michael...........................$225 - 250
Tinkerbelle ....$300 - 350
Set of four $1,000
Piper Laurie early 1950s , hard plastic
21" ....sold at auction for $2,000
Polly
   1965 only, vinyl and plastic
   17" ....$300 - 350
Polly Pigtails, 1949 -1951, hard plastic
   17" ....$450 - 500
Pollyanna
   1960 - 1961, vinyl, Marybel face
   16" ....$400 - 450
   1987 - 1988, Mary Ann face
   14" ....$45 - 55
   2000 - 2001, Wendy face
   8" ....$25 - 35
Portraits, 1960 on, Jacqueline face, 21",
early dolls have jointed elbows, later
one-piece arms,marked: "1961" For models made over long periods the older
dolls bring the higher end of the values
listed; later dolls bring the lower end
value can double for MIB
   Agatha, 1967 - 1980
   #2171 ....$160 - 325
   Coco, 1966 ....$250 - 300
   Cornelia, 1972
   #2191..............................$150 - 200

Gainsborough, 1968 - 1978
#2184 ....$250 - 300
Godey, 1977, in ecru and red
#2298 ....$125 - 150
Goya, 1968
#2183 ....$250 - 300
Jenny Lind, 1969 - 1970
#2193 ....$700 - 750
Lady Hamilton, 1968
#2182 ....$200 - 225
Madame Alexander
1988 - 1990 ....$100 - 175
Madame Pompadour, 1970
#2197 ....$200 - 250
Manet, 1982 - 1983
#2225 ....$160 - 190
Melanie, 1971
#2162 ....$100 - 200
Renoir, 1965
#2154 ....$650 - 700
Scarlett, 1975- 1977, green satin
gown with white lace at
cuffs ....$125 - 200
Southern Belle, 1965
#2155 ....$750 - 800
Prince Charming, 1948 - 1950, hard
plastic, Margaret face, brocade jacket,
white tights
   14".................................$700 - 775
   18".................................$825 - 875
Princess Margaret Rose
   1949 - 1953, hard plastic,
   Margaret face
   14" ....$750 - 800

16" Pollyanna, Alexander Doll Company, vinyl: $400.
Photo courtesy of McMasters Harris Apple Tree Doll Auctions.

Alexander Doll Company

18" Queen, Alexander Doll Company, hard plastic: $1,000. **Photo courtesy of Richard Withington, Inc.**

18" ....$875 - 925
1953 only, #2020B, hard plastic, Beaux Arts Series, pink taffeta gown with red ribbon, tiara, Margaret face
18" sold at auction $2,400
Queen, 1965, Elise face
18" ....$900 - 1,000
Quiz-Kin, 1953, hard plastic, back buttons, nods yes or no
8" ....$450 - 500
Renoir Girl, 1972 - 1986, vinyl body, pink multi-tiered dress
14" ....$25 - 35
Scarlett O'Hara
1950 on, hard plastic, Margaret face
14" - 16" ....$800 - 900
1966 - 1972, jointed knees, Wendy Ann face
8" ....$150 - 200
1969 - 1986, vinyl, Mary Ann face, white gown
14" ....$40 - 50
1970, #2180 green satin jacket with white trim
21" ....$350 - 450
Shari Lewis, 1958 - 1959
14" ....$600 - 1,000
21" ....$1,000 - 1,200
Sleeping Beauty, 1959, Disneyland Special
10" ....$300 - 350
16" ....$600 - 650

21" ....$850 - 900
Smarty, 1962 - 1963, vinyl body
12" ....$125 - 175
Snow White
1970 - 1985, Mary Ann face, Classic series, vinyl
14" ....$45 - 65
1990 - 1992, Wendy face, vinyl
8" ....$45 - 55
2002 - 2004, Cissette face, came with 5" dwarves
10", complete set..............$100 - 125
Sonja Henie, 1951 only, Madeline face, vinyl head
15" ....$300 - 400
Sound of Music, 1965 - 1970 (large), 1971 - 1973 (small), vinyl
Brigitta
10" ....$35 - 45
14" ....$50 - 80
Friedrich
8" ....$30 - 50
10" ....$45 - 75
Gretl
8" ....$35 - 55
10" ....$40 - 75
Liesl
10" ....$45 - 65

21" Coco, Alexander Doll Company, vinyl: $250. **Photo courtesy of Richard Withington, Inc.**

14" ....$60 - 75
Louisa
10" ....$60 - 75
14" ....$50 - 65
Maria
12" ....$40 - 65
17" ....$60 - 90
Marta
8" ....$50 - 75
10" ....$150 - 65
Suzy, 1970 only, vinyl head, Janie face
12"..............................$80 - 100
Timmy Toddler, 1960 - 1961, vinyl head,
hard-plastic body
23"..............................$125 - 150
1960 only
30"..............................$200 - 250
Tommy Bangs, 1952 only, hard plastic,
Little Men Series
11"..............................$825 - 875
Victorian Bride, 1951 only, hard-plastic
Portrait series of 6 models
21" ....sold at auction for $1,600
Wendy, Wendy Ann, Wendy-kin: See
Alexander-kins section.
Special Event dolls, limited editions
Collector's United

21" Godey portrait, Alexander Doll Company,
vinyl, circa 1969: $150. **Photo courtesy of
Alderfer Auction Company, Inc.**

Faith, 1992,
8"..............................$40 - 50
Sterling Light, Sterling Bright, 2000,
tree-top angel, lighted ....$75 - 100
Disney
Mousketeer, 1991, Disney theme
parks only
8"..............................$60 - 80
Morgan Le Fay, 1995, limit 500
10"..............................$125 - 150
Madame Alexander Doll Club Convention
Briar Rose, 1989, Cissette head,
limited edition of 804
8"..............................$200 - 225
Avalon Ball, 2008, limited edition of 100
10"..............................$75 - 100
Southern Belle Cissy, 2003,
limited edition of 65
21"..............................$450 - 500
U.F.D.C.
Empress Josephine, 2009,
limited edition of 185
10"..............................$125 - 145
Music, 2007, convention souvenir
in wardrobe trunk
10"..............................$90 - 100

HENRI ALEXANDRE

1888 - 1891, Paris. Succeeded by Tourrel
in 1892 and in 1895 merged with Jules
Steiner.
Incised HA model, bisque socket head,
paperweight eyes, closed mouth with
space between lips, straight wrist body
17" - 20" ....$5,500 - 6,900
Bébé Phénix, trademarked in 1895,
bisque socket head, paperweight eyes,
pierced ears, composition body
Child, closed mouth
10" - 14"..................$2,200 - 3,600
16" - 18" ....$5,000 - 5,500
20" - 24" ....$6,000 - 7,000
Child, open mouth
16" - 18"..................$2,100 - 2,400
20" - 24" ....$2,400 - 2,800

ALL-BISQUE FRENCH

1880 on, made by various French and German doll companies and sold as French products. Most are unmarked, some have numbers only. Allow more for original clothes and tags, less for chips or repairs.

Glass eyes, swivel head, molded shoes or boots

2½" - 3½" ....$800 - 1,200
4" - 5" ....$2,000 - 3,000
6" - 7" ....$4,000 - 6,000
10" ....$6,300 - 6,500

Five-strap boots, glass eyes, swivel neck
5" - 6" ....$2,000 - 2,800

Painted eyes
2½" - 3½" ....$600 - 700
4" ....$900 - 1,000

Bare feet
5" ....$2,500 - 2,800
6" ....$3,200 - 4,000

Later style, 1910 - 1920, glass eyes, molded shoes, swivel neck, long stockings
2½" ....$300 - 350
5" - 6" ....$575 - 625
7" ....$700 - 725

ALL-BISQUE GERMAN

1880s onward, made by various German doll companies including Alt, Beck & Gottschalk, Bähr & Pröschild, Hertel Schwab and Co., Kämmer & Reinhardt, Kestner, Kling, Limbach, Bruno Schmidt and Simon & Halbig. Some incised "Germany" with or without numbers, others have paper labels glued onto their torsos. Allow more for labels, less for chips and repairs.

All-Bisque, Black or Brown: See Black or Brown Dolls section.

Painted eyes, 1880 - 1910, stationary neck, molded painted footwear, dressed or undressed, all in good condition
2" - 3" ....$100 - 125
4" - 5" ....$125 - 200
6" - 8" ....$250 - 300

Black or brown stockings, tan slippers
4" - 5" ....$375 - 450
6" ....$475 - 525

Ribbed hose or blue or yellow shoes
4" - 5" ....$275 - 325
6" ....$425 - 475
8" ....$825 - 875

6" all bisque, French style, swivel neck: $5,000.
Photo courtesy of Richard Withington, Inc.

6.5" all bisque, swivel neck, glass eyes, all original: $700. **Photo courtesy of Morphy Auctions.**

21

All-Bisque German

6" all bisque, swivel neck, two rows of teeth: $1,000.
Photo courtesy of Richard Withington, Inc.

6" mold 211, all bisque, Kestner, swivel neck: $2,800.
Photo courtesy of Richard Withington, Inc.

Molded hair
4½" ....$125 - 200
6" ....$125 - 175
Early very round face
7" ....$2,100 - 2,300
Molded clothing, 1890 - 1910, jointed at shoulders only or at shoulders and hips, painted eyes, molded hair, molded shoes or bare feet, excellent workmanship, no breaks, chips or rubs
3½" - 4" ....$90 - 110
5" - 6" ....$100 - 160
7" ....$160 - 170
Lesser quality
3" ....$65 - 75
4" ....$75 - 85
6" ....$90 - 110
Molded-on hat or bonnet
5 - 6½" ....$365 - 395
8 - 9" ....$500 - 550
Stone bisque (porous)
4 - 5" ....$60 - 75
6 - 7" ....$85 - 95
Glass eyes, 1890 - 1910, stationary neck, molded painted footwear, excellent bisque, open or closed mouth, sleep or set eyes, good wig, nicely dressed, molded one-strap shoes, includes doll with sticker that reads: "Prize Baby"
3" - 4" ....$130 - 150
5" ....$160 - 225
6" - 7" ....$350 - 400
8" - 9" ....$450 - 600
Elaborate footwear or stockings

3" ....$275 - 300
4½" ....$350 - 400
6" - 7" ....$500 - 600
8" - 8½" ....$700 - 800
Mold 100, 125, 150, 225 (preceded by 83/), rigid neck, fat tummy, jointed shoulders and hips, glass sleep eyes, open mouth, molded black one-strap shoes with tan soles, white molded stockings with blue band. Similarly molded dolls, imported in 1950s by Kimport, have synthetic hair, lesser quality bisque. Allow more for original clothing. Mold number appears as a fraction with the following size numbers under 83; Mold "83/100," "83/125," "83/150," or "83/225." One marked "83/100" has a green label on torso that reads: "Princess//Made in Germany"
5½" - 6½" ....$400 - 500
7½" - 8½" ....$600 - 700
10" - 12" ....$1,000 - 1,100
Swivel neck and glass eyes, 1880 - 1910, molded painted footwear, pegged or wired joints, open or closed mouth, allow more for unusual footwear such as yellow or multi-strap boots or flirty eyes
3" - 4" ....$500 - 600
5" - 6" ....$700 - 800
7" - 8" ....$900 - 1,000
9" - 10" ....$1,100 - 1,500
Simon & Halbig or Kestner types, closed mouth, excellent quality, molds 130, 150, 160, 184, 208, 602, 881, 886, 890

All-Bisque German

and others
4" - 5"	$800 - 1,200
6" - 7"	$1,300 - 2,400
8"	$2,500 - 2,800
10"	$3,000 - 3,500

Jointed knees
6"	$3,000 - 3,500
8½"	$5,000 - 6,000
10"	$7,000 - 8,000

Bare feet
5" - 6"	$2,000 - 2,800
8" - 10"	$3,200 - 3,500

Early round face
6"	$1,600 - 1,800
8"	$2,200 - 2,300

Mold 102, Wrestler (so called), fat thighs, arm bent at elbow, open mouth (can have two rows of teeth) or closed mouth, stocky body, glass eyes, socket head, individual fingers or molded fist
3½" - 5"	$1,500 - 2,000
8" - 9"	$2,800 - 3,500

Slender dolls, 1900 on, stationary neck, slender arms and legs, glass eyes, molded footwear, usual wire or peg-jointed shoulders and hips. May wear regional costumes. Allow more for unusual color boots, such as gold, yellow or orange, all in good condition; allow much more for original clothes
3" - 4"	$200 - 250
5" - 6"	$275 - 325

Swivel neck, closed mouth
4"	$275 - 300

5" - 6"	$450 - 500
8½"	$800 - 900
10"	$1,000 - 1,100

Jointed knees and/or elbows with swivel waist
6"	$1,950 - 2,050
8"	$3,000 - 3,200

Swivel waist only
6"	$2,000 - 2,200

Baby, 1900 on, jointed at hips and shoulders, bent limbs, molded hair, painted features
2½" - 3½"	$80 - 90
5" - 6"	$175 - 225

Character Baby, 1910 on, jointed at hips and shoulders, bent limbs, molded hair, painted features
Glass eyes, molds 391, 830, 833, and others
4" - 5"	$325 - 425
6" - 7"	$425 - 500
8"	$600 - 625
11"	$750 - 850

Painted eyes
3½"	$95 - 125
4" - 5"	$150 - 200
7"	$250 - 300
8"	$350 - 400

Swivel neck, glass eyes
5" - 6"	$850 - 1,000
8" - 10"	$1,300 - 1,500

Swivel neck, painted eyes
5" - 6"	$325 - 350
7" - 8"	$550 - 600
16"	sold at auction for $1,150

Baby Bo Kaye, mold 1394, designed by

23

All-Bisque German

Joseph Kallus, distributed by Borgfeldt
5"..................................$1,500 - 1,400
7" - 8".........................$2,000 - 2,100
Baby Darling, mold 497, Kestner, one-piece body, painted eyes
6"....................................$850 - 950
8" ....$950 - 1,000
10" ....$1,100 - 1,200
Baby Peggy Montgomery, made by Louis Amberg, paper label, pink bisque with molded hair, painted brown eyes, closed mouth, jointed at shoulders and hips, molded and painted shoes/socks
3½" ....$325 - 375
5½" ....$525 - 575
Bonnie Babe, 1926 on, designed by Georgene Averill, glass eyes, swivel neck, wig, jointed arms and legs
5" ....$800 - 1,000
7" ....$1,100 - 1,200
8"..............................$1,300 - 1,400
Bye-Lo: See Bye-Lo section.
Mildred The Prize Baby, (not to be confused with all- bisque child dolls bearing the label "Prize Baby"- see page 22) mold 880, 1914 on, made for Borgfeldt; molded, short painted hair, glass eyes, closed mouth, jointed at neck, shoulders, and hips, molded and painted footwear, round paper label on chest
5" - 7".......................$3,100 - 3,500
Our Darling, open mouth with teeth, glass eyes

5½" ....$160 - 200
Tynie Baby, made for E.I. Horsman, wigged or painted hair, glass eyes
8" - 10" ....$1,600 - 2,200
Mold 231 (A.M.), toddler, swivel neck, glass eyes
9"................................$1,300 - 1,400
Mold 369, 372
7"...................................$650 - 725
9" ....$1,000 - 1,100
11"..............................$1,400 - 1,500
Mold 151, by Hertel and Schwab
10"...................................$650 - 750
Character Doll with Glass eyes, 1910
Molds 155, 156
5" - 6" ....$400 - 500
7"...................................$625 - 650
Heubach, Ernst, 1913 - 1920s, jointed at shoulders and hips, molded painted hair, some with ribbons etc., intaglio eyes, Our Golden Three, molds such as 9557, 9558, 10134, 10490, 10499, 10511, others
8" - 9" ....$1,500 - 1,700
9", swivel neck $2,400
Orsini, 1919 on, designed by Jeanne Orsini for Borgfeldt, produced by Alt, Beck & Gottschalk, Chi Chi, Didi, Fifi, Mimi, Vivi
Glass eyes
5"................................$2,200 - 2,700
7"................................$3,500 - 4,000
Painted eyes

5" Mimi designed by Orsini, all bisque: $2,700. **Photo courtesy of Richard Withington, Inc.**

2" teddy bear, all bisque, original crocheted outfit: $600. **Photo courtesy of The Doll Works.**

All-Bisque German

5" ....$900 - 1,100
Our Fairy, mold 222, wigged, glass eyes
4½" - 5" ....$800 - 1,000
6" - 7" ....$1,500 - 1,800
11"..............................$2,000 - 2,200
Painted eyes, molded hair
5"....................................$450 - 550
8"....................................$750 - 850
12" ....$950 - 1,500
Jointed animals, 1910 on, wire-jointed
shoulders and hips, crocheted clothing,
makers such as Kestner, others
2" - 3½"
Rabbit ....$500 - 700
Bear ....$500 - 600
Frog, Monkey, Pig, Mouse ......$700 - 1,000
Miniature dolls, painted eyes, crocheted
clothing, various makers
1" - 1¾" ....$70 - 90
Character Dolls, 1913 on, painted eyes
Campbell Kid, molded clothes, Dutch
bob
5"....................................$100 - 150
Chin-chin, Gebrüder Heubach, 1919,
jointed arms only, triangular label
on chest
4"....................................$275 - 300
Happifats, designed by Kate Jordan for
Borgfeldt, circa 1913 - 1921
4"....................................$150 - 200
HEbee, SHEbee
4" - 5" ....$500 - 650
7"....................................$750 - 800

Max, Moritz, Kestner, 1914, jointed at
the neck, shoulders and hips, many
companies produced these characters
from the Wilhelm Busch children's story
4½" - 5"..............each $1,700 - 2,000
Mibs, Amberg, 1921, molded blond hair,
molded painted socks and shoes, pink
bisque, jointed at shoulders, legs
molded to body, marked
"C.//L.A.andS.192//GERMANY"
3"....................................$150 - 200
5"....................................$325 - 375
8"....................................$400 - 475
Peterkin, 1912, one-piece baby, side-
glancing googly eyes, molded and
painted hair, molded blue pajamas on
chubby torso, arms molded to body
with hands clasping stomach
5" - 6" ....$200 - 250
September Morn, designed by Grace
Drayton for George Borgfeld, jointed at
shoulders and hips
4" - 5" ....$1,200 - 1,500
6" - 8" ....$1,800 - 2,200
Later issue with painted eyes, 1920 on,
painted hair or wigged, molded painted
single-strap shoes, white stockings,
makers such as Limbach, Hertwig and
Co, others
3½" ....$80 - 90
4" - 5"..............................$100 - 115
6" - 7"..............................$135 - 150
Molded "paper hat" and dagger in belt

3½" and 4" Happifats, all bisque: each $200.
**Photo courtesy of Alderfer Auction Company,
Inc.**

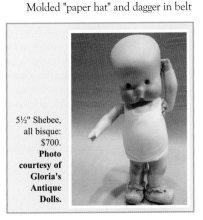

5½" Shebee,
all bisque:
$700.
**Photo
courtesy of
Gloria's
Antique
Dolls.**

All-Bisque German

3.5" flappers, all bisque, molded hats: each $250. **Photo courtesy of Morphy Auctions.**

4½" - 5½" ....$150 - 200
Infant, 1920 on, so-called candy babies
3" - 4" ....$50 - 65
Flapper (so-called) , 1920, tinted bisque, molded bobbed hairstyle, painted features, molded single-strap shoes
Child
2½" - 3½" ....$75 - 100
Adult
5½" ....$175 - 225
Molded loop for bow
2½" ....$125 - 175
5"..$225 - 300
6" - 7" ....$350 - 400
Molded hat
3½" - 4" ....$200 - 250
Aviatrix
5"..$325 - 375
Swivel waist
4½" ....$375 - 400
Wigged
3½" ....$95 - 125
Nodders, 1920 on, immobile body, head attached with elastic, makers such as Hertwig and Co., others, when their heads are touched, they "nod," molded clothes
Animals, cat, dog, rabbit
3" - 5" ....$100 - 150
Child/adult
3" - 4" ....$50 - 75
Comic characters
3" - 5"................................$120 - 135

2" - 4" boxed set of characters from Our Gang ......sold at auction for $2,000
Santa Claus or Indian ....$200 - 225
Teddy Bear................................$200 - 225
Immobiles, 1920, one-piece doll with molded clothing, top layer of paint not fired on and the color can be washed off, some have molded hats
Baby
3½" ....$30 - 40
5"..$40 - 50
Adults and Children
3"...$30 - 40
5"..$55 - 65
Bathing Beauties, 1910 - 1930s, various German porcelain factories made these bisque figures, painted features
3".......................................$100 - 300
6".......................................$400 - 600
10".....................................$800 - 900
Reclining woman, lying on stomach
2½" ....$135 - 165
4"..$375 - 425
Mermaid tail
4"..$300 - 325
Two figures molded together
4½" - 5½" ....$1,500 - 1,700
Wigged
5"..$700 - 7570
Too few in database for a reliable range
Painted bisque child, 1920 - 1930s, original clothing
3" - 4" ....$35 - 60

3" nodder, Hertwig, all bisque: $110. **Photo courtesy of Dolls and Lace.**

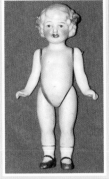

ALL-BISQUE JAPANESE

1915 on, made by a variety of Japanese companies. Quality varies widely, stationary dolls or jointed at shoulders and/or hips. Marked: "Made in Japan" or "Nippon."

Fired bisque, fired on color, some jointed at shoulders, some immobile *Characters* such as Que San Baby, Cho Cho San, etc.

4" - 4½" ....$175 - 250

Painted bisque, top layer of paint not fired on and the color can be washed off, usually one-piece figurines with molded hair, painted features, including clothes, shoes, and socks, some have molded hats

Baby
3" - 5"...................................$15 - 25
5" - 7" ....$30 - 40

Black baby, with pigtails
4" - 5" ....$30 - 55

Bye-Lo Baby-type, fine quality
3½" ....$60 - 75
5"..$100 - 120

Child
3" - 5"...................................$15 - 30

Child with molded clothes
4½" ....$30 - 45
6"...$50 - 60

Child, 1920s - 1930s, pink or painted bisque with painted features, jointed at shoulders and hips, has molded hair or wig, excellent condition
3" - 4" ....$25 - 35
4" - 6" ....$45 - 55

Betty Boop, bobbed hair style, large eyes painted to side, head molded to torso
4"...$18 - 25
6"...$30 - 40

Bride and Groom, all-original costume
4" ....$30 - 50

Happifats
3½" ....$100 - 125

Hebee, Shebee
4½" ....$70 - 90

Immobile characters, Indian, Pirate, etc.
5"...$15 - 25

Skippy
6"...$110 - 135

Snow White
5"...$90 - 110
Boxed with Dwarfs ....$450 - 650

Three Bears/Goldilocks
Boxed set ....$325 - 400

Nippon mark
4" - 6" ....$45 - 80

Occupied Japan mark
2" - 3" ....$20 - 30
4" - 6" ....$40 - 60
7"...$70 - 90

ALT, BECK & GOTTSCHALCK

1854, Nauendorf, Thüringia, Germany. Produced bisque and china-headed dolls for a variety of companies including Bergmann and Borgfeldt.

Shoulder Heads, china, 1880 on. Mold 639, 698, 784, 870, 890, 912, 974, 990, 1000, 1008, 1028, 1032, 1044, 1046, 1064, 1112, 1123, 1127, 1142, 1210, 1222, 1234, 1235, 1254, 1304, cloth or kid body, bisque lower limbs, molded hair or wig, no damage, nicely dressed, allow more for molded hat or fancy hairdo

15" - 18"	$250 - 300
19" - 22"	$300 - 400
23" - 26"	$450 - 525
28"	$675 - 750

Shoulder Heads, bisque, 1880. Cloth or kid body, bisque lower arms, closed mouth, molded hair or wig. Molds such as 784, 911, 912, 916, 990, 1000, 1008, 1028, 1044, 1046, 1064, 1127, 1142, 1210, 1234, 1254, 1304 and so-called Schoolboy style, allow more for molded hat or fancy hairdo

Glass eyes, closed mouth

9" - 11"	$325 - 375
15" -17"	$400 - 500
20" - 24"	$600 - 700

28" mold 639, ABG, bisque: $1,000. **Photo courtesy of Morphy Auctions.**

14" mold 1361, ABG, bisque, character baby: $425. **Photo courtesy of Richard Withington, Inc.**

Painted eyes, closed mouth

14" - 18"	$275 - 300
21" - 23"	$350 - 400

Turned bisque shoulder heads, 1885, solid-dome head or plaster pate, kid body, bisque lower arms, glass eyes, wigged, all in good condition, nicely dressed. Dolls marked 639, 698, 870, 1032, 1123, 1235, "DEP" or "Germany" after 1888. Some have head marked: "Wagner and Zetzsche," paper label inside top of body, allow more for molded bonnet or elaborate hairdo

Closed mouth, glass eyes

16" - 18"	$600 - 650
20" - 22"	$700 - 800
26"	$850 - 900

Open mouth

16" - 18"	$300 - 375
20" - 22"	$575 - 650

Character Baby, 1910s on, open mouth,

sleep eyes, bent-limb body. Allow more for flirty eyes or toddler body. Molds such as 1322, 1342, 1346, 1352, 1361

10" - 12"...........................$375 - 425
16" - 19"...........................$450 - 525
22" - 24" ....$575 - 650

Mold 1407, Baby Bo-Kaye

8" - 9" ....$2,300 - 2,400
15" - 19" ....$1,600 - 2,000

Child, All-Bisque: See All-Bisque section.

Child, 1880 on, bisque socket head, ball-jointed composition body, glass eyes, wig, closed mouth

Mold 630, glass eyes, closed mouth, circa 1880

20" - 22" ....$1,800 - 2,000

Mold 911, 915, 916, swivel head, closed mouth, circa 1890

16" - 18".....................$1,500 - 1,700
20" - 22".....................$1,900 - 2,100

Mold 938, swivel head, closed mouth, circa 1890

22" - 24".....................$2,500 - 3,100

Mold 1362, circa 1912, Sweet Nell, allow more for flapper body

14" - 16" ....$300 - 350
18" - 20" ....$350 - 400
22" - 24" ....$400 - 450
26" - 28" ....$500 - 600
29" - 32" ....$700 - 900

Character Child, circa 1910 on, bisque socket head, composition ball-jointed body

Mold 1357, circa 1912, solid dome or wigged, painted eyes, open mouth

15" - 20" ....$975 - 1,700

Mold 1358, circa 1910, molded hair, ribbon, flowers, painted eyes, open mouth

15" - 20" ....$975 - 1,700

Mold 1322, 1342, 1352, 1361, glass eyes

10" - 12"...........................$325 - 400
14" - 16"...........................$425 - 500
18" - 20" ....$550 - 650

Mold 1367, 1368, circa 1914

15"....................................$450 - 475

LOUIS AMBERG & SONS

1878 - 1930, Cincinnati, Ohio, and New York City. Importer, wholesaler and manufacturer. First company to manufacture all American-made composition dolls. Newborn Babe, Bottle Babe, 1914 on, bisque head on cloth body, hands of celluloid, bisque or rubber, sleep eyes, painted hair, closed or open mouth, molds such as 886, 371

Closed mouth

8" - 10"...........................$190 - 225
12" - 14"...........................$250 - 275
16" - 18"...........................$300 - 350

Charlie Chaplin, 1915, composition head with molded mustache, cloth body, composition hands, cloth label on sleeve

14"...................................$450 - 500

AmKid, 1918, composition shoulder head, kidolene body, composition arms, sleep eyes, wig

22"...................................$100 - 150

Happinus, 1918, all composition with head and torso molded in one piece, coquette-style, brown painted hair molded with hair ribbon

10"...................................$275 - 325

Baby Peggy, portrait of child actress Peggy Montgomery

Composition, 1923, composition head, arms and legs, cloth body, molded

18" Baby Peggy,
Amberg, bisque:
$2,000.
**Photo courtesy
of Joan & Lynette
Antique Dolls and
Accessories.**

bobbed hair painted brown, painted eyes

18" - 20" ....$600 - 800

Bisque, 1924, bisque socket head, composition or kid body, sleep eyes, brown mohair wig

Molds 972, 973, socket head

18" - 22" ....$2,300 - 2,500

Molds 982, 983, shoulder head

18" - 22"..................$1,100 - 1,400

Baby Peggy, All-Bisque: See All-Bisque, German section.

Composition Toddler, 1928, composition head and body, molded hair, painted eyes

13" - 15"..................$225 - 275

Little Phyllis May, 1921, composition shoulderhead and lower arms, cloth body, molded hair

14" ....$175 - 225

Mibs, 1921, designed by Hazel Drukker, composition turned shoulder head, cloth body, composition arms and legs, painted eyes, molded painted hair, molded painted shoes and socks or barefoot mama-style leg

16" ....$1,100 - 1,300

Mibs, All-Bisque: See All-Bisque, German section.

Miss Victory, composition dolly-face doll, ball-jointed composition body, wig, sleep eyes

22" - 24"..................$200 - 275

Sunny Orange Maid, 1924, composition shoulder head, cloth body, composition arms and legs, head has molded "orange" bonnet

14"..................$700 - 900

Vanta Baby, 1927 on, sold through Sears, advertising for Vanta baby clothes, bent-limb composition body, sleep eyes, open mouth with two teeth, painted hair

Bisque head

14" - 18"..................$500 - 700

22" - 27" ....$850 - 1,100

Composition head

10" - 14" ....$150 - 175

18" - 23" ....$225 - 250

Edwina, Sue, or It, 1928, all composition, painted features, molded side-part hair with swirl on forehead, body twist construction

12" - 14"..................$325 - 450

Tiny Tots, Body Twists, 1929, all composition, swivel waist attached to torso with a ball, molded hair, painted features, boy or girl

7½" - 8½" ....$90 - 125

Peter Pan, 1928, all composition, round joint at waist, wearing original Peter-Pan-fashion dress

14" ....$375 - 450

AMERICAN CHARACTER DOLL COMPANY

1919 - 1963, New York City. Made composition dolls, in 1923 registered the trademark "Petite" for mama and character dolls, later made cloth, rubber, hard plastic and vinyl dolls. In 1960 the company name was changed to American Character Doll and Toy Co.

"A.C." or "Petite" marked composition doll, 1923, composition heads and limbs, cloth body

Baby

11" - 14" ....$140 - 150

16" - 20"..................$150 - 225

Mama doll, sleep eyes, human-hair wig

16" - 18"..................$175 - 200

24" ....$250 - 300

Petite girls, 1930s, all-composition

16" - 18"..................$225 - 275

24"..................$300 - 325

Toddler

13"..................$200 - 225

Bottletot, 1926, composition head and bent limbs, cloth body, painted hair, open mouth, one arm molded to hold molded celluloid bottle

13"..................$200 - 225

American Character Doll Company

18"....................................$300 - 325

All-rubber, drink and wet, painted-eye doll in layette case, labeled Bottletot, A Petite Baby, back marked: "petite Dolls // Pt. Pending" and Horsman horseshoe

9½" ....$100 - 150

Puggy, 1928, all composition, character face with frown and side-glancing painted eyes, molded painted hair, jointed at neck, shoulders and hips, original outfits included baseball player, boy scout, cowboy and newsboy. Marked: "A // Petite // Doll," clothes tagged: "Puggy // A Petite Doll"

    13"....................................$400 - 475

    in cowboy outfit ....sold at auction $850

Sally, 1930, Patsy-type, all composition, molded hair or wig, painted or sleep eyes, marked: "Petite" or "American Char. Doll Co.,"

    12"....................................$75 - 125

    14" - 16"...........................$150 - 200

    18" - 22" ....$250 - 300

Sally, Shirley-type wig

    24" ....$350 - 375

16" Tiny Tears, American Character, hard plastic: $200. **Photo courtesy of Dollyology Vintage Dolls.**

22" Sweet Sue, American Character, hard plastic: $275. **Photo courtesy of American Beauty Dolls.**

Sally-Joy, composition head, cloth body

    16" ....$150 - 175

    18" ....$225 - 275

    21" ....$325 - 375

    24" ....$400 - 425

Carol Ann Beery, 1935, portrait doll of child-actor, daughter of Wallace Beery, all composition, mohair wig with two braids drawn up across top of head, marked: "Petite Sally" or "Petite"

    13"....................................$400 - 500

    16"....................................$600 - 700

    20"....................................$675 - 750

Little Love (also called Newborn Babe), 1942, composition flange-neck, head and hands, cloth body, molded hair, sleep eyes, Bye-Lo-type doll

    16" - 20" ....$200 - 300

Vinyl, sleep eyes, molded hair

    16" ....$125 - 150

Tiny Tears, 1950s, hard-plastic head with tear ducts, drink-and-wet doll. Value can double or more for doll in excellent condition with layette

Rubber body

    11½" ....$250 - 350

    13½" ....$350 - 400

    16"....................................$375 - 450

    18"....................................$450 - 500

    13½" black doll in layette, circa 1956 ....sold online for $1,895

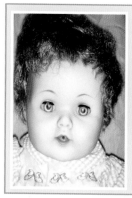

24" Toodles, American Character, vinyl: $175. **Photo courtesy of Charlotte's Web Vintage Dolls and Collectibles.**

11" Tressy, American Character Doll, vinyl: $40. **Photo courtesy of the Museum Doll Shop.**

Clothing and accessories
Bottle..$35
Bubble pipe...$25
Bracelet $30
Plastic cradle $200
Romper $35
All vinyl, 1963
　　11½" ....$150 - 200
　　13½" ....$225 - 250
　　16"..................................$250 - 275
　　20" ....$300 - 325
Danbury Mint, 2000, re-issue, porcelain, with layette, complete and perfect
　　10"......................................$85 - 95
Sweet Sue, 1953 - 1961, all hard plastic or hard plastic and vinyl, saran wig, some on walker bodies, others fully jointed including elbows, knees and ankles, marked: "A.C." "Amer. Char. Doll" or "American Character" in a circle
　　15"..................................$125 - 175
　　18" - 20" ....$200 - 250
　　22" - 25" ....$275 - 325
　　31" ....$400 - 425
Sweet Sue Sophisticate, vinyl head, earrings
　　20"..................................$200 - 295
Annie Oakley, 1953, hard-plastic walker
　　14"..................................$300 - 350
I Love Lucy Baby, 1952, girl dressed in pink, made for one year only as the birth of the baby was awaited on *I Love*

Lucy television show
　　14"..................................$550 - 600
Ricky Jr., 1954 -1956, personality doll based on character from *I Love Lucy* television show, baby
Hard plastic with rubber body, 1952
　　14" - 16" ....$200 - 400
All vinyl, 1953 - 1956
　　13"..................................$150 - 175
　　21"..................................$200 - 250
　　21" doll owned by Lucie Arnaz ....
　　　　sold at online auction for $1,776
Toodles, 1956, hard-rubber drink-and-wet doll
Teeny Toodles
　　11" ....$175 - 200
　　18" - 20"..........................$225 - 275
　　29"..................................$300 - 325
Toodles Toddler, 1960, vinyl and hard plastic, "Peek-a-Boo" eyes
　　24"..................................$300 - 375
　　30"..................................$425 - 500
Eloise, 1955, cloth with molded mask face, yarn hair
　　22"..................................$275 - 325
Toni, 1958, vinyl head with rooted hair
　　10½" ....$75 - 125
　　14"..................................$200 - 250
　　20"..................................$300 - 375
　　25"..................................$400 - 500
Little Miss Echo, 1964, vinyl, recorder mechanism in torso
　　30" ....$180 - 225

Miss America, 1963 ....$50 - 65
Tressy, 1963 - 1965, vinyl, grow-hair
doll, value can double for MIB, marked:
"American Doll and Toy Corp. //
19C.63" in a circle
    11" ....$50 - 65
    Black ....$150 - 200
Pre-teen Tressy, 1963
    15" ....$75 - 100
Tressy family and friends
Cricket
    9" ....$40 - 50
Mary Make-Up, non-grow hair
    11½" ....$40 - 60
Chuckles, 1969, vinyl, rooted hair,
painted eyes
    16" ....$90 - 115
    22" ....$225 - 250
Whimsies, 1960, all-vinyl characters
*Dixie the Pixie, Hedda Get Bedda (three
face), Miss Take, Tillie the Talker, Wheeler
the Dealer, and others*
    19" - 20" ....$150 - 200
Whimettes, 1963 smaller doll modeled
after the whimsies
    7½" ....$100 - 175
Cartwrights, Ben, Hoss, Little Joe,
1966, personality dolls based on
characters from BonanzaTV show, value
can double for MIB
    9" ....$75 - 90
Bonanza Outlaw
    9" ....$200 - 225

ANNALEE
MOBILITEE
DOLL COMPANY

1934 to present, Meredith, New Hampshire.
Dolls originally designed by Annalee
Thorndike, cloth with wire armature
"mobilitee" body, painted features.
Early dolls, 1934 - 1960
    9" - 10½" ....$300 - 500
Later dolls, must be in excellent
condition with tags

9" girl on bicycle, Annalee, felt, circa 1959:
$500. **Courtesy of private collection.**

10" Folk Hero dolls
Robin Hood and Johnny Appleseed,
    1983 - 1984 ....$70 - 90
Annie Oakley, 1985 ....$80 - 125
Mark Twain, 1986 ....$150 - 65
Ben Franklin, 1987 ....$70 - 90
Sherlock Holmes, 1988 ....$50 - 65
Abraham Lincoln, 1989 ....$50 - 65
Betsy Ross, 1990 ....$50 - 60
Christopher Columbus, 1991 ....$50 - 60
Uncle Sam, 1992 ....$60 - 80
Pony Express, 1993 ....$55 - 75
"50's Style" Bean Nose Santa,
    1994 ....$50 - 75
Pocahontas, 1995 ....$50 - 70
Logo Kid dolls
Milk and Cookies, 1985 ....$55 - $90
Sweetheart, 1986 ....$35 - 50
Naughty, 1987 ....$30 - 45
Raincoat, 1988 ....$30 - 40
Christmas Morning, 1989 ....$30 - 40
Clown, 1990 ....$25 - 35
Reading, 1991 ....$20 - 30
Back to School, 1992 ....$30 - 40
Ice Cream, 1993 ....$15 - 25
Dress-Up Santa, 1994 ....$20 - 30
Goin' Fishin', 1995 ....$25 - 35
Little Mae Flowers, 1996 ....$18 - 22
Tea for Two, 1997 ....$25 - 30

15th Anniversary Kid, 1998 ......$15 - 20
Mending My Teddy, 1999 ....$20 - 25
Precious Cargo, 2000 ....$18 - 25
Mother's Little Helper, 2001 ......$25 - 35
Sand Castle Susie, 2002............ $25 - 35
Museum Collection Dolls
1997 Woman ....$35 - 40

MAX OSCAR ARNOLD

1877 - 1930, Neustadt, Thüringia, Germany. Made dressed dolls and mechanical dolls including phonograph dolls.
Baby
Bisque socket head, composition body
12" ....$100 - 125
16" ....$225 - 250
19" ....$350 - 400
Child
Shoulder head, kid body, open mouth, glass sleep eyes, wigged
12" - 19"............................$250 - 325
Bisque socket head, composition body, glass sleep eyes, wigged, molds such as 200, 201, 250, or MOA
High-quality bisque
6½" on flapper body ......$300 - 325
12" ....$225 - 275
15" -18" ....$300 - 350
21" - 24"............................$425 - 500
32" - 35" ....$725 - 800
Low-quality bisque
15" ....$125 - 145

24" mold 201, Max Oscar Arnold, bisque: $400.
Photo courtesy of McMasters Harris Apple Tree Doll Auctions.

18" - 20"............................$225 - 275
24" ....$300 - 375

ARRANBEE DOLL COMPANY

1922 - 1958, New York City. Sold to the Vogue Doll Company, which continued to use their molds until 1961. Some bisque heads used by Arranbee were made by Armand Marseille and Simon & Halbig. The company also produced composition, rubber, hard-plastic, and vinyl dolls.
My Dream Baby, 1924 on
Bisque Head, head made by Armand Marseille, cloth body, celluloid hands, holding bottle, marked: "Germany"
16" ....$300 - 350
Composition head, 1927, composition, lower arms and legs, cloth body, metal sleep eyes
8" - 10".............................$100 - 125
17" - 21" ....$125 - 175
Composition
Baby
8"......................................$65 - 75
14" ....$100 - 150
23"....................................$200 - 225
Bottletot, 1926, all composition, molded bottle in hand
13" ....$175 - 200
16" ....$300 - 350
Child, 1930s and 1940s, all composition,

16" Bottletots, Arranbee, German, bisque, one open mouth, one closed mouth: each $350.
Photo courtesy of Memories of Things Past Antiques.

Arranbee Doll Company

12" Nancy with trunk set, Arranbee, composition: $400. **Photo courtesy of Minton's Doll and Curiosity Shop.**

14" Nancy Lee, Arranbee, composition: $300. **Photo courtesy of Gloria's Antique Dolls.**

mohair wig, marked: "Arranbee" or "R and B"

9" ....$90 - 110
15" ....$120 - 160

Debu 'Teen, 1938 on, all composition, elaborate costume brings higher end of price range

11" ....$175 - 275
14" ....$200 - 400
17" ....$200 - 400
21" ....$375 - 425

Skating costume

14" ....$225 - 250
17" ....$250 - 275
21" ....$350 - 375

WAC

18" ....$500 - 525

Kewty, 1934 - 1936, all composition, mohair wig, marked: "Kewty"

14" ....$250 - 300

Little Angel Baby, 1940s, composition head, cloth body, molded painted hair

11" ....$150 - 160
16" ....$200 - 250
18" ....$250 - 300

Hard Plastic

18" ....$150 - 225

Mama doll, 1920s on, composition and cloth

20" - 24" ....$100 - 150

Nancy, 1930s, Patsy-type, all composition, marked: "Arranbee" or "Nancy" Molded hair, painted eyes

12" ....$200 - 250

17" - 21" ....$300 - 350

Nancy Lee, all-composition, mohair wig, sleep eyes

12" - 14" ....$275 - 325
17" - 19" ....$250 - 300

Storybook dolls, 1935, composition dolls dressed as storybook charactors

8½" - 10" ....$100 - 200

Hard Plastic and Vinyl

Cinderella, 1952, hard plastic

14" ....$225 - 275
20" ....$375 - 400

Coty Girl, 1958, vinyl, fashion doll, high-heeled feet, allow more for rare outfits

10½" ....$100 - 150

Lil Imp, 1960, vinyl, red hair, freckles

10" ....$75 - 100

Littlest Angel, 1956, hard plastic, bent-knee walker, marked: "R and B"

14" Nanette, Arranbee, hard plastic: $225. **Photo courtesy of McMasters Harris Apple Tree Doll Auctions.**

8.5" Little Bo Peep, Storybook Series, Arranbee, composition, MIB: $300. **Photo courtesy of American Beauty Dolls.**

14" Nancy Lee Cinderella, Arranbee, hard plastic: $275. **Photo courtesy of McMasters Harris Apple Tree Doll Auctions.**

11" ....$100 - 150
My Angel, 1961, hard plastic and vinyl
   17" ....$45 - 55
   22" ....$75 - 100
   36" ....$155 - 165
Walker, 1957 - 1959
   30" ....$130 - 150
Vinyl head on oilcloth body, 1959
   22" ....$50 - 60
Nanette, 1949 - 1959, hard plastic, synthetic wig, sleep eyes, closed mouth
   14" ....$175 - 225
   17" ....$275 - 325
Nanette Walker, 1957 - 1959
   15" ....$100 - 150
   17" ....$150 - 200
   20" ....$225 - 275
Nancy, 1951 - 1952, vinyl head, hard-plastic body, wigged

11" Littlest Angel, Arranbee, hard plastic, blue hair, MIB: $200. **Photo courtesy of Memories of Things Past Antiques.**

14" ....$125 - 150
18" ....$170 - 190
Nancy Lee, 1950 - 1959, hard plastic
   14" ....$225 - 275
   17" ....$300 - 375
   20" ....$450 - 500
Nancy Lee Baby, 1952, painted eyes, crying face
   15" ....$125 - 145
Sweet Pea, 1956, vinyl drink-and-wet baby, rooted hair, sleep eyes
   12" ....$45 - 55
Taffy, 1956, Cissy-type
   23" ....$125 - 145

ARTIST DOLLS

Original artist dolls may be one-of-a-kind or limited-edition pieces made by the designing artist. Production artist dolls are artist series produced in workshop or factory settings, worked on by people other than the designing artist, often in limited editions. Values reflect secondary-market prices; the artist's retail prices will differ.

Original Artist Dolls
Martha Armstrong-Hand, porcelain
Babies...............................$1,200 - 1,300
Children
Brandon, Elizabeth, porcelain ..$450 - 500
Bob and June Beckett, wood
Baby ....$100 - 125
Children ....$250 - 300

Artist Dolls

Floyd Bell, wood
Historic figures ....$300 - 500
Jane Bradbury, cernit
    14" -15" ....$600 - 650
Carol Bowling, cloth over molded form
Baby
    11" ....$75 - 125
Frances Bringloe, wood
Pioneer Children or Parents
    6¼" ....$300 - 350
Muriel Bruyere, low-fire porcelain
Children
    8" ....$200 - 250
Helen Bullard, wood
Original artist dolls ....$350 - 500
Production artist dolls
    Holly, Barbry Allen ....$250 - 300
    Tennessee Mountain Kids........$50 - 60
Emma Clear, porcelain
China or bisque ladies
    15" - 22" ....$250 - 500
George and Martha Washington
    Painted eyes.................pair $400 - 500
    Glass eyes ....pair $500 - 600
Dewees Cochran, various media: latex
composition
Grow Up Series
    18".............................$2,500 - 2,600
Look Alikes, portrait children
    15" - 16" ....$2,000 - 2,500
    18" - 20" ....$2,500 - 2,800
Production doll, Cindy
    15" ....$900 - 1,000
Judith Condon, porcelain
Black children ....$250 - 400
Dianne Dengel, cloth
    3½" ....$100 - 125
    20" - 24" ....$200 - 250
Gertrude Florian, ceramic, composition
Ladies.....................................$250 - 375
Patti Hale, wood
    18"....................................$250 - 300
Cathy Hansen, porcelain
All-bisque child ....$250 - 300
Bisque-head lady ....$275 - 300
Dorothy Heizer, cloth
20th Century Fashion

12" Look-Alike, Dewees Cochran, composition: $1,900. **Photo courtesy of Morphy Auctions.**

Ladies................................$1,600 - 2,000
Historic Figures, 10" - 11"
    Men and more simple
    costumes.......................$2,600 - 3,200
    More elaborate costume
    (queens, etc.) ....$3,500 - 5,000
Maggie Head Kane,
    porcelain..........................$400 - 450
Avis Lee, wood
Americanettes
    11"....................................$500 - 800
Tykes, cloth body
    11" ....$400 - 500
Maryanne Oldenburg, porcelain
Children ....$200 - 250
Irma Park, wax
Wax-over-porcelain miniatures
    2" - 3" ....$125 - 225
Ann Parker, resin
Crepe paper
    8" - 11".............................$75 - 200
Frances and Bernard Ravca, various media
Crepe paper
    6" - 7"................................$90 - 120
Cloth, needle sculpted
    Peasants
    10" - 14" ....$100 - 150
    Other figures
    10" - 14"...........................$150 - 200
Composition, cloth and paper
    Historical figures
    10" - 14" ....$75 - 125

21" and 23" Laurel and Hardy..........
     sold at auction for $3,555
Kathy Redmond, porcelain
Ladies
  13" - 14"............................$350 - 500
Regina Sandreuter, wood ....$550 - 650
Madeline Saucier, cloth
  15" - 19" ....$225 - 300
Sherman Smith, wood, 5" - 6"
Simple style ....$250 - 325
More elaborate........................$375 - 500
Bisque head on wooden
boy ....$300 - 400
Lewis Sorenson, wax
Kewpie type
  15"....................................$100 - 150
Ladies
  14" - 25" ....$800 - 900
Peddler
  18" - 25" ....$900 - 1,700
Tamara Steinheil
Victorian lady ....$400 - 500
Martha Thompson, porcelain
Early reproductions of antique dolls
  13" - 18"............................$350 - 450
19th Century Fashion Ladies
  10" - 14"..........................$700 -1,200
Betsy..$675 - 750
Prince Charles and Princess Anne
  10" - 11" ....each $1,000 - 1,200
Fashion plate ladies
  8" - 14".........................$1,200 - 4,000
Little Women ....each $600 - 800
Ellery Thorpe, porcelain
Children ....$400 - 500
Vargas, wax
Ethnic figures
  10" - 11"...........................$600 - 700
Clara Wade, porcelain, marked
"Clarmaid"
Buster Brown, glass eyes
  18".....................................$250 - 300
Faith Wick, porcelain........$2,500 - 2,700
Fawn Zeller, porcelain
One-of-a-Kind ....$1,000 - 2,000
US Historical Society
  Holly................................$200 - 300

4¾" Martha Thompson, shoulder head, bisque: $600. **Photo courtesy of Richard Withington, Inc.**

Polly II.............................$175 - 225
Production Artist Dolls
Sabine Esche, vinyl by Sigikid
  22".....................................$250 - 300
Hildegard Gunzel, various media
Porcelain for Seymour Mann,
limited 1,200
  26"....................................$100 - 140
Vinyl
  Children
  24" - 30" ....$200 - 400
Sonja Hartmann, various media
Porcelain
  20"....................................$275 - 300
Vinyl
  23"....................................$150 - 200
Philip Heath, vinyl
World of Children
Collection ....$175 - 300
Karin Heller, cloth
Children ....$200 - 250
Annette Himstedt, 1986 on. Distributed
by Timeless Creations, a division of
Mattel, Inc. Swivel rigid vinyl head with
shoulder plate, cloth body, vinyl limbs,
inset eyes, real lashes, molded eyelids,
holes in nostrils, human-hair wig, bare
feet, original in box
Barefoot Children, 1986, Bastian,
Beckus, Ellen, Fatou, Kathe, Lisa, Paula
  26"....................................$150 - 350
The World Children Collection, 1988,
31"

Friederike ....$325 - 400
Kasimir ....$325 - 400
Makimura ....$275 - 350
Malin ....$275 - 350
Michiko ....$250 - 300
Reflections of Youth, 1989 - 1990,
Adrienne, Ayoka, Kai, Mia Yin,
Neblina, Tarea
    26" ....$150 - 225
World Children's Summit,
    35"...................................$600 - 900
Maggie Iacono, cloth
Children
    11" - 16".............................$400 - 600
Helen Kish, vinyl
Children
    7" ....$100 - 200
Lee Middleton, vinyl
Babies and toddlers ....$75 - 85
Bubba Chubbs
    22" ....$100 - 125
Harold Nabor, resin
Children
    14" - 15"..............................$75 - 125
Lynn and Michael Roche, porcelain
and wood Children
    17" - 22" ....$700 - 900
Robert Tonner, vinyl
Fashion Models
    19" ....$175 - 225
Robin Woods, 1980s on. Creative
designer for various companies,
including Le Petit Ami, Robin Woods

16" Lindsay,
R. John
Wright
Dolls, Inc.,
felt: $800.
**Photo
courtesy of
Richard
Withington,
Inc.**

Company, Madame Alexander (under
the name Alice Darling), Horsman
and Playtime Productions
Cloth
    1985, clowns ....$40 - 50
Vinyl
    2000, Halle Angel, for Home
Shopping Network
    14" ....$35 - 45
R. John Wright, cloth
Early adult peasant
characters ....$600 - 900
Children ....$750 - 1,000
Max and His Pinocchio
    17" ....$900 - 1,200
Kewpies ....$300 - 400
Raggedy Ann ....$500 - 525
U.F.D.C. souvenir dolls, various artists
for special events
Muriel Kramer, 1982, Rose O'Neill
    16" ....$40 - 65
Kathy Redmond, Christopher
Columbus, 1992, porcelain
    13" ....$100 - 200
Beverly Walters, Father Christmas,
1980, porcelain, kit head, arms boots
        Shoulder head 4" ....$45 - 60
Fawn Zeller, porcelain, 1966, Miss Miami
    13".......................................$40 - 65

ASHTON-DRAKE

1985 on, located in Niles, Illinois,
Ashton-Drake is a division of Bradford

20"
Susannah,
Lynn and
Michael
Roche,
porcelain,
wooden
body: $800.
**Photo
courtesy of
Richard
Withington,
Inc.**

15" Everything's Coming Up Roses Gene, Mel Odom/Ashton-Drake Galleries, vinyl: $90. **Photo courtesy of Charlotte's Web Vintage Dolls and Collectibles.**

Industries. Manufactures dolls designed by a number of well-known artists. Sells its dolls through distributors or via direct mail-order sales to the public. Dolls in perfect condition with original clothing and tags.

Yolanda Bello
Picture Perfect Babies
Jason, 1985.............................$100 - 140
Heather, 1986 ....$15 - 30
Jennifer, 1987 ....$15 - 30
Matthew, 1987 ....$15 - 30
Amanda, 1988 ....$15 - 30
Sarah, 1989 ....$15 - 30
Jessica, 1989..............................$15 - 30
Michael, 1990 ....$15 - 30
Lisa, 1990...................................$15 - 30
Emily, 1991 ....$15 - 30
Danielle, 1991 ....$15 - 30
Playtime Babies, 1994
Lindsey, Shawna, Todd ......each $25 - 30
Lullaby Babies ....$20 - 25
Blythe, 2005, vinyl, reissue of Hasbro doll
11½" ....$100 - 175
Brigitte Deval
Fairy Tale Princesses series
18".....................................$40 - 50
Dianna Effner

Heroines of Fairy Tale series,
Cinderella, Snow White, Goldilocks, Red Riding Hood, Rapunzel
16"...$40 - 60
Mother Goose series, Mary Mary, Curl with a Curl, Curly Locks, Snips and Snails
14"...$60 - 75
Julie Good-Krueger
Amish Blessings series
Rebeccah, Rachel, Adam............$25 - 35
Joan Ibarolle
Little House on the Prairie series, 1992 - 1995
Laura, Mary, Carrie,
Ma and Pa ....$35 - 50
Baby Grace.................................$45 - 50
Nellie, Almanzo ....$25 - 45
Wendy Lawton
Little Women, set of 5,
16".......................................$75 - 100
Mary Had a Little Lamb, Little Bo Peep, Little Miss Muffet ....$25 - 35
Others
Glamor of the Gibson Girl, 1987, porcelain, designed by Arlene Siegel
18"...$25 - 30
Patty Playpal Re-issues
35" - 37"...........................$100 - 150
Princess Diana, porcelain
19"...$40 - 75
Mel Odom
Gene
1995, designed by Mel Odom, marketed through Ashton-Drake
Premier, 1st
1995 ....$150 - 200
Monaco, 2nd
1995 ....$30 - 45
Red Venus, 3rd
1995 ....$40 - 50
Other Genes
Bird of Paradise
1997 ....$35 - 40
Blue Goddess ....$30 - 40
Breathless
1999 ....$40 - 60

Iced Coffee ....$35 - 45
Midnight Romance
1997 ....$35 - 55
Song of Spain
1999 ....$35 - 50
White Hyacinth
1997 ....$30 - 40
Gene Specials
Champagne Flight, MDCC,
limited edition of 250
2002 ....$200 - 250
Covent Garden, NALED
1998 ....$35 - 45
Diamond Evening
2001 ....$100 - 150
Dream Girl, Convention
1998 ....$225 - 250
Heart of Hollywood
2000 ....$35 - 45
Holiday Benefit Gala,
limited editon of 25
1998 ....$245 - 265
King's Daughter, NALED
1997 ....$30 - 45
Moments to Remember, MDCC,
limited edition of 250
2000 ....$100 - 125
Night at Versailles, FAO Schwarz
1997 ....$50 - 90
On the Avenue, FAO Schwarz
1998 ....$40 - 50
Priceless, FAO Schwarz exclusive
1999 ....$65 - 75
Sparkling Seduction, NALED
1997 ....$35 - 40
Titus Tomescu
From This Day Forward bridal series,
1994 ....$60 - 70
Barely Yours Series
Snug as a Bug in a Rug ....$30 - 40
Clean as a Whistle....................$40 - 50
Cool as a Cucumber ....$50 - 60
Cute as a Button, 1993 ....$30 - 40
Pretty as a Picture, 1996 ....$30 - 40
Special Delivery ....$50 - 65
I Am the Way, the Truth, and the
Life Collection ....$40 - 55

AUTOMATA

Various manufacturers used many different mediums including bisque, wood, wax, cloth and others to make dolls that performed some action. More complicated models performing more or complex actions bring higher prices. The unusual one-of-a-kind dolls in this category make it difficult to provide a good range. Values listed are auction prices for automata in good working order.

Autoperipatetikos, 1860 - 1870s
Bisque, china, or papier-mâché by American Enoch Rice Morrison, key-wound mechanism
12" ....$1,000 - 1,200
With more elaborate,
head ....$2,300 - 2,600
Ballerina
Bisque Simon & Halbig mold 1159, key rotates head and arms lower, leg extends, key wound, Leopold Lambert, circa 1900
20" $4,000
Bébé with Fan and Flowers
Bisque Paris Bébé head, key wound, moves hand, fans herself, sniffs flower, Leopold Lambert
19" $8,000
Clown Équilibriste
Roullet et Descamps, Jumeau head, clown raises his body to do a handstand

9" key-wind toy, parian (so called), shoulder head: $2,100.
Photo courtesy of Richard Withington, Inc.

41

15"
Roullet et
Descamps,
girl rock-
ing cradle,
Simon &
Halbig
bisque
head:
$4,000.
Photo courtesy of Alderfer Auction Company, Inc.

on the back of the chair, turns head, lifts one arm

18".....................$7,000 - 8,000

Edison Phonograph Doll
Simon & Halbig or Jumeau, bisque-head doll with mechanism in torso of composition body
Jumeau head

25" ....$8,000 - 10,000

Simon & Halbig head mold 719

23" ....$4,900 - 5,400

Flower Seller with Surprises
Black papier-mâché-headed lady selling flowers from a tray, when wound, each flower on tray lifts, revealing a monkee, a girl or a mouse (each has movements), lady nods heads and blinks, Gustav Vichy

25".....................$27,000

Girl with doll in arms
Bisque head by Jumeau, head turns, raises cage and puppy pokes out its head, Leopold Lambert, circa 1890

18"..................$9,000 - 12,000

Girl Hiding in Sugar Jar
Bisque head pops out of sugar jar when wound, Roullet et Descamps

8"..................$3,000 - 3,500

Girl Rocking Cradle
Bisque head by Simon & Halbig, moves head and rocks cradle with

bisque baby in it, Roullet et Descamps, circa 1890

15"..................$4,000 - 5,000

Lady Ironing
French bisque-headed lady ironing linens in a garden, key-wound mechanism, turns head, arm moves iron back and forth, Philabois, circa 1870

20" overall (10" doll)..............$5,000

Lady Cyclist
Jumeau head, pedals bike and turns head, Gustav Vichy

17" $14,000

Marquis Smoker
French bisque Jumeau portrait head, key wound, raises cigarette to mouth as music plays, Leopold Lambert

23".....................$8,000

Turc Fumeur
Papier-mâché-headed brown-skinned man with glass eyes, sits cross-legged while smoking a hooka, holds coffe cup in other hand, Leopold Lambert

25".....................$14,000 - 16,000

Pushing a Carriage, key-wind toy with pressed-fabric doll head

Goodwin...................$1,900 - 2,400

Riding Toy, key wind fur-covered horse with doll, metal with German bisque head, when wound the horse gallops across the floor, heads such as Cowboys, Indians, George Washington

6"........................$450 - 500

Waltzing Couple, Vichy, French poupée heads

13"..................$5,000 - 7,000

Waltzing Lady, Steiner

16"..................$5,000 - 6,000

Walking doll
Roullet et Descamps. Simon & Halbig 1078 head

23" ....$2,000 - 2,400

Steiner

15"..................$6,000 - 8,000

GEORGENE AVERILL

1913 - 1960s, New York City. Georgene and James Averill began their doll business dressing dolls. Georgene was the designer, James the businessman. They began as Averill Manufacturing Company. In 1915 they trademarked the name "Madame Hendron" for doll designs. In 1923 the Averills ended their association with Averill Manufacturing, which continued to make dolls designed by other artists. The Averills also continued to manufacture their own dolls under the name Georgene Novelties.

Allie Kat, bisque head by Alt, Beck & Gottschalk, glass eyes, open mouth with wobble tongue and teeth, plush Puss in Boots style body with composition boots

15".........................$10,000 - 14,000

Allie Dog, bisque head by Alt, Beck & Gottschalk, glass eyes, open mouth with tongue and teeth, mold 1405

12" - 15" ....$6,500 - 7,000

Baby Dawn, 1950, vinyl with cloth body

19"....................................$300 - 325

Baby Georgene or Baby Hendron, composition head, arms, and legs, cloth body, marked with name on head

13" ....$100 - 125
16" ....$125 - 175
20"...................................$225 - 275
26"...................................$425 - 475

Body Twists, 1927, composition with ball swivel joint in torso

Dimmie and Jimmie

14½" ....$425 - 475

Bonnie Babe, 1926 - 1930s, bisque heads made in Germany by Alt, Beck & Gottschalk, cloth bodies made in the USA by K&K toys

Bisque head, open mouth with two lower teeth, composition or celluloid lower arms and legs, cloth body, molds 1368, 1402

10" - 12".........................$850 - 900

21" Bonnie Babe, Georgene Averill, bisque: $275. **Photo courtesy of McMasters Harris Apple Tree Doll Auctions.**

15"...................................$850 - 900
18" ....$900 - 1,000
22" ....$1,100 - 1,200

Celluloid head

10"...................................$450 - 500
16"...................................$625 - 675

All-bisque Bonnie Babe:
See All-bisque, German section.

Brownies, Girl Scouts:
See Girl Scout section.

Character animals such as Uncle Wiggley, Nurse Jane, Krazy Kat and others

18"...................................$250 - 300

Character or ethnic doll, 1915 on, composition head, cloth or composition body, character faces, painted features

Indian, Sailor, Dutch Boy, etc.

12"...................................$75 - 125
16"...................................$200 - 250

Black

14" ....$350 - 375

Cloth, 1920s on, molded mask face, painted features, sometimes inset hair eyelashes, yarn hair, cloth body, many dressed in international costumes

12" - 15"...........................$75 - 110
18"...................................$120 - 150
24"...................................$250 - 300

Comic Characters, 1944 - 1965, cloth, molded mask face, cloth body, appropriate character clothing

Alvin, Nancy, Sluggo, Little Lulu, etc.

Georgene Averill

16" Little Cherub, Georgene Averill, composition: $300. **Photo courtesy of McMasters Harris Apple Tree Doll Auctions.**

14".....................................$300 - 400

Becassine, 1950s, French character doll
13"....................................$650 - 700

Dolly Reckord, 1922 - 1928, composition head, arms and legs, cloth body with record player inside, human-hair wig, sleep eyes, open mouth with teeth
26"..................................$700 - 800

Grace Drayton designs, 1923, flat-faced cloth dolls with painted features, some with yarn hair
Chocolate Drop
10".....................................$350 - 400
14".....................................$500 - 550
Dolly Dingle
11".....................................$375 - 400
15".....................................$525 - 550

Maude Tausey Fangel designs, 1938, flat-faced cloth dolls with painted features
Sweets, Snooks, etc.
12" - 14"............................$400 - 500
15" - 17"............................$600 - 675
21"....................................$750 - 800

Kris Kringle, cloth mask face
14"....................................$175 - 200

Little Cherub, designed by Harriet Flanders, composition with painted eyes
12"....................................$800 - 900
16"....................................$300 - 375

Lullabye Baby, 1920 - 1925, compo-

sition head and hands, cloth body
15" - 19"............................$175 - 250

Mama doll, 1918 on, composition head, arms and swing-style legs, cloth body, voice box in torso, molded hair or mohair wig, painted or sleep eyes
15" - 18"............................$150 - 200
20" - 22"............................$300 - 375
28"....................................$400 - 450

Peaches, 1928 on, Patsy-type, all composition, jointed at hips and shoulders, molded hair or wigged, painted eyes or glass, open mouth or closed
14"....................................$275 - 325
17"....................................$300 - 375

Snookums, 1927, based on child actor at Universal Stern Brothers studio, composition, laughing mouth with two rows of teeth
14"....................................$500 - 600

Sunny Girl, 1927, celluloid head, cloth body, turtle mark
15"....................................$375 - 425

Tear Drop Baby, designed by Dianne Dengel, cloth mask face, molded tear on cheek
16"....................................$200 - 250

Whistling doll, 1925 - 1929, doll makes a whistling noise when head is pushed down
Whistling Dan, etc.
14" - 15"............................$350 - 450

39" Little Lulu, Georgene Averill, cloth mask face: $600. **Photo courtesy of Sweetbriar Auctions.**

14"
Babyland
Rag,
painted
face, cloth:
$900.
**Photo
courtesy of
Alderfer
Auction
Company,
Inc.**

BABYLAND RAG DOLL

Babyland Rag dolls were sold by Horsman from 1893 to 1928. The actual manufacturer of these dolls is still unknown. The dolls were originally marked with paper tags that read "Genuine//Babyland//Trade//Mark." Dolls have flat cloth faces and cloth bodies, some have mohair wigs. Dolls listed are in good, clean condition with original clothing. Allow 50 percent of the value for faded, stained or worn examples.

Painted face
12" - 15" ....$850 - 950
18" - 22" ....$1,000 - 1,200
30"..............................$1,800 - 2,200
Black
15" - 17" ....$900 - 1,000
20" - 22"......................$1,100 - 1,400
Topsy-Turvy
13" - 15" ....$750 - 850
Lithographed face, 1907 on
12" - 15" ....$450 - 550
24" - 30" ....$675 - 1,000
Topsy-Turvy
14" ....$700 - 800

BADEKINDER

1860 - 1940. Most porcelain factories made china and bisque dolls in one-piece molds with molded or painted black or blond hair, and usually undressed. Sometimes called Bathing Dolls, they were dubbed "Frozen Charlotte" from a song about a girl who went dancing in light clothing and froze in the snow. They range in size from under 1" to over 19". Some were reproduced in Germany starting in the 1970s to the present. Allow more for pink tint, extra decoration or hairdo.

All china
Low quality
2" - 3" ....$20 - 35
4" - 5" ....$35 - 50
Good quality
2" - 3"................................$100 - 125
4" - 5"................................$150 - 175
6" - 7" ....$200 - 250
9" - 10"...............................$275 - 300
14" - 15"............................$500 - 575
Black china
5" - 6".................................$190 - 250
Blond hair, flesh-toned head
and neck
9" - 12" ....$600 - 900
14" - 15" ....$900 - 1,000
Molded boots
4"..$250 - 275
8"..$300 - 325
Molded clothes or hats
1½" - 3" ....$250 - 375
6"..$300 - 350
8" ....$425 - 475

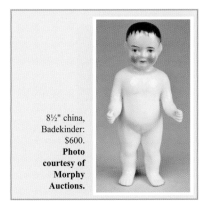

8½" china,
Badekinder:
$600.
**Photo
courtesy of
Morphy
Auctions.**

Pink tint, hairdo
3".....................................$200 - 325
5" - 8"..............................$375 - 400
13" - 14"..........................$600 - 700
Pink tint, bonnet-head
3".....................................$450 - 475
5".....................................$550 - 575
Bisque
Good quality
5".....................................$200 - 275
Fancy hair, molded boots
4" - 5"..............................$275 - 300
Stone bisque, molded hair, one piece
3"......................................$18 - 25
6"......................................$30 - 40
Parian-type, 1860
5".....................................$200 - 225
7".....................................$250 - 275

BÄHR & PRÖSCHILD

1871 - 1930s, Orhdruf, Thüringia, Germany. Porcelain factory that made its own dolls as well as providing heads for companies such as Kley & Hahn, Bruno Schmidt, Heinrich Stier and others.
Belton-type, 1880 on. Solid dome head with flat crown with small stringing holes in it, closed mouth, paperweight eyes, pierced ears, straight wrists, composition or kid body, molds in the 200 series
12"............................$1,900 - 2,000
14" - 16"....................$2,100 - 2,300

11" mold 604, Bähr & Pröschild, character baby: $500.
Photo courtesy of Richard Withington, Inc.

12" mold 343, Bähr & Pröschild, bisque: $800.
Photo courtesy of Hatton's Gallery of Dolls.

18" - 20" ....$2,600 - 2,700
Child, 1888, bisque head, open or closed mouth, human-hair or mohair wig, composition body in German or French style or kid body, molds 204, 213, 224 239, 246, 252, 273, 275, 277, 286, 289, 293, 297, 309, 325, 332, 340, 343, 379, 394
11" - 14" ....$700 - 1,200
16" - 18"....................$1,000 - 1,400
22" - 24" ....$1,600 - 1,800
Kid body
13" - 16"..........................$325 - 475
24".....................................$675 - 725
Mold 224, with dimples
14" - 16"..........................$800 - 900
22" - 24" ....$1,000 - 1,200
Character Child
Mold 247, open/closed mouth
26" ....$2,600 - 2,900
Mold 531
15" - 19" ....$800 - 1,200
Mold 536
18" - 20" ....$3,750 - 3,800
Mold 604
11" - 14" ....$900 - 1,000
18" - 22"....................$1,100 - 1,300
Mold 624, open mouth
12" - 17" ....$900 - 2,000
Too few in database for a reliable range
Character Baby, 1909 on, bisque socket head, solid dome or wigged, sleep eyes, open mouth, bent-limb

body, molds: 585, 586, 587, 602,
604, 619, 620, 624, 630, 641, 678

   9" - 10" ....$350 - 450
   12" - 14"..........................$650 - 750
   17" - 19"..........................$800 - 900
   22" - 24" ....$925 - 1,000
Toddler body
   10" - 12" ....$900 - 1,000
   18" - 20".....................$1,200 - 1,300

BARBIE®

Barbie®, 1959 to present, Hawthorne, California, 11½" fashion doll manufactured by Mattel, Inc. Values listed are for dolls in perfect condition, wearing original clothing and bearing all appropriate tags. Played-with and undressed dolls should be valued at one-fourth to one-third the listed values, which are for perfect dolls. Values can double or more for MIB.

Lilli, 1955 - 1964, a German cartoon character, created by Reinhard Beuthien for the tabloid Bild-Zeitung in Hamburg, Germany, inspiration for Barbie design

   7½ " ....$1,200 - 1,700
   12"..............................$3,000 - 3,500

#1 Barbie®, 1959, heavy, solid vinyl torso, faded to pale-white color, white irises, pointed arch eyebrows, soft texture ponytail hairstyle, black-and-white swimsuit, gold hoop earrings, metal lined holes in bottom of feet and shoes to accept doll stand

Blond ....$6,500 - 7,000
Brunette ....$7,000 - 9,000

#2 Barbie®, 1959, doll same as previous doll, but with no holes in feet, some wear pearl earrings

Blond ....$3,500 - 3,900
Brunette ....$3,800 - 4,000

#3 Barbie®, 1960, same as previous doll, but now has blue irises and curved eyebrows

Blond ....$1,000 - 1,100
Brunette...............$1,200 - 1,500

#4 Barbie¹, 1960, same as previous doll, but torso now has a flesh-tone color

Blond or brunette ....$300 - 350

#5 Barbie®, 1961, same as previous, but now has a hollow, hard-plastic torso, hair is now firmer texture saran

Blond, titian or brunette ....$300 - 375

#6 Barbie®, 1962, same as previous doll, but now available in many more hair and lipstick colors and wears a red swimsuit ....$200 - 250

Swirl Ponytail, 1964, smooth bangs swirled across forehead and to the side instead of the curly bangs of the previous ponytail dolls ....$200 - 300

Bubblecut Barbie®, 1961, same doll as others of this year but with new bubblecut hairstyle

Brown ....$400 - 450
White Ginger............................$300 - 325
Others ....$100 - 150
Side-part bubblecut ....$325 - 375

Barbie® Fashion Queen, 1963, doll has molded hair with a hair band and three interchangeable wigs, gold-and-white striped swimsuit and turban.....................................$175 - 200

Miss Barbie®, 1964, doll has molded bendable legs, hair with a hair band and three interchangeable wigs, sleep eyes ....$375 - 450

11½" Barbie®, #1, Mattel, vinyl: $8,000. Photo courtesy of McMasters Harris Apple Tree Doll Auctions.

American Girl Barbie®, 1965,
bobbed hairstyle with bangs,
bendable legs ....$275 - 325
Side-part American girl ....$400 - 500
Color Magic Barbie®, 1966, dolls
hair can change color
Blond ....$500 - 600
Midnight to ruby red.................$575 - 750
Twist N' Turn Barbie®, 1967,
swivel-jointed at waist ....$250 - 300
Talking Barbie®, 1968, doll now
has pull-string talker ....$250 - 300
Living Barbie®, 1970, joints at neck,
shoulders, elbows, wrists, hip, knees
and ankles ....$100 - 140
Other Barbie® dolls. Dolls listed are
in excellent condition, wearing original
clothing, value can double for MIB
Angel Face
    1983 ....$15 - 20
Ballerina
    1976 ....$25 - 35
Barbie Baby-sits
    1974 ....$20 - 40
Beautiful Bride
    1976 ....$95 - 120
Beauty Secrets
    1980 ....$50 - 60
Bicyclin'
    1994 ....$15 - 20
Busy Barbie
    1972 ....$75 - 100
Dance Club
    1989 ....$12 - 18
Day-To-Night
    1985 ....$20 - 25
Doctor
    1988 ....$12 - 15
Fashion Jeans, black
    1982 ....$12 - 16
Fashion Photo
    1978 ....$30 - 38
Free Moving
    1975 ....$50 - 70
Gold Medal Skater
    1975 ....$32.50 - 40
Golden Dream

11½" Barbie®,
bubble cut,
Mattel, vinyl,
MIB: $300.
**Photo courtesy of
McMasters
Harris Apple
Tree Doll
Auctions.**

    1980 ....$50 - 75
Growin' Pretty Hair
    1971....................................$75 - 100
Hair Fair
    1967 ....$50 - 65
Hair Happenin's
    1971....................................$375 - 550
Happy Birthday
    1981 ....$15 - 20
Ice Capades, 50th
    1990 ....$12 - 18
Kissing
    1979 ....$20 - 20
Live Action on Stage
    1971....................................$120 - 150
Loving You
    1983 ....$40 - 45
Magic Curl
    1982 ....$12 - 18
Magic Moves
    1986 ....$20 - 25
Malibu (Sunset)
    1971 ....$25 - 32
Miss America Walk Lively
    1972 ....$65 - 80
My First Barbie
    1981....................................$12 - 18
My Size
    1993 ....$75 - 100
Newport the Sport's Set
    1973....................................$62.50 - 82
Peaches 'n Cream
    1985 ....$40 - 50

Pink and Pretty
1982 ....$35 - 50
Rappin' Rockin'
1992 ....$12 - 15
Rocker
1986 ....$15 - 20
Roller Skating
1980 ....$20 - 25
Secret Hearts
1993 ....$10 - 12
Sensations
1988 ....$10 - 12
Silkstone Barbie, 2000
Lingere ....$45 - 60
Sun Lovin' Malibu
1979..................$12 - 16
Sun Valley, The Sports Set
1973..................$32.50 - 42
Super Fashion Fireworks
1976 ....$45 - 60
Super Size, 18"
1977 ....$35 - 60
Superstar Promotional
1978 ....$30 - 40
Talking Busy
1972 ....$40 - 55
Twinkle Lights
1993 ....$10 - 15
Walk Lively
1972 ....$50 - 60
Western (3 hairstyles)
1981 ....$25 - 30

Gift Sets
MIB values; allow more for NRFB
(never removed from box), less for worn
or faded
Barbie Hostess
1966 ....$4,750
Beautiful Blues, Sears
1967 ....$3,300
Color Magic Gift Set, Sears
1965 ....$2,000
Fashion Queen Barbie and Friends
1963 ....$2,250
Fashion Queen and Ken Trousseau
1963 ....$2,600
Little Theatre Set

1964 ....$5,500
On Parade
1960 ....$2,350
Party Set
1960 ....$2,300
Pink Premier
1969 ....$1,600
Round the Clock
1964 ....$5,000
Sparkling Pink
1964 ....$2,500
Travel in Style, Sears
1964 ....$2,400
Trousseau Set
1960 ....$2,850
Wedding Party
1964 ....$3,000
Store Specials or Special Editions, MIB
American Stories Series
1990s..................$20 - 30
Avon Winter Velvet
1996 ....$20
Billy Boy Feelin' Groovy
1986..................$80
Bloomingdales
Savvy Shopper
1994 ....$35
Donna Karan
1995 ....$45
Ralph Lauren
1996..................$40
Bob Mackie

11½" Barbie®,
swirl ponytail,
Mattel, vinyl:
$400.
**Photo
courtesy of
McMasters
Harris Apple
Tree Doll
Auctions.**

Gold
1990 ....$150
Platinum
1991 ....$175
Starlight Splendor, black
1992 ....$200
Empress
1992 ....$400
Neptune Fantasy
1992 ....$300
Masquerade Ball
1993 ....$150
Queen of Hearts
1994 ....$120
Goddess of the Sun
1995 ....$50
Moon Goddess
1996 ....$50
Madame du Barbie®
1997 ....$200
Goddess of the Africa
1999 ....$200
Goddess of the Americas
2000 ....$100
Goddess of the Arcitic
2001 ....$130
Sterling Silver Rose
2002 ....$25
Classique Series
Benefit Ball
1992 ....$30
City Style
1993 ....$35

11½" Barbie®, American Girl, Mattel, vinyl: $275. **Photo courtesy of McMasters Harris Apple Tree Doll Auctions.**

Opening Night
1994 ....$30
Evening Extravaganza
1994 ....$25
Uptown Chic
1994 ....$30
Midnight Gala
1995 ....$40
Disney
Euro Disney
1992 ....$40
Disney Fun
1993 ....$15
Disney World, 25th anniversary
1996 ....$15
FAO Schwarz
Golden Greetings
1989 ....$40
Winter Fantasy
1990 ....$90
Night Sensation
1991 ....$40
Madison Avenue
1991 ....$50
Rockette
1993 ....$50
Silver Screen
1994 ....$50
Jeweled Splendor
1995 ....$45
La Papillon, Bob Mackie
1999 ....$100
Great Eras
Gibson Girl
1993 ....$25
Flapper
1993 ....$30
Southern Belle
1994 ....$25
Lady Liberty
2000 ....$450
Hallmark
Holiday Memories
1995 ....$20 - 25
Holiday Voyage
1997 ....$15
Holiday Sensation

11½" Barbie®, Color Magic, Mattel, vinyl: $500. **Photo courtesy of McMasters Harris Apple Tree Doll Auctions.**

11½" Barbie®, Silkstone in Lingerie, Mattel, vinyl, MIB: $100. **Photo courtesy of McMasters Harris Apple Tree Doll Auctions.**

1998 ....$20 - 30
Hills
Party Lace
   1989 ....$10
Evening Sparkle
   1990 ....$8
Moonlight Rose
   1991 ....$10
Hula Hoop
   1997 ....$10
Holiday Barbie®
1988 ....$300
1989 ....$125
1990 ....$75
1991...$60
1992 ....$45
1993 ....$35
1994 ....$35
1995 ....$20
1996 ....$20
1997...$18
1998...$18
1999 ....$20
2000 ....$25
2001 ....$38
2002 ....$40
2003 ....$30
2004 ....$25
2005 ....$35
2006 ....$40
2007 ....$25
2008 ....$35
2009 ....$50

2010..$45
Hollywood Legends
Scarlett O'Hara,white gown
   1994 ....$20
Dorothy, Wizard of Oz
   1994 ....$38
Maria, Sound of Music
   1995 ....$35
Marilyn Monroe, Seven Year Itch
   1997 ....$30
Home Shopping Club
Evening Flame
   1991 ....$35
J.C. Penney
Evening Elegance
   1990 ....$35
Enchanted Evening
   1991 ....$25
Golden Winter
   1993 ....$30
Royal Enchantment, blond
   1995 ....$16
K-Mart
Peach Pretty
   1989 ....$35
Root 66 University
   2003 ....$25
Little Debbie
   1993 ....$10
Mervyns
Ballerina
   1983 ....$75
Fabulous Fur

1986 ....$70
Montgomery Ward
#1 Replica, shipping box
1972 ....$710
#1 Replica, pink box
1972 ....$840
Nostalgia Series
35th Anniversary
1994 ....$30
Solo in the Spotlight
1994 ....$18
Busy Gal
1995 ....$20
Enchanted Evening
1996 ....$25
Poodle Parade
1996 ....$20
Commuter Set
1998 ....$50
Sears
Celebration, 100th Anniversary
1986...$20
Lilac and lovely
1987 ....$25

11½" Barbie®, Gold Bob Mackie, Mattel, vinyl, 1990, MIB: $275. **Photo courtesy of McMasters Harris Apple Tree Doll Auctions.**

Star Dream
1987 ....$20
Evening Enchantment
1989 ....$20
Blossom Beautiful
1992 ....$50
Ribbons and Roses
1995 ....$15
Service Merchandise
Blue Rhapsody
1991 ....$45
Satin Nights
1992 ....$20
Sparkling Splendor
1993 ....$20
Sea Princess
1996 ....$20
Spiegel
Sterling Wishes
1991 ....$30
Regal Reflections
1992 ....$30
Royal Invitation
1993 ....$25
Theatre Elegance
1994 ....$25
Shopping Chic
1995 ....$25
Winner's Circle
1996 ....$22
Target
Gold 'n Lace
1989 ....$30
Party Pretty
1990 ....$20
Golden Evening
1991 ....$35
35th Anniversary Barbie
1997 ....$20
Barbie and Kelly Easter Egg Hunt set
1997 ....$12
Stars and Stripes Collection
Air Force
1990 ....$30
Navy
1991 ....$20
Marine

1992	$35
Army Gift Set	
1993	$40
Air Force Gift Set	
1994	$40
Toys R Us	
Dance Sensation	
1985	$40
Pepsi Spirit	
1989	$25
Vacation Sensation	
1989	$25
Radiant in Red	
1992	$16
Very Violet	
1992	$20
Moonlight Magic	
1993	$16
Harley-Davidson, #1	
1997	$225
Firefighter	
1995	$75
WalMart	
Pink Jubilee, 25th Anniversary	
1987	$25
Frills and Fantasy	
1988	$25
Tooth Fairy	
1994	$16
Skating Star	
1995	$18
Wholesale Clubs	
Party Sensation	
1990	$15
Fantastica	
1992	$20
Royal Romance	
1992	$45
Winter Royale	
1994	$25
After the Walk, Sam's Club	
1997	$35
Country Rose, Sam's Club	
1997	$20
Woolworths	
Special Expressions, white	
1989	$30

Sweet Lavender

1992	$25

Family and other related dolls.
Dolls listed are in excellent condition, wearing original clothing, value can double for MIB

Alan, 1964 - 1967

Straight legs	$75 - 100
Bendable legs	$100 - 125
Buffy and Mrs. Beasley	$100 - 125

Cara, Quick Curl, 1974,

African-American	$85 - 100

Casey, Twist 'n Turn

1967	$125 - 150
Non- twist 'n turn	$80 - 100

Chris, brunette, bendable legs

1967	$50 - 60

Francie
Bendable legs

1966	$150 - 200

Straight legs

1966	$75 - 100

Twist 'n Turn

1967	$150 - 200

11½" Barbie®, Classique Series, Benefit Ball, Mattel, vinyl, 1992: $30. **Photo courtesy of The Museum Doll Shop.**

11½" Francie, Twist n' Turn, Mattel, vinyl, MIB: $350. **Photo courtesy of McMasters Harris Apple Tree Doll Auctions.**

Black
1967 ....$850 - 950
Malibu
1971 ....$20 - 25
Growin' Pretty Hair
1971................................$100 - 120
Jamie, Walking
1970 ....$100 - 120
Julia, Twist 'N Turn
1969 ....$130 - 150
Talking
1969................................$100 - 110
Kelly
Quick Curl
1973 ....$80 - 100
Yellowstone
1974....................................$90 - 110
Ken, #1, straight legs, blue eyes,
hard-plastic hollow body, flocked
hair, 12", marked:
"Ken® MCMLX//by//Mattel//Inc."
1961 ....$70 - 80
Molded hair
1962 ....$60 - 70
Bendable legs
1965 ....$120 - 150
Talking
1968 ....$45 - 60

Mod Hair
1968 ....$50 - 60
Busy Talking
1971...................................$75 - 100
Walk Lively
1971 ....$50 - 60
Living Fluff
1971 - 1972 ....$40 - 50
Midge
Straight legs
1963 ....$75 - 100
No freckles
1963 ....$100 - 120
Bendable legs
1965 ....$100 - 125
P.J. Talking
1970................................$125 - 175
Twist 'N Turn
1970 ....$100 - 125
Live Action/Stage
1971................................$75 - 100
Ricky, straight legs
1965 ....$60 - 80
Skipper
Straight legs
1964 ....$75 - 100
Bendable legs
1965 ....$90 - 110

11½" Julia, Twist n' Turn, Mattel, vinyl, MIB: $300. **Photo courtesy of McMasters Harris Apple Tree Doll Auctions.**

Twist 'N Turn
1968 ....$125 - 150
Living
1969 ....$120 - 150
Growing Up
1975 ....$45 - 55
Skooter
Straight legs
1965 ....$45 - 60
Bendable legs
1966 ....$80 - 100
Stacey
Talking
1968 ....$100 - 120
Twist 'N Turn
1968 ....$120 - 150
Todd, bendable, posable
1966 ....$40 - 60
Tutti, bendable, posable
1967 ....$50 - 60
Pairs in sets
Tutti and Todd,
Sundae Treat..................$150 - 175
Angie and Tangie ....$150 - 200
Lori and Rorie ....$90 - 110
Twiggy, Twist 'N Turn
1967 ....$125 - 150

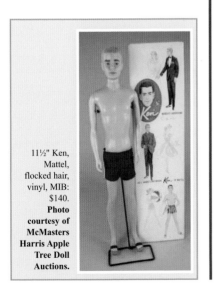

11½" Ken, Mattel, flocked hair, vinyl, MIB: $140.
Photo courtesy of McMasters Harris Apple Tree Doll Auctions.

9" Living Fluff, Mattel, vinyl: $50.
Photo courtesy of McMasters Harris Apple Tree Doll Auctions.

Barbie Accessories
Animals
All American (horse)
1991 ....$35
Blinking Beauty (horse)
1988 ....$25
Champion (horse)
1991 ....$40
Dancer (horse)
1971 ....$100
Midnight (horse)
1980 ....$40
Fluff (kitten)
1983 ....$20
Prancer (horse)
1984 ....$35
Prince (poodle)
1985 ....$35
Snowball (dog)
1990 ....$35
Cases
Fashion Queen, black, zippered
1964 ....$150
Barbie and Ken, black patent
1965 ....$35
Miss Barbie, zippered
1964 ....$160
Skooter, aqua
1965 ....$50

Clothing

Name of outfit, stock number; value listed is for mint in package; allow much less for loose

Aboard Ship
1631 ....$550

All That Jazz
1848 ....$350

Arabian Knights
874 ....$495

Ballerina
989 ....$325

Barbie in Japan
821 ....$500

Beautiful Bride
1698.......................................$2,100

Benefit Performance
1667.......................................$1,400

Black Magic Ensemble
1609 ....$420

Bride's Dream
947 ....$350

Busy Gal
981 ....$450

Campus Sweetheart
1616.......................................$1,750

Career Girl
954 ....$225

Cinderella
872 ....$550

Commuter Set
916..$1,400

Country Club Dance

11½" Barbie®, PJ In Motion set, Mattel, vinyl: $100. **Photo courtesy of McMasters Harris Apple Tree Doll Auctions.**

11½" Twiggy, Mattel, vinyl, MIB: $300. **Photo courtesy of McMasters Harris Apple Tree Doll Auctions.**

1627 ....$490

Dancing Doll
1626 ....$525

Debutante Ball
1666 ....$1,300

Dog 'n Duds
1613 ....$350

Drum Majorette
875 ....$225

Easter Parade
971 ....$4,500

Evening Enchantment
1695 ....$595

Fabulous Fashion
1676 ....$595

Formal Occasion
1697 ....$550

Fashion Editor
1635 ....$850

Formal Luncheon
1656 ....$1,400

Garden Wedding
1658 ....$575

Gay Parisienne
964 ....$4,300

Glimmer Glamour

1547 ....$5,000
Gold 'n Glamour
1647......................................$1,750
Golden Glory
1645 ....$495
Here Comes the Bride
1665 ....$1,200
Holiday Dance
1639 ....$625
International Fair
1653 ....$500
Intrigue
1470 ....$425
Invitation to Tea
1632 ....$600
Junior Prom
1614 ....$695
Knitting Pretty, pink
957 ....$450
Let's Have a Ball
1879 ....$325
Magnificence
1646 ....$625
Make Mine Midi
1861 ....$350
Masquerade
944......................................$250
Maxi 'n Midi
1799 ....$375
Midnight Blue
1617 ....$850
Miss Astronaut
1641 ....$700
On the Avenue
1644 ....$575
Open Road
985......................................$385
Orange Blossom
987 ....$600
Pajama Pow
1806 ....$300
Pan American Stewardess
1678 ....$5,000
Patio Party
1692 ....$375
Plantation Belle
966......................................$600

Poodle Parade
1643 ....$985
Rainbow Wraps
1798 ....$350
Reception Line
1654 ....$600
Red Fantastic, Sears
1817 ....$850
Riding in the Park
1668 ....$625
Roman Holiday
968 ....$5,000
Romantic Ruffles
1871 ....$250
Satin 'n Rose
1611 ....$395
Saturday Matinee
1615 ....$950
Sears Pink Formal
1681 ....$2,450
Shimmering Magic
1664 ....$1,550
Smasheroo
1860 ....$275
Solo in the Spotlight $200
Sorority Meeting
937......................................$300
Suburban Shopper
969......................................$350
Sunday Visit
1675 ....$595
Swirley-Cue

6"Tutti, Mattel,vinyl: each $60. **Photo courtesy of McMasters Harris Apple Tree Doll Auctions.**

1822 ....$300
Trailblazers
1846 ....$250
Travel Togethers
1688 ....$300
Tunic 'n Tights
1859 ....$300
Under Fashions
1655 ....$695
Velveteens, Sears
1818 ....$850
Weekenders, Sears
1815 ....$950
Wedding Wonder
1849 ....$375
Wild 'n Wonderful
1856 ....$300
Furniture, Suzy Goose
Canopy Bed, display box
1960s $250
Chifferobe, cardboard box
1960s $250
Queen Size Bed, pink
1960s $600
Vanity, pink $75
Vehicles
Austin Healy, orange and aqua
1964 ....$300
Beach Bus
1974 ....$45
Mercedes, blue-green
1968 ....$450
Speedboat, blue-green
1964 ....$1,100
Sport Plane, blue
1964 ....$3,000
Sun 'n Fun Buggy
1971 ....$150
United Airlines
1973 ....$75

E. BARROIS

1846 - 1877, Paris, France. Assembled, sold and distributed lady-type dolls with bisque heads and closed mouths, on kid and cloth bodies. It is still largely unknown which French and German

21" Barrois, bisque head, glass eyes: $11,000.
Photo courtesy of Morphy Auctions.

porcelain factories made heads for Barrois, although it is known that the heads Barrois supplied to Steiner and Blampoix were made by Frayon.
Marked: EB
Poupée (Fashion-type)
Painted eyes
14" - 16".....................$1,800 - 2,200
19" - 21"....................$2,600 - 3,000
Glass eyes
14" - 16"....................$8,000 - 9,000
19" - 21" ....$10,000 - 11,000
23" - 24"................$11,000 - 12,000

BELTON-TYPE

1875 on, made by various German manufacturers including Bähr & Pröschild, Kestner, Simon & Halbig and others. Solid dome bisque socket head doll with small holes in crown for stringing and/or wig application. Paperweight eyes, straight wristed wood and composition body, closed mouth, pierced ears. Belton-type is a name applied to this type of doll by modern doll collectors and is not a reference to a specific maker. Unmarked, or with mold numbers only.

C.M. Bergmann

13" French-Trade Belton, bisque, Germany: $1,400. **Photo courtesy of Alderfer Auction Company, Inc.**

Bru-look face
12" - 14"......................$2,000 - 2,600
French-Trade, dolls with a French look that were manufactured for the French market, some mold 137, 138
  9" - 15".........................$800 - 1,500
  18" - 20" ....$1,200 - 2,000
  22" - 24" ....$2,200 - 2,400
German-look dolls
  8" ....$900 - 1,300
  12" - 15" ....$900 - 1,000
  18" - 20" ....$1,000 - 1,200
Mold 200: See Bähr & Pröschild section.

C.M. BERGMANN

1888 - 1931, Walterhausen, Thuringia, Germany. Doll factory that distributed in the United States through L. Wolfe and Co., Bergmann had bisque doll heads made for them by Alt, Beck & Gottschalk, Armand Marseille, Simon & Halbig and others. Registered trademarks: Cinderella 1897, Columbia 1904, My Gold Star 1926. Dolls listed are in good condition, appropriately dressed.

Character Babies, bisque socket head on bent-limb composition body
Open mouth
  12" - 14".......................$325 - 400
  15" - 18" ....$450 - 600
Mold 612, open/closed mouth
  15".............................$2,000 - 2,200
Mold 134, character toddler
  12" ....$950 - 1,000
Child, bisque socket head, open mouth, wigged, sleep or set eyes, ball-jointed composition body, mold 1916 or others, some marked with Simon & Halbig/ Bergmann mark
  10"..................................$275 - 350
  14" - 18"..........................$475 - 550
  20" - 24" ....$650 - 800
  26" - 28" ....$800 - 850
  30" - 32" ....$750 - 825
  42" ....$1,100 - 1,300
Flapper-type body
  12"..................................$625 - 650
  16" ....$1,100 - 1,200
Eleonore
  18"..................................$550 - 600
  25"..................................$700 - 800

25" Eleanore, C M Bergmann, bisque: $800. **Photo courtesy of Richard Withington, Inc.**

BETSY MCCALL

Dolls based on *McCall's* magazine's paper doll Betsy McCall. Dolls listed are in excellent condition wearing original clothing. Value can double for MIB.

Ideal Toy Corp., 1952 - 1953
Doll with vinyl head, on a hard-plastic Toni body, saran wig

14" ....$200 - 275
1958, vinyl, four hair colors, rooted hair, flat feet, slim body, round sleep eyes, may have swivel waist or one-piece torso, marked: "McCall 19©58 Corp." in circle

14" ....$100 - 200
1959, vinyl, rooted hair, slender limbs, some with flirty eyes, one-piece torso, marked: "McCall 19©58 Corp." in circle

19" - 20"............................$225 - 275
1961, vinyl, five colors of rooted hair, jointed wrists, ankles and waist, blue or brown sleep eyes, four to six outfits available, marked: "McCall 19©61 Corp." in circle

22" ....$125 - 175
29".....................................$200 - 225

American Character Doll Co., 1957 to 1963, 8" hard-plastic doll with jointed knees, sleep eyes, molded eyelashes, metal barrettes in hair. In the first year these dolls had mesh cap saran wigs and plastic pin joints in knees; in the second year they had vinyl skull-caps on their wigs and metal knee pins

In undies ....$160 - 225
In street dress ....$200 - 300
In formalwear ....$350 - 425
8" doll clothing
Dresses ....$35 - 65
Shoes and socks..........................$28 - 30
Complete outfit ....$50 - 75
Boxed outfit ....$100 - 125
Vinyl doll, 1958 on, jointed at shoulder, neck and hip, sleep eyes, allow more for elaborate costumes

14".....................................$225 - 300
20".....................................$300 - 350
30".....................................$400 - 450
36".....................................$450 - 550
Additional joints at wrists, waist, knees and ankles

22"....................................$300 - 350
29"....................................$325 - 375
Companion-size Betsy McCall, 1959, vinyl, rooted hair, head marked: "McCall Corp//1959"

34"....................................$400 - 450
Linda McCall (Betsy's cousin), 1959, vinyl, Betsy face, rooted hair, head marked: "McCall Corp//1959"

34"....................................$350 - 450
Sandy McCall (Betsy's brother), 1959, vinyl, molded hair, sleep eyes, red blazer,

14" Betsy McCall, American Character, vinyl: $375. **Photo courtesy of American Beauty Dolls.**

29" Betsy McCall, American Character, vinyl: $350. **Photo courtesy of Sidney's Second Childhood.**

navy shorts, marked: "McCall 1959 Corp."; tag reads: "I am Your Life Size Sandy McCall"

35".....................................$350 - 450

Uneeda

1964, vinyl, rooted hair, rigid vinyl body, brown or blue sleep eyes, slim pre-teen body, wore mod outfits, some mini-skirts, competitor of Ideal's Tammy, unmarked

11½" ....$125 - 200

Horsman

1974, vinyl with rigid plastic body, sleep eyes, came in Betsy McCall Beauty Box with extra hair piece, brush, bobby pins on card, eye pencil, blush, lipstick, two sponges, mirror and other accessories, head marked: "Horsman Doll Inc.//19©67"; torso marked: "Horsman Dolls Inc."

12½" ....$85 - 95

1974, vinyl with rigid plastic teen type body, jointed wrists, sleep eyes, lashes, rooted hair with side part (some blond with ponytails), closed mouth, original clothing marked: "BMc" in two-tone blue box marked: "©1974//Betsy McCall - she WALKS with you," doll marked: "Horsman Dolls 1974"

29" ....$150 - 175

Tomy

1984, porcelain head, arms, legs, cloth bodies, stationary eyes, wigged

16" ....$10 - 15

Rothchild

1986, 35th anniversary Betsy, hard-plastic, sleep eyes, painted lashes below eyes, single stroke eyebrows, tied ribbon emblem on back, marks: hang tag reads: "35th Anniversary// BetsyMcCall//by Rothschild (number) 'Betsy Goes to a Tea Party,' or 'Betsy Goes to the Fair,'" box marked: "Rothchild Doll Company//Southboro, MA 01722"

8"..$25 - 35

Tonner Doll Company

1996 to present, vinyl (some porcelain), rooted hair, rigid vinyl body, glass eyes, closed smiling mouth, marked: "Betsy McCall//by//Robert Tonner// ©Gruner and Jahr USA PUB." Values listed are secondary-market prices; the dolls are still also available at retail

8"

In undies ....$20 - 30

Dressed.................................$35 - 50

14".......................................$40 - 70

29".......................................$70 - 85

BING ART DOLLS

Germany, 1921 - 1932. Gebrüder Bing was founded in 1882. In 1921 it became a part of a conglomerate called the Bing Werke Corporation and began making their cloth "art dolls." Molded cloth face,

12½" Betsy McCall, Horsman, vinyl, circa 1974, MIB: $175. **Photo courtesy of American Beauty Dolls.**

10" Bing, cloth: $475. **Photo courtesy of McMasters Harris Apple Tree Doll Auctions.**

sometimes with a heavy coating of gesso giving a composition appearance, cloth head and body, oil-painted features, wigged or painted hair, pin-jointed at neck, shoulders and hips, seams down front of legs, mitt hands.

Painted hair or wigged, cloth or felt, unmarked or bottom of foot marked: "Bing"

8" - 10"	$425 - 500
13"	$450 - 525
15"	$600 - 675

BISQUE, UNKNOWN OR LITTLE-KNOWN MAKERS

Various manufacturers of bisque-headed child dolls from 1870 on. No separate listing for these makers. No damage, appropriately dressed.

French

Unknown Maker

Early desirable very French-style face, marked: "J.D.," "J.M. Paris," and "H. G." (possibly Henri and Granfe-Guimonneau)

12"	$9,000 - 11,000
17"	$17,000 - 18,000
21"	$19,000 - 21,000
27"	$25,000 - 27,000

Jumeau or Bru style face, may be marked: "W. D." (Wilhalm Dehler, German doll for French trade)

14" WD, bisque head: $3,500. **Photo courtesy of Morphy Auctions.**

12" mold 136, bébé, bisque, seldom found: $3,900. **Photo courtesy of Richard Withington, Inc.**

or "R. R."

13" - 14"	$3,000 - 3,500
19"	$4,000 - 4,400
24"	$4,400 - 4,700
27"	$5,000 - 5,250

Closed mouth, marked: "J," "137," "136" or others

Excellent quality, unusual face

10" - 12"	$3,600 - 3,900
15" - 17"	$4,200 - 5,200
23" - 25"	$6,200 - 8,000

Standard quality, excellent bisque

13"	$2,200 - 2,450
18"	$3,200 - 3,450
23"	$4,300 - 4,500

Lesser quality, may have poor painting and/or blotches on cheeks

15"	$1,100 - 1,200
21"	$1,600 - 1,800
26"	$2,100 - 2,300

Open mouth

Excellent quality, circa 1890 on French body

15"	$1,300 - 1,500
18"	$2,100 - 2,300
21"	$2,300 - 2,400
24"	$3,000 - 3,100

High cheek color, circa 1920s, may have five-piece papier-mâché body

15"	$575 - 625
19"	$750 - 800
23"	$900 - 950

Danel et Cie., 1889 - 1895, Paris, France.

Bisque, Unknown or Little-Known Makers

18" Pintel & Godchaux, bisque: $4,000. **Photo courtesy of Richard Withington, Inc.**

15" Van Rozen, bisque: sold at auction for $15,930. **Photo courtesy of Morphy Auctions.**

Bisque socket head on composition body, paperweight eyes, wigged, pierced ears

Paris Bébé
10" .... $8,000 - 10,000
11" - 15" ....$4,500 - 5,000
18".............................$5,500 - 6,000
22" ....$6,500 - 7,000
24".............................$7,500 - 8,000
28"...........................$9,000 - 11,000
Bébé Francaise
14"............................$3,500 - 3,600
20" ....$4,300 - 4,400

Delcroix, Henri, 1887, Paris and Montreuil sous Bois. Pressed bisque socket head, closed mouth, paperweight eyes, marked: "Pan Bébé"
8"..............................$5,000 - 7,000
12"...........................$9,000 - 10,000
18" ....$14,000 - 17,000

Falck and Roussel, 1880s, socket head, closed mouth, paperweight eyes, wood and composition body, marked: "F.R."
15" - 16" ....$13,000 - 15,000
18" ....$16,000 - 17,000

Halopeau, A., 1881 - 1889, Paris, pressed bisque socket head, closed mouth, paperweight eyes, cork pate, French wood-and-composition body, marked: "H"
13" ....$36,000 - 50,000
16" - 18" ....$62,000 - 70,000
21" - 24"...............$80,000 - 100,000

Lefebvre et Cie., Alexander, 1875, pressed

bisque socket head, closed mouth, paperweight eyes, French wood-and-composition body, marked: "A.L."
22".......................................$35,000
Too few in database for a reliable range

Joanny, Joseph Louis, 1888, pressed bisque socket head, closed mouth, paperweight eyes, French wood-and-composition body, marked: "J"
12" - 15" ....$8,000 - 10,000
17" - 18"..................$12,000 - 14,000
22" - 23"..................$14,000 - 16,000
28" ....$16,000 - 18,000

J.M. Bébé 0, 1880s, pressed bisque socket head, closed mouth, paperweight eyes, French wood-and-composition body, marked: "J.M."
19" - 26"....................$9,000 - 14,000
Too few in database for a reliable range

M. Bebe, 1890s, pressed bisque socket head, closed mouth, paperweight eyes, pierced ears, French wood-and-composition body, marked: "M" with size number
12" - 14"......................$3,000 - 4,000
19" - 23" ....$2,900 - 3,900

Marque, Albert, 1914, fewer than 100 dolls are believed to have been made
21" - 22" ....sold at auction for $263,000

May Frères Cie, 1890 - 1897, later Steiner (1898 on), closed mouth, paperweight eyes, pierced ears, composition body, marked: "Bébé Mascotte"

63

Bisque, Unknown or Little-Known Makers

19" - 20" ....$3,000 - 4,500
Mothereau, Alexandre, 1880 - 1895, pressed bisque socket head, closed mouth, paperweight eyes, French wood-and-composition body, marked: "B.M."
12" - 15" ....$10,000 - 14,000
22" - 24" ....$20,000 - 22,000
28" - 29" ....$23,000 - 25,000
Pannier, 1875, pressed bisque socket head, closed mouth, paperweight eyes, French wood-and-composition body, marked: "C.P."
20" $59,000
Too few in database for a reliable range
Petite et Dumontier, 1878 - 1890, Paris. Pressed bisque socket head, closed mouth, paperweight eyes, French wood-and-composition body, some with metal hands, marked: "P. D." with size number
16" ....$10,000 - 11,000
18" - 19" ....$12,000 - 14,000
23" ....$15,000 - 16,000
Pintel et Godchaux, 1880 - 1889, Montreuil, France, pressed bisque socket head, closed mouth, paperweight eyes, French wood-and-composition body, marked: "Bébé Charmant"
10" .... $1,800 - 2,000
20" - 22" ....$5,000 - 6,000
Open mouth
18" - 20" ....$1,800 - 2,000
Van Rozen, 1912 - 1914, Paris, France, bisque character socket head, open mouth, glass eyes, composition body
16" - 17" ....$20,000 - 30,000
Verlingue, 1915 - 1921, Montreuil and Boulogne, France, bisque socket head, open mouth, glass eyes, composition body, marked: "J V" with anchor
14" ....$700 - 800
18" - 22" ....$900 - 1,000
German
Various German manufacturers of bisque-headed dolls working from 1870 on. No separate listing for these makers. May be unmarked or marked only with a mold or size number or "Germany"
Baby
Character Baby, 1910 on, solid dome or wigged, open mouth, glass eyes, bent-limb composition body, may be unmarked or marked: "G.B.," "P.M." (Porzellanfabrik Mengersgereuth), "F.B."
9" - 12" ....$175 - 225
14" - 16" ....$300 - 400
19" - 21" ....$450 - 550
My Sweet Baby
23" toddler ....$900 - 1,000
Newborn Baby, 1924, bisque head on cloth body, bisque or celluloid hands, marked: "Baby Weygh," or "IV," other marks, may be unmarked
10" - 12" ....$200 - 250
14" - 17" ....$300 - 350
Gerling Baby
17" ....$575 - 625
Dolly face child, 1880 on, bisque socket-head, wigged, glass eyes, open mouth, ball-jointed composition body or kid body with bisque lower arms, may be unmarked or marked: "G.B.," "K" inside "H," "L.H.K.," "P.Sch," "D.&K."
8" - 10" ....$225 - 275
12" - 15" ....$300 - 375
18" - 20" ....$375 - 450
23" - 25" ....$375 - 425
30" ....$475 - 550
Mold 50, 51, square teeth
14" - 16" ....$1,000 - 1,100

30" bisque socket, German, marked "Olimpia": $500. **Photo courtesy of Richard Withington, Inc.**

Bisque, Unknown or Little-Known Makers

Mold 422, 444, 457, 478
17".....................................$600 - 650
23".....................................$800 - 825
My Girlie, My Dearie, Olimpia, Pansy,
Princess, Special, Sweetheart,
Viola, G.&S., MOA, A.W.
13".....................................$250 - 275
18" - 20".............................$300 - 375
22" - 24".............................$425 - 475
26" - 28" ....$450 - 525
32".....................................$550 - 600
Shoulder head, wigged, 1880 - 1890,
glass eyes, open mouth, kid or cloth
body, special and other molds or no
mold mark
10" - 12"..............................$125 - 200
15" - 17"..............................$250 - 325
20" - 23" ....$300 - 400
Closed mouth
  Mold 50, shoulder head
  14" - 16"............................$450 - 650
  22" - 24"........................$1,200 - 1,275
  Mold 120, 126, 132, Bru-look
  13"..............................$2,500 - 2,600
  19" - 21"......................$3,800 - 4,000
  Mold 51, swivel neck, shoulder head
  17"..................................$950 - 1,100
  German-look doll, composition body
  11" - 13"......................$1,200 - 1,300
  16" - 18"......................$1,600 - 1,800
  Mold 136, French-look
  12" - 14"......................$1,900 - 2,000
  19" - 20"......................$1,600 - 1,700
  E.G., maker Ernst Grossman
  16"..............................$2,500 - 2,600
Shoulder head with molded hair,
1880 on
  American Schoolboy-type
  12" - 14"............................$300 - 375
  18" - 20" ....$400 - 500
Small Child, 1890 to mid 1910s, bisque
socket head, open mouth, set or sleep
eyes, five-piece composition body
  High-quality bisque, flapper-style body
  5" - 6"................................$375 - 425
  8" - 10" ....$400 - 500
Crude five-piece body

7" - 8"................................$175 - 200
Fully jointed body
  7" - 8" ....$575 - 600
Closed mouth
  4" - 5"................................$475 - 500
  8"......................................$750 - 800
Character, 1910 on, glass eyes, open or
open/closed mouth, solid dome or
wigged, composition body
Mold 125, smiling
  13"...............................$6,000 - 6,500
Mold 159
  23" ....$1,100 - 1,200
Mold 213, 214, maker Bawo & Dotter
  13" - 14" ....$4,900 - 5,200
Mold 221, toddler
  16".............................$2,500 - 2,600
Mold 411, shoulder-head lady
  14"...$3,500
Too few in database for a reliable range
Mold 838, P.M. Coquette
  11"....................................$550 - 575
K&K Mama doll, 1924, German
bisque shoulder head, American-
made cloth Mama-style body with
composition limbs, glass eyes, made for
George Borgfeldt
  15" - 23" ....$300 - 375
Wolfe, Louis & Co., 1870 - 1930 on,
Sonneberg, Germany, Boston, and
New York City. Made and distributed
dolls, also distributed dolls made for
them by other companies such as

23" dolly
face,
bisque,
incised
"Princess":
$400.
**Photo
courtesy
of The
Museum
Doll Shop.**

16" character baby, Morimura Brothers, bisque, Japan: $200. **Photo courtesy of McMasters Harris Apple Tree Doll Auctions.**

Hertel, Schwab & Co. and Armand Marseille. They made composition as well as bisque dolls and specialized in babies and Red Cross nurses before World War I. May be marked: "L.W. & C."

Baby, open or closed mouth, sleep eyes
12" - 14"...........................$250 - 350
28" toddler body........$1,000 - 1,100
26".................................$550 - 625
Sunshine Baby, solid dome, cloth body, glass eyes, closed mouth
15"..............................$1,000 - 1,300
Too few in database for a reliable range

Japanese
1915 on, Japan. Bisque-headed dolls often in imitation of the German bisque dolls. Distributed in the United States by companies such as Morimura Brothers, Yamato Importing Co., and others, from 1915 to 1921 marked: "Nippon;" after 1921 marked: "Japan"
Character baby, bisque socket head, solid dome or wigged, open mouth with teeth, bent-limb composition body
11" - 12"...........................$100 - 150
13" - 15" ....$150 - 200
19" - 21"...........................$175 - 225
Hilda look-alike
13".................................$400 - 475
19".................................$550 - 600
Heubach pouty look-alike, 300 series
17" ....$800 - 900

Child, bisque head, mohair wig, glass sleep eyes, open mouth, composition or kid body
9" - 11".............................$100 - 125
13" - 15" ....$150 - 200
19" - 21"...........................$200 - 300
Shoulder-head dolly
12" - 15"...........................$80 - 110
22" ....$150 - 225

BLACK OR BROWN DOLLS

Dolls both homemade and made by various European and American manufacturers. Shades range from black to tan. Sometimes Caucasian mold in dark color, other times sculpted ethnic mold. Values are for dolls in good condition, appropriately dressed.

All bisque
Glass eyes, wigged
4" - 5"..............................$375 - 475
Hertwig, character
2½" ....$85 - 100
Gebrüder Kuhnlenz
3½" - 4" ....$550 - 650
5" - 6".........................$1,100 - 1,200
Kestner, swivel neck
5" - 6" ....$1,800 - 1,900
7" - 8" ....$2,000 - 2,200
Simon & Halbig, 886
5" - 7" ....$1,200 - 1,700

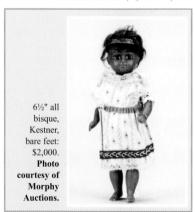

6½" all bisque, Kestner, bare feet: $2,000. **Photo courtesy of Morphy Auctions.**

Black or Brown Dolls

Bisque, 1880 on, French and German makers. Bisque socket head, painted black or black color in slip, brown composition or kid body

French

Poupée (Fashion-type), kid body
Unmarked
14" - 15" ....$3,000 - 3,400
FG
14"...............................$3,400 - 3,600
Bru
17"...........................$9,500 - 10,000
Jumeau
15"...............................$8,500 - 9,000
Bébé
Bru
Circle Dot
13"............................28,000 - 30,000
17" - 19"...................$32,000 - 42,000
Bru Jne
13" ....$22,000 - 28,000
E.D., open mouth
16"..............................$2,500 - 2,900
22"..............................$3,100 - 3,300
Eden Bébé, open mouth
15"..............................$2,300 - 2,500
Gaultier, François, closed mouth
12"..............................$5,000 - 6,000
Jumeau
E.J., closed mouth
10"..............................$6,500 - 7,500
15" - 17".....................$8,200 - 9,300

12" SFBJ, bisque, socket head: $1,500. **Photo courtesy of Morphy Auctions**.

15" Van Rozen, character, bisque: $20,000. **Photo courtesy of Richard Withington, Inc.**

Tête, open mouth
10" ....$1,800 - 2,100
15"..............................$2,500 - 2,700
20" ....$3,200 - 3,300
Tête, closed mouth
15"..............................$4,500 - 4,700
18" ....$4,900 - 5,100
22" - 24" ....$5,200 - 6,500
DEP, open mouth
16"..............................$2,400 - 2,600
Lanternier
18" - 20".....................$1,000 - 1,300
Mothereau
15" - 16".................$16,500 - 18,000
Paris Bébé, closed mouth
13"..............................$3,900 - 4,300
16"..............................$4,500 - 4,600
19"..............................$5,300 - 5,500
S.F.B.J.
Molds 226, 235
15" - 17".....................$2,600 - 3,000
Molds 301, 60 (Unis France mark also), jointed composition body, open mouth
8" - 10"..............................$175 - 225
14" - 17"...........................$350 - 525
Mold 307, googly, glass eyes, closed mouth, wigged
13" ....sold at auction for $2,800
Steiner
Figure A series, closed mouth
10" - 11"......................$5,000 - 5,500

14"............................$5,000 - 6,000
18" - 22"...................$6,500 - 7,000
Open mouth
   8"...........................$2,700 - 3,500
   13"..........................$3,800 - 4,000
   16"..........................$4,200 - 4,500
   23"...........................$6,000 - 6,500
Series C
   18"...........................$6,000 - 6,200
   21"............................$6,400 - 6,600
Van Rozen, 1912 - 1914, Paris,
France, bisque character socket
head, open mouth, glass eyes,
composition body
   16" - 17".................$20,000 - 30,000
German
Unmarked
   Closed mouth
   10 - 11" ....$350 - 400
   14"....................................$450 - 500
   17" ....$600 - 675
   21"....................................$825 - 875
   Open mouth
   5"......................................$150 - 200
   9" - 10" ....$400 - 500
   13"....................................$600 - 700
   15"....................................$800 - 900
   Painted bisque
   Closed mouth
   16"....................................$400 - 450
   19"....................................$550 - 600
   23" ....$900 - 1,000

Open mouth
   7"......................................$150 - 200
   12"....................................$200 - 250
   14"....................................$300 - 350
   18"....................................$500 - 550
   Ethnic features
   15"................................$3,000 - 3,200
   18"................................$3,800 - 4,000
Indian, open mouth, often with
scowling expression, glass eyes, wigged
   10" - 15" ....$225 - 300
Bähr & Pröschild, open mouth,
mold 277, circa 1891
   10"....................................$750 - 800
   12" ....$900 - 1,100
   Mold 244, Indian or native
   14" - 16" ....$900 - 1,200
Bye-Lo Baby
   9" ....$900 - 1,200
   16"...............................$3,200 - 3,000
Goebel, open mouth, dolly face
   10" ....$175 - 200
Handwerck, Heinrich, mold 79, 119
   Open mouth
   12" - 16" ....$800 - 1,000
   18" - 21"....................$1,400 - 1,600
   29" ....$2,200 - 2,400
Heubach, Ernst (Koppelsdorf)
   Mold 145, dolly face, socket head,
   glass eyes, open mouth, five-piece
   composition body
   10" ....$275 - 325

6" mold 134, Konig & Wernicke, toddler: $700. **Photo courtesy of Richard Withington, Inc.**

7" Hanna, Schoenau & Hoffmeister, bisque: $325. **Photo courtesy of Morphy Auctions.**

Black or Brown Dolls

Mold 271, 1914, shoulder head, painted eyes, closed mouth
10".................................$425 - 475
Mold 320, 339, 350
10".................................$375 - 425
13".................................$500 - 525
18".................................$650 - 700
Mold 399, allow more for toddler
10" - 14".........................$375 - 425
17".................................$550 - 600
Mold 414
9"...................................$340 - 450
17" ....$715 - 950
Mold 418 (grin)
9"...................................$675 - 725
14".................................$850 - 900
Mold 444, 451
9"...................................$250 - 300
14".................................$550 - 600
Mold 452, brown
7½" ....$425 - 475
10".................................$525 - 600
15".................................$675 - 700
Mold 458
10".................................$465 - 495
15".................................$700 - 775
Mold 463
12".................................$650 - 750
16" ....$950 - 1,050
Mold 473
13".................................$425 - 475
Mold 1900

14"...................................$500 - 600
17" ....$675 - 775
Heubach, Gebrüder, sunburst mark
Mold 344, glass eyes, open mouth, wigged
22" ....$5,500 - 6,000
Mold 7657, 7658, 7668, 7671
9" - 10"......................$1,800 - 2,100
12" - 13" ....$1,700 - 2,000
12" ..7671 sold at auction for $8,250
Mold 7620, 7661, 7686
10" ....$1,800 - 2,100
14"...........................$3,500 - 4,000
17" ....$4,100 - 4,200
Molds 8457, 9467, Indians
14"...........................$2,400 - 2,500
Kämmer & Reinhardt (K * R)
Child, no mold number
14" -16" ....$1,400 - 1,700
17" - 19" ....$1,900 - 2,100
Mold 100
10" - 11"..........................$850 - 950
11" with flocked hair.............sold at auction for $3,300
17" - 20".....................$1,600 - 1,900
Mold 101, painted eyes
15" - 18" ....$4,000 - 4,900
Mold 101, glass eyes
15" - 17".....................$4,300 - 4,800
Mold 114
13"............................$5,000 - 5,500
Mold 116, 116a

18" mold 1358, Simon & Halbig, bisque: $13,000. **Photo courtesy of Richard Withington, Inc.**

9½" squeeze toy, papier-mâché, German: $200. **Photo courtesy of Richard Withington, Inc.**

15"..............................$4,000 - 4,500
19"..............................$5,900 - 6,200
Mold 122, 126, baby body
7"......................................$400 - 500
12"....................................$700 - 750
18" ....$1,000 - 1,125
Mold 126, toddler
18"..............................$1,400 - 1,600
Mold 192, open mouth child
12" ....$900 - 1,100
Kestner, J. D.
    Baby, no mold number, open
    mouth, teeth
    10" $1,500
Too few in database for a reliable range
    Hilda, mold 245
    12" - 14" ....$2,800 - 3,100
    18"..............................$4,000 - 4,500
    Child, no mold number
    Closed mouth
    14" ....$900 - 1,100
    17" ....$1,500 - 1,700
    Open mouth
    12"..................................$550 - 6255
    16" - 18" ....$750 - 1,100
    Five-piece body
    9".......................................$285 - 300
    12"....................................$350 - 400
    AT-look, closed mouth
    15"..............................$6,000 - 6,500
Knoch, Gebrüder, mold 185 dolly-face
child, five-piece composition body

11" cloth, early 1900s: $1,500. **Photo courtesy of Morphy Auctions.**

8" - 10"..............................$150 - 250
König and Wernicke (KW/G)
    10" - 14"...........................$600 - 500
    18"- 20"..........................$900 - 1,200
    Ethnic features
    17" ....$1,000 - 1,100
Too few in database for a reliable range
Kuhnlenz, Gebrüder
    Closed mouth
    15".....................................$675 - 900
    18"..............................$1,350 - 1,800
    Open mouth, mold 34.14, 34.16,
34.24, etc.
    7" - 9" ....$500 - 700
    12" ....$1,000 - 1,100
    Ethnic features
    16"..............................$3,800 - 4,000
Marseille, Armand
    No mold number, ebony
    11" $850
Too few in database for a reliable range
    Mold 341, 351, 352, 362
    8" - 10" ....$450 - 550
    14" - 16"...........................$550 - 650
    18" - 20" ....$700 - 800
    Mold 390, 390n
    16".....................................$550 - 600
    19"....................................$775 - 825
    23"....................................$895 - 920
    28" ....$1,100 - 1,200
    Mold 966, 970, 971, 992, 995
    (some in composition)

12" Joel Ellis patent, wood: $2,000. **Photo courtesy of Richard Withington, Inc.**

Black or Brown Dolls

21" cloth, Brazilian: $700.
Photo courtesy of Richard Withington, Inc.

9".....................................$265 - 290
14"...................................$550 - 600
18"...................................$875 - 900
Mold 1894, 1897, 1902, 1912, 1914
12"...................................$300 - 400
14"...................................$500 - 600
18"...................................$700 - 800
Recknagel, marked: "R.A.," mold 126, 138
9" - 10"............................$375 - 425
16"...................................$800 - 950
19" ....sold at auction for $3,081
22".............................$1,275 - 1,430
Schmidt, Franz
Mold 1255, baby
14"...................................$800 - 900
21"............................... $900 - 1,000
Closed-mouth child, glass eyes, wig
15"............................$2,300 - 3,000
Schoenau Hoffmeister (S PB H)
Hanna
7" - 8" ....$300 - 400
10 - 12" ....$500 - 600
15"...................................$700 - 750
18"...................................$850 - 900
Painted bisque Hanna, glass eyes, wig
9".....................................$350 - 400
Mold 1909
16"...................................$575 - 625
19"...................................$750 - 850
Simon & Halbig
Mold 126
8" toddler body...............$875 - 925

Mold 639
14"............................$6,400 - 6,800
18"..........................$9,000 - 10,000
Mold 739, open mouth
10"............................$1,000 - 1,200
16"............................$1,500 - 1,800
22" ....$2,800 - 3,000
Closed mouth
13"...$1,500
Too few in database for reliable range
17"............................$2,400 - 2,600
Mold 939
Closed mouth
18"............................$3,000 - 3,300
21"............................$4,300 - 4,500
Open mouth
13", original outfit $2,300
Too few in database for reliable range
Mold 949
Closed mouth
18"............................$3,200 - 3,400
21"............................$3,750 - 3,950
Open mouth
15"............................$2,600 - 2,800
Mold 1009, 1039, 1078, 1079, 1248
open mouth
11" - 12".....................$1,000 - 1,200
15" - 16".....................$1,400 - 1,500
18" - 19".....................$1,900 - 2,100
34"............................$1,900 - 2,000
Pull-string sleep eyes
19"............................$2,200 - 2,300

28" Islander, Norah Wellings, cloth, glass eyes: $400.
Photo courtesy of Richard Withington, Inc.

Black or Brown Dolls

8" Dream Baby, Arranbee, composition, MIB: $400. **Photo courtesy of Memories of Things Past Antiques.**

Mold 1248, open mouth
15"............................$1,400 - 1,500
18"............................$1,600 - 1,800
Mold 1272
20"............................$1,800 - 2,000
Mold 1302, closed mouth, glass eyes, character face
18"..........................$9,000 - 10,000
Indian, sad expression, brown face
18"............................$7,000 - 7,400
Mold 1303, Indian, thin face, man or woman
15" - 16" ....$6,000 - 6,500
21"............................$7,800 - 8,000
Mold 1339, 1368
16"............................$5,700 - 5,900
Mold 1348
15"............................$5,000 - 6,000
Mold 1358
13" - 15" ....$10,000 - 12,500
19" - 24"................$13,000 - 17,000
28"........................$19,000 - 21,000
Herm Steiner, Mold 128
11" - 13"......................$150 - 200
Papier-mâché, shoulder head, cloth or leather body
10" - 13"......................$425 - 525
Squeeze toy, molded head, glass eyes

10" - 13".........................$200 - 300
Wood
Cooperative Manufacturing Co., 1873 - 1874, Joel Ellis manufactured wooden dolls with pressed heads and mortise and double tenon joints, with metal hands, black dolls were painted to order
12"............................$2,000 - 2,500
China
Frozen Charlie/Charlotte
3"..............................$100 - 135
6"..............................$225 - 250
8 - 9" ....$300 - 350
Shoulder-head doll
9" - 11" ....$400 - 1,000
Celluloid
All celluloid, German or American
10"..............................$150 - 200
15"..............................$275 - 350
18"..............................$500 - 600
Celluloid shoulder head, kid body, allow more for glass eyes
17" ....$275 - 350
21" ....$375 - 450
French-type, marked: "SNF"
14"..............................$350 - 400
16" - 18".......................$500 - 600
Kämmer & Reinhardt, mold 775, 778
11" ....$175 - 200
18"..............................$425 - 475
Cloth
Alabama Baby: See Alabama Baby section.
Babyland Rag Doll: See Babyland Rag Doll section.
Brazilian, embroidered features, shell fingernails
17" - 19"......................$400 - 600
Bruckner: See Bruckner section.
Homemade, painted, embroidered or appliquéd features, values vary according to the skill of the maker and the charm of the doll
Mid 1800s-early 1900s
8" - 12" ....$400 - 1,600
15" - 20" ....$600 - 1,800

Black or Brown Dolls

1900 - 1920
15" - 18" ....$250 - 600
1920 - 1940
15" - 18" ....$250 - 350
1930s Mammy-type
14" ....$400 - 500
18" ....$500 - 600
Chase: See Chase section.
Golliwog, 1895 to present. Character
from 1895 book *The Adventures of Two
Dutch Dolls and a Golliwogg,* all-cloth,
various English makers. See also
Deans Rag section.
1895 - 1920
13" ....$750 - 800
1930 - 1950
11" ....$400 - 500
15" ....$500 - 675
18" ....$600 - 700
1950 - 1970s
13" - 18" ....$250 - 325
Steiff, 1996
Molly Golli and Peg..................$450
Mask face, 1920 - 1930s, American
13" - 18" ....$65 - 100
Stockinette Baby (often mis-called
Black Beecher), embroidered features,
glass eyes
20" - 22" ....$2,200 - 2,800
Wellings, Norah, 1926 to 1960,
Wellington, Shropshire, England,
The Victoria Toy Works molded
heads and bodies of velvet, velveteen,
plush and felt
Black Islander, glass eyes
13" ....$180 - 250
16" ....$300 - 325
28" ....$450 - 500
Composition, doll in good condition
with original clothing
Unkown maker
Baby with three pigtails, painted eyes
8" - 10" ....$75 - 100
Arranbee Doll Co.
Dream Baby, 1927, composition,
lower arms and legs, cloth body,
metal sleep eyes

12" Kewpie, Cameo, composition: $200. **Photo courtesy of Richard Withington, Inc.**

8" - 10" ....$150 - 200
Averill
Madame Hendron, designed by
Grace Drayton
13" ....$400 - 500
Cameo
Kewpie , all composition, jointed body,
blue wings
8" ....$150 - 175
11" - 13" ....$200 - 250
Scootles, 1925 on, Rose O'Neill design,
all composition, painted side-glancing
eyes, paper wrist tag, unmarked
12" ....$400 - 500
Effanbee
Baby Grumpy
12" - 16" ....$525 - 700
Bubbles
17" - 22" ....$650 - 750
Candy Kid, original shorts, robe
and gloves
12" ....$300 - 350
Patsy baby
10" ....$575 - 625
Skippy, original outfit
14" $900
Too few in database for reliable range

Black or Brown Dolls

Horsman
Baby Bumps
12".....................................$200 - 225
Campbell Kid, 1910 on, designed by
Helen Trowbridge, based on Grace
Drayton's drawings, composition head,
painted and molded hair, side-glancing
painted eyes, closed smiling mouth
10" - 11"............................$250 - 300
Ideal
Marama, Shirley Temple body, based on
character from the movie *Hurricane*
13" ....$900 - 1,000
König & Wernicke, mold 134
14".....................................$450 - 500
Leo-Moss-type ....$2,500 - 8,000
Patsy-type
13" - 14"............................$200 - 300
Skookum Apple character head,
googly look
14" $300
Too few in database for reliable range
Tony Sarg Mammy with baby
18" ....$900 - 1,100
Topsy-type, cotton pigtails
10" - 12"............................$175 - 225
Rubber
Amosandra, from Amos and Andy radio

show
10" ....$225 - 275
Sun Rubber So-Wee,
10" ....$40 - 50
Hard Plastic
Pedigree
Many Lou, Ashtrakan wig, flirty eyes
16" ....$100 - 125
Walker 21".......................$150 - 175
Terri Lee
Benji, painted plastic, brown, 1946 -
1962, black lamb's wool wig
16"..............................$1,800 - 2,000
Patty Jo, 1947 - 1949
16"..............................$1,200 - 1,500
Bonnie Lou, black
16"..............................$1,200 - 1,800
Vogue
Strung Ginny, 1950 - 1953, hard plastic,
sleep eyes, strung joints, painted eyes,
molded hair with mohair wig, clothing
tagged: "Vogue Dolls" or "Vogue Dolls,
Inc. Medford Mass.," inkspot tag on
white with blue letters, head marked:
"Vogue"; body marked: "Vogue Doll"
8" ....sold at auction for $1,249
Vinyl
Baby Crissy, 1973 - 1976, all-vinyl

12" Scootles, Cameo, composition: $450.
Photo courtesy of Morphy Auctions.

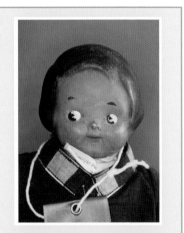

11" Horsman, composition: $300. **Photo cour-
tesy of Richard Withington, Inc.**

24" Baby Crissy, Ideal, vinyl, MIB: $275.
Photo courtesy of Charlotte's Web Vintage Dolls and Collectibles.

jointed body, foam-filled legs and arms, rooted auburn grow hair, two painted teeth, brown sleep eyes, marked: "©1972//IDEAL TOY COPR.//2M 5511//B orGHB-H-225"
24" ....$125 - 140
Drowsy, Mattel, 1965 - 1974, vinyl head, stuffed body, sleepers, pull-string talker
15½" ....$75 - 100
Dee and Cee, 1960- 1970s, Canada, vinyl head and body, rooted hair. See Vinyl section.
12" - 15"..............................$50 - 60
Effanbee Fluffy, 1957 on
8"..$30 - 40
FloJo, depicts Florence Griffin Joyner, made by LJN
11½" ....$15 - 20
Gotz
World of Children Series
23"....................................$150 - 180
Mindy, 1957, Earl Pullan Co. Canada, vinyl head with molded braids, stuffed vinyl body
15"....................................$200 - 250
Miss Peep, Cameo
18" ....$100 - 150
Sara Lee, Ideal, 1950, vinyl head and

limbs, cloth body, sleep eyes
17" ....$350 - 400

BLEUETTE

1905 - 1960, France. This premium doll was first made in bisque and later in composition for a weekly children's periodical, *La Semanine De Suzette* (The Week of Suzette), which also produced patterns for Bleuette. Premiere Bleuette was a bisque socket head, Tété Jumeau, marked only with a "1" superimposed on a "2," and 10⅝" tall. She had set blue or brown glass eyes, open mouth with four teeth, wig, and pierced ears. The composition jointed body was marked "2" on back and "1" on the sole of each foot. This mold was made only in 1905. S.F.B.J., a bisque socket head, began production in 1905, using a Fleischmann and Bloedel mold marked "6/0," blue or brown glass eyes, wig, open mouth, and teeth. S.F.B.J. mold marked "SFBJ 60" or "SFBJ 301 1" was a bisque socket head, open mouth with teeth, wig, and blue or brown glass eyes. All Bleuettes were 10⅝" tall prior to 1933, after that all Bleuettes were 11⅜".

10⅞" Bleuette, S.F.B.J., marked mold 301, bisque: $3,300. **Photo courtesy of Morphy Auctions.**

Bisque
Premiere, 1905, Jumeau head
    10⅝" ....$4,800 - 6,000
SFJB 6/0, 1905 - 1915, head made in
Germany by Fleischman
    10⅝" ....$2,800 - 3,100
SFBJ 60 8/0, 1916 - 1933
    10⅝" .... $2,200 - 3,000
SFBJ 301 1
    10⅝" ....$2,800 - 3,300
71 Unis France 149 60 8/0
    10⅝" ....$1,900 - 2,500
71 Unis France 149, 1933 on
    11⅜" ....$1,400 - 1,600
Composition, 1930 - 1933
SFBJ 301 or 71 Unis France 149 251,
1930 - 1933
    10⅝" ....$1,500 - 1,700
SFBJ or 71 Unis France 149 251, 1933 on
    11⅜" ....$600 - 900

BONNET HEADS

1860s - 1940s on, dolls made of a variety
of materials by numerous manufacturers,
all with molded bonnets or hats. More
elaborate hat brings higher end of range.
All-bisque, German immobiles, painted
eyes

10" bonnet heads, Hertwig, bisque: each $125.
Photo courtesy of Morphy Auctions.

11" bonnet head, papier-mâché: $1,000.
Photo courtesy of Richard Withington, Inc.

    5" ....$125 - 175
    7" - 8"...............................$275 - 325
    10" ....$350 - 375
Stone bisque immobile
    3½" - 5" ....$25 - 35
Bisque, socket or shoulder head,
five-piece composition body, kid body
or cloth body
Painted eyes
    5" - 8" ....$150 - 235
    11" - 14"...........................$300 - 500
    18" - 20" ....$400 - 500
Glass eyes
    7" - 9" ....$250 - 350
    12" - 15" ....$500 - 750
Alt, Beck & Gottschalk
Painted eyes
    16"............................$1,500 - 2,000
Glass eyes
    18" $1,530
Too few in database for a reliable range
Handwerck, Max, **WWI** military
figure, painted eyes, marked: "Elite"
Bisque socket head, glass eyes,
molded helmet
    10" - 14"......................$1,900 - 2,200
Heubach, Gebrüder
Mold 7975, "Baby Stuart," (so-called)

Bonnet Heads

20" bonnet head, parian (so called), German: $1,600. **Photo courtesy of Richard Withington, Inc.**

circa 1912, glass eyes, removable molded bisque bonnet

9" - 13" ....$1,600 - 3,000

Molds 7877, 7977, "Baby Stuart," (so-called) circa 1912, molded bonnet, closed mouth, painted eyes

8" - 9" ....$975 - 1,025
11" - 13" ....$1,400 - 1,600
15" ....$1,600 - 1,700

Hertwig, molded bonnet, jointed shoulders

8" - 10" ....$100 - 125
14" - 16" ....$150 - 200

Japan

8" - 9" ....$85 - 95
12" ....$125 - 145

Molded shirt or top

15" ....$750 - 850
21" ....$1,200 - 1,305

Recknagel, bonnet-head baby, painted eyes, open/closed mouth, teeth, molds 22, 28, 44, molded white boy's cap, bent-leg baby body

8" - 9" ....$450 - 550
11" - 12" ....$600 - 700

Stone bisque

8" - 9" ....$100 - 150
12" - 15" ....$175 - 225

Papier-mâché, leather body, wooden lower limbs

Painted eyes

12" - 18" ....$1,500 - 1,800

Man, molded military hat, 1840s - 1850s

16" ....$4,500 - 5,500

Glass eyes

13" ....$5,000 - 6,000

Parian-type, cloth body, composition or wooden lower limbs

Painted eyes

4" - 6" ....$400 - 900
10" - 17" ....$1,000 - 1,400

Glass eyes

10" - 14" ....$2,500 - 5,000

China, blond or black hair, painted eyes

Common style and quality

10" - 13" ....$150 - 200

High quality

8" -10½" ....$5,000 - 7,000
12" - 14" ....$6,000 - 8,000

Wax-over-composition, cloth body, composition or wooden lower limbs, glass eyes

7" - 13" ....$250 - 500
15" ....$575 - 800
19" - 23" ....$600 - 1,500
29" ....$2,000 - 2,200

12" bonnet head, common style, china: $175. **Photo courtesy of Richard Withington, Inc.**

26" boudoir, papier-mâché head: $300. **Photo courtesy of Pieces of Old.**

10½" Bru Smiler Poupée, bisque, original box: $4,200. **Photo courtesy of Richard Withington, Inc.**

BOUDOIR DOLLS

1915 - 1940s, usually made in France, Italy and United States. Long-limbed dolls of a variety of materials, used primarily as decorative items, fancy costumes, usually 28" - 30".

Cloth mask face, 1920s
High quality with silk
floss hair....................................$475 - 600
Average quality ....$250 - 350
Composition or papier-mâché head, 1920 - 1940s
Smoker ....$500 - 850
High quality ....$400 - 600
Average quality..........................$165 - 275
Hard plastic,
1940s ....$100 - 175

BRU

1866 - 1899, Bru Jne. & Cie, Paris and Montreuil-sous-Bois, France. Bru eventually became one of the members of the S.F.B.J. syndicate (1899 - 1953). Bébés Bru with kid bodies are some of the most collectible dolls, highly sought after because of the fine quality of bisque, delicate coloring and fine workmanship. Brus are made of pressed bisque and have a metal spring stringing mechanism in the neck. Allow more for original clothes and rare body styles.

Poupée (Fashion-type lady), 1866 -1877, pressed bisque socket head attached to bisque shoulder plate with metal spring stringing, painted or glass eyes, pierced ears, cork pate, mohair wig, kid body, some marked with numbers only, some with shoulder plate marked: " B. Jne et Cie"
12" - 13" ....$3,900 - 4,200
15" - 17"......................$3,200 - 3,500
20" - 21" ....$4,200 - 4,800
Wooden lower arms
16" - 19".....................$5,700 - 6,000
Wooden body
15" - 16" ....$8,900 - 9,500
26"..........................$12,000 - 14,000
Smiler, 1873 on, closed smiling mouth,

14" Bru Breveté, bisque: $20,000. **Photo courtesy of James D. Julia Auctioneers.**

Bru

14" Crescent Mark Bru, bisque: $24,000. **Photo courtesy of Richard Withington, Inc.**

marked with size letters A through O

Kid body with kid or bisque lower arms
11"	$3,600 - 3,800
13" - 15"	$4,000 - 5,000
20" - 21"	$7,500 - 8,500

Wooden lower arms
16" - 19"	$5,500 - 7,500

Wooden body
15" - 16"	$8,000 - 9,500
18" - 21"	$11,000 - 15,000

Surprise Doll, poupée with two faces
13"	$12,000 - 15,000

Bru Breveté, 1879 - 1880, pressed bisque socket head on bisque shoulder plate, paperweight eyes, multi-stroked eyebrows, closed mouth with space between the lips, full cheeks, pierced ears, cork pate, skin wig, kid or wooden articulated body, marked on head only with size number
10" - 12"	$18,000 - 23,000
14" - 16"	$20,000 - 26,000
19" - 22"	$24,000 - 28,000

Circle Dot or Crescent mark Bru, 1879 - 1884, pressed bisque socket head on bisque shoulder plate, paperweight eyes, multi-stroked eyebrows, open/closed mouth with molded, painted teeth, full cheeks, pierced ears, cork pate, mohair or human-hair wig, gusseted kid body with bisque lower arms
12" size 1	$25,000 - 30,000
13" - 14"	$22,000 - 24,000
18" - 19"	$23,000 - 29,000
22" - 24"	$28,000 - 31,000
31"	$32,000 - 35,000

Bru Jne, 1880 - 1891, pressed bisque socket head on bisque shoulder plate with deeply molded shoulders, paperweight eyes, multi-stroked eyebrows, open/closed mouth with molded, painted teeth, pierced ears, cork pate, mohair or human-hair wig, gusseted kid body with wooden upper arms, bisque lower arms and kid or wooden lower legs
12" - 14"	$28,000 - 32,000
15" - 17"	$33,000 - 40,000

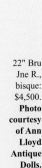

11" Bru Jne, size 1, bisque: $30,000. **Photo courtesy of Richard Withington, Inc.**

22" Bru Jne R., bisque: $4,500. **Photo courtesy of Ann Lloyd Antique Dolls.**

15" Bru Bébé Teteur, bisque: $9,000. **Photo courtesy of Richard Withington, Inc.**

20" - 24" ....$36,000 - 42,000
30" - 35" ....$35,000 - 40,000

Bru Jne R, 1891 - 1899, pressed bisque socket head on bisque shoulder plate with deeply molded shoulders, paperweight eyes, multi-stroked eyebrows, open/closed mouth with four to six teeth, pierced ears, cork pate, mohair or human-hair wig, articulated wood-and-composition body

Open mouth
12"...........................$2,000 - 2,500
18" - 21".....................$4,000 - 5,000

Closed mouth
10½" ....$4,500 - 5,000
12" - 13" ....$5,500 - 7,000
15" - 16"....................$9,500 - 10,000
19" - 21" ....$7,500 - 8,500
27" - 29" ....$8,500 - 9,500

Mechanical Specialty Dolls

Bébé Teteur (nursing), 1879 -1898, open mouth for insertion of bottle, screw key at back of head allowed doll to drink
13" ....$7,500 - 8,500
15" - 17"....................$9,000 - 10,000
19" - 24"..................$10,000 - 11,000

Bébé Gourmand (eating), 1880 on, open mouth with tongue, bisque lower legs, when fed, food pellets went in through mouth and out through holes on the bottom of the feet, special shoes with a flap opening on the bottom allowed for food removal
16" - 18" ....$40,000 - 50,000

Bébé Modele, 1880 on, Breveté face, carved wooden body
16" - 19"..................$31,000 - 36,000

Bébé Musique (musical), 1892 on, circle-dot head on wooden body, Swiss music box inside, 17" ....
        sold at auction for $44,000

Bébé Baiser (kiss throwing), 1892 on, pull-string mechanism raises doll's arm and simulates throwing a kiss
11"..............................$4,100 - 4,200
15"..............................$4,300 - 4,400
22" ....$5,500 - 6,000

Bébé Respirant (breathing), 1892 on, key or lever in torso activates mechanism to simulate chest movement
20" - 24" ....$12,000 - 15,000

Bru shoes ....$600 - 1,100

ALBERT BRUCKNER

1901 - 1930 on, Jersey City, New Jersey. Made some dolls with molded cloth mask faces, cloth bodies and printed features for the Horsman Babyland line. Later made flat-faced cloth dolls.

Molded cloth, mask faces
12" - 14" ....$175 - 225

Black......................................$300 - 400

Topsy-Turvy ....$400 - 475

12" Bruckner, cloth: $350. **Photo courtesy of Richard Withington, Inc.**

Flat faced, printed, 1925 on, such as
Dollypop, Pancake Baby, others
12" - 13".............................$150 - 200

BUCHERER

1921 -1930s, Armisil, Switzerland. Metal
bodies with metal ball joints, composition head, hands and feet, marked:
"MADE IN SWITZERLAND PATENTS
APPLIED FOR"
6½" - 7" ....$250 - 400
8" male aviator ....sold at
auction for $1,100
Regional and characters such as
baseball player, fireman, military,
Pinocchio, others....................$300 - 500
Comic characters such as Charlie
Chaplin, Happy Hooligan,
Katzenjammers, Maggie and Jiggs, Mutt
and Jeff, others ....$500 - 750

6" Bucherer,
metal: $325.
**Photo
courtesy of
Richard
Withington,
Inc.**

BUDDY LEE

1920 - 1962, United States. Made by the
H.D. Lee Co., Inc. as an advertising doll
to spotlight their overalls and work gear.
Doll with molded hair, painted side-
glancing eyes, jointed shoulders, legs
molded apart, all original clothing,
marked with embossed "Buddy Lee."
Composition, 1920 -1948, 13"
Engineer, Cowboy, Phillips 66 ....$350 - 500
Black Engineer

....sold at online auction for $2,750
*Football uniform, Gulf Oil, Minneapolis
Moline uniform* ....$1,500 - 2,000
Too few in database for reliable range
Hard Plastic, 1949 - 1962, 13"
Engineer, Phillips 66, others........$400 - 475
John Deere ....$500 - 600
Vinyl Reissue, 1997
13" ....$100 - 125

BURGARELLA

1925 - WWII, Rome, Italy. Made by Gaspare
Burgarella, designed by Ferdinando
Stracuzzi. Cloth label sewn into outfit
reads: "BURGARELLA Made in Italy."
Child, high-quality composition,
expressively painted eyes with heavy
shading, high-quality human-hair or
mohair wig, jointed at neck, shoulders,
hips and knees
16" - 18".....................$1,800 - 2,800
22" ....$3,000 - 3,800

BYE-LO BABIES

1922 - 1952. Baby doll designed by Grace
Storey Putnam to represent a three-day-
old infant. Distributed by George
Borgfeldt and Co. Bisque heads made by
German makers such as Hertel and
Schwab, Kestner, Kling, others. Cloth
bodies made by K and K in the United
States. Composition bodies made by
König & Wernicke in Germany.
Composition head made by Cameo Doll
Co.
All bisque, 1925 on, made by Kestner,
some with pink or blue booties, back
marked: "G. S. Putnam"; paper sticker
on chest reads:"Bye-Lo Baby"
Painted eyes
4" - 5" ....$225 - 300
6"....................................$350 - 400
8"....................................$500 - 600
Glass eyes, wigged
5" - 6" ....$650 - 750
8"....................................$850 - 950

Bye-Lo Babies

10" Bye-Lo baby, bisque, German: $350. **Photo courtesy of Morphy Auctions**

Swivel neck, glass eyes

5" - 6"	.........................$1,200 - 1,300
8"	...............................$1,300 - 1,500

Bisque head, flange-neck head on cloth body, "frog"-style legs or straight legs, closed mouth, molded, painted hair, blue sleep eyes, celluloid or composition hands, head incised" Copyright 1923 by//Grace S Putnam", some bodies stamped: "Bye-Lo Baby"

8" - 9"	..............................$250 - 300
10" - 12"	...........................$350 - 400
15" black	....sold at auction for $2,800
14" - 16"	...........................$400 - 450
18" - 22"	.........................$500 - 600

Socket head on composition body

13" - 15"	....................$1,000 - 1,400

Smiling face variation, circa 1927, flange-neck head on cloth body

17" - 18"

Painted eyes	..sold at auction for $2,000
Glass eyes	....sold at auction for $3,250

Composition head, 1924 on, molded painted hair, sleep or painted eyes, closed mouth, cloth body

12" - 13"	.........................$250 - 325
16"	..................................$450 - 500

Celluloid, made by Karl Standfuss,

Saxony, Germany

All celluloid

4"	....$150 - 200
6"	....$225 - 275

Celluloid head, cloth body

10"	.....................................$300 - 350
12"	.....................................$425 - 450

Wax, 1925, sold in New York boutiques

18" - 20"	....................$1,500 - 2,000

Wood, 1925, made by Schoenhut

	..................................$2,300 - 2,500

Vinyl, Horsman, 1972, head marked: "Grace Storey Putnam"

14"	....$25 - 30

Other Putnam dolls

Fly-Lo, 1926 -1930, bisque, ceramic or composition head, glass or metal sleep eyes, molded painted hair, flange neck on cloth body, celluloid hands, satin wings in pink, green or gold, head marked: "Corp. by //Grace S. Putnam"
Bisque, less for ceramic

9" - 11"	.....................$3,000 - 4,000

Composition

12" - 14"	...........................$700 - 900

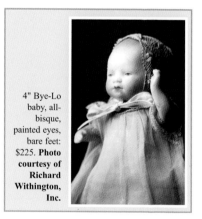

4" Bye-Lo baby, all-bisque, painted eyes, bare feet: $225. **Photo courtesy of Richard Withington, Inc.**

CABBAGE PATCH KIDS

1978 on, initially designed by Xavier Roberts as an all-cloth needle-sculpted doll. The dolls were made in varying skin tones and hair-and-eye color combinations, giving them each a unique look and "personality." Kids were 22", Newborns 17", and Preemies 15". Later licensing agreement led to vinyl-headed dolls made by Coleco. In 1988 rights for the vinyl-headed dolls went to Hasbro and in 1994 to Mattel. In 2004 rights for vinyl production were sold to Play Along Toys and 4Kids Entertainment. Dolls listed are in perfect condition with original clothing and tags or paperwork.

1978 on, Babyland General Hospital, Cleveland, GA, cloth, needle sculpture, signature color changes year to year. Value can double for MIB.

"A" blue edition
    1978 ....$600 - 700
"B" red edition
    1978 ....$500 - 550
"C" burgundy edition
    1979 ....$400 - 450
"D" purple edition
    1979 ....$350 - 450
    black $600
"E" bronze edition
    1980 ....$150 - 200
Preemie edition
    1980 ....$150 - 200
New Ears edition
    1981 ....$150 - 300
Ears edition
    1982 ....$250 - 200
Green edition
    1983 ....$150 - 200
"KP" dark-green edition
    1983 ....$150 - 200
"KPR" red edition
    1983 ....$150 - 200
"KPB" burgundy edition
    1983 ....$150 - 200
"KPZ" edition
    1983 - 1984.....................$40 - 75
Champagne edition
    1983 - 1984.....................$40 - 100
"KPP" purple edition
    1984 ....$40 - 100
"KPF," "KPG," "KPH," "KPI," "KPJ" editions

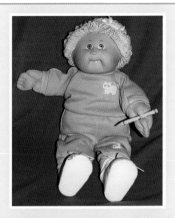

18" Cabbage Patch Kid, Coleco, vinyl head, circa 1989: $30. **Doll courtesy of private collection.**

    1984 - 1985.........................$50 - 75
Emerald edition
    1985 ....$50 - 75
Aquamarine
    1988 ....$50 - 125
Jade
    1989 ....$50 - 100
Garnet
    1991 ....$40 - 100
1989 through 1990s
Kid, Newborn or Preemie ....$35 - 90
2004 on
    Kid....................................$150 - 200
Coleco Cabbage Patch Kids, 1983 on, vinyl head, cloth body, black signature stamp. Value can double for MIB.
Kid, Newborn or Preemie ....$12 - 40
Popcorn hairdos, rare ....$85 - 100
Cornsilk Kid ....$40 - 50
Porcelain, 1985, made by Shaders
    Kid.......................................$40 - 90

CAMEO DOLL COMPANY

1922 - 1930 on, New York City, Port Allegheny, Pennsylvania. Joseph L. Kallus's company made composition dolls, some with wood segmented bodies and cloth bodies. All dolls listed are in good condition with original clothing; allow less for crazed or undressed dolls.

Bisque

Baby Bo Kaye

Bisque head, made in Germany, molded hair, open mouth, glass eyes, cloth body, composition limbs, good condition, marked: "J.L. Kallus: Corp. Germany//1394/30"

7" - 9" ....$1,000 - 1,400
17" - 20" ....$1,600 - 2,100

All bisque, molded hair, glass sleep eyes, open mouth, two teeth, swivel neck, jointed arms and legs, molded pink or blue shoes, socks, unmarked, some may retain original round sticker on body

5" ....$1,100 - 1,200
7" - 8" ....$1,500 - 1,600

Celluloid

Baby Bo Kaye

Celluloid head, made in Germany, molded hair, open mouth, glass eyes, cloth body

12" - 16"...........................$750 - 950

Composition

Annie Rooney, 1926, designed by Jack Collins, all composition, yarn wig, legs painted black, molded shoes

13"....................................$475 - 500
17"....................................$650 - 700

Baby Blossom, 1927, composition upper torso, cloth lower body and legs,

molded hair, open mouth, marked: "DES, J.L.Kallus"

19" - 20" ....$550 - 650

Baby Bo Kaye

Composition head, molded hair, open mouth, glass eyes, light crazing

14"...................................$650 - 675

Bandy, 1929, designed by J. Kallus, composition head, wood segmented body, hat marked: "General Electric Radio"

18½" ....$800 - 900

Betty Boop, 1932, composition-head character, wood segmented body, molded hair, painted features, label on torso

11"...................................$600 - 700
20" ....$1,000 - 1,100

Champ, 1942, composition with freckles

16" ....$575 - 600

Eugene the Jeep, composition and wood segmented doll based on character from Popeye comics

12" - 17" ....$800 - 1,000

Felix the Cat, composition and wood segmented doll

9" - 13"...........................$200 - 275

Giggles, 1946, composition with molded loop for ribbon, marked: "Giggles Doll, A Cameo Doll"

12" - 14"..........................$275 - 300

Ho-Ho, 1940, painted plaster, laughing

10" Margie, Cameo, composition: $175. **Photo courtesy of Joan & Lynette Antique Dolls and Accessories.**

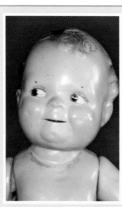

12" Scootles, Cameo, composition: $200. **Photo courtesy of Richard Withington, Inc.**

mouth

5½" ....$125 - 150

Joy, 1932, composition-head character, wood segmented body, molded hair, painted features, label on torso

10" ....$325 - 350

15" ....$425 - 475

Margie, 1929, composition-head character, wood segmented body, molded hair, painted features, label on torso

10" ....$225 - 250

15" ....$325 - 350

17" ....$400 - 450

Pete the Pup, 1930 - 1935, composition-head character, wood segmented body, molded hair, painted features, label on torso

9" - 12" ....$175 - 250

Pinkie, 1930 - 1935, composition-head character, wood segmented body, molded hair, painted features, label on torso

7" - 10" ....$375 - 425

Popeye, 1935, composition-head character, wood segmented body, molded hair, painted features, label on torso

14" ....$150 - 250

Pretty Bettsie, composition head, molded hair, painted side-glancing eyes, open/closed mouth, composition one-piece body and limbs, wooden neck joint, molded and painted dress with ruffles, shoes, and socks, triangular red tag on chest reads: "Pretty Bettsie//Copyright J. Kallus"

18" ....$400 - 450

Scootles, 1925 on, designed by Rose O'Neill, all composition, painted side-glancing eyes, paper wrist tag, unmarked

7" - 8" ....$225 - 275

12" ....$275 - 350

15" ....$400 - 425

22" ....$700 - 800

26" ....$950 - 1,150

Composition, sleep eyes

15" ....$575 - 650

Black composition

12" ....$400 - 475

Hard Plastic and Vinyl, dolls listed are in good condition wearing original clothing. Value can double for MIB.

Baby Mine, 1962 - 1964, vinyl and cloth, sleep eyes

16" ....$100 - 125

19" ....$150 - 200

Ho Ho, laughing mouth, squeaker, tag, marked: "Rose O'Neill"

White

7" ....$75 - 100

Black

7" ....$125 - 175

Miss Peep, 1957 - 1970s, pin-jointed shoulders and hips, vinyl

15" ....$60 - 80

18" ....$70 - 80

Black

18" ....$100 - 125

1984, Jesco re-issue, all vinyl

16" ....$25 - 30

Miss Peep, Newborn, 1962, vinyl head, rigid plastic body

14" - 18" ....$50 - 100

Pinkie, 1950s

10" - 11" ....$125 - 150

Scootles, 1964, vinyl

14" ....$65 - 75

18" Miss Peep, Cameo, vinyl, MIB: $300. **Photo courtesy of Hatton's Gallery of Dolls.**

20" ....$125 -175
1980s, Jesco
12"...................................$25 - 30
16"...................................$40 - 50
19"...................................$60 - 80

CATTERFELDER PUPPENFABRIK

1906 on, Catterfeld, Thuringia, Germany. Had heads made by Kestner. Trademark: My Sunshine

C.P. Child, 1902 on, dolly face, bisque socket head, glass sleep eyes, wigged, open mouth with teeth, ball-jointed composition body
Mold 264 and others
9".....................................$250 - 300
14" - 16"............................$325 - 375
25" - 28" ....$450 - 550

C.P. Character child, 1910 on, bisque socket head, painted eyes, wigged, open mouth with teeth, ball-jointed composition body
Mold: 207, 210, 215, 219, 217, others
12"...............................$5,500 - 6,000
15" -16" ....$8,500 - 9,000
Mold 220, glass eyes
14"...............................$8,300 - 8,500
Mold 524, painted eyes, closed mouth, wigged
18" ....sold at auction for $5,750
Character Baby, 1910 on, bisque socket

head, molded hair or wig, painted or glass sleep eyes, composition baby body
Mold: 200, 201, 207, 208, others
8" - 10" ....$550 - 650
14" - 16"...........................$750 - 800
19" - 21"...........................$875 - 925
201, toddler
8" - 10" ....$900 - 1,200
Mold 262, 263
15" - 17"...........................$450 - 500
20" - 22" ....$550 - 600
262 toddler, five-piece composition body
18" ....$775 -825

CELLULOID

Early form of plastic made from nitrocellulose and a plasticizer such as camphor. Came into use in 1869 and an improved version became popular about 1905. Made in numerous countries by various manufacturers:
England - Wilson Doll co., Cascelliod Ltd. (Palitoy)
France - Petitcollin (profile of eagle head), Widow Chalory, Convert Cie, Parisienn Cellulosine, Neuman & Marx (dragon), Société Industrielle de Celluloid (SIC), Société Nobel Francaise (SNF in diamond), Sicoine, others.
Germany - Bähr & Pröschild, Buschow & Beck (helmet Minerva), Catterfelder Puppenfibrik Co., Cuno & Otto

16" mold 262, Catterfelder Puppenfabrik, bisque: $475. **Photo courtesy of Morphy Auctions.**

17" babies, celluloid: each $200. **Photo courtesy of Richard Withington, Inc.**

Celluloid

5" celluloid, French, MOC: $250. **Photo courtesy of Pieces of Old.**

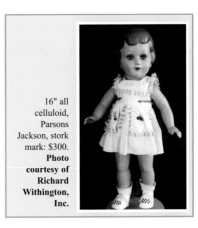

16" all celluloid, Parsons Jackson, stork mark: $300. **Photo courtesy of Richard Withington, Inc.**

Dressel, E. Maar & Sohn (3M), Emasco, Kämmer & Reinhardt, Kestner, Koönig & Wernicke, A. Hagendorn & Co., Hermsdorfer Celluloidwarenfabrik (lady bug), Dr. Paul Hunaeus, Kohn & Wengenroth, Rheinsche Gummi und Celluloid Fabrik Co. later known as Schildkröte (turtle mark), Max Rudolph, Bruno Schmidt, Franz Schmidt & Co., Schoberl & Becker (mermaid), which used Cellba as a trade name, Karl Standfuss, Albert Wacker, others. USA - Averill, Bo-Peep (H.J. Brown), DuPont Viscaloid Co., Horsman, Irwin, Marks Bros., Parsons-Jackson (stork mark), Celluloid Novelty Co. others.

All Celluloid

Baby, 1910 on, painted eyes
  4" - 8" ....$65 - 90
  12" - 15".............................$160 - 180
  19" - 21" ....$210 - 225

Marked "France"
  3".......................................$100 - 125
  5" - 9" ....$120 - 250
  16" - 18".............................$350 - 450

Marked German character baby
  12".....................................$325 - 400

Marked "Japan"
  4" - 5"...................................$18 - 22
  8" - 10"..................................$65 - 75
  13" - 15" ....$145 - 165

Marked: "Occupied Japan"

24" ....$150 - 175

Child, painted eyes, jointed at shoulder and hips
  5" - 7"...................................$75 - 100
  11" - 14" ....$125 - 175
  18" - 20"..............................$225 - 275

Glass eyes
  12" - 13" ....$200 - 250
  15" - 16".............................$250 - 300
  24" ....$350 - 375

Marked "France"
  7" - 9"..................................$150 - 175
  14" - 18".............................$300 - 325
  22" - 24".............................$375 - 425

Marked "Japan"
  With molded clothing
    3" - 4" ....$50 - 60
    8" - 9"................................$125 - 150
  Jointed shoulders only
    3" - 4" ....$18 - 22
    8" - 10"..................................$30 - 40

Marked: "Occupied Japan"
  6" - 8"....................................$90 - 100

In regional costume, tagged: LeMinor, Poupée Magali, others
  8"...$40 - 55
  12" - 15" ....$90 - 115
  19" ....$125 - 150

Carnival-type, may have feathers glued on head or body
  8" - 12"..................................$25 - 35

Kewpie: See Kewpies section.

Celluloid

Shoulder-head child, 1900 on, German, molded hair or wig, open or open/closed mouth, kid or cloth body, sometimes arms of other materials
Painted eyes
    11" - 14" ....$100 - 160
    16" - 18".............................$200 - 225
Glass eyes
    16" - 18".............................$225 - 300
    22" - 24" ....$300 - 400
Bye-Lo Baby: See Bye-Lo section.
Socket-head child, 1910 on, open mouth, glass sleep eyes, wig, composition body
French, such as Petitcolin, others, glass eyes, wigged
    18" - 19"..............................$350 - 400
Jumeau
    13"....................................$450 - 500
    16" ....$575 - 600
German, various makers
Molded hair, painted eyes
    11" - 13" ....$200 - 300
    16" - 19"..............................$225 - 325
    Glass eyes
    14" - 17" ....$200 - 400
Heubach Koppelsdorf, mold 399
    11" ....$75 - 100
Kämmer & Reinhardt
Shoulder-head child, mold 255, 406, others
    21" - 23".............................$200 - 300
Baby, mold 721, 728
    10" - 15".............................$275 - 325
    17" - 21".............................$450 - 500
Toddler, flirty eyes
    17" ....$500 - 600
Socket-head child, socket head, mold 701, 717, and others
    8"......................................$350 - 400
    12" - 14".............................$550 - 650
    18" - 25" ....$750 - 850
Kestner, mold 203 character baby
    12"....................................$425 - 450
König & Wernicke (K & W)
Toddler
    15" - 19"..............................$375 - 500
Max and Moritz

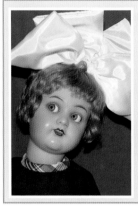

24" mold 717, Kammer & Reinhardt, celluloid, flirty eyes: $800. **Photo courtesy of The Museum Doll Shop.**

    7" ....each $300 - 350
American
Parsons-Jackson (stork mark)
    Baby
    10" - 12".............................$100 - 150
    14" ....$175 - 225
    Toddler
    12" - 15" ....$150 - 200

CENTURY DOLL COMPANY

1909 - 1930, New York City. Founded by Max Scheuer and sons, used bisque heads on many later dolls. In about 1929, Century merged with Domec to become the Doll Corporation of America. Some heads were made by Kestner, Herm Steiner and other firms for Century. Dolls listed are in good condition, with original clothes or appropriately dressed. Allow more for boxed, tagged, or labeled exceptional doll.
Bisque
Baby, 1926, Kestner, bisque head, molded and painted hair, sleep eyes, open/closed mouth, cloth body
    13"....................................$275 - 300
    16" - 18".............................$325 - 450
Mold 275, solid dome, glass eyes, closed mouth, cloth body, composition limbs
    14"....................................$800 - 850
Child
Molds 285, 287, Kestner, bisque socket

head, glass eyes, wig, ball-jointed body

14"....................................$600 - 625

19" - 24"............................$625 - 650

Molds 279, Kestner, bisque socket head, molded bobbed hair, glass eyes, wig, ball-jointed body—looks like Patsy

15"....................................$425 - 475

Composition

Child, composition shoulder head, cloth body, composition arms and legs, molded hair, painted eyes

13" - 17"............................$100 - 175

Century Baby, 1920s, composition flange head and hands, open mouth, cloth baby body, resembles Marseilles's Dream Baby

13" - 15"............................$125 - 175

Chuckles, 1927 - 1929, composition shoulder head, arms, and legs, cloth body, crier, open mouth, molded short hair, painted or sleep eyes, two upper teeth, dimples in cheeks, bent-leg baby or toddler

14" - 16"............................$125 - 200

18" - 22"............................$200 - 300

Mama dolls, 1922 on, composition head, tin sleep eyes, cloth body, crier, composition swing legs and arms

16"....................................$175 - 200

23"....................................$300 - 325

Bisque shoulder head, mold 281

21"....................................$600 - 700

CHAD VALLEY

1917 - 1930s, Harbonne, England. Founded by Johnson Bros. in 1897, in 1917 began making all types of cloth dolls. Early ones had stockinette faces, later ones were felt, with velvet bodies, jointed necks, shoulders and hips, glass or painted eyes, mohair wigs. Used designers such as Mabel Lucie Atwell and Norah Wellings.

Animals

Cat

12"....................................$215 - 230

Bonzo, cloth dog with painted, almost-closed, eyes, and smile

4"....................................$210 - 230

12"....................................$750 - 800

Bonzo, open eyes

5½"....................................$275 - 300

14"....................................$575 - 600

Dog, plush

12"....................................$260 - 280

Characters

Captain Blye, Fisherman, Long John Silver, Pirate, Policeman, Train Conductor, etc.

Glass eyes

10" - 12"............................$200 - 225

18" - 20"............................$850 - 950

Painted eyes

13" - 15"............................$325 - 350

18" - 20"............................$625 - 725

Ghandi/India

13"....................................$625 - 675

Rahmah-Jah

26"....................................$850 - 900

Child

Glass eyes

12" - 16"............................$200 - 375

18" - 21"............................$400 - 500

Painted eyes

9" - 10"............................$125 - 200

12" - 15"............................$200 - 250

18"....................................$300 - 375

Mabel Lucy Atwell design, wide impish face, glass eyes

14"....................................$550 - 650

18"....................................$800 - 1,000

15" Chad Valley, felt, designed by Mabel Lucy Atwell, felt: $650. **Photo courtesy of Richard Withington, Inc.**

Royal Family, glass eyes, 16" - 18"
Princess Alexandra ....$1,400 - 1,500
Prince Edward,
Duke of Windsor ....$1,000 - 1,300
Princess Elizabeth ....$1,500 - 2,000
Princess Margaret Rose ....$1,500 - 2,000
Storybook Dolls
Snow White and Dwarfs
Dwarf, 6½" ....$250 - 275
Set 10" dwarves,
16" Snow White ....$2,200 - 2,800
Red Riding Hood
    14" - 19"............................$350 - 500
Golliwog
    14" - 16"............................$150 - 300

CHASE DOLL COMPANY

1889 - 1981, Pawtucket, Rhode Island, founded by Martha Chase. Earlier dolls had heads of molded stockinette with heavily painted features including thick lashes, closed mouth, painted textured hair, jointed shoulders, elbows, knees and hips, later dolls were jointed only at shoulders and hips, had latex heads on vinyl-coated bodies, all in good condition with original or appropriate clothing.

Baby or child, short hair with curls around face
    12" - 16"............................$750 - 800
    17" - 20"............................$600 - 700
    22 " - 24" ....$700 - 800
    26" - 30" ....$900 - 1,000
Hospital-type, weighted doll with pierced nostrils and ear canals
    20"....................................$475 - 500
    29"....................................$400 - 500
Child
Molded bobbed hair
    12" - 15"......................$1,200 - 1,400
    20" - 22" ....$1,700 - 2,200
Side-part painted hair
    15" - 16"......................$1,800 - 2,500
Characters, 1905 to 1920s, produced characters based on Alice in Wonderland, George Washington and books by Charles Dickens and Joel Chandler Harris
Dickens Characters, needle-sculpted hairstyles including buns, curls, etc.
    15"
      Lady or man ....$2,800 - 4,000
      Little Nell, braids ......$1,500 - 2,000
George Washington
    15" - 25"....................$3,900 - 4,200
Mammy
    26"..........................$10,000 - 12,000
Later Dolls, latex heads
Hospital Baby
    14" - 15"............................$200 - 250
    19"....................................$250 - 300
Baby
    12"....................................$75 - 150
Black
    12" ....$175 - 200
Child
    15" ....$95 - 175
Black
    15" ....$125 - 200

16" Chase, cloth: $800. **Photo courtesy of Morphy Auctions.**

CHINA OR GLAZED-PORCELAIN HEADS

1840 on. Most china shoulder-head dolls were made in Germany by various firms. Prior to 1880, most china heads were pressed into the mold; later ones were poured. Pre-1880, most china heads were sold separately with purchasers buying commercial bodies or making them at home. Original commercial costumes are rare; most clothing was homemade. Early unusual features are glass eyes or eyes painted brown. Heads made after 1870 may have pierced ears and blond hair and, after 1880, more child chinas with shorter hair and shorter necks were popular. Most common in this period were flat tops and low brows; the latter were made until the mid-1900s. Later innovations were china arms and legs with molded boots. Most heads are unmarked or marked only with size or mold number, usually on the back shoulder plate. Hair styles, color, complexion tints and bodies help date the doll. Dolls listed are in good condition with original or appropriate clothes. Allow more for exceptional quality.

1840 Styles

China shoulder head with long neck, painted features, black or brown molded hair, may have exposed ears and pink complexion, with red-orange facial detail, may have bust modeling, cloth, leather, or wood body, nicely dressed, good condition

Early marked china (Nuremberg, Rudolstadt, Schlaggenwald)
  12" - 14".....................$1,800 - 2,800
  17" - 24".....................$3,500 - 5,500
Pink complexion, bun or coronet
  13" - 15" ....$7,000 - 9,000
  18" - 21"..................$11,000 - 12,000
Wooden body, with china lower arms, 1840s on
  5" - 8" .... $4,000 - 6,000

Covered Wagon
Center part, combed back to form sausage curls, pink-tint complexion
  7" - 10" ....$500 - 600
  14" - 17"...........................$750 - 900
  20" - 25" ....$1,000 - 1,200
  31" ....$1,400 - 1,500

Kinderkopf (child head)
Pink tint child-head doll, brush strokes around face
  12" - 16".....................$1,900 - 3,200
  21"..............................$3,500 - 4,000

K.PM (KPM - Königliche Porzellanmanufaktur, Berlin) -1840s - 1850s on, marked inside shoulder plate: "KPM"
Brown-haired man

10½" china, pink tint, circa 1840s: $1,500.
Photo courtesy of Richard Withington, Inc.

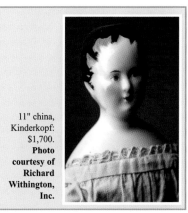

11" china, Kinderkopf: $1,700.
Photo courtesy of Richard Withington, Inc.

China or Glazed-Porcelain Heads

16" - 18".....................$6,500 - 9,000
22" - 23" ....$12,000 - 14,000
Lady, brown hair in bun
   14" - 18"....................$8,000 - 11,000
   20" - 24" ....$12,000 - 15,000
1850 Styles
China shoulder head, painted features, bald with black spot or molded black hair, may have pink complexion, cloth, leather or wood body, china arms and legs, nicely dressed, good condition
Various unnmamed styles, variations of buns and side waves
   12" - 16" ....$6,000 - 8,000
   24" - 26" ....$6,000 - 12,000
Alice in Wonderland, snood, headband
   12" - 14"............................$550 - 650
   16" - 18"...........................$800 - 900
   20" - 22" ....$900 - 1,000
   On Taufling-style body
   14"............................$9,000 - 12,000
Bald head (so-called Biedermeier style), glazed china with black spot, painted eyes, human-hair or mohair wig

7" - 12" ....$225 - 650
14" - 16"...........................$800 - 900
20" - 24" ....$1,500 - 2,000
17" with glass eyes ....sold at
                auction for $4,900
Badekinder (Frozen Charlies or Charlottes): See Badekinder section.
Greiner-type with painted black eyelashes
Painted eyes
   14" - 15"......................$1,000 - 1,200
   18" - 22"......................$1,300 - 1,500
Glass eyes
   13" - 15" ....$3,700 - 4,200
   18" - 22" ....$4,400 - 5,200
French, 1850s on, some heads may have been made in Germany for French makers
Morning Glory, brown hair with molded morning glories
   21" - 24"....................$9,000 - 10,250
Poupée-type, glass or painted eyes, open crown, cork pate, wig, kid body, china arms

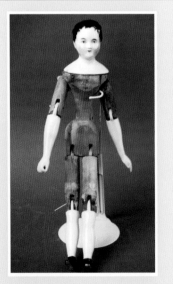

10½" china, Kinderkopf, wooden body: $8,000. **Photo courtesy of Richard Withington, Inc.**

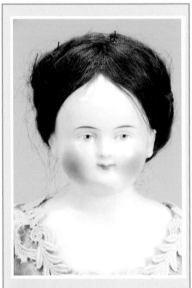

19" china, Beidermeier style: $1,200. **Photo courtesy of Morphy Auctions.**

China or Glazed-Porcelain Heads

12" - 14"......................$4,500 - 5,000
17" - 21"......................$8,500 - 9,000
Slit head, molded slot on top of head
to receive human hair
17"..............................$3,000 - 4,500
Sophia Smith, straight sausage curls
ending in a ridge around head, rather
than curved to head shape
17" - 24"......................$4,000 - 6,000
Young Queen Victoria, molded braids
looped around ears, bun in back
16" - 18"......................$3,000 - 4,000
22" - 23" ....$4,500 - 5,000
1860 Styles
China shoulder head, center part,
smooth black curls, painted features,
seldom brush marks or pink tones,
all-cloth bodies or cloth with china
arms and legs, may have leather arms.
Decorated chinas with fancy hair
styles embellished with flowers,
ornaments, snoods, bands or ribbons,
may have earrings
Flat-top Civil War

Black hair, center part, with flat top,
curls on sides and back
5" - 7" ....$200 - 250
10" - 14"..........................$300 - 375
18" - 22" ....$450 - 550
24" - 26" ....$550 - 650
34".....................................$625 - 675
Swivel neck
15".................................$1,300 - 1,500
Molded necklace
21" - 24"..........................$700 - 800
High brow, curls, high forehead,
round face
9".......................................$150 - 250
12" - 13" ....$300 - 400
15" - 18" ....$450 - 500
19" - 22" ....$450 - 500
25" - 32" ....$500 - 650
Conta and Boehme, pierced ears
9" - 10" ....$400 - 700
14" - 16" ....$900 - 1,100
18" - 20"....................$1,100 - 2,000
Curly Top
11" - 12"..........................$700 - 800

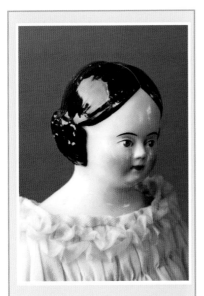

17" china, Greiner style: $1,250. **Photo courtesy of Richard Withington, Inc.**

23" china, brown eyes, circa 1850s: $1,700. **Photo courtesy of Richard Withington, Inc.**

China or Glazed-Porcelain Heads

23" china, slit head, rarely found: $6,000. **Photo courtesy of Richard Withington, Inc.**

23" china, Sophia Smith style, circa 1850s: $4,000. **Photo courtesy of Gloria's Antique Dolls.**

18" - 19" ....$800 - 1,200
Currier and Ives, long hair lying on shoulders
   15" - 17".............................$600 - 700
Dagmar, curls on forehead, curls gathered at nape with barrette
   13" - 18" ....$600 - 1,000
   22" - 25" ....$1,200 - 1,400
Dolley Madison, with molded bow
   9".......................................$300 - 350
   14" - 16".............................$450 - 550
   20" - 24" ....$700 - 800
Man or boy with curls
   17" - 19".......................$1,300 - 1,800
Grape Lady, with cluster of grape leaves and blue grapes
   15" - 20" ....$1,800 - 2,200
Mary Todd Lincoln, black hair, gold snood, gold luster bows at ears
   14" - 15".............................$700 - 800
   18" - 21" ....$900 - 1,200
Blond with snood
   15" - 16".............................$800 - 900
   18" - 21".......................$1,000 - 1,300
Spill Curls, with or without headband, lots of single curls across forehead, around back to ringlets in back
   13" - 15" ....$800 - 900
   18" - 20".......................$1,000 - 1,100
   24" - 26" ....$1,200 - 1,400
1870 Styles
China shoulder head, poured, finely

painted, well molded, black or blond hair, cloth or cloth-and-leather bodies, pink facial details instead of earlier red-orange
   14" - 16".............................$350 - 400
   18" - 24".............................$425 - 475
Adelina Patti, hair pulled up and away, center part, brush-stroked at temples, partly exposed ears, ringlets across back of head
   13" - 15" ....$600 - 700
   18" - 22" ....$800 - 900
   26" ....$1,000 - 1,100
Bangs, full cut across forehead, sometimes called *Highland Mary*
   14" - 16".............................$300 - 350
   19" - 21".............................$375 - 425

18" china, flat-top, pink tint: $450. **Photo courtesy of Richard Withington, Inc.**

China or Glazed-Porcelain Heads

16" china, Countess Dagmar style: $900.
Photo courtesy of Richard Withington, Inc.

17" china, Mary Todd Lincoln style: $850.
Photo courtesy of Morphy Auctions.

Jenny Lind, black hair pulled back into a bun or coronet

12" - 15"	$900 - 1,200
20" - 24"	$1,400 - 1,700

1880 Styles

May also have many blond as well as black hair, more curls, and overall curls, narrower shoulders, fatter cheeks, irises outlined with black paint, may have bangs, china legs have fat calves and molded boots

Child, short black or blond curly hairdo with exposed ears, makers such as Alt, Beck & Gottschalk, Kling and others.

14" - 18"	$200 - 300
20" - 24"	$350 - 450
27" - 30"	$550 - 650

Bawo & Dotter, patented 1880

13" - 14"	$200 - 225
18" - 20"	$275 - 325
24" - 27"	$350 - 400

1890 Styles

Shorter, fatter arms and legs, may have printed body with alphabet, emblems, flags

Common or low brow, black or blond center part wavy hairdo that comes down low on forehead

4" - 8"	$75 - 125
10" - 14"	$125 - 150
16"	$175 - 200
19" - 23"	$225 - 250
27" - 28"	$275 - 300

17" china, spill curls style: $950.
Photo courtesy of Morphy Auctions.

17" china, bangs style: $350.
Photo courtesy of Richard Withington, Inc.

With jewel necklace
8" ....$140 - 160
17" ....$200 - 225
20" - 22" ....$325 - 425
Pet Names, 1899 - 1930 on
Agnes, Bertha, Daisy, Dorothy, Edith,
Esther, Ethel, Florence, Helen, Mabel,
Marion, Pauline and Ruth, made for
Butler Brothers by various German
firms, china head and limbs on cloth
body, molded blouse marked in front
with name in gold lettering, molded
blond or black allover curls
9" ....$100 - 125
12" - 14" ....$150 - 225
17" - 21" ....$275 - 350
Japanese, 1910 - 1920, marked or
unmarked, black or blond hair
10" ....$100 - 125
15" ....$160 - 190

15" china,
Bawo &
Dotter: $225.
**Photo
courtesy of
Richard
Withington,
Inc.**

24" china,
Jenny Lind
style:
$1,700.
**Photo
courtesy of
Richard
Withington,
Inc.**

CLOTH

Various American and European manufacturers of cloth-headed dolls working
from 1850 on. No separate listing for these
makers. Many are unmarked or have
paper hang tags.
Becassine, French comic character,
originally drawn by Emile Joseph
Porphyre Pinchon for *La Semaine de
Suzette*. Made in doll form by various
makers; needle-sculpted nose,
painted features
Reine Dégrais, 1947 - 1972,
8" - 14" ....$150 - 200
Minerve, 1972 on
12" - 16" ....$90 - 150
See Averill section for additional listing.
Homemade, 1800s and early 1900s.
Makers unknown, many one-of-a- kind
type dolls. Embroidered or painted
features. Dolls vary greatly according
to the skill of the maker. Values may
differ substantially for individual
examples.
Mid 1800s - 1900
8" - 12" ....$300 - 900
15" - 20" ....$900 - 2,000
1900 - 1930
15" - 18" ....$250 - 600
16" - 24" ....$700 - 1,200

3¼"-6" Baps Theater, cloth: set $2,500. **Photo
courtesy of Morphy Auctions.**

Cloth

18" Baby Sister, Tebbetts Sisters, cloth: $1,800. **Doll courtesy of private collection.**

4½" Tiny Town Swiss, cloth: pair $300. **Photo courtesy of Memories of Things Past Antiques.**

Baps, 1946 on, Burgkunstadt, Germany. Made by Edith von Arps. Felt doll with felt-over-wire armature body, yarn hair, metal feat, painted features. Many represent storybook characters. Allow more for sets

2½" - 6"

Single figures ....$50 - 150

Blossom, 1920s on, New York, New York. Made cloth mask-faced dolls depicting children as well as long-limbed lady dolls (See Boudoir Dolls section)

11" ....$65 - 100

Hol-Le Toy, 1950s, New York, NY. Eloise, cloth mask face based on the fictional character created by Kay Thompson

21" ....$165 - 200

Junel Novelties, 1930s on, cloth doll with mask face, painted features, yarn hair,

18" ....$100 - 125

Maggie Bessie dolls, 1890s on, Salem, North Carolina. Margaret and Elizabeth Pfohl made cloth dolls with oil painted faces in three sizes, 13/14", 17/18", and 20/22"

13" - 18" ....$15,000 - 17,000

Molded cloth shoulder-head dolls, mid 1800s on. Makers such as George H. Hawkins, Carl Weigand, and others, both known and unknown. Dolls resemble the china and papier-mâché

dolls of the era

19" - 24"......................$1,500 - 2,500

Nelke, 1917 to 1930, Philadelphia, Pennsylvania. Harry Nelke founded the Elke Knitting Mills Co. in 1901 and began making stockinette crib dolls in 1917. The dolls were made of a silky stockinette fabric with painted features. Clothing integral to body, added band of stockinette around neck, and/or added collars, hats, etc. Doll in clean, un-faded condition

8" - 10"................................$60 - 75

13" - 15"............................$100 - 125

Tebbetts Sisters, 1922 on, Pittsburgh, Pennsylvania. Mary, Elizabeth, Marion, and Ruth Tebbetts patented and made cloth dolls

Petiekins, cloth mask face, crepe or flannel body

6½" ....$375 - 425

Baby Sister, needle-sculpted stockinette doll with painted features, wigged

18"............................$2,200 - 2,800

Tiny Town, 1949 into the 1950s, San Francisco, California. Alma LeBlanc took out a patent under the business name of Lenna Lee's Tiny Town Dolls for these dolls, which have felt faces with painted features, mohair wigs and wrapped-wire-armature bodies with metal feet. Value can double for MIB.

4" - 7" ....$75 - 100
Worsted dolls, 1878 - 1900s, Emil Wittzack of Gotha, Thuringia, Germany. Woolen crib dolls with needle-sculpted features, bead eyes, chenille embroidered designs on bodies, some have bells sewn on them
7" - 10" ....$45 - 65
15" - 18" ....$115 - 125

CLOTH, PRINTED

1876 on. Made by various American, British and German firms including Arnold Print Works, North Adams, Massachusetts , Cocheco Manufacturing Co., Art Fabric Mills, and other lesser or unknown firms who printed fabric for making cutout dolls to be sewn together and stuffed. Dolls listed are in good, clean condition; uncut sheets bring double the values listed.

Improved Life Size Doll, with printed underwear
16" - 18" ....$150 - 200
20" - 24" ....$225 - 275
26" - 30" ....$300 - 350
Punch and Judy
27" ....pair $550 - 650
Brownies, 1892 - 1907, produced by Aronld Printworks. Printed cloth dolls based on copyrighted figures of Palmer Cox; 12 different figures, including Canadian, Chinaman, Dude, German, Highlander, Indian, Irishman, John Bull, Policeman, Sailor, Soldier, and Uncle Sam
7½" ....each $125 - 175

8" Brownies, uncut cloth panel, circa 1892: $750. **Photo courtesy of Richard Withington, Inc.**

Printed underwear, Dolly Dear, Flaked Rice, Merry Marie, etc.
7" - 9" ....$95 - 115
16" - 18" ....$200 - 250
20" - 24" ....$250 - 300
Child with printed clothing, 1903
12" - 14" ....$175 - 225
17" - 19" ....$225 - 275
Columbian Sailor, Arnold Printworks, 1892
16" ....$250 - 300
Foxy Grandpa
18" ....$200 - 225
Gutsell, Ida, 1893 on, made by Cocheco Manufacturing. Designed and patented by Ida Gutsell of Ithaca, New York. Printed boy doll with a center-seam face, removable clothing with printed detail
16" ....$250 - 250
Mother's Congress, 1900 on, Philadelphia, Pennsylvania. Designed and patented by Madge L. Meade. The uniquely styled pattern piece used for the head included a round section to produce the crown and several darts in the neck area. Unbleached muslin doll with lithographed facial features, blond hair with a blue bow and black Mary-Jane-style shoes, marked with a stamp: "Mother's Congress Doll//Baby Stuart//

20" Cut & Sew doll in bathing costume, cloth: $275
Photo courtesy of Richard Withington, Inc.

Children's Favorite// Philadelphia, Pa.//
Pat. Nov. 6, 1900"
    17" - 24".............................$500 - 700
Our Soldier Boys ....$125 - 150
Red Riding Hood ....$150 - 175
Peck, 1886 Santa Claus/St. Nicholas
    15"....................................$200 - 250

COLUMBIAN

1891 on, Oswego, New York. Emma E.
Adams designed and made rag dolls, sold
directly or through stores such as
Marshall Field. Won awards at the 1893
Chicago World Fair. Succeeded by her
sister, Marietta Adams Ruttan. Cloth
dolls had hand-painted features, stitched
fingers and toes. Values are for dolls in
good condition wearing appropriate
clothing; allow more for examples in
exceptional condition.
    14" - 15" ....$7,000 - 8,000
    19" - 23" ....$9,000 - 12,000
    28"........................$10,000 - 14,000

15" Columbian, cloth: $7,500. **Photo courtesy
of Dollsantique.**

COMPOSITION

Dolls listed are in good condition with
original or appropriate dress. Allow more
for exceptional dolls with elaborate costume or accessories.
American
Animal-head doll, 1930s, all composition
on Patsy-type five-piece body, could be

wolf, rabbit, cat, monkey
    10".....................................$300 - 350
Baby, 1910 on, wigged or molded hair,
painted or sleep eyes, composition or
cloth body with bent legs
    12" - 14"............................$175 - 225
    18" - 20" ....$250 - 300
Bester Doll Company, 1918 - 1921,
Bloomfield and Newark, New Jersey.
Composition doll in the style of
German dolly-faced dolls, ball-jointed
body, sleep eyes, wigged
    18" - 22" ....$400 - 425
Character Baby
    18"....................................$250 - 300
Child, costumed in ethnic or theme
outfit, all composition, sleep or painted
eyes, mohair wig, closed mouth, original
costume
Lesser quality
    9" - 11"................................$65 - 75
Better quality
    9" - 11".............................$100 - 125
    16"....................................$200 - 250
Coleman Walker
    24" - 28" ....$125 - 175
Denny Dimwitt, Toycraft Inc, 1948, all-
composition, nodder, painted clothing
    11½" ....$200 - 225
Early child, 1910 - 1920, all composition,

11" compo-
sition,
painted eyes,
circa 1940s:
$125.
**Photo
courtesy of
Joan &
Lynette
Antique
Dolls and
Accessories.**

Composition

unmarked, painted features, may have molded hair

    12" ....$145 - 165

    18" - 19"...........................$200 - 250

Elektra Toy and Novelty Co, New York

    Rosie Posie, Stationary legs, Kewpie-type, Black

    11".....................................$325 - 350

    Character Baby

    22" - 23" ....$300 - 350

Character face, 1910 - 1920, unmarked, cork-stuffed cloth body, painted features, may have molded hair

    12" - 15" ....$150 - 200

    18" - 20" ....$250 - 300

    24" ....$375 - 400

Jackie Robinson, complete in box

    13" ....$900 - 1,000

Kewty, 1930, made by Domec of Canada, all-composition Patsy-type, molded bobbed hair, closed mouth, sleep eyes, bent left arm

    14".....................................$300 - 350

Little Annie Rooney, Colonial Toy Co, painted eyes, yarn hair

    15".....................................$175 - 225

Lone Ranger (or Tonto), cloth body, hat marked: "TLR Co, Inc.//Doll Craft

Novelty Co. NYC"

    20"....................................$350 - 450

Louis Vuitton, 1955, ceramic, composition, with labeled case and wardrobe

    19"...$2,200

Too few in database for a reliable range

Maiden America, 1915, all composition, patriotic ribbon, marked: "Kate Silverman"

    8½" ....$165 - 185

Mama doll, 1922 on, wigged or painted hair, sleep or painted eyes, cloth body, crier, swing legs, composition lower legs and arms

    16" - 18"............................$225 - 275

    20" - 22" ....$325 - 375

    24" - 26" ....$425 - 500

Miss Curity, composition, eye shadow, nurse's uniform

    18" - 21"............................$250 - 300

Our Gang's Mary, based on character created by Hal Roach, made by Sayco, New York City

    11½" $1,100

Patsy-type girl, 1928 on, molded and painted bobbed hair, sleep or painted eyes, closed pouty mouth, composition or hard stuffed cloth body

    9" - 10".............................$125 - 150

    14" - 16"............................$225 - 275

    19" - 20"............................$275 - 300

With molded hair loop

13" Jackie Robinson, composition: $600. **Photo courtesy of Minton's Doll and Curiosity Shop.**

11½", Character Mary from Hal Roach's Our Gang, Sayco, composition: $1,100. **Photo courtesy of Richard Withington, Inc.**

12" - 15"............................$125 - 150
Pinocchio, composition and wood character
16½" ....$400 - 425
Puzzy, 1948, "H of P"
15"....................................$375 - 400
Quintuplets, 1934 on, all-composition jointed five-piece baby or toddler body, molded hair or wig, painted or sleep eyes, closed or open mouth
7" - 8"..............................$140 - 160
13"....................................$225 - 250
Santa Claus, composition molded head, composition body, original suit, sack
19"....................................$450 - 500
Shimmy Doll, 1920s, key-wind shimmy dancer
12" - 18"............................$150 - 300
Shirley Temple-type girl, 1934 on, all-composition five-piece jointed body, blond curly wig, sleep eyes, open mouth, teeth, dimples
16" - 19"............................$250 - 300
Sizzy, 1948, "H of P"
14"....................................$350 - 400
Thumbs-Up, made as fundraiser for ambulances during WWII
8"......................................$140 - 155
Uncle Sam, various makers
All original, cloth body
13" $900
Too few in database for reliable range
Whistler, composition head, cotton body, composition arms, open mouth
14½" ....$200 - 225
Canadian, Pullan
Eskimo
13" ....$60 - 100
Little Lulu
14"....................................$350 - 450
German, composition head, composition or cloth body, wig or molded and painted hair, closed or open mouth with teeth, dressed, may be Amusco, Sonneberger Porzellanfabrik, Winkler or others

15" Puzzy, composition: $400.
Photo courtesy of Skinner, Inc.

Character Baby
Cloth body
18"....................................$275 - 325
Composition baby body, bent limbs
16"....................................$275 - 325
Child
Composition shoulder head, cloth body, composition arms
20"....................................$275 - 300
Socket head, all-composition body
12" - 14"............................$200 - 300
19" - 21"............................$425 - 450
Japanese
Quintuplets
7" - 9"................................$175 - 250

COSMOPOLITAN DOLL AND TOY CORPORATION

1950s on, Jackson Heights, New York. Dolls listed are in perfect condition with original clothing. Value can double for MIB; allow one-third of value listed for undressed dolls.
Ginger, 1955 on, 7½", hard plastic
Painted lash straight-leg walker........$35 - 45
Molded lash straight-leg walker........$30 - 40
Bent-knee walker ....$25 - 35

8" Ginger, hard plastic, painted lashes: $45. **Photo courtesy of Charlotte's Web Vintage Dolls and Collectibles.**

Vinyl head ....$20 - 35
Boxed outfit ....$50 - 60
Cardboard house and furniture ..$130 - 150
Miss Ginger, 1957 on, vinyl, rooted hair, sleep eyes, teen doll, tagged clothes
10½" ....$55 - 75
Boxed outfit ....$80 - 90
Little Miss Ginger, 1958 on, vinyl, rooted hair, sleep eyes, teen doll, tagged clothes
8"...$60 - 85

CRÈCHE FIGURES

Figures of various materials made especially for religious scenes such as the Christmas manger. Usually not jointed, some with elaborate costumes. Some early created figures have gesso-over-wood head and limbs, fabric-covered bodies with wire frames, later figures are made of terra-cotta or other materials, some with inset eyes.
Wood, carved
Man or woman, shoulder head, glass eyes, wire body
8"....................................$400 - 500
10" - 14" ....$700 - 1,000
17" - 19".....................$1,400 - 1,800
Angel
10" - 16".....................$2,000 - 2,800
Too few in database for reliable range
Terra Cotta, mid 1800s, shoulder head, wire frame

11½" crèche figure, wood: $600. **Photo courtesy of Richard Withington, Inc.**

Man or woman
7" - 10" ....$600 - 1,300
12" -15" ....$1,400 - 2,000
17" - 22" ....$2,000 - 2,500
Elaborate figure such as King or Angel
15" -19" ....$3,500 - 6,000

29" De Fuisseaux, bisque, portrait style: sold at auction for $2,250. **Photo courtesy of Morphy Auctions.**

DE FUISSEAUX

1909 - 1912, Baudour, Belgium. Porcelain heads, often highly colored. Marked: "D.F.B," or "F1" (and other #s)," D1" (and other numbers).
Open-mouth dolly face, sleep eyes, wig, cardboard-and-composition ball-jointed body
18" - 22" ....$300 - 350
Character doll
Painted eyes, resembles Kämmer & Reinhardt 101, various body types
8".....................................$400 - 450
Glass eyes, resembles Heubach, ball-jointed composition body
12" - 18"......................$1,200 - 1,700
Portrait-style girl or lady, cloth body
19" - 23".....................$1,800 - 2,100

DEANS RAG BOOK COMPANY

1905 on, London. Subsidiary of Dean and Son, Ltd., a printing and publishing firm, used "A1" to signify quality, made Knockabout Toys, Tru-to-Life, Evripoze, and others. An early designer was Hilda Cowham.
Child, painted eyes
10"..................................$225 - 250
16" - 17"..........................$450 - 500
24"..................................$550 - 600
Printed cloth, cut-and-sew type
9" - 10"..............................$85 - 95
15" - 16"..........................$125 - 200
Mask face, velvet, cloth body and limbs
12" - 15"..........................$100 - 150
18" - 24"..........................$200 - 275
30" - 34" ....$325 - 400
40" .... $500 - 600
Dancing Dolls, cloth dolls sewn together at hands to look like a dancing couple, on a string
12" - 14" ....$100 - 110
Lupino Lane
12" ....$175 - 200
Mickey Mouse

15" Lillibet, Deans Rag Book Co., cloth: $500. **Photo courtesy of Memories of Things Past Antiques.**

12" - 13" ....$400 - 500
Golliwog
11"..................................$350 - 425
15"..................................$450 - 550
18"..................................$600 - 650
Ronnie, 1950s, molded-rubber head, plush body
15" ....$150 - 175

DELUXE READING

1955 - 1972, Elizabeth, New Jersey. Also used the names Deluxe Toy Creations, Deluxe Premium Corp., Deluxe Topper, Topper Toys, and Topper Corp. Dolls listed are complete, all original, in good condition, wearing original clothes, hard plastic or vinyl; value can double for MIB.
Baby
Baby Boo, 1965, battery-operated
21" ....$75 - 100
Baby Catch A Ball, 1969 (Topper Toys), battery-operated
18" ....$65 - 75
Baby Magic, 1966, blue sleep eyes, rooted saran hair, magic wand has magnet that opens/closes eyes
18" ....$60 - 100
Baby Party, 1968, blows horns, balloons, etc.

Deluxe Reading

24" Nancy Nurse, Deluxe Reading, vinyl, MIB: $200. **Photo courtesy of Charlotte's Web Vintage Dolls and Collectibles.**

30" Sweet Ann, Deluxe Reading, vinyl, MIB: $225. **Photo courtesy of Charlotte's Web Vintage Dolls and Collectibles.**

18"...$25 - 35
Baby Peek 'N Play, 1969, battery-operated
18"...$20 - 25
Baby Tickle Tears
14"...$20 - 30
Nancy Nurse, 1963
21"...$25 - 30
Suzy Cute, move arm and face changes expressions
7"...$30 - 40
Tickles, 1963, battery-operated, talks and laughs
20"...$65 - 75
Child or Adult
Betty Bride, 1957, also called Sweet Rosemary, Sweet Judy, Sweet Amy, one-piece vinyl body and limbs, allow more for many accessories
30"...$55 - 65
Candy Fashion, 1958, made by Deluxe Premium, a division of Deluxe Reading, sold in grocery stores, came with three dress forms, extra outfits
21" ....$70 -75
Dawn Series, circa 1969 - 1970s, all-vinyl doll with additional friends, Angie, Daphne, Denise, Glori, Jessica, Kip, Long Locks, Majorette, Maureen, black versions of Van and Dale, accessories available, included Apartment, Fashion

Show, outfits
Dawn and friends
6"...$20 - 25
Dawn and other outfits
Loose, but complete ....$10+
NRFP ....$35 - 45
Go Gos, 1965, soft vinyl bendable body; Cool Cat, Private Ida, Tom Boy
6"...$30 - 35
Little Miss Fussy, battery-operated
18"...$55 - 60
Little Red Riding Hood, 1955, vinyl, synthetic hair, rubber body, book, basket
23"...$50 - 75
Nancy Nurse, hard plastic and vinyl
24"...$85 - 100
Penny Brite, 1963 on, all vinyl, rooted blond hair, painted eyes, bendable and straight legs, extra outfits, case, furniture available, marked: "A - 9/B150 (or B65) DELUXE READING CORP.//c. 1963"
8"...$20 - 30
Outfit, NRFP.........................$30 - 40
Kitchen set.................................$50 - 60
Suzy Homemaker, 1964, hard plastic and vinyl, jointed knees, marked: "Deluxe Reading Co."
21"...$40 - 50
Suzy Smart, circa 1962, vinyl, sleep eyes, closed mouth, rooted blond ponytail,

hard-plastic body, The Talking School Doll, desk, chair, easel

25".....................................$90 - 140

Sweet Ann, vinyl head, soft-vinyl body, high-heeled feet

30".....................................$95 - 115

Sweet Rosemary, vinyl head, soft-vinyl body, high-heeled feet

28".....................................$70 - 80

DEP

The "DEP" mark on the back of bisque heads stands for the French "Deposé" or the German "Deponirt," which means registered claim. Some dolls made by Simon & Halbig have the "S&H" mark hidden above the "DEP" under the wig. Bisque head, swivel neck, appropriate wig, paperweight eyes, open or closed mouth, good condition, nicely dressed on French-style wood-and-composition body. Dolls listed are in good condition with original or appropriate clothing.

Closed mouth

15"......................$1,800 - 2,000

18" - 20" ....$2,000 - 2,500

23" - 25" ....$3,000 - 3,300

Open mouth, including those marked Jumeau

13" - 15"......................$1,000 - 1,300

18" - 20"......................$1,500 - 1,800

23" - 25" ....$2,000 - 2,200

28" - 30" ....$2,400 - 2,600

DOLLHOUSE DOLLS

Small German dolls generally under 8", usually dressed as member of a family or in household-related occupations, often sold as a group. Made of any material, but by 1880 were usually made with bisque heads.Dolls listed are in good condition with original clothes.

Bisque

Adult, man or woman,

Painted eyes, molded hair or wig

4" - 5"...............................$100 - 350

6" - 7" ....$250 - 450

Glass eyes

Molded hair

6".....................................$350 - 450

Wigged

6".....................................$500 - 550

Black man or woman, molded hair, original clothes

6".....................................$400 - 650

Chauffeur, molded cap

6".....................................$245 - 285

Grandparents, or with molded-on hats

6".....................................$235 - 265

Military man, mustache, original clothes

6".....................................$575 - 650

With molded-on helmet

6".....................................$600 - 900

9" man with molded full beard, painted eyes ....sold at auction for $1,500

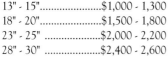

22" DEP, bisque: $1,800.
Photo courtesy of Dolls and Lace.

4½" dollhouse maid, bisque, circa 1920s: $200.
Doll courtesy of private collection.

Children, all-bisque
4".....................................$100 - 150
China
With early hairdo
4"....................................$300 - 600
With low brow or common hairdo, 1900 on
4"......................................$75 - 125
Composition, papier-mâché, plaster, etc.
5"....................................$150 - 200

DOOR OF HOPE

1901 - 1950, Shanghai, China. Cornelia Bonnell started the Door of Hope Mission in Shanghai to help poor girls who had been sold by their families. As a means to learn sewing skills, the girls dressed carved pear-wood heads from Ning-Po. The heads and hands had a natural finish; the stuffed cloth bodies were then dressed in correct representation for 26 different Chinese classes. Carved wooden heads with cloth or wooden arms, original handmade costumes, in very good condition. Dolls listed are in good condition with clean, bright clothing. Allow more for exceptional dolls; less for dolls in faded costumes.

Adult, man or woman
11" - 13".....................$1,100 - 2,500
Amah with Baby.............$2,000 - 2,800
Boy or girl in silk
6" - 9" ....$2,000 - 3,900

8"& 10" Door of Hope, wood, boy in silk, girl in cotton with carved bun; $1,100 (boy); $4,500 (girl). **Photo courtesy of The Doll Works.**

Boy with western hairstyle
8" - 9" ....$850 - 1,100
Bride and Groom
12"............................$2,700 - 3,500
Farmer in bamboo raincoat
12"............................$1,500 - 2,000
Kindergarten child
6"..............................$3,800 - 4,200
Male Mourner
12"............................$1,500 - 2,000
Manchu Woman
11"............................$7,500 - 8,500
Policeman
11½" ....$5,000 - 7,000
Priest
11½" ....$2,600 - 3,400

CUNO & OTTO DRESSEL

1857 - 1943, Sonneberg, Thüringia, Germany. The Dressel family began its business in the early 1700s and was dealing in toys from a very early date. Cuno and Otto became involved in the 1880s. The Dressels made wood, wax, wax-over-composition, papier-mâché, composition, china and bisque heads for their dolls which they produced, distributed and exported. Their bisque heads were made by Simon & Halbig, Armand Marseille, Ernst Heubach, Schoenau and Hoffmeister and others. Dolls listed are in good condition with appropriate clothing.

Bisque
Baby, 1910 on, character face, allow more for toddler body, marked: "C.O.D."
12" - 14"..........................$325 - 375
15" - 17"..........................$375 - 425
19" - 23" ....$550 - 600
Child, mold 1912, others, open mouth, jointed composition body
14" - 16".........................$350 - 400
18" - 24".........................$400 - 500
Flapper body, flirty eyes

25" mold 1349, Cuno & Otto Dressel, bisque: $700. **Photo courtesy of Dolls and Lace.**

15" Uncle Sam, Cuno & Otto Dressel, bisque: $1,700. **Photo courtesy of Richard Withington, Inc.**

22".....................................$800 - 900
Shoulder-head child
   Molds 93, 1896, or no mold #, bisque, wigged, open mouth, kid or cloth body, glass eyes
   13" - 15"............................$150 - 175
   18" - 24"............................$250 - 275
   Bisque, closed mouth, molded hair, kid or cloth body, glass eyes
   14"....................................$300 - 325
Child, character face, closed mouth, jointed child or toddler body
Painted eyes
   14" - 16".......................$1,200 - 1,300
   18" - 20".......................$1,500 - 1,700
Glass eyes
   12" - 15"....................$2,400 - 2,700
   18" - 20"....................$3,000 - 3,200
Flapper, molds 1468, 1469, lady doll, closed mouth, five-piece composition body, thin legs, high-heeled feet, painted-on hose up entire leg, mold 1469
   12" - 15"....................$3,000 - 4,000
Composition
Holz-Masse, 1875 on, shoulder head, wigged or molded hair, painted or glass eyes, cloth body, composition limbs, molded-on boots
   13" - 15"...........................$300 - 350
   18" - 20"...........................$400 - 475
   24" - 29"...........................$525 - 600
Glass eyes
   12"....................................$400 - 450

16" - 18"...........................$500 - 600
Wigged
   18"....................................$650 - 750
Jutta
Baby open mouth, bent-leg body
   16" - 18"...........................$325 - 375
   20" - 24"...........................$400 - 550
Child, 1906 - 1921, open mouth, marked: "Jutta" or "S&H" mold 1914, 1348, 1349, etc.
   14" - 16"...........................$350 - 400
   17" - 19"...........................$450 - 500
   21" - 24"...........................$550 - 650
   25" - 29" ....$700 - 750
Toddler
   8"....................................$525 - 550
   14" - 16"...........................$575 - 625
   17" - 19"...........................$700 - 750
Portrait dolls, 1896 on, bisque head, glass eyes, composition body
Admiral Dewey, Admiral Byrd, other military
   8"..............................$1,200 - 1,500
   12" - 14"....................$2,000 - 3,000
Buffalo Bill
   8" - 10" ....$2,000 - 2,500
Farmer, Old Rip, Witch
   8"..............................$1,200 - 1,500
   12"...........................$2,600 - 3,000
Father Christmas
   18".............................$4,000 - 4,500
Uncle Sam
   10" - 13" .... $1,300 - 1,600

E.D.

1857 - 1899, Paris. E.D. Bébés marked with "E.D." and a size number and the word "Deposé" were made by Etienne Denamur. It is important to note that other dolls marked E.D. with no Deposé mark were made when Emile Douillet was director of Jumeau and should be priced as Jumeau Tété face dolls. Denamur had no relationship with the Jumeau firm and his dolls do not have the spiral spring used to attach heads used by Jumeau. Denamur bébés have straighter eyebrows, the eyes are slightly more recessed, the lips are large and the bisque is of lesser quality. Smaller sizes of Denamure E.D. bébés may not have the Deposé mark. Dolls listed are in good condition, appropriately dressed. Allow more for exceptional clothing.

Closed mouth
11" - 15" ....$4,000 - 5,000
18" - 22" ....$5,000 - 6,000
25" - 28" ....$7,000 - 8,000
Open mouth
14" - 16"....................$2,000 - 2,300
18" - 21" ....$3,000 - 3,100
25" - 27" ....$3,500 - 3,800

22" ED, bisque, closed mouth: $5,500. **Photo courtesy of Dolls and Lace.**

16" bébé, bisque, open mouth, French, marked "ED": $2,300. **Photo courtesy of Morphy Auctions.**

EDEN BÉBÉ

1890 - 1899, made by Fleischmann & Bloedel; 1899 - 1953, made by Société Francaise de Fabrication de Bébés and Jouet (S.F.B.J.). Dolls had bisque heads, jointed composition bodies. Dolls listed are in good condition, appropriately dressed.

Closed mouth, pale bisque
14" - 16"....................$2,200 - 2,800
18" - 24" ....$3,000 - 4,600
Open mouth
15" - 18" ....$2,000 - 2,500
20" - 26" ....$2,700 - 2,900
High color, five-piece body
13" ....$600 - 1,000
19"...........................$1,300 - 1,500
22"...........................$1,900 - 2,100

24" bébé, Eden, bisque, open mouth: $2,800. **Photo courtesy of Morphy Auctions.**

EEGEE

1917 on, Brooklyn, New York. Owned by E. G. Golderberger, assembled and made dolls; some of their dolls had bisque heads imported from Armand Marseille. Eegee also made their own heads and complete dolls of composition, hard plastic and vinyl. Dolls listed are in all original, good condition. Add more for exceptional doll, tagged, extra outfits, or accessories.

Composition

Baby, cloth body, bent limbs
16".....................................$65 - 100
Child, open mouth, sleep eyes
14".....................................$135 - 150
18".....................................$175 - 200
MaMa Doll, 1920s - 1930s, composition head, sleep or painted eyes, wigged or molded hair, cloth body, crier, swing legs, composition lower arms and legs
16".....................................$200 - 225
20".....................................$300 - 325
Miss Charming or Little Miss Movie, 1936, all composition, Shirley Temple look-alike
19" - 22" ....$250 - 300
Pin-back button $50
Hard Plastic and Vinyl
Andy, 1963, vinyl, teen-type, molded painted hair, painted eyes, closed mouth
12".....................................$25 - 35
Annette or Babette, 1963, vinyl, teen-type fashion, rooted hair, painted eyes
11½" ....$25 - 40
Annette, 1961 on, PlayPal type
19".....................................$40 - 50
32" - 35"............................$100 - 140
Walker, all vinyl, rooted long blond hair or short curly wig, blue sleep eyes, closed mouth
25".....................................$60 - 75
28".....................................$50 - 55
36".....................................$65 - 75
Babette, 1970, vinyl head, stuffed limbs, cloth body, painted or sleep eyes, rooted hair
15".....................................$30 - 40
25".....................................$55 - 65
Baby Care, 1969, vinyl, molded or rooted hair, sleep or set glassine eyes, drink-and-wet doll, with complete nursery set
18".....................................$35 - 45
Baby Carrie, 1970, rooted or molded hair, sleep or set glassine eyes, with plastic carriage or carry seat
24".....................................$60 - 80
Baby Luv, 1973, vinyl head, rooted hair, painted eyes, open/closed mouth, cloth body, pants are part of body, marked: "B.T. Eegee"
14".....................................$30 - 40
Baby Susan, 1958, head marked: "Baby Susan"
8".....................................$30 - 40
Baby Tandy Talks, 1963, pull string activates talking mechanism, vinyl head, rooted hair, sleep eyes, cotton-and-foam-stuffed body and limbs
14".....................................$25 - 35
20".....................................$55 - 65
Ballerina
1964, vinyl head and hard-plastic body
31".....................................$75 - 100
1967, vinyl head, foam-filled body
18".....................................$30 - 40

15" Miss Debby, Eegee, vinyl: $125. **Photo courtesy of American Beauty Dolls.**

Barbara Cartland, painted features, adult
15".................................$45 - 52

Beverly Hillbillies, based on Clampett family from *The Beverly Hillbillies* 1960s television show

Car $350

Granny Clampett, gray rooted hair
14"...................................$55 - 65

Bundle of Joy, 1964, vinyl head, arms, legs, cloth body, rooted hair, sleep eyes
19".....................................$30 - 40

Fields, W. C., 1980, vinyl ventriloquist doll by Juro, division of Goldberger
30"...................................$65 - 75

Flowerkins, 1963, seven dolls in series, head marked: "F-2"
Boxed
16"....................................$35 - 45

Gemmette, 1963, rooted hair, sleep eyes, jointed vinyl, wearing gem-colored dress, includes child's jeweled ring
Misses Amethyst, Diamond, Emerald, Ruby, Sapphire and Topaz
15½".................................$50

Georgie, Georgette, 1971, vinyl head, cloth bodies, red-headed twins
22" ....each $35 - 45

Gigi Perreau, 1951, early vinyl head, hard-plastic body, open/closed smiling mouth
17"..................................$550 - 700

Honey, 1949, hard plastic
12"...................................$45 - 55

Karena Ballerina, 1958, vinyl head, rooted hair, sleep eyes, closed mouth, hard-plastic body, jointed knees, ankles, neck, shoulders and hips, head turns when walks
21"...................................$45 - 55

Lil' Sister, vinyl head, rooted hair, painted eyes, looks like Mattel's Skipper®
9"....................................$20 - 25

Little Debutantes, 1957, vinyl head, rooted hair, sleep eyes, closed mouth, hard-plastic body, swivel waist,

high-heeled feet
15"...................................$35 - 90
17"...................................$60 - 100

Debutante, 1958
28'"..................................$80 - 100

Little Miss Debutante, 1958
10 1/2" ....$60 - 90

Miss Debby, all vinyl, high-heel fashion type, swivel waist, fully jointed
20"...................................$65 - 75

My Fair Lady, 1958, all vinyl, fashion type, stufed vinyl body
15"..................................$100 - 125

Parton, Dolly, 1978
11½" ....$15 - 20
18"...................................$25 - 35

Posi Playmate, 1969, vinyl head, foam-filled vinyl body, bendable arms and legs, painted or rooted hair, sleep or painted eyes
12"...................................$15 - 20

Puppetrina, 1963 on, vinyl head, cloth body, rooted hair, sleep eyes, pocket in back for child to insert hand to manipulate doll's head and arms
22"...................................$65 - 75

Shelly, 1964, Tammy-type, grow hair
12"...................................$12 - 18

Sniffles, 1963, vinyl head, rooted hair, sleep eyes, open/closed mouth, marked: "13/14 AA-EEGEE"
12"...................................$15 - 20

Susan Stroller, 1955, vinyl head, hard-plastic walker body, rooted hair, closed mouth
20"...................................$40 - 60
23"...................................$75 - 100
26"...................................$80 - 100

Tandy Talks, 1961, vinyl head, hard-plastic body, freckles, pull-string talker
20"...................................$35 - 45

Ventriloquist dolls, 1960s, Bozo, Charlie McCarthy, Howdy Doody, Suzie Sez, vinyl and cloth
14" - 31" ....$45 - 75

Winky the Wurlitzer Walking doll, vinyl
36"...................................$75 - 100

EFFANBEE

1910 to present, New York City. Founded by Bernard Fleischaker and Hugo Baum. This company began selling composition-headed dolls, which were made for them by Otto Ernst Denivelle (marked Deco). Effanbee eventually did their own manufacturing; by the late 1920s they were one of the leading manufacturers of American composition dolls. They went on to make dolls of hard plastic and vinyl. In 2002 the company was purchased by Robert Tonner, who is re-issuing many of the designs from the past, as well as new pieces. Values listed are for early dolls in good condition with original clothing and dolls from 1950 on in perfect condition with appropriate tags. Allow more for exceptional dolls with wardrobes or accessories.

Bisque/Composition

Mary Jane, 1920, dolly-faced doll to compete with German bisque. Some have bisque heads, others have composition; bisque head, manufactured by Lenox Potteries, NJ, for Effanbee, sleep eyes, composition body, wooden arms and legs, also kid body with wood and composition limbs

Composition shoulder head, wooden ball-jointed arms and legs, composition hands, wigged, sleep eyes, marked on kid body: "Effanbee" (marked with Effanbee sticker)

24" ....$375 - 450

Early Composition

Babies

Baby Bud, 1918 on, all composition, painted features, molded hair, open/closed mouth, jointed arms, legs molded to body, one finger goes into mouth

6" ....$175 - 195

Black ....$200 - 225

Baby Dainty, 1912 on, name given to a variety of dolls with composition heads, cloth bodies, some toddler types, some mama-types with crier

12" - 14" ....$170 - 190

15" ....$200 - 250

Vinyl

10" ....$30 - 40

Baby Effanbee, 1925, composition head, cloth body

12" - 13" ....$165 - 185

Baby Evelyn, 1925, composition head, cloth body

17" ....$250 - 275

Baby Grumpy, 1915 on, also later variations, composition character, heavily molded, painted hair, frowning eyebrows, painted intaglio eyes, pin-jointed limbs, cork-stuffed cloth body, gauntlet arms, pouty mouth

Mold #172, 174, 176

12" - 16" ....$425 - 500

Black ....$550 - 600

Baby Grumpy Gladys, 1923, composition shoulder head, cloth body, marked in oval: "Effanbee//Baby Grumpy//corp. 1923"

15" ....$300 - 350

Grumpy Aunt Dinah, black, cloth body, striped stocking legs

14½" ....$400 - 425

Grumpykins, 1927, composition head, cloth body, composition arms, some

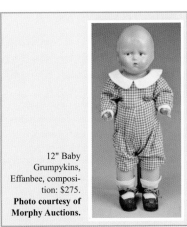

12" Baby Grumpykins, Effanbee, composition: $275.
Photo courtesy of Morphy Auctions.

Effanbee

28" Lovums, Effanbee, composition: $600. **Photo courtesy of Richard Withington, Inc.**

with cloth legs, others with composition legs

12".....................................$225 - 275
Black ....$325 - 375

Grumpykins, Pennsylvania Dutch Dolls, 1936, dressed by Marie Polack in Mennonite, River Brethren, and Amish costumes

12"...................................$225 - 250

Bubbles, 1924 on, composition shoulder head, open/closed mouth, painted teeth, molded painted hair, sleep eyes, cloth body, bent-cloth legs, some with composition toddler legs, composition arms, finger of left hand fits into mouth, heart necklace, various marks including: "Effanbee//Bubbles//Copr. 1924//Made in U.S.A."

16" - 18"...........................$150 - 200
20" - 22" ....$250 - 300
24" - 29" ....$300 - 400

Lamkin, 1930 on, composition molded head, sleep eyes, open mouth, cloth body, crier, chubby composition legs, feet turned in, fingers curled, molded gold ring on middle finger

16".....................................$325 - 375

Lovums, 1928 on, child doll, composition swivel head, shoulder plate and limbs, cloth body, sleep eyes, molded and painted hair or wigged, can have

bent baby legs or toddler legs

16" - 18"...........................$300 - 375
20" - 22" ....$400 - 450
24" - 28" ....$500 - 600

Pat-o-Pat, 1925 on, composition head, painted eyes, cloth body with mechanism which, when pressed, causes hands to clap

13"...................................$200 - 250
15"...................................$250 - 275

Cloth mask faced

15"...................................$575 - 600

Sugar Baby, 1936 on, composition molded head, sleep eyes, cloth body, composition legs and hands

22" - 25" ....$150 - 200

Character Children, 1912 on, composition, heavily molded hair, painted eyes, pin-jointed cloth body, composition arms, cloth or composition legs, some marked: "Deco"

Cliquot Eskimo, 1920, painted eyes, molded hair, felt hands, mohair suit

18"...................................$450 - 525

Coquette, Naughty Marietta, 1915, composition girl, molded bow in hair, side-glancing eyes, cloth body

12" - 14"...........................$375 - 600

Harmonica Joe, 1923, cloth body, with rubber ball, when squeezed provides air to open mouth with harmonica

15"...................................$425 - 450

Irish Mail Kid, 1915, or Dixie Flyer, composition head, cloth body, arms sewn to steering handle of wooden wagon

10"...................................$300 - 325

Johnny Tu-face, 1912, composition head with faces on front and back, painted features, open/closed crying mouth, closed smiling mouth, molded and painted hair, cloth body, red striped legs, cloth feet, wearing knitted romper and hat

16"...................................$275 - 325

Effanbee

Pouting Bess, 1915, composition head with heavily molded curls, painted eyes, closed mouth, cloth cork-stuffed body, pin-jointed, back of head marked: "162" or "166"
15"...................................$275 - 300
Whistling Jim, 1916, composition head, heavily molded hair, painted intaglio eyes, perforated mouth, cork-stuffed cloth body, black sewn-on cloth shoes, wearing red striped shirt, blue overalls, label reads: "Effanbee//Whistling Jim//Trade Mark"
15"...................................$300 - 325
MaMa Dolls, 1921 on, including Rosemary and Marilee, composition shoulder head, painted or sleep eyes, molded hair or wigged, cloth body, swing legs, crier, composition arms and lower legs
    14" ....$175 - 200
    17" - 19"............................$200 - 225
    24" - 27" ....$250 - 300
Late Composition
American Children, 1936 - 1939 on, all composition, designed by Dewees Cochran, open mouth, separated fingers may wear gloves, marks: heads may be unmarked or body marked: "Effanbee//Anne Shirley"
    Barbara Joan, Barbara Ann
    14" - 17"............................$600 - 750
    Barbara Lou
    21"...................................$900 - 925
Closed mouth, separated fingers, sleep or painted eyes, head marked: "Effanbee//American//Children;" body marked: "Effanbee//Anne Shirley"
    Painted eyes such as Peggy Lou and others
    14" - 17"............................$600 - 900
    19" - 21".......................$1,200 - 1,500
    Sleep eyes such as Gloria Ann and others
    17" - 21" ....$1,400 - 1,900

Anne Shirley, 1936 - 1940, never advertised as such, same mold used for Little Lady, all composition, more grown-up body style, marked: "EFFANBEE//ANNE SHIRLEY"
    10"...................................$300 - 350
    14" - 15" ....$450 - 500
    17" - 18"............................$500 - 550
    21"...................................$500 - 550
    27"...................................$550 - 600
Movie Anne Shirley, 1935 - 1940. 1934 RKO movie character, Anne Shirley from *Anne of Green Gables* movie, all composition, red braids, wearing Anne Shirley movie costume and gold paper hang tag reading: "I am Anne Shirley." Marked: "Patsy" or other Effanbee doll name. The Anne Shirley costume changes the identity of these dolls.
Mary Lee/Anne Shirley, open mouth, head marked: "©Mary Lee"; body marked: "Patsy Joan"
    16"...................................$300 - 400
Patsyette/Anne Shirley, body marked: "Effanbee// Patsyette// Doll"
    9½" ....$325 - 375
Patricia/Anne Shirley, body marked: "Patricia"
    15"...................................$500 - 550
Patricia-kin/Anne Shirley, hang tag reads: "Anne Shirley;" head marked:

25"
Rosemary,
Effanbee,
composition,
Mama doll:
$275.
**Photo
courtesy of
Dollsantique.**

Effanbee

"Patricia-kin"; body marked:
"Effanbee//Patsy Jr."
11½" ....$325 - 375
Babyette, 1943, eyes molded closed,
composition head, hands, legs,
cloth body
13" ....$150 - 200
Bright Eyes, 1940, composition head,
hands, legs, cloth body, molded hair
14" - 16" ....$175 - 250
Brother or Sister, 1943, composition
head, hands, cloth body, legs, yarn hair,
painted eyes
12" - 16" ....$125 - 275
Butin-nose: See Patsy family, and vinyl.
Candy Kid, 1946 on, all composition,
sleep eyes, toddler body, molded and
painted hair, closed mouth
13" ....$250 - 300
in boxing outfit ....$500 - 550
Charlie McCarthy, 1937, composition
head, hands, feet, painted features,
mouth opens, cloth body, legs,
marked: "Edgar Bergen's Charlie
McCarthy//An Effanbee Product"
17" - 19" ....$400 - 600
25" ....sold at auction for $1,100
Happy Birthday Doll, 1940, music box
in body, heart bracelet
17" ....$450 - 550
Historical Dolls, 1939 on, all-composition

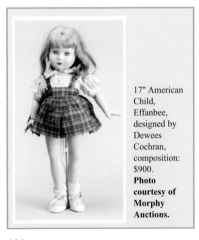

17" American
Child,
Effanbee,
designed by
Dewees
Cochran,
composition:
$900.
**Photo
courtesy of
Morphy
Auctions.**

jointed body, human-hair wig,
painted eyes, only three sets of thirty
dolls depicting history of apparel,
1492 - 1939, very elaborate original
costumes, metal heart bracelet,
head marked:
"Effanbee//American//Children";
body marked: "Effanbee//Anne Shirley"
21" ....$2,250 - 2,500
Historical Replicas, 1939 on, all-composition jointed body, copies of sets
above, but smaller, human-hair wig,
painted eyes, original costumes
14" ....$400 - 550
Honey, 1947 - 1948, all-composition
jointed body, human-hair wig, sleep
eyes, closed mouth
18" - 21" ....$200 - 325
**All hard plastic, circa 1949 - 1955,
see Vinyl and Hard Plastic below in
this category.**
Ice Queen, 1937 on, composition,
open mouth, skater outfit
17" ....$625 - 750
Little Lady, 1939 on, used Anne
Shirley mold, all composition, more
grown-up body, wigged, sleep eyes,
separated fingers, gold paper hang tag,
many wearing formals, as brides, or
fancy gowns with matching parasol,
during war years yarn hair was used,
may have gold hang tag bearing name
like Gaye or Carole
15" ....$225 - 275
18" ....$275 - 325
21" ....$350 - 400
27" ....$425 - 500
Mae Starr, 1928, talking doll, composition shoulder head, cloth body, open
mouth, four teeth, with cylinder
records, marked: "Mae//Starr// Doll"
29" ....$500 - 700
Marionettes, 1937 on, puppets designed
by Virginia Austin, composition,
painted eyes
Clippo, clown
15" ....$95 - 125

Effanbee

Emily Ann
14".....................................$75 - 125
Kilroy Cop
15".....................................$80 - 100
Portrait Dolls, 1940 on, all composition,
Bo-Peep, Ballerina, Bride, Groom,
Gibson Girl, Colonial Maid, etc.
12".....................................$275 - 350
Suzanne, 1940, all-composition jointed
body, sleep eyes, wigged, closed mouth,
may have magnets in hands to hold
accessories, allow more for additional
accessories or wardrobe
14".....................................$150 - 225
Suzette, 1939, all-composition fully
jointed body, painted side-glancing
eyes, closed mouth, wigged
12".....................................$250 - 275
Sweetie Pie, 1939 on, also called Baby
Bright Eyes, Tommy Tucker, Mickey,
composition bent limbs, sleep eyes,
caracul wig, cloth body, crier, issued
again in 1952 on in hard plastic, cloth
body and vinyl limbs, painted hair or
synthetic wigs, wearing same pink
rayon taffeta dress with black and
white trim as Noma doll
16" - 18".....................................$275 - 300
20" - 24".....................................$350 - 425
W. C. Fields, 1929 on, composition
shoulder head, painted features, hinged
mouth, painted teeth
17½".....................................$900 - 950
Patsy Family, 1928 on, composition
through 1947, later issued in vinyl and
porcelain, many have gold paper hang
tag and metal bracelet that reads:
"Effanbee Durable Dolls,"allow more
for black, special editions, costumes
or with added accessories
Babies
Patsy Baby, 1931, painted or sleep eyes,
wigged or molded hair, composition
baby body, advertised as Babykin, came
also with cloth body, in pair, layettes,
trunks, head marked: "Effanbee//Patsy
Baby"; body marked: "Effanbee

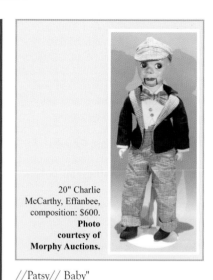

20" Charlie
McCarthy, Effanbee,
composition: $600.
**Photo
courtesy of
Morphy Auctions.**

//Patsy// Baby"
10" - 13".....................................$300 - 400
Patsy Babyette, 1932, sleep eyes, head
marked: "Effanbee"; body marked:
"Effanbee//Patsy //Babyette"
9".....................................$175 - 225
Patsy Baby Tinyette, 1934, painted
eyes, bent-leg composition body, head
marked: "Effanbee"; body marked:
"Effan-bee//Baby//Tinyette"
7".....................................$250 - 300
Quints, 1935, set of five Patsy Baby
Tinyettes in original box, from FAO
Schwarz, organdy christening gowns
and milk glass bottles, excellent
condition
Set of five
7".....................................$1,700 - 2,100
Children
Patsy
     1924, cloth body, composition
legs, open mouth, upper teeth, sleep
eyes, painted or human hair wig,
with composition legs to hips,
marked in half oval on back shoulder
plate: "Effanbee//Patsy"
15".....................................$300 - 350
     1928, all-composition jointed body,
painted or sleep eyes, molded headband
on red molded bobbed hair, or wigged,

Effanbee

bent right arm, gold paper hang tag,
metal heart bracelet, body marked:
"Effanbee//Patsy//Pat. Pend.//Doll"
    14".................$450 - 500
    Oriental with black painted hair,
    painted eyes, wearing fancy silk
    pajamas and matching shoes
    14".................$750 - 800
    1946, all-composition jointed
    body, bright facial coloring, painted
    or sleep eyes, wearing pink or blue
    checked pinafore
    14".................$400 - 450
Patsy Ann, 1929, all-composition,
closed mouth, sleep eyes, molded
hair, or wigged, body marked:
"Effanbee//'Patsy-Ann'//©//Pat.
#1283558"
    19".................$375 - 425
    1959, limited edition, vinyl, sleep
    eyes, white organdy dress, with pink
    hair ribbon, head marked
    "Effanbee//Patsy Ann//©1959";
    body marked: "Effanbee"
    15".................$225 - 275
Patsyette, 1931, composition
    9".................$300 - 325
    Black, Dutch, George and Martha
    Washington
    9" ....each $350 - 400

14" Suzanne, Effanbee, composition, with trunk:
$375. **Photo courtesy of Richard Withington,
Inc.**

Patsy Fluff, 1932, all cloth, painted
features, pink checked rompers
and bonnet
    16".................$1,000
Too few in database for reliable range
Patsy Joan, 1931, composition
    16".................$450 - 500
    1946, body marked: "Effandbee"
    (with added "d")
    17".................$325 - 425
Patsy Jr., 1931, all-composition,
advertised as Patsykins, marked:
"Effanbee//Patsy Jr.//Doll"
    11½".................$400 - 450
Patsy Lou, 1930, all-composition,
molded red hair or wigged, body
marked: "Effanbee//Patsy Lou"
    22".................$350 - 425
Patsy Mae, 1934, shoulder head,
sleep eyes, cloth body, crier, swing
legs, head marked: "Effanbee//Patsy
Mae;" shoulder plate marked:
"Effanbee// Lovums//c//Pat. No.
1283558"
    29".................$1,500 - 1,600
Patsy Ruth, 1934, shoulder head,
sleep eyes, cloth body, crier, swing legs,
head marked: "Effanbee//Patsy Ruth;"
shoulder plate marked:
"Effanbee//Lovums//©//Pat. No.
1283558"
    26".................$1,400 - 1,700
Patsy Tinyette Toddler, 1935, painted
eyes, head marked: "Effanbee"; body
marked: "Effanbee// Baby//Tinyette"
    7¾".................$325 - 375
Tinyette Toddler, tagged: "Kit and Kat"
    In Dutch costume ....pair $800
Wee Patsy, 1935, head molded to body,
molded and painted shoes and socks,
jointed arms and hips, advertised only
as "Fairy Princess," pin back button,
body marked: "Effanbee//Wee Patsy"
    5¾".................$400 - 500
Related items
    Metal heart bracelet, reads "Effanbee

Durable Dolls" $25
Metal personalized name bracelet
for Patsy family $65
Patsy Ann, Her Happy Times, circa
1935, book by Mona Reed King ..$75
Patsy For Keeps, circa 1932, book by
Ester Marian Ames $125
Patricia Series, 1935, all sizes
advertised in *Patsytown News*,
all-composition slimmer bodies, sleep
eyes, wigged, later WWII-era Patricia
dolls have yarn hair and cloth bodies
Patricia, wig, sleep eyes, body marked:
"Effanbee Patricia"
15"....................................$375 - 450
Patricia Ann, wig, marked:
Effanbee//Patricia Ann
19"....................................$600 - 650
Patricia Joan, wig, slimmer legs,
marked: Effanbee//Patricia Joan
16"....................................$500 - 550
Patricia-Kin, wig, head marked: "Patricia-
Kin"; body marked: "Effanbee//Patsy Jr."
11½" ....$350 - 400
Patricia Lou, wig, marked:
Effanbee//Patricia Lou
22"....................................$475 - 525
Patricia Ruth, head marked:
"Effanbee//Patsy Ruth," no marks
on slimmer composition body
27"..............................$1,200 - 1,350
Patsy Related Dolls and Variants
Betty Bee, 1932, all composition,
short tousle wig, sleep eyes, body
marked: "Effanbee//Patsy Lou"
22"....................................$375 - 400
Betty Bounce, tousle head, 1932 on,
all composition, sleep eyes, Lovums
head marked: "Effanbee//'Patsy Ann'/
/©//Pat. #1283558" on body
19"....................................$350 - 400
Betty Brite, 1932, all composition,
short tousle wig, sleep eyes, gold hang
tag reads: "This is Betty Brite, The
lovable Imp with tiltable head and
movable limb, an Effanbee doll." some

with body marked: "Effanbee//Betty
Brite;" others with head marked:
"© Mary-Lee"; body marked "Effanbee
Patsy Joan"
16"....................................$300 - 350
Butin-nose, 1936 on, all composition,
molded and painted hair, features,
distinct feature is small nose, usually
wearing regional or special costume
8"......................................$200 - 300
Oriental, with layette
8" $525
Mary Ann, 1932 on, composition,
sleep eyes, wigged, open mouth, head
marked: "Mary Ann"; body marked:
"Effanbee//'Patsy Ann'//©//Pat.
#1283558"
19"....................................$350 - 375
Mary Lee, 1932, composition, sleep
eyes, wigged, open mouth, head
marked: "©//Mary Lee"; body marked:
"Effanbee//Patsy Joan"
16½" ....$325 - 350
Patsy/Patricia, 1940, marked Patsy head
on marked Patricia body, all composi

19" Patsy Ann, Effanbee, composition, wigged:
$400. **Photo courtesy of Morphy Auctions.**

tion, painted eyes, molded hair, may have magnets in hands to hold accessories, marked: "Effanbee//'Patricia'"on body
15".....................$400 - 450
Skippy, 1929, advertised as Patsy's boyfriend, composition head, painted eyes, molded painted blond hair, composition or cloth body, composition molded shoes and legs, head marked: "Effanbee//Skippy//©//P. L. Crosby": body marked: "Effanbee//Patsy// Pat. Pend// Doll"
14"
Military outfit ....$300 - 500
Boy's outfit.............................$300 - 400
Rubber
Dy-Dee, 1934 on, hard-rubber head, sleep eyes, jointed rubber bent-leg body, drink/wet mechanism, molded and painted hair. Early dolls have molded ears, after 1940 have applied rubber ears, nostrils and tear ducts, later made in hard plastic and vinyl, value can double (or more) for mint condition or layette packaging marked: "Effanbee//Dy-Dee Baby" with four patent numbers.
Dy-Dee-Wee
9"......................$275 - 300
Dy-Dee-Ette
11"......................$300 - 350
Dy-Dee-Kin
13"......................$350 - 400
Other Dy-Dee dolls
15"......................$425 - 475
20"......................$475 - 525
Dy-Dee in Layette Trunk, with accessories
11" - 13"......................$700 - 850
Vinyl Re-issue, 1984 molded hair or curly rooted hair
14"......................$60 - 75
Hard Plastic and Vinyl, dolls listed are in good condition wearing original clothing, value can double for MIB
Alyssa, 1960 - 1961, vinyl head,

hard-plastic jointed body, walker, including elbows, rooted saran hair, sleep eyes
23".....................$200 - 225
Baby Lisa, 1980, vinyl, designed by Astri Campbell, represents a three-month-old baby
11"......................$10 - 15
with lyette ....$45 - 55
Baby Lisa Grows Up, 1983, vinyl, toddler body, in trunk with wardrobe ....$40 - 50
Brenda Starr, 2002 - 2007
16".....................$75 - 100
Butterball, 1969, all vinyl, molded hair or rooted, sleep eyes
12"......................$30 - 40
1989, molded hair
12"......................$18 - 22
Button Nose, 1968 - 1971, vinyl head, cloth body
18"......................$25 - 35
2004
18"......................$45 - 60
Champagne Lady, 1959, vinyl head and arms, rooted hair, blue sleep eyes, lashes, hard-plastic body, based on performer on The Lawrence Welk Show TV show, Miss Revlon-type
21"......................$150 - 200
23"......................$250 - 300
Currier and Ives, vinyl and hard plastic
12"......................$10 - 15
Disney dolls, 1977 - 1978, Snow White, Cinderella, Alice in Wonderland, Sleeping Beauty
14"......................$50 - 75
16½"......................$100 - 175
Fluffy, 1954 on, all vinyl
Molded hair
8"......................$20 - 28
Rooted hair
8"......................$22 - 30
11"......................$35 - 45
Grand Dames, 1970 on, vinyl, sleep eyes, rooted hair, elaborate costumes
11"......................$12 - 18

Effanbee

15" ....$20 - 25
18" ....$18 - 22
Gumdrop, 1962 on, vinyl, jointed
toddler, sleep eyes, rooted hair
16" ....$15 - 20
Hagara, Jan, designer, all vinyl,
jointed, rooted hair, painted eyes,
Christina-1984, Larry-1985,
Laurel-1984, Lesley-1985
15" ....$25 - 30
Half Pint, 1966 - 1983, all vinyl,
rooted hair, sleep eyes, lashes
11" ....$10 - 20
Happy Boy, 1960, vinyl, molded hair,
tooth, freckles, painted eyes
11" ....$45 - 50
Hibel, Edna, designer, 1984 only,
all vinyl
Flower Girl................................$20 - 30
Contessa ....$25 - 35
Honey, 1949 - 1958, hard plastic
(see also Composition), saran wig,
sleep eyes, closed mouth, head and
body marked: "Effanbee," gold paper
hang tag reads: "I am//Honey//An//
Effanbee//Sweet/ /Child"
Honey, 1949 - 1955, all hard plastic,
closed mouth, sleep eyes
14" ....$350 - 400
18" ....$400 - 500
24" ....$500 - 525
Honey Walker, 1952 on, all hard plastic
with walking mechanism, Honey Walker
Junior Miss, 1956 - 1957, hard plastic,
extra joints at knees and ankles permit
her to wear flat or high-heeled shoes,
add $50 for jointed knees and ankles
14" ....$225 - 275
19" ....$275 - 325
Humpty Dumpty, 1985 ....$55 - 75
Katie, 1957, molded hair
8½" ....$40 - 50
Legend Series, vinyl, 15½", value can
double for MIB
1980, W.C. Fields ....$30 - 35
1981, John Wayne, cowboy ....$25 - 30
1982, John Wayne, cavalry ....$25 - 30

9" Patsyette, Effanbee, composition, original
boxes: each $450. **Photo courtesy of Morphy
Auctions.**

1982, Mae West..........................$20 - 30
1983, Groucho Marx..................$15 - 20
1984, Judy Garland, Dorothy ....$20 - 25
1985, Lucille Ball.......................$35 - 40
1986, Liberace ....$25 - 30
1987, James Cagney...................$20 - 25
Lil Sweetie, 1967, nurser with no lashes
or brow
16" ....$35 - 40
Limited Edition Club, vinyl
1975, Precious Baby...............$100 - 125
1976, Patsy Ann ....$100 - 110
1977, Dewees Cochran ....$35 - 45
1978, Crowning Glory ....$20 - 30
1979, Skippy ....$75 - 100
1980, Susan B. Anthony ....$20 - 30
1981, Girl with Watering Can ..$60 - 70
1982, Princess Diana ....$100 - 125
1983, Sherlock Holmes.............$35 - 45
1984, Bubbles ....$45 - 50
1985, Red Boy ....$25 - 30
1986, China head ....$25 - 30
1987 - 1988, Porcelain Grumpy
(2,500) ....$100 - 125
Vinyl Grumpy.....................$40 - 50
Martha and George Washington,
1976 - 1977, all vinyl, fully jointed,
rooted hair, blue eyes, molded lashes
11" pair ....$40 - 50
Mickey, 1956 - 1972, all vinyl, fully
jointed, some with molded hat,
painted eyes

10" ....$30 - 40
Miss Chips, 1966 - 1981, all vinyl,
fully jointed, side-glancing sleep eyes,
rooted hair
17" ....$25 - 35
Black
17" ....$30 - 45
Most Happy Family, 1958, vinyl, 21"
mother, 10" brother and sister, 8" baby
Set ....$100 - 125
Noma, The Electronic Doll, 1950, hard
plastic, cloth body, vinyl limbs,
battery-operated talking doll, wearing
pink rayon taffeta dress with
black-and-white check trim
27" ....$300 - 350
Polka Dottie, 1954, vinyl head,
molded pigtails on fabric body, or
hard-plastic body
21" ....$145 - 165
Latex body
11" ....$100 - 120
Personality Series
1984, Sir Winston Churchill ....$20 - 30
1984, Louis Armstrong ....$15 - 25
1984, Mark Twain ....$20 - 30
1985, Eleanor Roosevelt ....$20 - 30
Presidents, 1984 on
Abraham Lincoln
18" ....$20 - 25

15" Dy-Dee Jane, Effanbee, hard rubber, layette: $650. **Photo courtesy of Sweetbriar Auctions.**

George Washington
16" ....$25 - 30
Teddy Roosevelt
17" ....$20 - 25
Franklin D. Roosevelt
1985 ....$20 - 25
Andrew Jackson
1989 ....$20 - 25
Princess Diana, 1982, vinyl
18" ....$20 - 25
Pun'kin, 1966 - 1983, all vinyl,
fully jointed toddler, sleep eyes,
rooted hair
11" ....$15 - 20
Regal Heirloom Collection, 1965, vinyl,
rooted hair, sleep eyes
18" ....$10 - 15
Rootie Kazootie, 1954, vinyl head,
cloth or hard-plastic body, smaller
size has latex body
11" ....$100 - 120
21" ....$145 - 165
Santa Claus, 1982 on, designed by
Faith Wick, "Old Fashioned Nast
Santa," No. 7201, vinyl head, hands,
stuffed cloth body, molded and
painted features, marked:
"Effanbee//7201 c//Faith Wick"
18" ....$20 - 30
Sugar Pie, 1960, vinyl nurser, rooted
or molded hair, sleep eyes
14" - 16" ....$30 - 40
Storybook Series, 1976, Heidi, Red
Ridinghood, Alice In Wonderland,
others
11" ....$10 - 15
Suzie Sunshine, 1961 - 1979, designed
by Eugenia Dukas, all vinyl, fully
jointed, rooted hair, sleep eyes, lashes,
freckles on nose, add $25 for black
18" ....$30 - 35
Sweetie Pie, 1952, hard plastic
27" ....$200 - 250
Tintair, 1951, hard plastic, hair color
set, made to compete with Ideal's Toni
14" - 16" ....$150 - 200
20" ....$200 - 300

Wicket Witch, 1981 - 1982, designed by Faith Wick. No. 7110, vinyl head, blond rooted hair, painted features, cloth stuffed body, dressed in black, with apple and basket, head marked: "Effanbee//Faith Wick//7110 19cc81"

18".....................................$20 - 25

FARNELL-ALPHA TOYS

1915 - 1930s, Acton, London. Cloth dolls with molded felt or velvet heads, cloth bodies, painted features, mohair wigs.

Baby

15"....................................$300 - 350
18"....................................$400 - 500

Child

10"....................................$300 - 350
14" - 15" ....$400 - 425
20"....................................$425 - 475

Black

13" - 15" ....$500 - 600

Too few in database for reliable range

15" George VI, Farnell, cloth: $550.
Photo courtesy of Morphy Auctions.

Characters such as Islanders, pirates etc.

15" ....$100 - 175

Long-limbed Lady

26"....................................$700 - 750

Too few in database for reliable range

King George VI, "H.M. The King"

15"....................................$450 - 550

Palace Guard, "Beefeater"

15" ....$175 - 250

FISHER-PRICE

1931 on, New York. Began by making infants' and children's toys. Eventually the product line was expanded to include dolls. Values are for secondary-market dolls in perfect condition wearing original clothing, many are still available at retail sources.

My Friend Mandy Series, 1977 on, vinyl head and limbs, cloth body, rooted hair, painted eyes

16".....................................$15 - 25

My Baby Beth, 1978, vinyl head and limbs, cloth body, rooted hair, painted eyes

18" ....$50 - 60

FRANKLIN MINT

1964 on, Wawa and Exton, Pennsylvania. Began by making legal tender coins for foreign countries, as well as commemorative medallions, casino tokens and precious metal ingots. Eventually the product line was expanded to include sculptures, deluxe games, precision die-cast models, and collector dolls. Since 2003 the doll lines have been reduced in production, and some have been phased out completely. Values are for secondary-market dolls in perfect condition wearing original clothing, many are still available at retail sources. Value can double for MIB.

Vinyl

Cinderella

15½" ....$75 - 85

15" Jackie, Franklin Mint, porcelain, extra outfits: $200. **Photo courtesy of Morphy Auctions.**

Jackie Kennedy
14½" ....$30 - 50
Marilyn Monroe
16" ....$75 - 125
Princess Diana
15½" ....$90 - 100
Porcelain
Arwen Evenstar
22" ....$75 - 90
Country Store Advertising Logo Dolls, 1986
on
13" ....$15 - 25
Gibson girl
21" ....$55 - 75
Jackie Kennedy
15" ....$40 - 70
With trunk and wardrobe
......................$200 - 300
Wedding Portrait
16" ....$125 - 150
Marilyn Monroe
19" ....$40 - 65
Scarlett O'Hara, in wedding gown
19" ....$100 - 125
Princess Diana
18½" ....$70 - 130

FRENCH POUPÉES

1869 on. Glass eyes, doll modeled as an adult lady, with bisque shoulder head, stationary or swivel neck, closed mouth, earrings, kid or kid and cloth body, nicely dressed, good condition. Add more for original clothing, special body such as Gesland, Kintzbach, Terrenne, black or exceptional doll.

Poupée Peau (kid body), unmarked or with size number only
Glass eyes
12" - 14" ....$2,000 - 4,000
16" - 18" ....$4,000 - 7,000
21" ....$6,000 - 9,000
27" ....$10,000 - 12,000
Painted eyes, kid body
14" - 16" ....$1,600 - 1,900
Poupée Bois (wooden body), unmarked or with size number only, articulated body, glass eyes
13" ....$6,500 - 9,000
15" ....$7,000 - 8,500
18" ....$7,500 - 8,000
Kid-over-wood body
15" - 18" ....$6,000 - 8,000
Blown-kid body
14" ....$8,000 - 10,000

Too few in database for a reliable range

Barrois: See Barrios section.

B.S., Blampoix
12" - 14" ....$2,600 - 3,000
16" - 17" ....$4,000 - 7,000
A. Dehors, 1860, swivel neck, bisque lower arms
Generic face, wooden body
14" - 15" ....$4,000 - 5,000
17" - 20" ....$7,000 - 9,000

Portrait face
17" - 18"..................$17,000 - 20,000
L.D., Louis Doleac, kid body
17" - 20" ....$3,000 - 5,300
Wooden body
18" ....$12,000 - 15,000
Too few in database for a reliable range
Simonne
Kid body
12"............................$4,900 - 5,200
16" - 17"......................$6,000 - 7,000
Wooden body
14"............................$7,500 - 8,500
18"..........................$10,500 - 12,000
Fortune Teller Dolls, fashion-type head with swivel neck, glass or painted eyes, kid body, skirt made to hold many paper "fortunes," allow more for exceptional doll
Closed mouth
15" - 18".....................$4,100 - 7,000
Open mouth
18" ....$3,100+
China, glazed finish, 1870 - 1880 hairstyle
14" - 15" ....$5,000 - 5,500
18"............................$8,500 - 9,000

Accessories
Dress ....$600+
Shoes marked by maker.................$500+
Unmarked.......................................$250
Trunk ....$250+
Wig ....$250+

RALPH A. FREUNDLICH

1924 - 1945, New York City, later Clinton, Massachusetts. Ralph Freundlich worked for Jeanette Doll Co. then opened Silver Doll and Toy Manufacturing Co. in 1923. In 1924 became Ralph Freundlich, Inc. and made composition dolls. Dolls listed are in good condition wearing original clothing.
Baby Sandy, 1939 - 1942, all-composition jointed toddler body, molded hair, painted or sleep eyes, smiling mouth
8"......................................$150 - 200
12"....................................$175 - 225
15"....................................$275 - 325
20"....................................$350 - 450

16" Poupée peau, bisque, unmarked: $4,000.
Photo courtesy of Morphy Auctions.

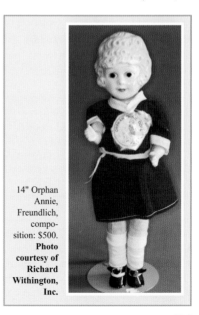

14" Orphan Annie, Freundlich, composition: $500.
Photo courtesy of Richard Withington, Inc.

Dummy Dan, ventriloquist doll,
Charlie McCarthy look-alike

15"...$50 - 75
21"..$75 - 100

General Douglas MacArthur, 1942,
all-composition jointed body, bent arm
salutes, painted features, molded hat,
jointed, in khaki uniform, paper tag

18"......................................$200 - 275

Military dolls, 1942 on, all composition, molded hats, painted features,
original clothes, paper tag, Soldier,
Sailor, WAAC, or WAVE

15"......................................$150 - 200

Orphan Annie and her dog, Sandy

12".....................................$500 - 600

Pig Baby, 1930s, composition pig
head, painted features, unmarked
five-piece body, Freundlich presumed
maker of similar composition cat,
rabbit and monkey dolls

9".......................................$350 - 400

Pinocchio, composition and cloth,
molded hair, painted features,
brightly colored cheeks, large eyes,
open/closed mouth, tagged:
"Original as portrayed by C. Collodi"

16".....................................$400 - 425

Red Riding Hood, Wolf, Grandma,
1934, composition, set of three, in
schoolhouse box, original clothes
Set of three

9"......................................$775 - 875

Trixbe (Patsy-type), all-composition
girl, painted features, molded painted
hair with bow pined into head

11"....................................$100 - 125

FULPER POTTERY COMPANY

1918 - 1921, Flemington, New Jersey.
Made dolls with bisque heads and all-
bisque dolls. Sold dolls to Amberg,
Colonial Toy Mfg. Co., and Horsman.
"M.S." monogram stood for Martin
Stangl,who was in charge of production.

17" baby, Fulper, bisque, socket head, for Amberg: $400. **Photo courtesy of Morphy Auctions.**

Dolls listed are in good condition with
original or appropriate clothes.

Baby, bisque socket head, glass eyes,
open mouth, teeth, mohair wig,
bent-leg body

14" - 16"..........................$300 - 350
17" - 22" ....$400 - 500

Toddler

16" - 18"..........................$575 - 625

Child, socket head, glass eyes,
open mouth

Kid body

18" - 22" ....$250 - 325
27".................................$400 - 450

Composition body

16" - 18".........................$250 - 350
22" - 24".........................$475 - 550

GABRIEL

The Lone Ranger Series, 1970s, vinyl
action figures with horses, separate accessory sets available. Dolls in very good
condition with original clothing and
accessories. Value can double for MIB.

Dan Reed on Banjo, blond hair, figure
on palomino horse

9"..$50 - 65

Butch Cavendish on Smoke, black hair,
mustache, on black horse

9".......................................$90 - 130

Hopi medicine man

9" ....$110 - 120

Lone Ranger on Silver, masked figure on
white horse

9"..$80 - 125
Lone Ranger, no horse
9"..$65 - 85
Mysterious Prospector set, Mule and
mining items
$50 - 60
Tonto on Scout, Indian on brown-and-
white horse
9"......................................$110 - 125
Tonto, no horse
9"..$65 - 75

GANS AND SEYFARTH PUPPENBABRIK

1908 - 1922, Waltershausen, Thüringia,
Germany. Made bisque dolls; had a
patent for flirty and googly eyes. Partners
separated in 1922; Otto Gans opened his
own factory.
Baby, bent leg, original clothes
or appropriately dressed, allow more
for toddler
10" - 14"...........................$350 - 375
16" - 20" ....$425 - 500
25"...................................$650 - 725
Child, open mouth, composition body,
original clothes or appropriately dressed,
molds 120, 6589, or none
13" - 15"...........................$325 - 375
21" - 24"...........................$400 - 475
28"...................................$550 - 600

FRANÇOIS GAULTIER

1860 - 1899. After 1899, became part of
S.F.B.J., located near Paris. Made bisque
doll heads and parts for lady dolls and for
bébés and sold to many French makers of
dolls including Gesland, Jullien, Petite et
Dumontier, Rabery et Delphieu and
Thuillier. Also made all-bisque dolls
marked "F.G." Dolls listed are in good
condition, appropriately dressed.
Poupée (fashion-type), 1860 on,
swivel head on bisque shoulder plate,
kid body, may have bisque lower arms,
head marked: "F.G."
Glass eyes
10" - 11".....................$1,900 - 2,200
12" - 13" ....$2,400 - 3,000
15" - 17".....................$3,200 - 3,600
18" - 20" ....$4,000 - 5,000
23" - 24" ....$6,000 - 6,200
30" - 32" ....$4,000 - 5,000
Painted eyes
16" - 17".....................$1,800 - 2,000
Wooden body
16" - 18" ....$8,000 - 9,000
Later one-piece shoulder head, kid
body, often in regional dress
Painted eyes
12" - 15" ....$700 - 900
Glass eyes
18" ....$900 - 1,000

9½" mold 301, toddler, Gans & Seyfarth,
bisque: $650. **Photo courtesy of Gloria's
Antique Dolls.**

27" bébé,
FG, bisque,
scroll mark:
$400.
**Photo
courtesy of
Morphy
Auctions.**

Bébé (child), 1879 - 1887, closed mouth, excellent quality bisque socket head, glass eyes, pierced ears, cork pate, marked in block letters: "F.G."

Composition-and-wood body with straight wrists

    10" - 11" ....$8,000 - 11,000
    13" - 16" ....$7,000 - 9,000
    18" - 22" ....$7,000 - 8,000
    27" - 29" ....$8,000 - 10,000

Kid body, may have bisque forearms

    10" - 12" ....$4,900 - 6,000
    13" - 15" ....$7,000 - 9,000
    17" - 19" ....$10,000 - 11,000

Bébé (child), 1887 - 1900, composition body, closed mouth, marked: "F.G." inside scroll,

    9½" size 0 ....$5,000 - 5,500
    12" - 13" ....$4,500 - 5,000
    15" - 17" ....$4,000 - 4,800
    22" - 24" ....$4,800 - 5,100
    28" ....$5,200 - 5,300

Composition body, open mouth

    14" - 16" ....$1,700 - 1,900
    20" - 24" ....$2,500 - 3,000
    27" ....$4,000 - 4,200

GESLAND

1860 - 1928, Paris. Made, repaired, exported and distributed dolls, patented a doll body, used heads from François Gaultier with "F.G." block or scroll mark. In 1926 became part of the Société Industrielle de France. Gesland's doll bodies have metal articulated armature covered with padding and stockinette, with bisque or wood/composition hands and legs. Dolls listed are in good condition, appropriately dressed. Allow more for exceptional original clothing.

Poupée (fashion-type) Gesland, stockinette covered metal articulated fashion-type body, bisque lower arms and legs

    14" - 15" ....$4,500 - 5,000
    16" - 17" ....$5,000 - 7,000
    23" - 24" ....$6,000 - 9,000

Bébé (child), marked Gesland body,

closed mouth

    12" - 15" ....$4,800 - 5,000
    17" - 20" ....$5,200 - 5,800
    22" - 24" ....$6,100 - 6,500
    28" - 30" ....$5,000 - 7,000

RUTH GIBBS

1946 on, Flemington, New Jersey. Made dolls with china heads and limbs on cloth bodies. The dolls were designed by Herbert Johnson. Dolls listed are in good condition wearing original clothing; value can double if in original box.

Godey's Lady Book Dolls, pink-tint or white shoulder head, cloth body

    7" ....$60 - 75
    12" ....$85 - 100

Blond special for G Fox 100th anniversary CT

    12" MIB.........................$150 - $180

With molded necklace

    12" ....$120 - 145

Black

    12" ....$145 - 155

Caracul wig, original outfit

    10" ....$150 - 225

7" Godey lady, Ruth Gibbs, china: $70. **Doll courtesy of Elaine Holda.**

GILBERT TOYS

1909 - 1966, New Haven, Connecticut. Founded on the invention of the Erector Set, went on to make dolls based on popular television characters. Dolls listed are in very good condition with all original clothing and accessories; value can double for MIB.

Honey West, 1965, vinyl head and arms, hard-plastic torso and legs, rooted blond hair, painted eyes, painted beauty spot near mouth, head marked: "K73" with leopard

11½" ....$100 - 125

Accessories MOC .... $60 - 80

Characters from *The Man From U.N.C.L.E.* TV show of the 1960s

Ilya Kuryakin (David McCallum)

12¼" ....$100 - 150

Napoleon Solo (Robert Vaughn)

12¼" ....$125 - 150

James Bond, Secret Agent 007, character from James Bond movies

12¼" ....$75 - 100

Odd Job ....$85 - 115

GIRL SCOUT DOLLS

1917 on, listed chronologically. Dolls made for the Girl Scouts of America, various manufacturers. Dolls listed are in good condition with original clothing; value can double for MIB.

1917, all-composition doll, painted features, mohair wig

6½" ....$225 - 250

1920s Girl Scout doll in camp uniform, pictured in Girl Scout 1920 handbook, all cloth, mask face, painted features, wigged, gray-green uniform

13" ....$600+

Grace Corry, Scout 1929, designed by Grace Corry, composition shoulder head, cloth body with crier, molded hair, painted features, original uniform, shoulder plate marked: "by Grace Corry," body stamped: "Madame Hendren

13" Girl Scouts, Georgene Novelties, cloth mask faces: each $125. **Photo courtesy of Alderfer Auction Company, Inc.**

Doll//Made in USA"

13" ....$550 - 675

Averill Mfg. Co, 1936, all cloth, printed and painted features

16" ....$300 - 350

Georgene Novelties

1940 - 1946, all cloth, flat-faced painted features, yellow yarn curls, wearing original silver-green uniform with red triangle tie, hang tag reads: "Genuine Georgene Doll//A product of Georgene Novelties, Inc., NY//Made in U.S.A."

15" ....$200 - 250

1946 - 1955, all cloth, mask face, painted features, string hair

13½" ....$75 - 125

1955 - 1957, same as previous listing, but now has stuffed vinyl head

13" ....$150 - 200

Terri Lee, 1949 - 1958, hard plastic, felt hat, oilcloth saddle shoes

16" ....$400 - 500

Outfit only $160

Tiny Terri Lee, 1955 - 1958, hard plastic, walker, sleep eyes, wig, plastic shoes

10" ....$125 - 175

Ginger, 1956 - 1958, made by Cosmopolitan for Terri Lee, hard plastic, straight-leg walker, synthetic wig

7½" - 8" ....$65 - 90

Effanbee Honey, 1949 - 1957, hard plastic, mohair wig

14" ....$100 - 125

18" ....$200 - 250

Vogue, Painted Lash Walker Ginny, 1954, hard plastic

8" ....$225 - 275

Nancy Ann Storybook, 1957, Muffie, hard plastic

8" ....$100 - 140

Effanbee, Patsy Ann, 1959 on, all-vinyl jointed body, saran hair, sleep eyes, freckles on nose, Brownie or Girl Scout

15" ....$75 - 125

Effanbee Suzette, circa 1960, jointed vinyl body, sleep eyes, saran hair, thin body, long legs

15" ....$250 - 300

Uneeda, 1961 - 1963, Ginny look-alike, vinyl head, hard-plastic body, straight-leg walker, Dynel wig, head marked: "U"

8" ....$65 - 80

Effanbee Fluffy, 1964 - 1972, vinyl dolls, sleep eyes, curly rooted hair, Brownie has blond wig, Junior is brunette, box has clear acetate lid, printed with Girl Scout trademark and catalog number

8" ....$45 - 55

Related, Fluffy Camp Fire Girl

8" ....$65 - 75

Effanbee Fluffy Cadette, 1965, vinyl, rooted hair, sleep eyes

11" ....$150 - 200

Effanbee Pun'kin Jr., 1974 - 1979, all vinyl, sleep eyes, long straight rooted hair, Brownie and Junior uniforms

11½" ....$25 - 35

Related, Fluffy Camp Fire Girl

11½" ....$45 - 55

Hallmark, 1979, all cloth, Juliette Low, from 1916 handbook, wearing printed 1923 uniform

6½" ....$20 - 25

Jesco, 1985, Katie, all vinyl, sleep eyes, long straight rooted hair, look-alike Girl Scout, dressed as Brownie and

Junior

9" ....$35 - 45

Dakin, Ginny, 1986 - 1995, all vinyl

8" ....$60 - 90

Alexander Doll Company, 1992, vinyl, unofficial Girl Scout, sleep eyes

8" ....$55 - 75

Avon, 1995, Tender Memories series, porcelain, carrying box of cookies

14" ....$25 - 35

GLADDIE

1928 - 1930 on. Trade name of doll designed by Helen Webster Jensen, made in Germany, body made by K&K for Borgfeldt. Flange heads made of bisque or biscaloid (a ceramic imitation of bisque), with molded hair, glass or painted eyes, open/closed mouth with two upper teeth and laughing expression, composition arms, lower legs, cloth torso, some with crier and upper legs, marked: "copyriht" (misspelled). Dolls listed are in good condition, appropriately dressed.

Biscaloid ceramic head

18" - 20" ....$800 - 1,100

23" - 24" ....$1,200 - 1,500

29" ....$1,500 - 1,900

Bisque head

14" ....$2,600 - 2,800

18" - 20" ....$3,800 - 4,800

18" Gladdie, biscaloid: $1,000. **Photo courtesy of Joan & Lynette Antique Dolls and Accessories.**

WM. AND
F. & W. GOEBEL

1867 - 1930 on, Oeslau, Thüringia, Germany. Made porcelain and glazed china dolls, as well as bathing dolls, Kewpie-types and others. Earlier mark was triangle with half moon. Supplied heads to other doll-makers including Max Handwerck. Dolls listed are in good condition appropriately dressed. Allow more for exceptional dolls.

Child, 1895
Socket head, open mouth, composition body, sleep or set eyes, mold 120 or none

7" - 10"	$100 - 150
12" - 16"	$225 - 275
17" - 23"	$325 - 375
25" - 27"	$425 - $500

Baby body

13"	$200 - 225

Shoulder head, open mouth, kid or cloth body, glass eyes

20" - 24"	$200 - 225

Character Child, after 1909
Molded hair, may have flowers or ribbons, painted features, five-piece papier-mâché body

5½" - 7"	$300 - 500

Molded on bonnet or hat, closed mouth, five-piece papier-mâché body, painted features

9"	$525 - 550

Character Baby, after 1909, open mouth, sleep eyes, five-piece bent-leg baby body

13" - 15"	$375 - 425
18" - 21"	$475 - 525

Toddler body

14"	$450 - 500

GOOGLIES

Popular 1900 - 1925, various manufacturers. Most doll manufacturers of the period made dolls with exagerated, round "googly" eyes. Painted eyes, looking to side or straight ahead or inserted glass, tin or celluloid eyes. For inserted eye dolls the same head can be found with and without flirty eyes (flirty eyes refers to eyes which move side to side). May have closed smiling mouth, composition or papier-mâché body, molded hair or wigged. Dolls listed are in good condition appropriately dressed. Allow more for exceptional dolls.

All bisque, jointed shoulders, hips, molded shoes, socks
Painted intaglio eyes, unmarked

3"	$350 - 400
5" - 6"	$500 - 600

Rigid neck, glass eyes, unmarked

3"	$325 - 375
4" - 5"	$500 - 550

6" Goebel, bisque, painted eyes, molded hairband and bow: $400.
Photo courtesy of The Museum Doll Shop.

8" googly, mold 208, Goebel, bisque, glass eyes: $1,200.
Photo courtesy of Morphy Auctions.

129

Googlies

7" googly, mold 264, Ernst Heubach, bisque: $500.
Photo courtesy of McMasters Harris Apple Tree Doll Auctions.

6" - 7" ....$600 - 775
Swivel neck, glass eyes, unmarked
5".....................................$525 - 600
7".....................................$800 - 850
No mold number, jointed knees
7"..............................$2,500 - 2,800
Marked by maker, Molds 217, 330, 501
4" - 5" ....$725 - 775
6" - 7" ....$900 - 950
Hertwig, molded clothing, wire-jointed at shoulders and hips, painted eyes
4" - 7"................................$100 - 125
Hertel, Schwab, Mold 189
5" - 6½" ....$800 - 1,300
8"............................$1,500 - $1,600
Kestner, Mold 111, jointed knees and elbows
4½" - 6" ....$1,500 - 2,100
Molds 192, 292, glass eyes, watermelon smile
4" - 5" ....$800 - 900
Mold 211, jointed elbows, knees and neck
5"..............................$2,800 - 3,000
Too few in database for reliable range
7"..............................$3,750 - 4,200
Too few in database for reliable range
Our Fairy, mold 222, circa 1914, wigged, glass eyes
4½" - 5" ....$800 - 1,000
6" - 7" ....$1,500 - 1,800
11"..............................$2,000 - 2,200

Painted eyes, molded hair
5"......................................$450 - 550
8"......................................$750 - 850
12" ....$950 - 1,500
Limbach, mold 1920, molded cloche, painted eyes, jointed shoulders
7½" ....$450 - 500
Peek-a-boo kids, designed by Chloe Preston, 1914 on, bisque immobile, painted features including wide lashes
1¾" - 2½" ....$35 - 50
4" - 5" ....$135 - 250
Bisque Head, painted or glass eyes, composition body
Bähr & Pröschild, mold 608, circa 1914, glass eyes, wigged, marked: "B.P."
8"..............................$1,500 - 1,800
Demacol, made for Dennis Malley and Co., London, bisque socket head, glass eyes, closed watermelon mouth, mohair wig, five-piece composition toddler body
8" - 13" ....$750 - 1,200
Goebel, mold 208, 268, others
Painted eyes
6" - 7" ....$600 - 650
9" - 10" ....$800 - 850
12"..................................$900 - 1000
Glass eyes
7" - 8" ....$900 - 1,200
10" - 11".....................$1,500 - 1,600
13"............................$2,200 - 2,500

7" googly, mold 262, Ernst Heubach, bisque: $500.
Photo courtesy of Morphy Auctions.

Googlies

Round open/closed mouth, molded painted hair, toddler body, resembles Recknagel mold 50
    Painted eyes
        7" ....$900 - 1,050
    Glass eyes
        9½" ....$3,400 - 3,600
Handwerck, Max
Marked "Elite," molded military helmet, bisque socket head, glass eyes, closed mouth
        10" - 14"....................$1,200 - 1,500
Marked "Elite," bellhop-style molded hat
        11" - 12"....................$2,900 - 3,200
Hertel Schwab & Co., 1914 on
Mold 163, solid dome, glass eyes, molded hair, closed smiling mouth, toddler body
        12"............................$5,000 - 6,500
        16" - 18"....................$7,900 - 8,800
        21½".................................. $13,000
Jubilee, socket head, glass eyes, closed smiling mouth
    Mold 165, toddler
        11" - 12"....................$7,000 - 9,000
        15" - 16" ....$12,000 - 15,000
        22" ....sold at auction for $29,000
    Mold 172, baby, solid dome
        11" - 12"....................$4,000 - 4,500
        16"............................$5,500 - 6,000
Mold 173, solid dome, glass eyes, closed smiling mouth

6½" googly, mold 210, Armand Marseille, bisque: $500. **Photo courtesy of Morphy Auctions.**

9" googly, mold 323, Armand Marseille, bisque: $1,200. **Photo courtesy of Richard Withington, Inc.**

    Baby
        10" - 11"....................$3,500 - 3,800
        16"............................$5,800 - 6,200
    Toddler
        10" - 12" ....$4,000 - 5,000
        16"............................$7,000 - 7,400
Heubach, Ernst
    Molds 262, 264, circa 1914, painted eyes, closed mouth, marked: "EH"
        6" - 8" ....$450 - 550
        10" - 12"..........................$650 - 900
Mold 276, bug mold on nose, googly crossed eyes
        7" ....$2,500 - 3,000
Mold 318, circa 1920, character, closed mouth, marked: "EH"
        11" ....$1,100 - 1,285
        14"............................$1,900 - 2,050
Mold 319, circa 1920, character, painted eyes, tearful features, marked: "EH"
        12" ....sold at auction for $24,000
Mold 417, character, small eye cuts, glass eyes, closed mouth with pursed lips, wigged
        11".....................................$750 - 900
Heubach, Gebrüder
No mold number, painted eyes
        6" - 7" ....$575 - 650
        9" - 11" ....$800 - 1,000
        13"............................$1,500 - 1,700

Googlies

7" mold 208, Walthur & Sohn, bisque: $400. **Photo courtesy of McMasters Harris Apple Tree Doll Auctions.**

Mold 8556, painted eyes, molded hair, button nose, O-shaped lips
13" ....sold at auction for $2,300
Mold 8590, painted eyes, molded touseled hair with pronounced curl on top
15" - 16" ....$6,500 - 6,700
Mold 8676, painted eyes
9"......................................$800 - 850
11" ....$950 - 1,050
Mold 8678, glass eyes
6" - 7" ....$900 - 1,000
9" - 11".......................$1,400 - 1,600
Mold 8723, 8995, glass eyes
13"..............................$2,600 - 2,900
Mold 8764, Einco, for Eisenmann and Co., shoulder head, glass eyes, closed mouth
11"..............................$4,500 - 5,000
18" - 20"..................$11,500 - 13,500
Mold 9056, circa 1914, square painted eyes, closed mouth
8"..$650 - 700
Mold 9141, winker, one eye painted closed
7" - 10" ....$900 - 1,100
Mold 9573, glass eyes
6" - 8"...........................$1,000 - 1,100
9" - 11"........................$1,500 - 2,000
Mold 10342, wigged, glass eyes, rosebud mouth
8" ....$1,300 - 1,600
Kämmer & Reinhardt

Mold 131, circa 1914, glass eyes, closed mouth, marked: "S&H//K*R"
7" - 8½"....................$4,500 - 5,500
11" - 13" ....$5,000 - 6,500
15" - 16" ....$9,000 - 12,000
Kestner
Mold, 221, circa 1913, character, glass eyes, smiling closed mouth, marked: "JDK ges. gesch"
7"................................$6,500 - 6,700
11" - 13"...................$6,000 - 10,000
14" - 16"................$12,000 - 14,000
Kley & Hahn, mold 180, circa 1915, by Hertel Schwab and Co. for Kley & Hahn, character, glass eyes, laughing open-closed mouth; marked "K&H"
15"..............................$2,700 - 3,000
17"..............................$3,400 - 3,500
Knoch, Gebrüder
Mold, 246, molded cap, winking left eye
12" ....sold at auction for $11,500
Lenci: See Lenci section.
Limbach, socket head, large round glass eyes, pug nose, closed smiling mouth, marked with crown and cloverleaf
7" - 8" ....$2,200 - 2,400
Armand Marseille
Mold 200, circa 1911, glass eyes, closed mouth
8" - 9" ....$1,250 - 1,400
11" - 14"....................$2,000 - 2,500
Mold 210, circa 1911, painted intaglio eyes, character, solid-dome head, painted eyes, closed mouth
6" - 8" ....$500 - 600
11" - 12"..........................$800 - 900
Mold 232, circa 1913, character, closed mouth
7" ....$900 - 1,200
11" ....$1,200 - 1,300
Molds 241, circa 1914, wigged, glass eyes, closed mouth
9" - 10"......................$3,600 - 4,100
Mold 252, "AM 248," circa 1912, solid dome, painted intaglio eyes,

molded tuft, painted eyes, closed mouth
9".................................$1,000 - 1,200
12" - 15".....................$1,800 - 1,900
Mold 253, circa 1925, marked: "AM
Nobbikid Reg. U.S. Pat. 066 Germany"
6" - 7" ....$1,300 - 1,700
9" - 11".......................$1,400 - 1,800
Mold 254, circa 1912, painted eyes,
closed mouth, dome marked: "AM"
6" ....$500 - 550
8" - 9" ....$525 - 625
Mold 258, circa 1913, wigged,
sleep eyes, marked: "AM 255"
12"...............................$1,600 - 1,900
Mold 322, circa 1914, dome,
painted eyes, marked: "AM"
8" - 9" ....$600 - 650
11"....................................$800 - 850
Mold 323, 1914 - 1925, glass eyes,
also composition
7" - 9".........................$1,100 - 1,200
11" - 12" ....$1,100 - 1,800
Mold 325,circa 1915, character,
closed mouth
9"....................................$675 - 725
14" ....$900 - 1,000
Nippon, baby, painted eyes, five-piece
body
6½" - 7½" ....$100 - 150
15" glass eyes, molded tuft of
hair ....sold at auction for $567
Peek-a-boo kids, designed by
Chloe Preston, 1914 on, bisque
flange-neck head, cloth body
4" - 5"...............................$275 - 350
P.M. Porzellanfabrik Mengersgereuth,
circa 1926, character, closed mouth,
previously thought to be made by Otto
Reinecke, mold 950, marked "PM"
6½" - 7".............................$800 - 900
Recknagel, no mold number, glass eyes
7" - 8" ....$900 - 1,100
10" - 11".....................$1,500 - 1,600
13"..............................$2,200 - 2,500
Mold 43, intaglio eyes, molded hat
and hair tufts, closed mouth
7" - 8" ....$700 - 900

14" googly,
Hug Me
Kiddie, com-
position:
$1,800.
**Photo
courtesy of
McMasters
Harris
Apple Tree
Doll
Auctions.**

Mold 45, 46, 49, 54, 55, intaglio eyes,
molded hair, closed mouth
7" - 9"................................$375 - 500
20" $900
Mold 50, round open/closed mouth,
intaglio eyes, molded hair
7" - 8" ....$600 - 850
Simon & Halbig
Mold 605, socket head, sleep eyes
8"..............................$2,800 - 3,200
S.F.B.J.
Mold 245, glass eyes
7" - 8" ....$4,000 - 6,000
Fully jointed body
10"..............................$5,800 - 6,500
Steiner, Hermann, mold 133, circa 1920,
closed mouth, papier-mâché body,
marked: "HS"
7" - 8" ....$1,400 - 1,800
11"..............................$2,300 - 2,500
Walthur & Sohn, mold 208,
circa 1920, closed mouth, five-piece
papier-mâché body, painted
socks/shoes, marked: "W&S"
7" - 9" ....$400 - 700
Composition Face, 1911 - 1914,
all-composition head or composition
mask face, cloth body, includes
Hug Me Kids, Little Bright Eyes
and others
9" - 12" ....$900 - 1,200
12" - 14".................................$1,800

133

LUDWIG GREINER

1840 - 1874. Succeeded by sons, 1890 - 1900, Philadelphia, Pennsylvania. Papier-mâché shoulder-head dolls, with molded hair, painted/glass eyes, usually large dolls. Dolls listed are in good condition, appropriately dressed. Some wear is acceptable for these dolls, but highly worn examples will bring half the value of examples in good condition.

With label reading: "1858"

12" - 13"	$1,100 - 1,200
15" - 17"	$800 - 900
20" - 23"	$800 - 1,100
28" - 30"	$1,200 - 1,600

Glass eyes

21"	$2,100 - 2,200
26"	$2,500 - 2,800

With label reading: "1872"

15"	$250 - 350
18" - 24"	$500 - 625
26" - 30"	$650 - 700
32" - 33"	$700 - 750

GUND

1898 on, Connecticut and New York. Adolph Gund founded the company making stuffed toys.

Character

Cloth mask face, painted features, cloth body

14" - 16"	$70 - 80
19"- 24"	$100 - 150

Little Lulu

16"	$40 - 50

Flat-faced cloth

6½"	$20 - 25

Mary Poppins, crepe-fabric-over-wire armature

11" - 13"	$30 - 35

Plastic mask face, 1940s - 1950s, cloth body, Perki and others

14" - 16"	$30 - 40
21"	$40 - 50

Vinyl mask face, 1950s - 1960s, plush body, characters such as Popeye, Disney Pinocchio, Seven Dwarves and others

9" - 12"	$35 - 40

28" Greiner, papier-mâché, 1858 patent mark: $1,200. **Photo courtesy of Sweetbriar Auctions.**

16" Perki, Gund, vinyl mask face: $400. **Doll courtesy of private collection.**

Christopher Robin, cloth body
18".......................................$75 - 100

The Now Kids, 1970s, cloth dolls, yarn
hair, hippies named Desmond and
Rhoda
    Pair ....$50 - 60

HALF DOLLS

1900 - 1930s, Germany, Japan. Half dolls
can be made of bisque, china, composition or papier-mâché, and were used not
only for pincushions but on top of jewelry or cosmetic boxes, brushes, lamps and
numerous other items of decor. The
hardest to find have arms molded away
from the body, as they were more break-
able with the limbs in this position, and
thus fewer survived. Dolls listed are in
good condition; allow more for extra
attributes. Rare examples may bring
more. Dolls listed are German except if
otherwise noted.

Arms Away

Lady, good quaility, molded hair,
marked by maker or mold number

3" - 4".................................$100 - 140
5" - 6" ....$225 - 500
8"..$375 - 600
12"......................................$850 - 900

Bald head with wig
    4" ....$100 - 140
    6" ....$150 - 210

Child, molded hair
    2½" ....$40 - 80

*Elaborate hat or special headwear, or
applied décoration in hair*
    3½" - 4½" ....$450 - 550
    5" - 6" ....$500 - 600

Medieval lady by Galluba &
Hoffman, arms raised holding
platter of fruit
    4" ....sold at online auction for $2,200

Galluba & Hoffman, unglazed area at
base that flares out, wigged
    4" - 5"................................$275 - 500
    7½" ....$500 - 1,200

Holding items in hand, such as letter,
flower, book, etc.
    3½" - 4" ....$300 - 400
    4½" - 5" ....$500 - 600

4½" half doll, Egyptian style, china, both arms away: $550. **Photo courtesy of Morphy Auctions.**

4½" half doll, china, both arms molded to body, holding fan: $200. **Doll courtesy of private collection.**

Half Dolls

Flapper

   3½" - 4" ....$150 - 300

   4½" - 5" ....$400 - 600

One arm away and back to body,
common German type

   2" - 3½" ....$50 - 75

   4½" - 6½" ....$60 - 100

Flapper

   2 ½" - 3" ....$80 - 120

   4" - 5"................................$100 - 200

Both arms away and back to body

   2½" - 3½" ....$20 - 30

   5"...$45 - 75

   7".......................................$60 - 130

Flapper

   2½" - 4" ....$40 - 90

Arms in, close to figure

   3" - 4"..................................$40 - 100

   5" - 6".................................$75 - 125

Bald head, wigged

   3" - 4" ....$50 - 60

   6"...$80 - 100

Decorated bodice, necklace, fancy hair
or holding article

   3" - 5" ....$200 - 250

Double faced

   2.5" - 3.5" ....$325 - 375

Man .... `$375 - 400

Papier-mâché or composition

   2" - 3½".................................$20 - 30

   5" - 6" ....$45 - 60

China lady, marked: "Japan"

   3"...$15 - 25

   6"...$40 - 50

China lady, marked: "Occupied Japan"

   3"...$55 - 60

Jointed Shoulders

China or bisque, molded hair

   3" - 4" ....$50 - 80

   5" - 7" ....$120 - 200

HEINRICH HANDWERCK

1855 - 1932, Waltershausen, Thüringia,
Germany. Made composition doll bodies, sent Handwerck molds to Simon &

Halbig to make bisque heads.
Trademarks include an eight-point star
with French or German wording, a shield
and "Bébé Cosmopolite," "Bébé de
Reclame" and "Bébé Superior." Sold dolls
through Gimbels, Macy's, Montgomery
Ward and others. Bodies marked
"Handwerck" in red on lower back.
Patented a straight-wrist body. Dolls listed
are in good condition, appropriately
dressed. Allow more for exceptional
dolls.

Socket-Head Child, 1885 on. Open
mouth, sleep or set eyes, ball-jointed
body, bisque socket head, pierced ears,
appropriate wig, nicely dressed

*Molds 69, 79, 89, 99, 109, 119, or
no number*

   10" - 12"...........................$575 - 600

   14" - 16" ....$575 - 625

   18" - 24"...........................$700 - 750

   26" - 28" ....$700 - 750

   30" - 33" .... $800 - 900

Mold 79, 89 closed mouth

   15"..............................$1,500 - 1,600

   18" - 20".....................$2,000 - 2,100

   24"..............................$2,500 - 2,700

Mold 189, open mouth

   15"................................$700 - 750

   18" - 22" ....$850 - 1,000

Bébé Cosmopolite

   19" - 20".....................$1,000 - 1,200

23"
mold 69,
Heinrich
Handwerck,
bisque, dolly
face: $725.
**Photo
courtesy of
Richard
Withington,
Inc.**

24" - 28" ....$1,200 - 1,400
Shoulder-Head Child, 1885 on, open mouth, glass eyes, kid or cloth body
Molds 139 or no numbers
    12" ....$100 - 125
    15" - 16" ....$150 - 175
    18" - 22" ....$200 - 250
    24" - 25"...........................$275 - 300

MAX HANDWERCK

1899 - 1928, Waltershausen, Thüringia, Germany. Made dolls and doll bodies, registered trademark, "Bébé Elite."
Used heads made by Goebel.
Child
Bisque socket head, open mouth, sleep or set eyes, jointed composition body, marked with size numbers only or molds 283, 285, 286, 291, 297, 307 and others
    16" - 18"...........................$300 - 325
    22" - 26" ....$400 - 550
    28" - 32" ....$600 - 750
Bébé Elite, 1900 on, bisque socket head, mohair wig, glass sleep eyes, mohair lashes, open mouth, pierced ears, jointed composition/wood body, back of head marked: "Max Handwerck Bébé Elite 286 12 Germany"
    13" - 15"...........................$300 - 375
    19" - 21"...........................$425 - 500
    27" - 29"...........................$575 - 625
Googly: See Googlies section.

36" mold 283, Max Handwerck, bisque: $750.
Photo courtesy of McMasters Harris Apple Tree Doll Auctions.

HARD PLASTIC

Hard plastic was developed during WWII and became a staple of the doll industry after the war ended. Numerous companies made hard-plastic dolls from 1948 through the 1950s; dolls have all hard-plastic jointed bodies, sleep eyes, lashes, synthetic wigs, open or closed mouths. Marked with letters, little known, unidentified companies or unmarked.
Hard-Plastic Child, 1950s, maker unknown, some on "magic skin" laytex bodies, original clothing and wig, some marked:"U.S.A."
    14" - 16" ....$125 - 175
    18" - 20" ....$200 - 250
Advance Doll & Toy Company, 1954 on, made heavy walking hard-plastic dolls, metal rollers on molded shoes, named Winnie and Wanda, later models had vinyl heads
    18" - 24".............................$75 - 100
Artisan Novelty Company, 1950s, hard plastic, wide crotch
Raving Beauty
    20"...................................$100 - 125
Black ....$225 - 275
Duchess Doll Corporation, 1948 - 1950s, made small hard-plastic adult dolls, mohair wigs, painted or sleep eyes, jointed arms, stiff or jointed neck, molded and painted shoes, about 7" - 7½" tall, costumes stapled onto body, elaborate costumes, allow more for exceptional dolls
    7"...$12 - 15
Eugenia Doll Co., 1950s, New York City
    16" - 20"..............................$80 - 150
Fortune Doll Company, a subsidiary of the Beehler Arts Company
Pam (Ginny-type), hard plastic, sleep eyes, synthetic wig, closed mouth
    8"...$35 - 45
Imperial Crown Toy Co. (Impco), 1950s, made hard-plastic and vinyl

Hard Plastic

12" Sayco, hard-plastic heads, latex "magic skin" bodies, MIB: pair $300. **Photo courtesy of Sweetbriar Auctions.**

dolls, rooted hair, synthetic wigs
Hard-Plastic Walker
    14" ....$45 - 55
    20"..$70 - 80
Vinyl
    16" ....$55 - 65
Kendall Company
Miss Curity, 1953, hard plastic, jointed only at shoulders, blond wig, blue sleep eyes, molded-on shoes, painted stockings, uniform sheet vinyl, marked in blue on hat: "Miss Curity"
    7½" ....$20 - 30
Nun Doll, all hard plastic, sleep eyes, unmarked
    12"...$45 - 65
    17" ....$100 - 125
Pedigree Dolls and Toys, England, 1950s on, made hard-plastic and vinyl dolls
Posey Walker, walker, sleep eyes, wig
    20" - 22' ....$125 - 150
Roberta Doll Co.
Walker
    14" ....$30 - 40
Roddy of England, 1950 - 1960s, made by D.G. Todd and Co. Ltd., Southport, England, hard-plastic walker, sleep or set eyes

    11" - 12½" ....$75 - 100
    22" ....$125 - 175
Rosebud of England, 1950s - 1960s, started in Raunds, Northamptonshire, England, by T. Eric Smith shortly after WWII
Miss Rosebud, hard plastic, various shades of blue sleep eyes, glued-on mohair wig, jointed at the neck and hips, allow more for rare examples or MIB, head and back marked in script: "Miss Rosebud"; upper back marked: "MADE IN ENGLAND,
    7½" .... $75 - 100
Ross Products
Tina Cassini, designed by Oleg Cassini, hard plastic, back torso marked: "TINA CASSINI," clothes tagged: "Made in British Crown Colony of Hong Kong"
    12" ....$175 - 200
Costume, MIB ....$100 - 125
Royal Doll Co.
Hard-plastic girl, 1950s, similar to Sweet Sue by American Character Wearing formal
    20"....................................$200 - 225
Virga, a subsidiary of the Beehler Arts Company, marketed Ginny-type dolls under various lines such as Playmates, Lolly Pop, Play-Pals, Lucy and Schiaparelli GoGo

15" Eugenia Doll Co, hard plastic, circa 1952: $125. **Photo courtesy of Emmie's Antique Doll Castle.**

138

14" Hoyer type, hard plastic: $125. **Photo courtesy of Pieces of Old.**

Lolly Pop dolls, hair colors such as pink, blue, bright yellow
8"......................................$50 - 70

HARTLAND PLASTICS

1954 - 1963, Hartland, Wisconsin. Made action figures and horses, many figures from Warner Brothers television productions. Purchased by Revlon Cosmetics in 1963 and stopped making toys. Others have bought the molds and make these products today. Dolls listed are those made from 1954 to 1963s. Values listed are for good condition with approriate accessories; value can double for MIB.
Television or Movie Characters
Annie Oakley, 1953 - 1956, played by Gail Davis in *Annie Oakley*
8" with horse......................$160 - 200
Bret Maverick, circa 1958, played by James Garner in *Maverick*
8"......................................$100 - 125
Clint Bonner, 1957 - 1959, played by John Payne in *The Restless Gun*
8"......................................$100 - 120
Colonel Ronald MacKenzie, circa 1950s, played by Richard Carlson in *Mackenzie's Raiders*
8" with horse ....$200 - 250
Dale Evans, circa 1958, #802, with horse, Buttermilk, in *The Roy Rogers Show*
8"......................................$75 - 125
Davy Crockett, 1956 played by Fess Parker in *Davy Crockett*
8" with horse....................$100 - 150
Jim Hardie, 1958, played by Dale Robertson in *Tales of Wells Fargo*
8"......................................$125 - 150
Josh Randall, circa 1950s, played by Steve McQueen in *Wanted Dead or Alive*
8" with horse ....$300 - 400
Major Seth Adams, 1957 - 1961, #824, played by Ward Bond in *Wagon Train*
8" with horse $100
Paladin, 1957 - 1963, played by Richard Boone in *Have Gun, Will Travel*
8" with horse......................$75 - 100
Roy Rogers, circa 1955, and Trigger in *The Roy Rogers Show*
8"......................................$95 - 115
The Rifleman, Chuck Connors in *The Rifleman*
8"......................................$125 - 140
Sgt. Lance O'Rourke RCMP
8" with horse......................$90 - 140
Sgt. William Preston, circa 1958, #804, played by Richard Simmons in *Sgt. Preston of the Yukon*
8" with horse ....$250 - 265
Tom Jeffords, circa 1958 - 1961, played by John Lupton in *Broken Arrow*
8" with horse ....$225 - 255
Other Figures
Brave Eagle, #812, with horse, White Cloud in *Brave Eagle*
Buffalo Bill, #819, Pony Express Rider
Chief Thunderbird, with horse, Northwind
Cochise, #815, with pinto horse, in *Broken Arrow*
Jim Bowie, #817, with horse, Blaze

General George Custer, #814, with horse, Bugler
General George Washington, #815 with horse, Ajax
General Robert E. Lee, #808, with horse, Traveler
Lone Ranger, #801, with horse, Silver
TontoTonto, #805, with horse, Scout
    8" ....each $70 - 125
All others
    8"..............................each $60 - 100

CARL HARTMANN

1889 - 1930s, Neustadt, Germany. Made and exported bisque and celluloid dolls, especially small dolls in regional costumes called Globe Babies.
Child, bisque socket head, open mouth, jointed composition-and-wood body
    22" - 24" ....$450 - 625
Globe Baby, bisque socket head, glass sleep eyes, open mouth, four teeth, mohair or human-hair wig, five-piece papier-mâché or composition body, painted shoes and stockings
    8" ....$325 - 375
    12"....................................$400 - 425

6½" Globe Baby, Carl Hartmann, bisque: $275. **Photo courtesy of McMasters Harris Apple Tree Doll Auctions.**

KARL HARTMANN

1911 - 1926, Stockheim, Germany. Doll factory, made and exported dolls.

25" mold 305, Karl Hartmann, bisque: $350. **Photo courtesy of McMasters Harris Apple Tree Doll Auctions.**

Advertised ball-jointed dolls, characters and papier-mâché dolls. Marked: "KH."
Child, bisque socket head, open mouth, glass eyes, composition body
    No Mold Number
    18" - 22"...........................$275 - 300
    24" - 26" ....$350 - 400
    27" - 32" ....$425 - 525
    Mold 283, 287, 305
    22 - 24" ....$350 - 400

HASBRO

1923, Pawtucket, Rhode Island. Founded by the Hassenfeld Brothers. Began making toys in 1943. One of their most popular toys was the G.I. Joe series, which came out in 1964. Dolls listed are in good condition with original clothing and accessories, value can double for mint-in-package. Allow one-third to one-half the value for dolls in played-with condition.
Aimee, 1972, rooted hair, amber sleep eyes, jointed vinyl body, long dress, sandals, earrings
    18".......................................$30 - 35
Baby Alive, 1992, vinyl, eats, drinks, wets
    14" ....$30 -35
Bridal Sewing doll, 1950s, hard-plastic

doll, boxed with fabric and sewing
supplies

    1 doll set ....$40 - 45
    6 doll set ....$100 - 120
Charlie's Angels, 1977, vinyl, Jill,
Sabrina, Kelly, Kris
    8½" ....$18 - 20
Dolly Darling, 1965
    4½" ....$30 - 50
John and his pets ....$45 - 50
Flying Nun
    4¾" ....$25 - 35
    12" ....$100 - 120
Jem: See Jem section.
Leggie, 1972
    10" ....$30 - 40
Black ....$35 - 45
Little Miss No Name, 1965
    15" ....$75 - 125
Maxie, 1987, her friends Rob, Ashley,
Kimberly and others, vinyl fashion doll
    11½" ....$10 - 15
My Buddy, 1985, vinyl and cloth boy
    24" ....$100 - 135
My Buddy's Kid Sister
    20" ....$30 - 40
Peteena Poodle, 1966, vinyl fashion doll
poodle
    9½" ....$275 - 325
Pippi Longstocking, 1973, vinyl
    12" ....$20 - 30
Real Baby, 1984, designed by J. Turner
    18" ....$35 - 45
Show Biz Babies, 1967, 4"
Mama Cass Elliott ....$150 - 180
Mitch Rider ....$175 - 200
Monkees
Individual ....$75 - 80
Set of four ....$325 - 350
Storykins, 1967, 3", includes
Cinderella, Goldilocks, Prince
Charming, Rumpelstiltskin, Sleeping
Beauty ....each $40 - 50
Prince Charming
    MIB ....sold at auction for $100
Sweet Cookie, 1972, vinyl, with cooking
accessories

4½" Dolly
Darling
Party Time
"sweet-
heart,"
Hasbro,
vinyl,
MOC: $60.
**Photo
courtesy
of The
Museum
Doll Shop.**

    18" ....$100 - 125
World of Love Dolls, 1971,
Love, Peace, Flower
    9" ....$25 - 35
Soul (black) ....$50 - 60
Adam ....$30 - 40
G.I. Joe Action Figures, 1964,
hard-plastic head with facial scar,
painted hair and no beard. Dolls listed
are in good condition with original
clothing and accessories, value can
double for MIB
G.I. Joe Action Soldier, flocked hair,
Army fatigues, brown jump boots,
green plastic cap, training manual,
metal dog tag, two sheets of stickers
    11½" ....$100 - 175
Painted hair ....$100 - 150
    Black ....$300 - 350
Green Beret, teal-green fatigue jacket,
four pockets, pants, Green Beret cap
with red unit flashing, M-16 rifle, 45
automatic pistol with holster, tall brown
boots, four grenades, camouflage scarf,
field communication set
    11" ....$125 - 175
G.I. Joe Action Marine, camouflage shirt,
pants, brown boots, green plastic cap,
metal dog tag, insignia stickers, training
manual
    11" ....$125 - 200
G.I. Joe Action Sailor, blue chambray

Hasbro

11½" Ashley, from the Maxie line, Hasbro, vinyl: $10. **Photo courtesy of The Museum Doll Shop.**

work shirt, blue denim work pants, black boots, white plastic sailor cap, dog tag, rank insignia stickers
11" ....$150 - 175
G.I. Joe Action Pilot, orange flight suit, black boots, dog tag, stickers, blue cap, training manual
11"....................................$150 - 250
Dolls only, nude ....$75 - 95
G.I. Joe Action Soldier of the World, 1966, figures in this set may have any hair and eye-color combination, no scar on face, hard-plastic heads
Australian Jungle Fighter ......$395 - 450
British Commando, boxed ....$525 - 600
French Resistance Fighter......$425 - 500
German Storm Trooper ....$500 - 600
Japanese Imperial Soldier ......$500 - 600
Russian Infantryman..............$475 - 500
Talking G.I. Joe, 1967 - 1969, talking mechanism added, semi-hard vinyl head, marked: "G.I. Joe®//Copyright 1964//By Hasbro®//Pat. No. 3,277,602//Made in U.S.A. "
Talking G.I. Joe Action Soldier, green fatigues, dog tag, brown boots, insignia, stripes, green plastic fatigue cap, comic book, insert with examples of figure's speech....................................$175 - 225

Talking G.I. Joe Action Sailor, denim pants, chambray sailor shirt, dog tag, black boots, white sailor cap, insignia stickers, Navy training manual, illustrated talking comic book, insert examples of figure's speech ....$250 - 350
Talking G.I. Joe Action Marine, camouflage fatigues, metal dog tag, Marine training manual, insignia sheets, brown boots, green plastic cap, comic, and insert ....$175 - 225
Talking G.I. Joe Action Pilot, blue flight suit, black boots, dog tag, Air Force insignia, blue cap, training manual, comic book, insert..................$250 - 350
G.I. Joe Action Nurse, 1967, vinyl head, blond rooted hair, jointed hard-plastic body, nurse's uniform, cap, red cross armband, white shoes, medical bag, stethoscope, plasma bottle, two crutches, bandages, splints, marked: "Patent Pending//©1967 Hasbro®//Made in Hong Kong" ....$1,300 - 1,500
G.I. Joe, Man of Action, 1970 - 1975, flocked hair, scar on face, wearing fatigues with Adventure Team emblem on shirt, plastic cap, marked: "G.I. Joe®//Copyright 1964//By Hasbro®//Pat. No. 3, 277, 602//Made in U.S. A."
Kung Fu Grip ....$200 - 250
Talking....................................$250 - 300
G.I. Joe, Adventure Team, flocked hair and beard, six team members, marked: "©1975 Hasbro ®//Pat. Pend. Pawt. R.I."
Air Adventurer, orange flight suit ....$265 - 285
Astronaut, talking, white flight suit, molded scar, dog tag pull string..............................$150 - 200
Land Adventurer, black, tan fatigues, beard, flocked hair, scar ....$275 - 300
Land Adventurer, talking, camouflage fatigues ....$200 - 225
Sea Adventurer, light-blue shirt, navy pants ....$250 - 300

Hasbro

Talking Adventure Team Commander, flocked hair, beard, green jacket, pants ....$400 - 450

G.I. Joe Land Adventurer, flocked hair, beard, camouflage shirt, green pants..$100 - 150

G. I. Joe Negro Adventurer, flocked hair ....$250 - 300

G. I. Joe, Mike Powers, Atomic Man................................$55 - 75

G.I. Joe Eagle Eye Man of Action ....$100 - 125

G.I. Joe Secret Agent, unusual face, mustache ....$400 - 450

Sea Adventurer, with Kung Fu Grip ....$125 - 145

Bulletman, muscle body, silver arms, hands, helmet, red boots........$200 - 250

Others

G.I. Joe Air Force Academy, Annapolis, or West Point Cadet ....$350 - 400

G.I. Joe Secret Service Agent, limited edition of 200 ....$225 - 275

Accessory sets, mint in package, no doll included

Adventures of G.I. Joe
    Adventure of the Perilous
    Rescue $250
    Adventure Capture of the
    Pygmy Gorilla $130
    Eight Ropes of Danger
    Adventure $200
    Fantastic Free Fall Adventure ..$275
    Hidden Missile Discovery
    Adventure $150
    Mouth of Doom Adventure $150

Accessory Packs or Boxed Uniforms and Accessories

Air Force, Annapolis, West Point Cadet................................$200

Action Sailor....................................$350

Astronaut $250

Crash Crew Fire Fighter.................$275

Deep Freeze with Sled $250

Deep Sea Diver $250

Frogman Demolition Set $375

Green Beret $450

Landing Signal Officer....................$250

Marine Communications Set..........$100

Marine Medic Pack.........................$155

Military Police.................................$325

Pilot Scramble Set...........................$200

Rescue Diver $350

Scramble Pilot Crash Helmet Pack ..$150

Sonic Blaster Set..............................$150

Ski Patrol..$350

G.I. Joe Vehicles and Other Accessories, mint in package

Adventure Team Helicopter, yellow $70

Amphibious Duck, green plastic, Irwin $600

Armored Car, green plastic, one figure $150

Crash Crew Fire Truck, blue........$1,400

Desert Patrol Attack Jeep, tan, one figure......................................$1,400

Footlocker, with accessories ....$400+

Iron Knight Tank, green plastic ..$1,400

Jeep Combet set $200

Jet Aeroplane, dark blue plastic $550

Jet Helicopter, green, yellow blades $350

Motorcycle and Side Car, by Irwin $225

Personnel Carrier and Mine Sweeper...$700

Sea Sled and Frogman $325

Space Capsule and Suit, gray plastic.......................................$425

12" GI Joe Land Adventurer, Hasbro, vinyl, MIB: $300.
Photo courtesy of Morphy Auctions.

Hasbro

Staff Car, four figures, green plastic, Irwin $900

Jem, 1986 - 1987

The line of 27 Jem dolls was based on characters in the animated *Jem* television series, circa 1985 - 1988. All-vinyl fashion type with realistically proportioned body, jointed elbows, wrists and knees, swivel waist, rooted hair, painted eyes, open or closed mouth, and hole in bottom of each foot. All boxes read: "Jem" and "Truly Outrageous!" Most came with cassette tape of music from *Jem* cartoon, plastic stand, poster and hair pick. All 12½" tall, except Starlight Girls, 11". Dolls listed are in excellent condition, wearing complete original outfit; value can double for MIB.

Jem and Rio
Jem/Jerrica 1st issue
   4000 ....$35 - 45
Jem/Jerrica, star earrings............$50 - 60
Glitter 'n Gold Jem
   4001 ....$25 - 45
Rock 'n Curl Jem
   4002 ....$20 - 25
Flash 'n Sizzle Jem
   4003 ....$48 - 56
Rio, 1st issue
   4015 ....$25 - 35
Glitter 'n Gold Rio
   4016 ....$25 - 30
Glitter 'n Gold Rio, pale vinyl
   4016 ....$125 - 150

Holograms
Synergy
   4020 ....$40 - 50
Aja, 1st issue
   4201/4005 ....$32 - 40
Aja, 2nd issue
   4201/4005 ....$60 - 75
Kimber, 1st issue
   4202/4005 ....$32 - 40
Kimber, 2nd issue
   4202/4005 ....$60 - 70
Shana, 1st issue

   4203/4005 ....$32 - 40
Shana, 2nd issue
   4203/4005 ....$100 - 125
Danse
   4208 ....$50 - 55
Video
   4209 ....$25 - 30
Raya
   4210 ....$125 - 150
Starlight Girls, 11", no wrist or elbow joints
Ashley 4211/4025, Krissie 4212/4025, Banee 4213/4025 ....$25 - 35
Misfits
Pizzazz, 1st issue
   4204/4010 ....$60 - 75
Pizzazz, 2nd issue
   4204/4010 ....$55 - 65
Stormer, 1st issue
   4205/4010 ....$40 - 50
Stormer, 2nd issue
   4205/4010 ....$50 - 70
Roxy, 1st issue
   4206/4010 ....$55 - 60
Roxy, 2nd issue
   4206/4010 ....$40 - 50
Clash
   4207/4010 ....$20 - 30

12½" Jem, Hasbro, vinyl, MIB: $55. **Doll courtesy of private collection.**

Jetta
4214 ....$50 - 65
Accessories
Concert Clash game, by Milton Bradley, 1986 ....$25
Glitter 'n Gold Roadster ....$100 - 150
Rock 'n Roadster ....$35 - 40
Jem Guitar ....$30 - 40
Backstager ....$30 - 35
Star Stage ....$40 - 45
MTV jacket (promo) ....$100 - 125
Jem Fashions
Prices are for NRFB (never removed from box or card) examples, with packaging in excellent condition. Allow approximately 25 percent less for damaged boxes, or mint and complete, or with no packaging.................$32 - 60

HERTEL, SCHWAB & COMPANY

1910 - 1930s, Stutzhaus, Germany. Porcelain factory founded by August Hertel and Heinrich Schwab, both designed doll heads used by Borgfeldt, Kley & Hahn, König & Wernicke, Louis Wolf and others. Made china and bisque heads as well as all-bisque dolls, most with character faces. Molded hair or wigs, painted blue or glass eyes (often blue-gray), open mouth with tongue or closed mouth, socket or shoulder heads. Usually marked with mold number and "Made in Germany" or mark of company that owned the mold.
Baby, 1910 on, bisque head, molded hair or wig, open or open/closed mouth, teeth, sleep or painted eyes, bent-leg baby composition body
Mold 130, 142, 150, 151, 152, 159
9" - 12" ....$225 - 300
15" - 16"..........................$250 - 300
19" - 21".........................$350 - 450
22" - 24" ....$500 - 550
Toddler body
14"..................................$400 - 450

20".................................$550 - 600
Mold 1125 (so-called Patsy Baby)
12"..................................$800 - 900
Mold 126 (so-called Skippy Baby)
9".................................$825 - 875
Child
Mold 111, character face, closed mouth, glass sleep eyes, wigged
11"............................$7,200 - 7,400
17" - 18" ....$16,000 - 17,000
Mold 127, circa 1915, character face, solid dome with molded hair, sleep eyes, open mouth, Patsy-type
15"............................$1,500 - 1,800
17"............................$2,000 - 2,400
Mold 131, circa 1912, character face, solid dome, painted closed mouth
18" $1,300
Too few in database for reliable range
Mold 134, circa 1915, character face, sleep eyes, closed mouth
15" - 18" ....$4,500 - 5,000
Mold 136, circa 1912, character face, open mouth, marked: "Made in Germany"
7"....................................$300 - 325
18" - 20"..........................$350 - 375
24" - 25" ....$425 - 475
Mold 140, circa 1912, character, glass eyes, open/closed laughing mouth
12" - 15" ....$3,400 - 4,200

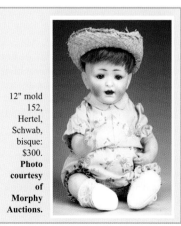

12" mold 152, Hertel, Schwab, bisque: $300. **Photo courtesy of Morphy Auctions.**

145

13" Patsy Baby, Hertel, Schwab, bisque, solid dome, glass eyes: $1,000. **Photo courtesy of Richard Withington, Inc.**

Mold 141, circa 1912, character, painted eyes, open/closed mouth

    12" - 14" ....$2,800 - 3,300
    17" - 18".....................$7,400 - 9,000

Mold 178, character, open/closed mouth, wigged, ball-jointed body

    6" - 7".............................$375 - 435

Mold 182, dolly-faced doll, open mouth, wigged, ball-jointed body

    18" - 23" ....$600 - 700

Googly: See Googlies section.

HERTWIG & COMPANY

1864 - 1940s, Kutzhütte, Thüringia, Germany. Porcelain factory producing china and bisque dolls. Some distributed by Butler Brothers.

Half-Bisque Dolls, 1911 on, bisque head and torso, molded clothing, lower body cloth, lower arms and legs bisque

Child

    4½" ....$75 - 100

Adult

    6½" ....$150 - 225

All Bisque, including animals in crochet outfits: See All-Bisque section.
China Name Dolls: See China section.
Bisque Bonnet-Head: See Bonnet-Heads section.

ERNST HEUBACH

1887 - 1930s, Köppelsdorf, Germany. In 1919, the son of Armand Marseille married the daughter of Ernst Heubach and merged the two factories. Mold numbers range from 250 to 452. They made porcelain heads for Dressel (Jutta), Revalo, and others. Dolls listed are in good condition, appropriately dressed.

Child, 1888 on

Mold 1900, 225, 275, or Horseshoe Mark, shoulder head, open mouth, glass eyes, kid or cloth body

    10" - 12" ....$95 - 110
    18" - 22"..........................$180 - 220
    26"...................................$275 - 300

Molds 250, 251, 302, and others, socket head, composition body, open mouth, glass eyes

    8" - 10"............................$175 - 225
    8" - 9" flapper body..........$350 - 400
    13" - 15" ....$225 - 250
    16" - 19"...........................$300 - 325
    23" - 25" ....$350 - 400
    27" - 32" ....$400 - 450
    36"...................................$500 - 575

Painted bisque

    8" - 12"..............................$90 - 100
    16" ....$125 - 150

24" Ernst Heubach, mold 320, bisque head: $400. **Photo courtesy of Morphy Auctions.**

Baby, 1910 on, open mouth, glass eyes, socket head, wig, five-piece bent-leg composition body, allow more for toddler body, flirty eyes
Molds 300, 320, 321, 342 and others
  5" - 6½" ....$250 - 275
  8" - 11" ....$150 - 175
  14" - 17" ....$250 - 325
  19" - 21" ....$350 - 400
  25" - 27" ....$475 - 550
Painted bisque, flirty eyes
  16" - 24" ....$325 - 450
Character Child, 1910 on, painted eyes
Molds 261, 262, 271, and others, bisque shoulder head, cloth body
  12" ....$300 - 400
Molds 267, bisque-headed boy, molded hair and glass eyes
  25" ....sold at auction for $2,700
Mold 312 (for Seyfarth & Reinhard)
  14" ....$275 - 300
  18" ....$350 - 375
  28" ....$500 - 550
Mold 417, glass eyes, resembles Armand Marseille Just Me
  11" - 12" ....$1,200 - 1,400
Baby, Newborn, 1925 on, solid dome, molded painted hair, glass eyes, closed mouth, cloth body, composition or celluloid hands
Molds 338, 339, 340, 348, 349
  10" - 12" ....$225 - 325
  14" - 16" ....$375 - 475
  17" ....$500 - 550
Black, mold 444
  12" ....$375 - 425

GEBRÜDER HEUBACH

1910 - 1938, Lichte, Thüringia, Germany. Porcelain factory founded in 1804, but did not make dolls until 1910. Made bisque heads and all-bisque dolls, characters, either socket or shoulder head, molded hair or wigs, sleeping or intaglio eyes, in heights from 4" to 26". Provided

12" mold 7602, Gebruder Heubach, bisque, closed mouth, socket head: $600. **Photo courtesy of Morphy Auctions.**

heads to other companies including Bauersachs, Cuno and Oto Dressel, Eisemann and Co. and Gebrüder Ohlhaver. Mold numbers from 556 to 10633. Sunburst or square marks, more dolls with square marks. Dolls listed are in good condition, appropriately dressed.
Marked: "Heubach," no mold number
Closed mouth, intaglio eyes, wigged
  8" ....$400 - 700
Closed mouth, intaglio eyes, deeply sculpted molded hair
  15" ....sold at auction for $3,000
Closed mouth pouty, intaglio eyes
  6½" ....$150 - 200
  14" ....$500 - 600
Smile, painted eyes
  15" ....$3,400 - 3,500
Lady doll, open or closed mouth, glass eyes, mold 7625, 7635, 7925, 7926, others
  10" - 11" ....$2,000 - 2,400
  14" - 16" ....$2,800 - 3,500
  22" ....$4,000 - 4,500
Animal head, bears, cats, etc., five-piece composition child bodies
  6" - 8" ....$1,600 - 1,800
Marked Heubach Googly: See Googlies section.

Gebrüder Heubach

Character Child
Shoulder Head
Mold 5392, boy, molded hair, closed mouth, painted eyes
17" - 19".........................$300 - 400
Mold 5777, Dolly Dimple, shoulder-head version
17" - 19".......................$1,600 - 1,700
Mold 6692, circa 1912, shoulder-head version, intaglio eyes, closed mouth, pouty, sunburst mark
14" - 16"..........................$700 - 750
20".....................................$875 - 900
Mold 6736, circa 1912, painted eyes, laughing mouth, square mark
9" - 13" ....$250 - 350
16"....................................$800 - 900
Mold 7072, circa 1912, closed mouth, molded hair, painted eyes
22" - $750 - 850
Mold 7644,circa 1910, "Our Pet," (so-called) painted eyes, open/closed laughing mouth, sunburst or square mark
9" - 10" ....$350 - 400
14"....................................$750 - 850
17" ....$1,000 - 1,100
20"..............................$1,450 - 1,550
Mold 7844,circa 1912, open/closed laughing mouth, molded hair, intaglio eyes
12" - 13"..........................$275 - 300
Mold 7850, circa 1912, "Coquette"

9" mold 8193, Gebrüder Heubach, bisque: $650. **Photo courtesy of Richard Withington, Inc.**

(so-called), open/closed mouth
10" - 12"..........................$550 - 650
15"...................................$625 - 675
Mold 7852,circa 1912, open/closed mouth with row of teeth showing, molded hair in coiled braided buns over ears, upward side-glancing intaglio eyes
16"...........sold at auction for $1,100
Too few in database for reliable range
Mold 7853, circa 1912, downcast eyes
14"..............................$1,600 - 1,800
Mold 8191, baby, solid dome, molded hair, open/closed mouth, intaglio eyes
8" - 12"............................$700 - 875
Mold 8221, dome, intaglio eyes, open/closed mouth, square mark
14"....................................$650 - 700
Mold 8457, Princess Angeline, Native American woman, believed to be a portrait of the daughter of Chief Seattle, wigged, wrinkled face, downcast eyes
13"...........................$7,500 - 10,000
Mold 8792, closed mouth, intaglio eyes, hair molded
16"....................................$750 - 800
Too few in database for reliable range
Mold 9355,circa 1914, glass eyes, open mouth, square mark
13"....................................$800 - 850
19" ....$1,100 - 1,250
Socket Head
Mold 5636, circa 1912, glass eyes, open/closed laughing mouth, teeth
12" - 13" ....$1,000 - 1,100
15" - 18".....................$1,200 - 1,600
21" ....$1,800 - 1,900
Mold 5689, circa 1912, smiling open mouth, sunburst mark
14"..............................$1,600 - 1,700
17" ....$2,000 - 2,100
22" ....$2,700 - 2,800
Mold 5730, circa 1912, made for Hamburger and Co., sunburst mark, marked: "Santa"
14" - 16".....................$1,000 - 1,200
19" - 22".....................$1,400 - 1,800
24" - 26" ....$2,000 - 2,200

Gebrüder Heubach

Mold 5777, circa 1913, open mouth,
for Hamburger and Co., marked:
"Dolly Dimple"
    12" - 14"....................$1,000 - 1,200
    16" - 19"....................$1,400 - 1,800
    22" - 24" ....$2,000 - 2,400
Mold 6682, intaglio eyes,
closed mouth
    14"....................................$350 - 400
Mold 6894, intaglio eyes,
closed mouth
    9" - 12" ....$400 - 450
    20" - 22" ....$800 - 900
Mold 6969, circa 1912, socket head,
glass eyes, closed mouth, square mark
    7" - 9" ....$1,050 - 1,250
    12" - 13"....................$1,400 - 1,600
    16" - 18"....................$2,000 - 2,300
    20" - 24" ....$2,500 - 3,000
Mold 6970, circa 1912, glass eyes,
closed mouth, sunburst mark
    7" - 9" ....$900 - 1,000
    12" - 13" ....$2,000 - 2,200
    16" - 18"....................$2,400 - 2,700
    20" - 24" ....$3,000 - 3,300
Molds 7246, 7247, 7248, circa 1912,
closed mouth, glass eyes, sunburst
or square mark
    7" - 10" ....$1,000 -1,200
    12" - 13" ....$1,700 - 2,000
    16" - 18"....................$2,200 - 2,400
    20" - 24"....................$2,800 - 3,100
    26" - 28" ....$3,300 - 3,500
Mold 7307, character, glass eyes,
open/closed mouth, two upper teeth
    15" - 18" ....$2,200 - 2,400
Mold 7550, character, glass eyes,
open/closed mouth
    12"............................$1,200 - 1,500
Mold 7602, 7603, circa 1912, molded
hair tufts, intaglio eyes
    10" - 12"......................$500 - 600
    15" - 18" ....$700 - 800
Mold 7604, circa 1912, open/closed
mouth, intaglio eyes
    12" - 14"..........................$650 - 700
    20" ....$1,100 - 1,200

Mold 7608, pouty
    9"....................................$400 - 500
Mold 7622, 7623, circa 1912, intaglio
eyes, closed or open/closed mouth
    16" - 18" ....$1,100 - 1,300
Mold 7644, circa 1912, child,
open/closed laughing mouth,
intaglio eyes, molded hair
    12" - 13" ....$500 - 600
Mold 7711, circa 1912, flapper body,
glass eyes, open mouth
    9" - 10"........................$1,000 - 1,200
    18"............................$6,000 - 7,000
Mold 7759, circa 1912, dome,
painted eyes, closed mouth
    10" - 12"...........................$500 - 600
Molds 7763, 7788, 7850 Coquette
(so-called), circa 1912, molded hair
with bow
    11"....................................$900 - 950
    14" - 15" ....$1,100 - 1,300
    20"............................$1,500 - 1,600
Mold 8004, circa 1912, intaglio eyes,
closed mouth, molded hair
    9" - 11"............................$500 - 550
Mold 8145, small side-glancing
intaglio eyes, molded hair
    20" $11,258
Mold 8191, Crooked Smile
(so-called), circa 1912, intaglio eyes,
laughing mouth, square mark
    11½" ....$1,200 - 1,300
    14" ....$1,500 - 1,600
    16"............................$2,800 - 3,000

Mold 8193, dolly face, sleep eyes,
open mouth
11" - 13".............................$750 - 800
Mold 8192, circa 1914, sleep eyes,
open mouth, sunburst or square mark
11" - 13" ....$900 - 1,000
16" - 20"......................$1,500 - 2,100
Mold 8317, wig, open/closed smiling
mouth, eight teeth, glass eyes
16"............................$3,200 - 3,400
19"............................$4,600 - 4,800
Mold 8381, Princess Juliana
(so-called), molded hair, ribbon,
painted eyes, closed mouth,
14" - 16".................$10,000 - 13,000
Mold 8413, circa 1914, wig, sleep eyes,
open/closed mouth with teeth
16"............................$2,800 - 3,437
Mold 8469, open/closed mouth
with two lower teeth, glass eyes, wig
8" - 10" ....$300 - 400
Mold 8535 boy, open/closed mouth
with dimples by lips, painted eyes,
molded hair, ears slightly protruding
17" ....sold at auction for $8,500
Mold 8774, Whistling Jim, circa 1914,
smoker or whistler, flange neck,
intaglio eyes, molded hair, cloth
body, bellows, square mark
9" ....$900 - 1,000
13" - 14" ....$1,100 - 1,200
Mold 8950, laughing girl, blue hair
bow
18".............................$6,900 - 7,200
Mold 8970, closed mouth, intaglio
eyes, wigged
9"...............................$1,200 - 1,300
Mold 9457, Eskimo, circa 1914, dome,
intaglio eyes, closed mouth, square
mark
15"............................$2,300 - 2,500
18"............................$3,800 - 4,000
Mold 9590, closed mouth, intaglio
eyes, molded page-boy hair style
with molded bow
7" ....$650 - 800
Mold 10532, circa 1920, open mouth,

five-piece toddler body, square mark
8½" ....$1,000 - 1,100
13½" ....$1,450 - 1,550
20" - 22"....................$1,900 - 2,100
25" ....$2,400 - 2,500
Mold 11173, Tiss Me, socket head, wig
8"...............................$3,000 - 3,500
Too few in database for reliable range
Character Baby, 1911 on, bisque
socket head, bent-limb body
Mold 6894, 6897, 7759, 7602, 7604,
all circa 1912, intaglio eyes, closed
mouth, molded hair, sunburst or
square mark
6" - 7"...........................$475 - 525
9" - 12"..........................$575 - 675
15"..................................$700 - 800
20" ....$900 - 1,000
Toddler
14"...................................$850 - 950
Molds 7877, 7977, Baby Stuart
(so-called),circa 1912, molded bonnet,
closed mouth, painted eyes
8" - 9" ....$1,200 - 1,400
11" - 13"....................$1,400 - 1,600
15"............................$1,700 - 2,000
Mold 7975, Baby Stuart (so-called),
circa 1912, glass eyes, removable
molded bisque bonnet
9" - 13" ....$2,200 - 2,400
Mold 8420, circa 1914, glass eyes,
closed mouth, square mark
10"..................................$650 - 750
15"............................$1,200 - 1,400
Mold 9377, sleep eyes, open mouth,
dimples, prominent ears, wigged
27".............................$2,000 - 2,400
Too few in database for reliable range
All Bisque: See All-Bisque section.

E.I. HORSMAN

1878 - 1980s, New York City. Founded by
Edward Imeson Horsman to import,
assemble, wholesale and distribute various dolls and doll lines. From 1909 to
1919 they distributed Aetna Doll and Toy
company's dolls; in 1919 the two compa-

E.I. Horsman

13" Gene Carr Kid, Horsman, composition: $300. **Photo courtesy of Richard Withington, Inc.**

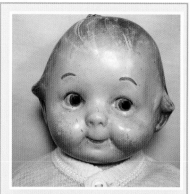

13" Peterkin, Horsman, composition: $300. **Photo courtesy of Joan & Lynette Antique Dolls and Accessories.**

nies merged. Eventually Horsman made their own dolls as well as distributing other lines. They took out their first patent for a complete doll in 1909 for a Billiken doll. They made dolls of composition, rubber, hard plastic and vinyl.

Early Composition on Cloth Body, composition head, sometimes lower arms, cloth body. Dolls listed are in good condition with original clothing, add more for exceptional dolls.

Baby Bumps, 1910 - 1917, composition head, cloth cork-stuffed body, blue-and-white cloth label on romper, copy of K*R #100 Baby mold

11" $250
Black ....$300 - 350

Baby Butterfly, 1914 on, composition head, hands, cloth body, painted hair and features

13".................................$250 - 300
15".................................$350 - 400

Billiken, 1909, composition head, molded hair, slanted eyes, smiling closed mouth, on stuffed mohair or velvet body, cloth label on body, right foot marked: "Billiken"

12"..................................$200 - 350

Campbell Kids, 1910 on, designed by Helen Trowbridge, based on Grace

Drayton's drawings, composition head, painted and molded hair, side-glancing painted eyes, closed smiling mouth, composition arms, cloth body and feet, marked: "EIH © 1910"; cloth label on sleeve reads: "The Campbell Kids// Trademark by //Joseph Campbell// Mfg. by E.I. Horsman Co."

10" - 11"............................$200 - 250
15" - 16"............................$300 - 350

Can't Break "Em Characters, 1911 on
Child, boy or girl

11" - 13"............................$200 - 275
Cotton Joe, black

13"....................................$350 - 400
Little Mary Mix-up

15"....................................$350 - 375
Master and Miss Sam, in patriotic outfits

15"....................................$350 - 375
Polly Pru

13"....................................$325 - 350

Fairy, 1911, composition head and hands, molded hair, painted side-glancing eyes, cloth body, designed by Helen Trowbridge, based on Little Fairy Soap advertising by N.K. Fairbanks Co., marked: "EIH © 1911"

13"....................................$325 - 400

Gene Carr Kids, 1915 - 1916, compo-

sition head, molded and painted hair, painted eyes, open/closed smiling mouth with teeth, big ears, cloth body, composition hands, original outfit, cloth tag reads: "MADE GENE CARR KIDS U.S.A.//FROM NEW YORK WORLD'S//LADY BOUNTIFUL COMIC SERIES//By E.I. HORSMAN CO. NY"
Blink, Lizzie, Mike, Skinney
 14".................................$250 - 300
Snowball, black ....$450 - 500
Gold Medal Baby, 1911 on, baby dolls with composition head and limbs, upper and lower teeth, included Baby Suck-a-Thumb, Baby Blossom, Baby Premier and others
 10"..................................$150 - 175
 12"..................................$200 - 225
 19"..................................$275 - 300
Early All Composition
Peek-a-Boo, 1913, designed by Grace Drayton
 8"....................................$100 - 125
Peterkin, 1914 - 1930
 11" - 13" ....$300 - 400
Puppy and Pussy Pippin, 1911, designed

18" Baby Dimples, Horsman, composition: $275. **Photo courtesy of McMasters Harris Apple Tree Doll Auctions.**

by Grace Drayton, composition head, plush body
 11"..................................$450 - 550
Composition on Cloth Body, 1920 on
Brother and Sister, 1937, marked: "Brother//1937//Horsman//©" and: "Sister//1937//Horsman//©"
Brother 21" and Sister 23"
 ....each $300 - 400
Ella Cinders, 1928 - 1929, based on cartoon character, composition head, black painted hair or wig, round painted eyes, freckles under eyes, open/closed mouth, also came as all-cloth, marked: "1925//MNS"
 14"..................................$500 - 650
 18" ....$950 - 1,500
Jackie Coogan, "The Kid," 1921 - 1922, composition head, hands, molded hair, painted eyes, turtleneck sweater, long gray pants, checked cap, button reads: "HORSMAN DOLL// JACKIE// COOGAN// KID// PATENTED"
 13½" ....$550 - 600
 15½" ....$600 - 650
Jeanie Horsman, 1937, composition head and limbs, painted molded brown hair, sleep eyes, marked: "Jeanie© Horsman"
 14"..................................$225 - 250
All Composition, 1930 on
Body Twist, 1930, jointed waist
 11" ....$125 - 175
Bright Star, 1937 - 1946,
 14"..................................$100 - 150
 20"..................................$200 - 250
Campbell Kids, 1930 - 1940s, all composition
 13"..................................$200 - 250
Child, including Gold Medal child
 13" - 14"..........................$125 - 150
 16" - 18" ....$175 - 200
 21"..................................$225 - 250
HEbee-SHEbees, 1925 - 1927, based on drawings by Charles Twelvetrees, painted features, molded undershirt

and booties, or various costumes

10½" ....$200 - 250

All-bisque HEbee and SHEbee:
See All-Bisque section.

JoJo, 1937, blue sleep eyes, wig over molded hair, toddler body, marked: "HORSMAN JO JO//©1937"

13" ....$150 - 175

Naughty Sue, 1937, jointed body

16" ....$600 - 700

Patsy-Type, names such as Sue, Babs, Joan were given to the various sizes

12" ....$150 - 200

14" ....$200 - 250

Roberta, 1937, all composition

16" ....$375 - 450

Sweetheart, 1938, composition, hard-rubber arms

24" - 28" ....$325 - 400

Composition Baby, 1920s - 1940s

Buttercup, 1931, composition flange-neck head, arms, legs, cloth body, closed mouth, sleep, marked

12" - 19"..........................$500 - 950

Dimples, 1927 - 1937 on, composition head, arms, cloth body, bent-leg body or bent-limb baby body, molded dimples, open mouth, sleep or painted eyes, marked: "E.I. H."

13" - 14" ....$125 - 175

16" - 18" ....$225 - 275

20" - 22" ....$300 - 350

Toddler

20"...................................$300 - 350

24"...................................$400 - 425

Tynie Baby, circa 1924 - 1929, bisque or composition head, sleep or painted eyes, cloth body, some all-bisque, composition marked: "©1924//E.I. HORSMAN//CO. INC." or "E.I.H. Co. 1924"; bisque heads incised: "©1924 by//E I Horsman Co. Inc//Germany//37"

All bisque, with wardrobe, cradle

9"..$2,500

Bisque, closed mouth, sleep eyes

12" - 15" ....$200 - 250

20" Rosebud, Horsman, composition, Mama doll: $250. **Photo courtesy of Joan & Lynette Antique Dolls and Accessories.**

Composition, head and arms, cloth body

14" ....$90 - 110

18" ....$130 - 145

21" ....$175 - 200

Vinyl, 1950s, boxed

15".......................................$40 - 50

Mama Dolls, 1920 on, composition head, arms and lower legs, cloth body, crier, stitched hip joints to allow lower legs to swing, painted or sleep eyes, mohair or molded hair, models including Peggy Ann, Rosebud and others

14" - 15" ....$125 - 175

19" - 21"...........................$200 - 250

23" - 24" ....$300 - 350

Hard Plastic and Vinyl, dolls listed are in excellent condition with original clothing and tags, allow more for MIB or for accessories or wardrobe

Angelove, 1974, plastic/vinyl made for Hallmark

12".......................................$15 - 20

Answer Doll, 1966, button in back moves head

10".......................................$10 - 15

Baby Dimples, vinyl re-issue

19" - 21"...............................$45 - 55

36" Mary Poppins, Horsman, vinyl: $375. **Photo courtesy of Charlotte's Web Vintage Dolls and Collectibles.**

Baby First Tooth, 1966, vinyl head, limbs, cloth body, open/closed mouth with tongue and one tooth, molded tears on cheeks, rooted blond hair, painted blue eyes, marked: "©Horsman Dolls Inc. //10141"

16".........................$30 - 40

Baby Grow Up, 1966, vinyl, one body with interchangable child arms and legs, girl's head, baby arms, legs and baby head

16".........................$15 - 20

Baby Sofskin, 1972 on, vinyl

12" - 15" ....$25 - 30

Baby Tweaks, 1967, vinyl head, cloth body, inset eyes, rooted saran hair, head marked: "54//HORSMAN DOLLS INC.//Copyright 1967/67191"

20".........................$30 - 40

Ballerina, 1957, vinyl, one-piece body and legs, jointed elbows

18".........................$60 - 75

Betty, 1951, all vinyl, one-piece body and limbs

14".........................$50 - 60

Vinyl head, hard-plastic body

16".........................$20 - 25

Betty Ann, vinyl head, hard-plastic body

19".........................$40 - 50

Betty Jane, vinyl head, hard-plastic body

25".........................$65 - 75

Betty Jo, vinyl head, hard-plastic body

16".........................$20 - 30

Bright Star, circa 1952 on, all hard plastic

15".........................$175 - 300

Bye-Lo Baby, 1972, reissue, molded vinyl head, limbs, cloth body, white nylon organdy bonnet dress, marked: "3 (in square)//HORSMAN DOLLS INC.//©1972"

14".........................$25 - 30

1980 - 1990s

14".........................$15 - 20

Celeste, portrait doll, in frame, eyes painted to side

12".........................$35 - 40

Cinderella, 1965, vinyl head, hard-plastic body, eyes painted to side

11½".........................$25 - 30

Cindy, 1950s, all hard-plastic child, marked: "170"

15".........................$100 - 125

17".........................$150 - 175

19".........................$200 - 225

Cindy fashion-type doll, vinyl head, soft vinyl stuffed body, high-heeled feet

15".........................$70 - 80

18".........................$125 - 150

Vinyl head, solid vinyl body jointed at shoulders and hips, high-heeled feet

10".........................$30 - 40

Cindy Kay, 1950s on, all-vinyl child, long legs

15".........................$70 - 80

20".........................$110 - 125

27".........................$200 - 225

Crawling Baby, 1967, vinyl, rooted hair

14".........................$20 - 25

Disney Exclusives, 1981, Cinderella, Snow White, Mary Poppins, Alice in Wonderland

8".........................$20 - 35

Elizabeth Taylor, 1976

E.I. Horsman

11½" ....$25 - 35
Floppy, 1958, vinyl head, molded
foam body and legs
   18" ....$20 - 25
Flying Nun, 1965, character played
by Sally Field in *The Flying Nun*
TV show of the 1960s
   12" ....$100 - 125
Gold Medal Doll, 1953, vinyl head, soft
vinyl foam-stuffed body, molded hair
   17" - 26"............................$80 - 125
1954, vinyl, boy
   12"......................................$35 - 40
   15"......................................$65 - 75
Hansel and Gretel, 1963, vinyl head,
hard-plastic body, rooted synthetic
hair, closed mouth, sleep eyes, body
marked: "MADE IN USA"; tag reads:
"HORSMAN, Michael Meyerberg, Inc.,
Reproduction of the famous Kinemins
in Michael Myerberg's
marvelous Technicolor production
of Hansel and Gretel"
   15" ....pair $60 - 70
HEbee-SHEbees, 1987,
vinyl re-issues ....$15 - 25
Jackie, 1961, designed by Irene Szor
(according to Szor, this doll named
Jackie was not meant to portray Jackie
Kennedy), vinyl, rooted hair, blue sleep
eyes, long lashes, closed mouth, high-
heeled feet, small waist, nicely dressed,
marked: "HORSMAN//19©61//BC"
   18" - 25" ....$70 - 85
Lil' David and Lil' Ruth, 1970s, all vinyl,
anatomically correct babies
   12" ....$12 - 18
Lullabye Baby, 1967 - 1968, vinyl
bent-leg body, rooted hair, inset blue
eyes, drink-and-wet feature, musical
mechanism, Sears 1968 catalog,
suedette pillow, wearing terry-cloth
p.j.s, marked: "2580//B144 8 //
HORSMAN DOLLS INC//19©67"
   12" ....$10 - 15
Mary Poppins, 1965, all in good
condition with original clothing, value

can double for MIB
   12"......................................$35 - 50
   16"......................................$60 - 70
   26", 1966............................$75 - 90
   36"..................................$300 - 375
Mary Poppins with Michael and
Jane, 1966
   12" and 8" ....$150 - 160
Mary Poppins, 1970s
   12" ....$10 - 20
Patty Duke, circa 1965, vinyl, rooted
hair, painted eyes
   12"...................................$100 - 125
Peggy Pen Pal, circa 1970, vinyl, rooted
hair, came with writing desk and pen
   18"......................................$20 - 30
   Black ....$40 - 50
Pipi Longstocking, circa 1972, vinyl,
rooted hair, painted eyes
   11"......................................$30 - 40
Police Woman, circa 1976, vinyl, plastic
fully articulated body, rooted hair
   9".......................................$15 - 20
Poor Pitiful Pearl, 1963, from cartoon
by William Steig, neck marked:
"Horsman 1963"

17" Poor Pitiful Pearl, Hasbro, vinyl, MIB:
$200. **Photo courtesy of Charlotte's Web
Vintage Dolls and Collectibles.**

11" ....$50 - 60
17" ....$75 - 100
Ruthie, 1962
   15" ....$25 - 35
   19" ....$45 - 50
Softee, 1959, vinyl baby
   15" ....$20 - 25
Thirsty Walker, 1962
   26" ....$35 - 40
Ventriloquist dolls, 1973 on, Tessi Talk,
Willie Talk, Simon Sez
   16" ....$30 - 40

MARY HOYER DOLL MANUFACTURING COMPANY

1937 - 1968, 1990 to present, Reading, Pennsylvania. Designed by Bernard Lipfert, all composition, later hard plastic, then vinyl, swivel neck, jointed body, mohair or human-hair wig, sleep eyes, closed mouth, original clothes or knitted from Mary Hoyer patterns, company reopened by Hoyer's granddaughter in 1990. Dolls listed are in good condition with appropriate clothing.

Composition, allow less for painted eyes
   14" ....$200 - 325

Hard Plastic
In knit outfit
   14" ....$250 - 400
In tagged Hoyer outfit
   14" ....$700 - 900
Boy in original wig
   14" ....$425 - 475
Modern, values are for secondary market dolls, dolls are still available at retail
   14" MIB.............................$80 - 100
Gigi, circa 1950, with round Mary Hoyer mark found on 14" dolls, only 2,000 made by the Frisch Doll Company
   18" ....$700 - 1,300
Vinyl, circa 1957 on
Vicky, all vinyl, body bends at waist, high-heeled feet, rooted saran hair, two larger sizes 12" and 14" were discontinued
   10½" ....$90 - 100
Margie, circa 1958, toddler, rooted hair, made by Unique Doll Co.
   10" ....$80 - 100
Cathy, circa 1961, infant, made by Unique Doll Co.
   10" ....$20 - 25
Janie, circa 1962, baby
   8" ....$20 - 25
Becky, circa 1967, girl
   14" ....$75 - 100

14" Mary Hoyer, composition: $275. **Photo courtesy of Richard Withington, Inc.**

18" Gigi, Mary Hoyer, hard plastic: $650. **Photo courtesy of Alderfer Auction Company, Inc.**

ADOLPH HÜLSS

1915 - 1930 on, Waltershausen, Germany. Made dolls with bisque heads, jointed composition bodies. Trademark: "Nesthak-chen," "h" in mold mark often resembles a "b." Heads made by Simon & Halbig.

Baby, bisque socket head, sleep eyes, open mouth, teeth, wig, bent-leg baby, composition body, allow more for flirty eyes

Mold 156

9"	$275 - 300
14" - 15"	$400 - 475
17" - 19"	$625 - 675
23"	$800 - 825

Toddler

9" - 10"	$850 - 900
16"	$775 - 800
20"	$900 - 925

Painted bisque

22"	$200 - 225

Child, bisque socket head, jointed composition body, wig, sleep eyes, open mouth, teeth, tongue

Mold 176

15"	$650 - 675
18"	$650 - 750
22"	$950 - 975

MAISON HURET

1812 - 1930 on, France. May have pressed, molded bisque or china heads, painted or glass eyes, closed mouths, bodies of cloth, composition, gutta-percha, kid or wood and sometimes metal hands. Wigs are fur or mohair; fashion-type body with defined waist. Look for dolls with beautiful painting on eyes and face; painted eyes are more common than glass, but the beauty of the painted features and/or wooden bodies increases the value.

Poupée

Bisque shoulder head, kid body, bisque lower arms, glass eyes

15"	$13,000 - 14,000
17" - 18"	$16,000 - 20,000

Gutta-percha body

17"	sold at auction for $58,000

Round face, painted blue eyes, cloth body

16" - 18"	$11,000 - 14,000

Wooden body

17"	$19,000 - 28,000

China shoulder head, kid body, china lower arms

17"	$15,000 - 20,000

Wooden body

17"	$30,000 - 33,000

Gutta-percha body

17"	$20,000 - 25,000

Huret Bébé, 1878, bisque head, glass eyes, closed mouth

Composition body

13"	$7,000 - 11,000
20"	$19,000 - 21,000

Gutta-percha body

18"	$70,000 - 80,000

Wooden body

18"	$34,000 - 36,000

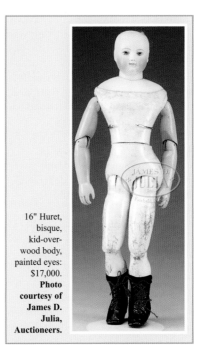

16" Huret, bisque, kid-over-wood body, painted eyes: $17,000. **Photo courtesy of James D. Julia, Auctioneers.**

18" Huret, bisque, Prevost era: $8,500. **Photo courtesy of Richard Withington, Inc.**

Prevost Era Lady or Gentleman, 1914 - 1918, elongated face on composition body
17" - 18".....................$7,000 - 8,500

IDEAL NOVELTY AND TOY COMPANY

1906 - 1980s, Brooklyn, New York. Produced their own composition dolls in early years and later made dolls of rubber, hard plastic, vinyl and cloth. For values listed, dolls made up to 1950 are in good condition with appropriate clothing; dolls made after 1950 dolls are in excellent condition with original clothing and tags.

Cloth

Dennis the Menace, 1976, based on character in comic strip by Hank Ketcham, all cloth, printed doll, blond hair, freckles, wearing overalls, striped shirt
7".........................$10 - 15
14".......................$30 - 35

Internationals, 1920s on, cloth mask faces, cloth bodies
13"....................$75 - 100

Peanuts Gang, 1976 - 1978, all-cloth stuffed printed dolls based on characters in comic strip by Charles Schulz:
Charlie Brown, Lucy, Linus, Peppermint

Patty, Snoopy
7".........................$18 - 22
14".......................$25 - 30

Snow White and the Seven Dwarfs, 1939 on, cloth mask face dolls, cloth body Snow White, black mohair wig, dress with dwarfs printed on skirt
16"....................$300 - 350

Dwarfs
10"...........................each $175 - 200

Strawman, 1939, all-cloth, based on character played by Ray Bolger in *The Wizard of Oz* movie, yarn hair, all original, wearing dark jacket and hat, tan pants, round paper hang tag
17" ....$900 - 1,200
21" ....$1,400 - 1,500

Composition

Early Composition Character Children, composition heads, lower arms, sometimes shoes on cloth body, excelsior stuffed

Cracker Jack Boy, 1917, sailor suit, carries package of Cracker Jacks
14"....................$350 - 375

Happy Hooligan, 1910
21" ....$475 - 525

21" Deanna Durbin, Ideal, composition: $800. **Photo courtesy of McMasters Harris Apple Tree Doll Auctions.**

Liberty Boy, 1917, molded uniform
12" ....$125 - 175
Naughty Marietta (coquette-type), 1912
14" ....$250 - 300
Snookums, 1910, plush body
14" ....$500 - 600
Uneeda Kid, 1914 - 1919, original
clothing, including rain slicker and
biscuit box
15" ....$425 - 475
Zu Zu Kid, 1916 - 1917
14" ....$225 - 275
Child or Toddler, 1913 on, composition
head, molded hair, or wigged, painted
or sleep eyes, cloth or composition
body, original clothes, may have Ideal
diamond mark or hang tag
13" ....$155 - 225
15" - 16" ....$230 - 255
18" ....$295 - 325
Baby Doll, 1913 on, composition head,
molded hair or wigged, painted or
sleep eyes, cloth or composition body,
models such as Baby Mine, Our Pet,
Prize baby and others
15" - 16" ....$120 - 180
Mama Doll, 1921 on, composition
head and arms, molded hair or wigged,
painted or sleep eyes, cloth body, crier,
stitched swing leg, composition lower leg
16" ....$225 - 250
20" ....$275 - 300
24" ....$325 - 350
Babies, mid 1920s - 1940s, composition
head, arms and legs, cloth body
Flossie Flirt, 1924 - 1931, composition
head and limbs, cloth body, crier, tin
flirty eyes, open mouth, upper teeth,
original outfit, dress, bonnet, socks and
shoes, head marked: "IDEAL" in diamond with "U.S. of A"
14" ....$200 - 225
18" ....$250 - 275
20" ....$300 - 325
22" ....$350 - 375
24" ....$375 - 400
28" ....$400 - 525

25"
Lone
Ranger,
Ideal,
compo-
sition:
$400.
**Photo
courtesy of
Morphy
Auctions.**

Tickletoes, 1928 - 1939, composition
head, rubber arms and legs, cloth body,
squeaker in each leg, flirty sleep eyes,
open mouth, two painted teeth, original
organdy dress, bonnet, paper hang tag,
head marked: "IDEAL" in diamond
with "U.S. of A.
14" ....$225 - 275
17" ....$275 - 300
20" ....$325 - 350
Snoozie, 1933 on, designed by Bernard
Lipfert, composition head, painted
hair, hard rubber hands and feet, cloth
body, open yawning mouth, molded
tongue, sleep eyes, head marked: "©B.
Lipfert//Made for Ideal Doll and Toy
Corp. 1933" or "©by B. Lipfert" or
"IDEAL SNOOZIE//B. LIPFERT"
on head
14" ....$150 - 175
16" ....$200 - 275
18" ....$300 - 325
20" ....$350 - 375
Princess Beatrix, 1938 - 1943,
represents Princess Beatrix of the
Netherlands, composition head,
arms and legs, cloth body, flirty sleep
eyes, fingers molded into fists, original
organdy dress and bonnet

11" Pinocchio, Ideal, composition and wood: $300. **Photo courtesy of Morphy Auctions.**

14".................................$200 - 250
16".................................$300 - 350
22".................................$350 - 425
26".................................$450 - 500

Soozie Smiles, 1923, two-faced composition doll with smiling face, sleep or painted eyes, crying face with tears, molded painted hair, cloth body and legs, composition arms, original clothes, also in gingham check romper, tag

15" - 17"............................$375 - 425

Composition Child, 1920s - 1940s
Buster Brown, 1929, composition head, hands and legs, cloth body, tin eyes, red outfit, marked: "IDEAL" in diamond

17" ....$325 - 375

Charlie McCarthy, 1938 - 1939, hand puppet, composition head, felt hands, molded hat, molded features, wire monocle, cloth body, painted tuxedo, marked: "Edgar Bergen's//©CHARLIE MCCARTHY//MADE IN U.S.A."

8"...................................$450 - 60

Cinderella, 1938 - 1939, all composition,

brown, blond or red human-hair wig, flirty brown sleep eyes, open mouth, six teeth, same head mold as Ginger, Snow White, Mary Jane with dimple in chin, some wear formal evening gowns of organdy and taffeta, velvet cape, rhinestone tiara, silver snap shoes, Sears catalog version wears Celanese rayon gown, body marked: "SHIRLEY TEMPLE//13"

13"..................................$300 - 325
16"..................................$325 - 350
20"..................................$350 - 375
22"..................................$375 - 400
25"..................................$400 - 425
27"..................................$425 - 450

Deanna Durbin, 1938 - 1941, all composition, fully jointed, dark-brown human-hair wig, brown sleep eyes, open mouth, six teeth, felt tongue, original clothes, allow more for fancy outfits,pin reads: "DEANNA DURBIN//A UNIVERSAL STAR,"head marked: "DEANNA DURBIN//IDEAL DOLL"; body marked: "IDEAL DOLL//21"

15"..................................$300 - 400
18"..................................$500 - 600
21"..................................$700 - 900
24"...............................$1,100 - 1,300

21" costumed as Gulliver ......sold at
auction for $1,300

Flexy, 1938 - 1942, composition head, gauntlet hands, molded painted hair, painted eyes, wooden torso and feet, flexible wire tubing for arms and legs, original clothes, paper tag, head marked: "IDEAL DOLL//Made in U.S. A." or: "IDEAL DOLL"

Black Flexy, closed smiling mouth, tweed patched pants, felt suspenders

13½" ....$275 - 300

Baby Snooks, (based on character created by actress Fannie Brice), open/closed mouth with teeth

13½" ....$325 - 400

Clown Flexy, looks like Mortimer Snerd (see below), painted white as clown

13½" ....$175 - 200
Mortimer Snerd, Edgar Bergen's
dummy, closed smiling mouth,
two teeth
13½" ....$325 - 400
Soldier, closed smiling mouth,
khaki uniform
13½" ....$200 - 225
Sunny Sam and Sunny Sue, girl
bobbed hair, pouty mouth, boy with
smiling mouth
13½" ....$250 - 300
Judy Garland
1939 - 1940, as Dorothy from *The
Wizard of Oz* movie, designed by
Bernard Lipfert, all composition,
jointed, wig with braids, brown sleep
eyes, open mouth, six teeth, blue or
red checked rayon jumper, white blouse,
head marked: "IDEAL" and size
number; body marked "USA"
13" ....$1,100 - 1,200
15½" ....$1,500 - 1,700
18"..............................$1,900 - 2,200
1940 - 1942, teen, all composition,
wig, sleep eyes, open mouth, four teeth,
original long dress, hang tag reads:
"Judy Garland// A Metro Goldwyn
Mayer//Star//in//'Little Nellie//Kelly,"
pin reads "JUDY GARLAND METRO
GOLDWYN MAYER STAR," head
marked: "IN U.S.A."; body marked:
"IDEAL DOLLS" and backwards "21"
15"...................................$700 - 800
21" ....$1,100 - 1,400
Lone Ranger (or Tonto), composition
head, cloth body, hat marked with
character's name on band
20"...................................$350 - 450
Seven Dwarfs, 1938 on, composition
head, cloth body, head turns,
removable clothes, each dwarf has
name on cap, pick and lantern
12" ....$175 - 200
Dopey, 1938, one of Seven Dwarfs,
ventriloquist doll, composition head
and hands, cloth body, arms and legs,

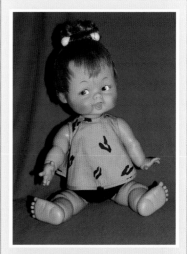
16" Baby Pebbles toddler, Ideal, all vinyl, circa
1964-1966: $120. **Photo courtesy of The
Museum Doll Shop.**

hinged mouth with drawstring,
molded tongue, painted eyes, large
ears, long coat, cotton pants, felt
shoes sewn to leg, felt cap with name,
can stand alone, neck marked:
"IDEAL DOLL"
20"...................................$700 - 800
Snow White, 1938 on, all-composition
jointed body, black mohair wig, flirty
glass eyes, open mouth, four teeth,
dimple in chin, Shirley Temple body,
red velvet bodice, rayon taffeta skirt
pictures seven Dwarfs, velvet cape,
some unmarked, some marked on
back: "Shirley Temple/18" or other
size number
11½" ....$400 - 450
13" - 14"...........................$425 - 475
19" - 21"...........................$550 - 650
Snow White, 1938 - 1939, as above,
but with molded and painted bow and
black hair, painted side-glancing eyes,
allow 50 percent more for black
version, head marked: "IDEAL DOLL"
14½" ....$300 - 350
17½" - 19½" ....$450 - 550

161

Ideal Novelty and Toy Company

13½" Betsy Wetsy, Ideal, hard-plastic head, vinyl body, mint with tag: $350. **Photo courtesy of Dollyology Vintage Dolls.**

Shirley Temple, 1934 on: See Shirley Temple section.

Composition-and-Wood Dolls, 1940 on, segmented wood body, strung with elastic

Gabby
    10½" ....$425 - 500
Jiminy Cricket
    9"..................................$450 - 525
Ferdinand the Bull
    9"..................................$200 - 250
Pinocchio, 1939
    8"..................................$150 - 200
    11"................................$275 - 325
    20"................................$500 - 625
Superman, 1940s, painted features
    13"................................$800 - 900
Magic Skin Dolls, 1940 on, stuffed latex body, original clothing. These doll bodies are prone to disintegration.
Baby Coos, 1948 - 1953, also Brother and Sister Coos, designed by Bernard Lipfert, hard-plastic head, jointed arms, sleep eyes, molded painted hair, closed mouth, squeeze box voice, later on cloth and vinyl body, unmarked or head marked: "16 IDEAL DOLL// MADE IN U.S.A."
    14" ....$100 - 150
    16" - 18" ....$165 - 180
    20" - 22".........................$175 - 200

27" - 30" ....$225 - 250
Bonnie Braids, 1951 - 1953, character based on daughter of Dick Tracy and Tess Trueheart in Chester Gould's comic strip *Dick Tracy*, vinyl head, jointed arms, one-piece body, open mouth, one tooth, painted yellow hair, two yellow saran pigtails, painted blue eyes, coos when squeezed, long white gown, bed jacket, toothbrush, Ipana toothpaste, neck marked: "©1951//Chi. Tribune//IDEAL DOLL//U.S.A."
Baby
    11½" ....$150 - 200
    14"..................................$250 - 300
Toddler, 1953, vinyl head, jointed hard-plastic body, open/closed mouth with two painted teeth, walker
    11½" ....$100 - 125
    13½" ....$150 - 175
Magic Skin Baby, 1940, 1946 - 1949, hard-plastic head, one-piece body and legs, jointed arms, sleep eyes, molded painted hair, latex usually darkened with time, some with fancy layettes or trunks
    13" - 14"..............................$40 - 65
    15" - 16"..............................$65 - 80
    17" - 18" ....$190 - 110
    20" ....$110 - 125
Joan Palooka, 1953, character based on daughter of Joe Palooka from Ham Fisher's comic strip *Joe Palooka*. Vinyl head, "Magic Skin" body, jointed arms and legs, yellow molded hair, yellow saran topknot, blue painted eyes, open/closed mouth, smells like baby powder, original pink dress with blue ribbons, came with Johnson's baby powder and soap, head marked: "©1952//HAM FISHER//IDEAL DOLL"
    14" ....$100 - 150
Snoozie, 1951, vinyl head, open/closed mouth
    11" ....$100 - 125

16" ....$125 - 150

20" ....$150 - 175

Sparkle Plenty, 1947 - 1950, based on character from Dick Tracy comics in Chester Gould's comic strip *Dick Tracy*, hard-plastic head, "Magic Skin" body may have darkened with time, yarn hair

14" ....$275 - 350

MIB ....sold at online auction for $689

Hard-Plastic and Vinyl Dolls, good condition, original clothing, value can double for MIB

Baby

11" ....$25 - 35

14" ....$45 - 55

20" $75

Child

14" ....$25 - 35

Andy Gibb, 1979

7½" ....$18 - 23

April Shower, 1969, vinyl, battery-operated, splashes hands, head turns

14" ....$25 - 30

Baby Pebbles, 1963 - 1964, based on character from television cartoon series *The Flintstones*, Hanna Barbera Productions, vinyl head, arms and legs, soft body, side-glancing blue painted eyes, rooted hair with topknot and bone, leopard-print nightie and trim on flannel blanket, also produced as a 16" all-vinyl toddler, jointed body, leopard-print outfit

14" ....$75 - 90

Tiny Pebbles, 1964 - 1966, hard-vinyl body, in 1965 had plastic-log cradle

12" ....$85 - 95

Bamm-Bamm, 1964, based on character from television cartoon series *The Flintstones*, Hanna Barbera Productions, vinyl head, jointed body, rooted blond saran hair, painted blue side-glancing eyes, leopard-print suit, cap, club

12" ....$50 - 60

16" ....$95 - 125

Belly Button Babies, 1971, Me So Glad,

Me So Silly, Me So Happy, boy and girl versions, vinyl head, rooted hair, painted eyes, when button in belly is pressed, arms, head and bent legs move

White

9½" ....$20 - 25

Black

9½" ....$25 - 30

Betsy McCall, 1952 - 1953: See Betsy McCall section.

Betsy Wetsy, 1937 - 1938, 1954 - 1956, 1959 - 1962, 1982 - 1985, open mouth for bottle, drinks, wets, came with bottle, some in layettes, head marked: "IDEAL"; body marked: "IDEAL"

Hard-rubber head, soft-rubber body, sleep or painted eyes

11" ....$95 - 125

13½" ....$150 - 175

15" ....$200 - 225

17" ....$225 - 250

19" ....$275 - 300

Hard-plastic head, vinyl body

11½" ....$150 - 175

13½" ....$200 - 250

16" ....$250 - 300

20" ....$325 - 275

All vinyl

18" Giggles, Ideal, vinyl: $350. **Photo courtesy of Charlotte's Web Vintage Dolls and Collectibles.**

8" ....$60 - 75
11½".........................$75 - 100
13½".........................$80 - 110
16" ....$100 - 150
Bizzie-Lizzie, 1971 - 1972, vinyl head, jointed body, rooted blond hair, sleep eyes, when plugged into power pack, irons, vacuums, uses feather duster, two D-cell batteries, allow 50 percent of value for doll without accessories
White
18" ....$65 - 75
Black
18" ....$75 - 85
Blessed Event, crying baby, vinyl head, squinting eyes
21" ....$150 - 200
Butterick Sew Easy Designing Set, 1953, hard-vinyl mannequin of adult woman, molded blond hair, came with Butterick patterns and sewing accessories
14" ....$100 - 125
Captain Action® Superhero, 1966 - 1968, represents a fictional character who changes disguises to become a new identity, vinyl articulated figure, dark hair and eyes, value can double for MIB
Captain Action

13½" Cinnamon, Ideal, vinyl, grow-hair doll: $45. **Photo courtesy of Charlotte's Web Vintage Dolls and Collectibles.**

12" ....$160 - 200
Batman disguise ....$80 - 100
Silver Streak box only $400
Too few in database for a reliable range
Aquaman ....$100 - 125
Capt. Flash Gordon accessories $150
Dr Evil lab set ....$550 - 650
Phantom set.........................$100
Steve Canyon disguise.........................$200
Superman set w/dog $160
Lone Ranger outfit only $150
Spiderman ....$175 - 200
Tonto outfit only.........................$150
Action Boy
9".........................$375
Robin Accessories $150
Special Edition $300
Super Girl
11½" ....$350 - 400
Clarabelle, 1954, based on clown from *Howdy Doody* TV show of the 1950s, mask face, cloth body, wearing satin Clarabelle outfit, noise box and horn, later dolls have vinyl face
16" ....$200 - 225
20" ....$225 - 250
Crissy® Family of Dolls, 1969 - 1974, 1982, vinyl grow-hair dolls, all good condition, original clothing, value can double for MIB
Baby Crissy, 1973 - 1976, all vinyl, jointed body, foam-filled legs and arms, rooted auburn growing hair, two painted teeth, brown sleep eyes, back marked: "©1972//IDEAL TOY COPR.//2M 5511//B" or "GHB-H-225
White
24" ....$110 - 120
Black
24" ....$125 - 130
Beautiful Crissy, 1969 - 1974, all vinyl, dark-brown eyes, long hair, hair grows when knob in back is turned, some with swivel waist (1971), head turns when string is pulled (1972), talks when string is pulled (1971), reissued

circa 1982 - 1983, first year hair grew to floor length
White
18" ....$90 - 120
Black
17½".................................$80 - 90
1982 doll ....$35 - 40
Crissy's Friends, Brandi, 1972 - 1973; Kerry, 1971; Tressy, 1970 (Sears Exclusive), vinyl head, painted eyes, rooted growing hair, swivel waist
White
18" ....$55 - 60
Black
18" ....$60 - 70
Cinnamon, Velvet's Little Sister, 1972 - 1974, vinyl head, painted eyes, rooted auburn growing hair, orange polka-dotted outfit, additional outfits sold separately, head marked: "©1971//IDEAL TOY CORP.//G-H-12-H18//HONG KONG//IDEAL 1069-4 b"; back marked: "©1972//IDEAL TOY CORP.//U.S. PAT-3-162-976//OTHER PAT. PEND.//HONG KONG"
White
13½" ....$40 - 45
Black
13½" ....$60 - 70
Cricket, 1971 - 1972 (Sears Exclusive); Dina, 1972 - 1973; Mia, 1971, vinyl, members of the Crissy® family, growing-hair dolls, painted teeth, swivel waist
15" ....$75 - 80
Tara, 1976, all-vinyl black growing-hair doll, long black rooted hair, sleep eyes, head marked: "©1975//IDEAL TOY CORP//H-250//HONG KONG"; buttocks marked: "©1970//IDEAL TOY CORP//GH-15//M5169-01//MADE IN HONG KONG"
15½" ....$75 - 85
Velvet, 1971 - 1973, Crissy's younger cousin, talker
15" ....$80 - 125
1974, non-talker, other accessories, grow hair

White
15" ....$65 - 75
Black
15" ....$60 - 65
Movin' Groovin Velvet ......$75 - 95
Movin' Groovin Dina ......$45 - 50
Movin' Groovin Kerri ....$100 - 125
Movin' Groovin Mia ....$75 - 95
Daddy's Girl, 1961, vinyl head and arms, plastic body, swivel waist, jointed ankles, rooted saran hair, blue sleep eyes, closed smiling mouth, preteen girl, label on dress reads: "Daddy's Girl,"head marked: "IDEAL TOY CORP.//g-42-1"; body marked: "IDEAL TOY CORP.//G-42"
38" ....$1,500 - 1,800
42" ....$2,200 - 3,000
Davy Crockett and his horse, 1955 - 1956, all plastic, can be removed from horse, fur cap, buckskin clothes
4¾" ....$40 - 50
Diana Ross, 1969, based on lead singer of The Supremes, all vinyl, rooted black bouffant hairdo, wearing gold sheath, feathers, gold shoes, or chartreuse mini-dress, print scarf, black shoes

16" Tiny Kissy, Ideal, vinyl: $80. **Photo courtesy of Alderfer Auction Company, Inc.**

18" Miss Revlon Kissing Pink, Ideal, vinyl, MIB: $575. **Photo courtesy of American Beauty Dolls.**

17½" ....$300 - 350

Dorothy Hamill, 1978, based on Olympic skating star, vinyl head, plastic posable body, rooted short brown hair, comes on ice rink stand with skates, extra outfits were available

11½" ....$15 - 20

Evel Knievel, 1974 - 1977, all-plastic stunt figure, helmet, allow more if has stunt cycle

7" ....$25 - 35

Flatsy, 1969, flat vinyl doll with wire armature, rooted hair

6" ....$20 - 45

Giggles, 1960, vinyl head, giggling doll

18" ....$240 - 290

Harmony, 1972, vinyl, battery-operated, makes music with guitar

21" ....$175 - 200

Harriet Hubbard Ayer, 1953, cosmetic doll, vinyl stuffed head, hard-plastic (Toni) body, wigged or rooted hair, came with eight-piece H. H. Ayer cosmetic kit, beauty table and booklet, head marked: "MK 16//IDEAL DOLL"; body marked: "IDEAL DOLL//P-91"

14" ....$90 - 120

16" ....$125 - 140

19" ....$150 - 165

21" ....$175 - 190

Honeybunch, 1956 - 1957, soft-vinyl head, cotton-stuffed vinyl body and limbs, curlable hair

15" - 23" ....$100 - 125

Hopalong Cassidy, 1949 - 1950, vinyl stuffed head, vinyl hands, molded, painted gray hair, painted blue eyes, one-piece body, wearing black cowboy outfit, leatherette boots, guns, holster, black felt hat, buckle marked: "Hopalong Cassidy"

20" ....$185 - 200

24" ....$200 - 225

Plastic, with horse, Topper

4½" ....$40 - 50

Howdy Doody, 1950 - 1953, based on television personality, hard-plastic head, red molded painted hair, freckles, ventriloquist doll, mouth operated by pull string, cloth body and limbs, wearing cowboy outfit, scarf reads: "HOWDY DOODY," head marked: "IDEAL"

18" ....$450 - 500

20" ....$500 - 525

24" ....$525 - 550

1954, with vinyl hands, wearing boots, jeans

20½" ....$250 - 275

25" ....$300 - 350

Jet Set Dolls, 1967, vinyl head, posable body, rooted straight hair, mod fashions, earrings, strap shoes, Chelsea, Stephanie, and Petula

24" ....$45 - 55

Jody, An Old Fashioned Girl, 1975, vinyl, long rooted red hair

9" ....$15 - 25

Jody with her Schoolhouse, 1976 ....$50 - 60

Joey Stivic, based on the character of Archie Bunker's grandson in *All In The Family*, 1976, vinyl, rooted hair

14" ....$35 - 50

Judy Splinters, 1949 - 1950, vinylite, based

on character created by Shirley Dinsdale for the *Judy Splinters* TV show, ventriloquist doll, open/closed mouth

18" ....$180 - 200

22" ....$225 - 250

36" ....$280 - 300

Baby

15" ....$275 - 300

Kissy, 1961 - 1964, vinyl head, rigid vinyl toddler body, rooted saran hair, sleep eyes, jointed wrists, when hands are pressed together, mouth puckers and makes kissing sound, original dress, panties, t-strap sandals, head marked: "©IDEAL CORP.//K-21-L"; body marked: "IDEAL TOY CORP.// K22//PAT. PEND."

White

22½" ....$75 - 85

Black

22½" ....$125 - 150

Kissy Baby, 1963 - 1964, all vinyl, bent legs

22" ....$45 - 65

Tiny Kissy, 1963 - 1968, smaller toddler, red outfit, white pinafore with hearts, head marked: "IDEAL CORP.//K-16-1"; body marked: "IDEAL TOY CORP./K-16-2"

White

16" ....$80 - 90

Black

16" ....$90 - 100

Lori Martin, 1961, based on character from *National Velvet* TV show, all vinyl, swivel waist, jointed body, including ankles, blue sleep eyes, rooted dark hair, individual fingers, wearing shirt, jeans, black vinyl boots, felt hat, head marked: "Metro Goldwyn Mayer Inc.//Mfg. by//IDEAL TOY CORP//38"; body marked: "©IDEAL TOY CORP.//38"

30" ....$500 - 600

38" ....$700 - 750

Little Lost Baby, 1968, three-faced doll

22" ....$75 - 100

Mary Hartline, 1952, based on personality

16" Saucy Walker, Ideal, hard plastic: $150. **Photo courtesy of McMasters Harris Apple Tree Doll Auctions.**

on *Super Circus* TV show, hard plastic, fully jointed, blond nylon wig, blue sleep eyes, lashes, black eye shadow over and under eye, red, white or green drum majorette costume with baton, original box, red heart paper hang tag, head marked: "P-91//IDEAL DOLL//MADE IN U.S.A."; back marked "IDEAL DOLL//P-91 or IDEAL//16"

7½" ....$80 - 110

16" ....$300 - 400

22½" ....$500 - 600

Miss Clairol, Glamour Misty, 1965 - 1966, vinyl head and arms, rigid plastic body and legs, rooted platinum blond saran hair, side-glancing eyes, high-heeled feet, teen doll has cosmetics to change her hair, all original, neck marked: "©1965//IDEAL TOY CORP//W-12-3"; lower rear torso marked "©1965 IDEAL" in oval

12" ....$35 - 45

Miss Curity, 1953, hard plastic, Toni body saran wig, sleep eyes, black eye shadow, nurse's outfit, navy cape, white cap, Bauer and Black first aid kit and book, curlers, head marked: "P-90 IDEAL DOLL, MADE IN U.S.A."

11½" Mitzi, Ideal, vinyl: $85. **Photo courtesy of Charlotte's Web Vintage Dolls and Collectibles.**

14½" ....$150 - 200

Miss Ideal, 1961, all vinyl, rooted nylon hair, jointed ankles, wrists, waist, arms and legs, closed smiling mouth, sleep eyes, original dress, with beauty kit and comb, head marked: "©IDEAL TOY CORP.//SP-30-S"; back marked: "©IDEAL TOY CORP.//G-30-S"

25" ....$100 - 125
30" ....$150 - 200

Miss Revlon, 1956 - 1959, vinyl, hard-plastic teenage body, jointed shoulders, waist, hips and knees, high-heeled feet, rooted saran hair, sleep eyes, lashes, pierced ears, hang tag, original dress, some came with trunks, dolls listed are in good condition with original clothing, value can double for MIB, marked: "VT 20//IDEAL DOLL"

15" ....$225 - 275
18" ....$175 - 275
20" ....$200 - 250
23" ....$225 - 300
26", 1957 only ....$300 - 350

Little Miss Revlon, 1958 - 1960, vinyl head and body, jointed head, arms, legs, swivel waist, high-heeled feet, rooted hair, sleep eyes, pierced ears with earrings, original clothes, with box, many extra boxed outfits available

10½" ....$125 - 200

Mini Monsters, 1865, Wolfy, Vampy, Franky, others

8 1/4" ....$100 - 150

Mitzi, 1961 - 1962, vinyl fashion doll similar to Mattel's Barbie®

11.5".................................$75 - 85

Plassie, 1942, hard-plastic head, molded painted hair, composition shoulder plate, composition limbs, stuffed pink oilcloth body, blue sleep eyes, original dress, bonnet, head marked: "IDEAL DOLL//MADE IN USA//PAT.NO. 225 2077"

16" ....$120 - 140
19" - 22" ....$130 - 145
24" ....$160 - 180

Play Pal Family of Dolls, 1959 - 1962 Patti, all vinyl, jointed wrists, sleep eyes, curly or straight saran hair, bangs, closed mouth, blue- or red-and-white checked dress with pinafore, three-year-old size, reissued in 1981 and 1982 from old molds, allow more for redheads, head marked: "IDEAL TOY CORP.//G 35//B-19-1"

35".................................$200 - 325
Carrot- red hair ....$600 - 700

Bonnie Play Pal, 1959, Patti's three-month-old sister, made only one year, rooted blond hair, blue sleep eyes, blue-and-white checked outfit, white shoes and socks

24" ....$325 - 375

Johnny Play Pal, 1959, Patti's three-month-old brother, blue sleep eyes, molded hair

24".................................$350 - 400

Pattite, 1960, rooted saran hair, sleep eyes, red-and-white checked dress, white pinafore with her name on it,

looks like Patti Playpal

18".....................................$750 - 800

Penny Play Pal, 1959, Patti's two-year-old sister, made only one year, rooted blond or brown curly hair, blue sleep eyes, wears organdy dress, vinyl shoes, socks, head marked: "IDEAL DOLL//32-E-L" or "B-32-B PAT. PEND."; back marked: "IDEAL"

32".....................................$300 - 350

Peter Play Pal, 1960 - 1961, gold sleep eyes, freckles, pug nose, rooted blond or brunette hair, original clothes, black plastic shoes, head marked: "©IDEAL TOY CORP.// BE-35-38"; body marked "©IDEAL TOY CORP.//W-38//PAT. PEND."

38".....................................$700 - 750

Walker

38".....................................$850 - 875

Suzy Play Pal, 1959, Patti's one-year-old sister, rooted curly short blond saran hair, blue sleep eyes, wearing purple-dotted dress

28".....................................$375 - 400

Reissue Patti ....$200 - 225

Posie Walker, 1954 - 1956

17".....................................$100 - 125

23".....................................$150 - 200

25".....................................$175 - 225

Rub-A-Dub Dolly, 1989

15" - 18"..............................$70 - 80

Samantha, 1965 - 1966, based on role played by Elizabeth Montgomery on *Bewitched* TV show, vinyl head, body, rooted saran hair, posable arms and legs, wearing red witch's costume, with broom, painted side-glancing eyes, other costume included negligee, head marked: "IDEAL DOLL//M-12-E-2"

12".....................................$200 - 250

All original, with broom ....$550 - 600

Saucy Walker, 1951 - 1955, all hard plastic, walks, turns head from side to side, flirty blue eyes, open/closed mouth, teeth, holes in body for crier, saran wig, plastic curlers, came as

toddler, boy and Big Sister

14".....................................$130 - 155

16".....................................$150 - 175

22".....................................$200 - 250

Black

16".....................................$250 - 275

Big Sister, 1954

25".....................................$425 - 475

Snoozie

1958 - 1965, all vinyl, rooted saran hair, blue sleep eyes, open/closed mouth, cry voice, knob makes doll wiggle, close eyes, crier, wearing flannel pajamas

14".....................................$90 - 120

1964 - 1965, vinyl head, arms, legs, soft body, rooted saran hair, sleep eyes, when knob is turned, doll squirms, opens and closes eyes and cries

20".....................................$70 - 80

Storybook dolls, 1985, all vinyl, rooted hair

8"...$10 - 15

Tabitha, 1966, based on baby character from *Bewitched* TV show, vinyl head, body, rooted platinum hair, painted blue side-glancing eyes, closed mouth,

10½" Thumbelina toddler, Ideal, vinyl: $80.
Photo courtesy of McMasters Harris Apple Tree Doll Auctions.

wearing pajamas, head marked: "©1965//Screen Gems, Inc.//Ideal Toy Corp.//T.A. 18-6//H-25"

    12½" ....$260 - 300

    MIB $1,500

Tammy Family Dolls, dolls listed are in good condition wearing original clothing, value can double for MIB Tammy, 1962 on, vinyl head, arms, plastic legs and torso, head jointed at neck base, head marked: "©IDEAL TOY CORP.//BS12"; back marked: "©IDEAL TOY CORP.//BS-12//1"

    White

    12"...............................$45 - 60

    Black

    12"...............................$55 - 90

    Pos'n

    12" ....$60 - 70

    Mom

    12½" ....$40 - 50

    Dad

    13"...............................$40 - 50

14" Toni, Ideal, marked P90, hard plastic: $250.
Photo courtesy of Morphy Auctions.

    Dodi

    9"............................$65 - 75

    Ted

    12½" ....$25 - 35

    Pepper

    9"............................$65 - 90

    Pos'n Pepper

    9"............................$40 - 50

    Salty

    9"............................$65 - 85

Clothing (MIP) ....$50 - 90

Tearie Dearie, 1964

    9" .... $30 - 40

Thumbelina

1961 - 1962, vinyl head and limbs, soft cloth body, painted eyes, rooted saran hair, open/closed mouth, body moves when knob on back is wound, crier in 1962

    16" ....$130 - 165

    20"..................................$225 - 300

1982 - 1983, all-vinyl one-piece body, rooted hair, non-moving, comes in quilted carrier, also black

    7"..........................$20 - 30

1982, 1985, reissue from 1960s mold, vinyl head, arms, legs, cloth body, painted eyes, crier, open mouth, molded or rooted hair, original with box

    18" ....$30 - 40

Thumbelina, Ltd. Production Collector's Doll, 1983 - 1985, porcelain, painted eyes, molded and painted hair, beige crocheted outfit with pillow booties, limited edition of 1,000

    18" ....$65 - 75

Tiny Thumbelina, 1962 - 1968, vinyl head, limbs, cloth body, painted eyes, rooted saran hair, wind key in back makes arms and head wriggle like newborn baby, original tagged clothes, head marked: "IDEAL TOY CORP.//OTT 14"; body marked: "U.S. PAT. #3029552"

    14" ....$150 - 225

Newborn Thumbelina, 1968, vinyl head and arms, foam-stuffed body, rooted hair, painted eyes, squirms when string is pulled
9" ....$80 - 110
Toddler Thumbelina, 1969 - 1971, vinyl head and arms, cloth body, rooted hair, painted eyes
9"..$70 - 80
Tiffany Taylor, 1974 - 1976, all vinyl, rooted hair, when head turns, hair color changes, painted eyes, teenage body, high-heeled, extra outfits available
19"...$65 - 80
Tuesday Taylor, 1976 - 1977, vinyl, posable body, when head turns, hair color changes, tag on clothing reads: "IDEAL Tuesday Taylor"
11½" ....$22 - 35
Tippy Tumbles, 1977
17"..$30 - 40
Toni, 1949, designed by Bernard Lipfert, all hard plastic, jointed body, DuPont nylon wig, usually blue eyes, rosy cheeks, closed mouth, came with Toni wave set and curlers in original dress, with hang tag, value can double for MIB, head marked: "IDEAL DOLL//MADE IN U.S.A."; body marked: "IDEAL DOLL" and P-series number
P-90
14" ....$250 - 325
P-91
16" ....$300 - 375
P-92
19"..................................$450 - 500
P-93
21" ....$450 - 500.
P-94
22½" ....$600 - 750
Tubsy, 1967
18"...$40 - 50
Whoopsie, 1978 - 1981, vinyl, reissued in 1981, marked: "22//©IDEAL TOY CORP//HONG KONG// 1978//H298"

13"...$20 - 25
Wizard of Oz Series, 1984 - 1985, Tin Man, Lion, Scarecrow, Dorothy, and Toto, all-vinyl six-piece posable bodies
9" ....each $15 - 20
Batgirl, Mera Queen of Atlantis, Wonder Woman, and Super Girl, 1967 - 1968, all vinyl, posable body, rooted hair, painted side-glancing eyes, wearing costume
11½" ....$350 - 400

JULLIEN

1827 - 1904, Paris, France. After 1904 became a part of S.F.B.J. Had a porcelain factory, won some awards, purchased bisque heads from François Gaultier. Dolls listed are in good condition, appropriately dressed.

Child, bisque socket head, wig, glass eyes, pierced ears, open mouth with teeth or closed mouth, jointed composition body

Closed mouth
17" - 19" ....$3,600 - 4,100
24" - 26" ....$4,600 - 5,000
Open mouth
18" - 20" ....$1,800 - 2,200
29" - 30" ....$2,600 - 2,800

20" bébé, Jullien, bisque, open mouth: $2,200.
Photo courtesy of Richard Withington, Inc.

JUMEAU

1842 - 1899, Paris and Montreuil-sous-Bois. In 1899 joined S.F.B.J., which continued to make dolls marked Jumeau through 1958. Founder Pierre Francois Jumeau made fashion dolls with kid or wooden bodies, heads marked with size number, bodies stamped "JUMEAU// MEDAILLE D'OR//PARIS." Early (pre-1890) Jumeau heads were pressed. By 1878, son Emile Jumeau was head of the company and made Bébé Jumeau, marked on back of head, on chemise, band on arm of dress. Tête Jumeaux have poured heads. Registered trademarks Bébé Protige and Bébé Jumeau in 1886, Bee mark in 1891, Bébé Marcheur in 1895, Bébé Francaise in 1896. Mold numbers of marked EJs and Têtes approximate the following heights: 1 - 10," 2 - 11," 3 - 12," 4 - 13," 5 - 14," 6 - 16," 7 - 17," 8 - 18," 9 - 20," 10 - 21," 11 - 24," 12 - 26," 13 - 30". Dolls listed are in good condition, nicely wigged, and with appropriate clothing. Exceptional dolls may be much more.

Poupée Jumeau French Fashion-type (so called), 1860s on, paperweight eyes, closed mouth, pierced ears, stamped kid body, allow more for original clothes, marked on swivel head with

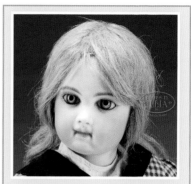

18½" Portrait Jumeau, bisque: $35,000. **Photo courtesy of James D. Julia, Auctioneers.**

size number
Poupée Peau (kid body)
    11" - 13" ....$3,500 - 5,000
    15" - 16" ....$4,000 - 6,000
    17" - 18"......................$7,000 - 8,000
    20" ....$7,000 - 9,000
Poupée Bois (wooden body), bisque
lower arms
    10" - 11"......................$8,000 - 9,000
    14" - 16" ....$10,000 - 11,000
Portrait face (so called)
    17" - 19" .... $6,000 - 7,000
    21" - 23" .... $8,000 - 10,000
Wooden body
    19" - 21"..................$10,000 - 12,000
Child Doll
Portrait, 1877 - 1883, paperweight eyes, closed mouth, pierced ears, wigged (sometimes skin wig), composition body, straight wrists, separate balls at joints, head marked with size number only
First Series, almond-shaped eyes
    12" - 14½" ....$24,000 - 30,000
    16" - 18½" ....$30,000 - 35,000
    19" - 20" ....$27,000 - 32,000
    23"..........................$39,000 - 41,000
    25" ....$53,000 - 58,000
Second Series
    11" - 12"....................$7,000 - 9,000
    13" - 15" ....$10,000 - 12,000

21" Portrait Poupée, bisque, kid-over-wood body: $12,000. **Photo courtesy of Richard Withington, Inc.**

18" - 20" ....$15,000 - 18,000
22"..........................$18,000 - 20,000
25"..........................$21,000 - 22,000
Long Face Triste Bébé, 1879 - 1886, pierced applied ears, paperweight eyes,closed mouth, straight wrists,Jumeau marked body, head marked with number only
20" - 23" ....$20,000 - 25,000
26" - 27" ....$26,000 - 30,000
31" - 33" ....$29,000 - 32,000
Premiere, 1880, unmarked bébé, allow more for exceptional couturier outfit
9" - 12" ....$7,000 - 9,000
15" - 16"..................$11,000 - 13,000
17" - 19" ....$14,000 - 17,000
E.J. Bébé, 1881 - 1886, , pressed bisque socket head, wig, paperweight eyes, pierced ears, closed mouth, jointed body, straight wrists, marked with earliest "EJ" mark above with number over initials
12" - 16"..................$10,000 - 11,000
17" - 18"..................$12,000 - 15,000
19" - 21" ....$16,000 - 21,000
23" - 24" ....$23,000 - 27,000
EJ/A marked Bébé
25" ....$32,000 - 36,000
Mid EJ, marked with size number centered between "E" and "J" ("E 8 J"), later with "Déposé" above marking

8"...............................$8,000 - 9,000
10" - 14"..................$10,000 - 12,000
16" - 20"..................$12,000 - 14,000
23" - 26" ....$15,000 - 17,000
Déposé Jumeau, 1886 - 1889, poured bisque head, pierced ears, paperweight eyes,closed mouth, composition-and-wood body, straight wrists: marked "Medaille d'Or Paris,"head marked: "Déposé Jumeau" and size number
10" - 14" ....$8,000 - 9,000
16" - 18" ....$9,000 - 10,000
20" - 23" ....$10,000 - 12,000
25" - 26" ....$12,000 - 14,000
Tête Jumeau, 1885 on, poured bisque socket head, wig, glass eyes, pierced ears, closed mouth, uses tête face, jointed composition body, straight wrists,red stamp on head, stamp or sticker on body, may also be marked "E.D." with size number (when Douillet ran factory). The following sizes were used for Têtes: 0 - 9," 1 - 10," 2 - 11," 3 - 12," 4 - 13," 5 - 14 ½," 6 - 16," 7 - 17," 8 - 19," 10-21 ½," 11 - 24," 12 - 26," 13 - 29," 14 - 31," 15 - 33," 16 - 34" - 35"
Bébé (Child), closed mouth
9" - 10" ....$7,000 - 7,500
12" - 13" ....$6,000 - 7,000
16" - 17".....................$6,000 - 7,000
19" - 22" ....$7,000 - 8,000

22" Triste (Long Face) Jumeau, bisque: $23,000. **Photo courtesy of Richard Withington, Inc.**

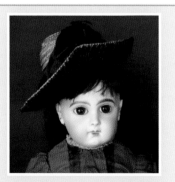

20" E.J. Jumeau, bisque: $18,000. **Photo courtesy of Sweetbriar Auctions.**

14" Jumeau, bisque, closed-mouth tête: $7,000. **Photo courtesy of Richard Withington, Inc.**

36" mold 1907, Jumeau, bisque: $4,200. **Photo courtesy of Richard Withington, Inc.**

24" - 26" ....$8,000 - 9,000
29" - 31"...................$9,000 - 11,000
Lady body
    14" - 16".......................$4,000 - 5,000
    18" - 22" ....$6,000 - 7,000
Open mouth, child
    12"..............................$2,500 - 3,000
    17" - 22" ....$3,200 - 3,500
    24" - 25" ....$4,000 - 4,500
    27" - 29" ....$5,000 - 5,500
    32" - 35" ....$5,500 - 6,000
    42" ....$6,000 - 6,500
B. L. Bébé, 1892 on, socket head, wig, pierced ears, paperweight eyes, closed mouth, jointed composition body, marked: "B. L." for the Louvre department store
    15" - 16" ....$3,500 - 4,500
    18" - 23".....................$4,700 - 5,100
Phonographe Jumeau, 1894 - 1899, bisque head, open mouth, phonograph in working condition in torso
    24" - 25" ....$8,000 - 10,000
R.R. Bébé, 1892 on, wig, pierced ears, paperweight eyes, closed mouth, jointed composition body, straight wrists
    21" - 23" ....$4,400 - 4,800
    Open mouth
    18" .... $3,000 - 3,100

Child, 1907 on, jointed French body, sleep or set eyes, open mouth, some with Tété Jumeau stamp
    14" - 16".....................$1,400 - 1,700
    19" - 20" ....$1,900 - 2,200
    23" - 26" ....$2,500 - 2,800
    29" - 32" ....$3,200 - 3,800
    35"..............................$4,000 - 4,100
Character Child
Mold 203, 208, and other 200 series, 1882 - 1899, glass eyes
    20" $70,000
Too few in database for reliable range
Mold 217, crier
    20"......................................$88,000

10" Great Lady of Fashion, Jumeau, bisque: $500. **Photo courtesy of The Museum Doll Shop.**

21" $110,000
Too few in database for reliable range
Mold 230 *child*, 1910 on, sockethead, glass eyes, open mouth, wig, composition body
  12" - 14"..........................$650 - 700
  20 - 23" ....$1,100 - 1,300
Two-Faced Jumeau, crying and smiling
  18" ....$15,000 - $16,000
Too few in database for reliable range
Princess Elizabeth, made after Jumeau joined S.F.B.J. and adopted Unis label, bisque socket head with high color, flirty eyes,closed mouth, jointed composition body, marked: "71 Unis//France 149//306//Jumeau// 1938//Paris,"
Mold 306
  15"............................$1,500 - 1,800
  18" - 19" ....$2,000 - 2,200
  32" - 33" ....$5,000 - 6,000
Great Ladies of Fashion, Mold 221, 1940s - 1950s, bisque head, five-piece composition body, hole in one foot for stand, elaborate costumes and wigs representing Queen Victoria, Marie Antoinette, etc.
  10"....................................$400 - 550
Accessories
Marked Jumeau shoes
  5" - 6" ....$300 - 400
  7" - 10" ....$600 - 700

KAMKINS

1919 - 1928, Philadelphia, Pennsylvania, and Atlantic City, New Jersey. Cloth dolls made by Louise R. Kampes Studio. Clothes made by cottage industry workers at home. All-cloth, molded mask face, painted features, swivel head, jointed shoulders and hips, mohair wig. Dolls listed are in good, clean, un-faded condition, allow 50% less for soiled or faded examples.
  18" - 20" ....$2,200 - 3,800

19" Kamkins,
cloth: $3,200.
Photo courtesy of Morphy Auctions.

KÄMMER & REINHARDT

1885 - 1933, Waltershausen, Germany. Registered trademark K R, Majestic Doll, Mein Leibling, Die Kokette, Charakterpuppen (character dolls). Designed doll heads, most bisque were made by Simon & Halbig; in 1918 Schuetzmeister & Quendt also supplied heads; Rheinische Gummi und Celluloid Fabrik Co. made celluloid heads for Kämmer & Reinhardt. Kämmer & Reinhardt dolls were distributed by Bing, Borgfeldt, B. Illfelder, L. Rees & Co., Strobel & Wilken and Louis Wolfe & Co. Also made heads of wood and composition, later cloth and rubber dolls. Mold numbers identify heads starting with 1) bisque socket heads, 2) shoulder heads, as well as socket heads, of black or mulatto babies, 3) bisque socket heads or celluloid shoulder heads, 4) heads having eyelashes, 5) googlies, black heads, pincushion heads, 6) mulatto heads, 7) celluloid heads, bisque-headed walking dolls, 8) rubber heads, 9) composition heads, some rubber heads. Other letters refer to style or material of wig or clothing. All dolls listed are in good condition with appropriate clothing.

20" Kämmer & Reinhardt, bisque: $850. **Photo courtesy of McMasters Harris Apple Tree Doll Auctions.**

10" mold 100 baby, Kämmer & Reinhardt, bisque: $300. **Photo courtesy of Dollsantique.**

Child
Bisque socket-head child
Mold 192 (possibly as early as 1892), jointed composition body, sleep eyes
  Closed mouth
  6" - 7" ....$600 - 700
  10" - 11" ....$900 - 1,000
  16" - 18"....................$2,000 - 2,200
  22" - 24" ....$2,400 - 2,600
  Open mouth
  7" - 8"...............................$475 - 575
  12" - 14".............................$700 - 750
  16" - 18" ....$850 - 1,000
  20" - 22" ....$1,200 - 1,500
  26" - 28" ....$1,600 - 1,900
Child, dolly face, 1910 to 1930s, bisque head, jointed composition body, sleep eyes, open mouth
No mold number or Molds 191, 401, 402, 403
  Five-piece flapper-style body
  5" - 6" ....$350 - 450
  7" - 8" ....$450 - 500
  Jointed composition body
  8" - 10" ....$450 - 550
  12" - 14"............................$650 - 750
  16" - 18"............................$800 - 900
  19" - 21"............................$800 - 900
  23" - 26" ....$1,000 - 1,200
  28" - 30" ....$1,200 - 1,500
Child shoulder head, kid body
  14" ....$325 - 375

  19" - 22" ....$400 - 425
Character Dolls, 1909 on
Mold 100, Baby, Kaiser Baby (so-called), solid-dome head, intaglio eyes, open/closed mouth, composition bent-limb body. Allow more for toddler body.
  11" - 12"............................$300 - 400
  14" - 15" ....$450 - 500
  18" - 20" ....$600 - 700
Mold 101, Peter or Marie, painted eyes, closed mouth, jointed body
  7 - 8" ....$1,300 - 1,500
  10" - 12"....................$1,600 - 2,000
  14" - 15" ....$2,400 - 3,200
  17" - 18"....................$3,400 - 4,000
  19" - 20" ....$4,500 - 5,000
Glass eyes
  12"............................$7,000 - 8,000

17" mold 101, Marie, Kämmer & Reinhardt, bisque: $3,400. **Photo courtesy of Richard Withington, Inc.**

15" mold 114, Gretchen, Kämmer & Reinhardt, bisque: $4,000.
Photo courtesy of Richard Withington, Inc.

15" mold 115, Kämmer & Reinhardt, bisque: $4.500.
Photo courtesy of Richard Withington, Inc.

18" - 20" ....$9,000 - 12,500
Mold 102, Elsa or Walter, painted eyes, molded hair, closed mouth, very rare
12"..........................$19,000 - 22,000
Too few in database for reliable range
Mold 103, painted eyes, closed mouth
19".....................................$80,000+
Too few in database for reliable range
Mold 104, circa 1909, painted eyes, laughing closed mouth, very rare
18".....................................$80,000+
Too few in database for reliable range
Mold 105, painted eyes, open/closed mouth, very rare
21" $170,956
Too few in database for reliable range
Mold 106, painted intaglio eyes to side, closed mouth, very rare

11½" mold 115A toddler, Kämmer & Reinhardt, bisque: $3,000.
Photo courtesy of Richard Withington, Inc.

22"......................................$145,000
Too few in database for reliable range
Mold 107, Karl, painted intaglio eyes, closed mouth
21" - 22" ....$58,000 - 65,000
Too few in database for reliable range
Mold 108, one example
reported ....$275,000+
Too few in database for reliable range
Mold 109, Elise, painted eyes, closed mouth
9" - 10" ....$6,000 - 8,000
12" - 14".................$12,000 - 17,000
20" - 24".................$21,000 - 24,000
Mold 112, painted open/closed mouth
9"...$5,000
13" - 15" ....$9,000 - 10,000
17" - 18".................$10,000 - 12,000
Glass eyes
12" - 16" ....$14,000 -18,000
Too few in database for reliable range
Mold 112X, flocked hair
17" ....$13,000 - 15,000
Mold 114, Hans or Gretchen, painted eyes, closed mouth
8" - 9" ....$2,000 - 2,200
12" - 15" ....$3,000 - 4,000
18" - 20" ....$5,000 - 6,000
23" - 25" ....$6,500 - 7,500
Glass eyes
15" - 20" ....$8,000 - 10,000

Kämmer & Reinhardt

19" mold 126 & 15" mold 122 character babies, Kämmer & Reinhardt, bisque, open mouth: $800 (19") & $650 (15"). **Photo courtesy of Morphy Auctions.**

Mold 115, solid dome, painted hair, sleeping eyes, closed mouth, toddler
12" - 15" ....$3,500 - 4,500
Mold 115A, sleep eyes, closed mouth, wig
Baby, bent-leg body
10" - 12" ....$900 - 1,400
14" - 16".....................$1,600 - 2,000
19" - 22" ....$2,500 - 3,000
Toddler, composition, jointed body
15" - 16" ....$3,750 - 4,300
18" - 22" ....$4,900 - 5,500
Mold 116, dome head, sleep eyes, open/closed mouth
10" - 13"......................$1,500 - 1,800
Mold 116A, sleep eyes, open/closed mouth or open mouth, wigged, bentleg
Baby
10" - 12" ....$1,100 - 1,400
15" - 18" ....$1,600 - 2,000
21" - 23" ....$2,500 - 3,000
Toddler body
15" - 18" ....$3,200 - 4,000
21" - 23" ....$5,000 - 7,000
Mold 117, 117A Mein Liebling (My Darling), glass eyes, closed mouth
8" - 11" ....$3,200 - 3,600
14" - 16".....................$3,800 - 4,000
18" - 20" ....$4,500 - 5,000
22" - 24" ....$5,500 - 6,000

28" - 30" ....$7,000 - 8,000
Flapper-style body
8"..............................$3,500
Too few in database for reliable range
Mold 117N, Mein NeuerLiebling (My New Darling), flirty eyes, open mouth
14" - 16" ....$1,500 - 1,900
20" - 22" ....$2,200 - 2,600
28" - 30" ....$3,000 - 3,400
Mold 117X, socket head, sleep eyes, open mouth
14" - 16"......................$850 - 950
22" - 24" ....$1,300 - 1,400
30" - 32" ....$1,600 - 1,800
Molds 118, 118A, sleep eyes, open mouth, baby body
11" ....$1,100 - 1,200
15".............................$1,300 - 1,500
18".............................$1,900 - 2,200
Mold 119, sleep eyes, open/closed mouth, five-piece baby body,marked: "Baby"
24" - 25"......................$16,000
Too few in database for reliable range
Molds 121, 122, sleep eyes, open mouth
Baby
10" - 11".......................$550 - 600
15" - 16" ....$650 -800
20" - 26" ....$900 - 1,000
Toddler body
10" ....$900 - 1,000
13" - 14" ....$1,150 - 1,250
18" - 20".....................$1,300 - 1,500
Mold 123 Max and Mold 124 Moritz, flirty sleep eyes, laughing/closed mouth, special body with molded shoes
16" ....$48,000 - 55,000 pair
Mold 126 Mein Liebling Baby (My Darling Baby), sleep or flirty eyes, bent leg, values are for sleep eyes, allow more for flirty or naughty eyes, or wobble tongue
Baby
10" - 12"........................$500 - 600
14" - 16".......................$700 - 900
18" - 20" ....$700 - 900
22" - 24" ....$600 - 700

Toddler body
   Five-piece body, with starfish
(so called) hands
   6" - 8" ....$800 - 900
   9" - 10" ....$1,000 -1,200
   20" - 25" ....$900 - 1,100
   Jointed composition body
   15" - 17"...........................$750 - 850
   22" - 24" ....$900 - 1,200
Mold 127, 127N, domed-head-like mold
126, bent-leg body, allow more for
flirty eyes
Baby
   10" - 11"...........................$750 - 800
   14" - 15" ....$900 - 1,000
   18" - 22" ....$1,100 - 1,200
Toddler body
   15" - 16".....................$1,300 - 1,500
   20" - 22" ....$1,600 - 1,700
   26"...........................$1,900 - 2,000
Mold 128, sleep eyes, open mouth, baby
body
   10"...................................$550 - 600
   13" - 15" ....$700 - 800
   20" - 24" ....$1,200 - 1,600
Mold 131: See Googlies section.
Mold 135, sleep eyes, open mouth,
baby body
   13" - 16" ....$950 - 1,100
Mold 171 Klein Mammi (Little Mammy),
dome, open mouth
   14" - 15" ....$3,000 - 3,500
Too few in database for reliable range
Mold 214, shoulder head, painted eyes,
closed mouth, similar to mold 114,
muslin body
   15"...........................$3,100 - 3,400
Too few in database for reliable range
Mold 314, socket head, composition
body, painted eyes, flocked hair
   14" $6,250
Puz, composition head, cloth body
   16" - 17".....................$1,000 - 1,300
   25"...........................$1,400 - 1,500
Cloth Character Dolls, 1927, wire-
armature body, needle-sculpted

13"
character,
Kämmer
&
Reinhardt,
cloth:
$400.
**Doll
courtesy of
Alfred
Edward.**

stockinette head, painted features,
wooden feet, all in good clean,
unfaded condition
   12" - 13"...........................$300 - 475
Composition, 1930s on, sleep eyes,
wigged
Baby, Mold 926
   22"...................................$150 - 200
Adult
Fat Character Man & Woman pair
   8"....................................$600 - 800
Too few in database for reliable range
Celluloid: See Celluloid section.

KENNER

1947 - 2000, Cincinnati, Ohio. Purchased
by Tonka Toys in 1987 and then by
Hasbro in 1991, run as a separate division by both. Dolls listed are in very good
condition with all-original clothing and
accessories. Value can double for MIB.
Baby Alive, 1990, vinyl head, eats and
drinks
   16".....................................$22 - 30
Baby Bundles
   16".....................................$10 - 15
Baby Yawnie, 1974, vinyl head, cloth
body
   15".....................................$12 - 18

11½" Blythe, Kenner, vinyl: $1,400. **Photo courtesy of Charlotte's Web Vintage Dolls and Collectibles.**

Blythe, 1972, eyes change color when string is pulled, mod-style clothes
11½" ....$1,500 - 2,000
Butch Cassidy or Sundance Kid
4".............................$30 - 40
with horse............................$40 - 50
Charlie Chaplin, 1973, all cloth, walking mechanism
14" ....$80 - 90
Cover Girls, 1978, posable elbows and knees, jointed hands
Dana, black
12½" ....$30 - 40
Darci, 1979
12½" ....$25 - 30
Erica, redhead
12½" ....$20 - 25
Crumpet, 1970, vinyl and plastic
18"..$35 - 40
Dusty, 1974, vinyl teenage doll
11" ....$15 - 20
Skye, black, teenage friend of Dusty
11" ....$15 - 20
Gabbigale, 1972
White
18" ....$20 - 25
Black
18" ....$30 - 35

Garden Gals, 1972, hand bent to hold watering can
6½" ....$6 - 10
Hardy Boys, 1978, based on characters played by Shaun Cassidy, Parker Stevenson in TV show of the same name
12"..$15 - 20
International Velvet, 1976, based on character played by Tatum O'Neill in movie of the same name
11½" ....$10 - 15
Jenny Jones and baby, 1973, all vinyl Jenny, 9"; Baby, 2½"
Set ....$18 - 22
Nancy Nonsense, 1975, pull-string talker
17" ....$40 - 50
Rose Petal, 1984, scented, various flowers and colors
7"...$12 - 25
Sabrina the Teenage Witch, 1997, based on character played by Mellissa Joan Hart in TV show of the same name
11½" ....$10 - 15

11½" Sabrina the Teenage Witch, Kenner, vinyl, MIB: $30. **Photo courtesy of The Museum Doll Shop.**

Sea Wees, 1979 - 1984, mermaid dolls
7"..$15 - 25

Six Million Dollar Man Figures,
1975 - 1977, based on character played
by Lee Majors in TV show of the same
name, value can double or more for
MIB, and even more for rare figures

Bionic Man, Big Foot
13"..$65 - 75

Bionic Man, Masketron Robot
13"......................................$100 - 125

Bionic Woman, Robot
13"..$75 - 85

Jaime Sommers, Bionic Woman
13"......................................$75 - 100

Oscar Goldman, 1975 - 1977, with
exploding briefcase
13"..$35 - 40

Steve Austin, The Bionic Man
13" ....$75 - 125

Steve Austin, Bionic Grip, 1977
13" ....$75 -125

Transport and Repair play set
MIB ..sold at online auction for $95

Star Wars Figures, 1974 - 1978, large-
size action figures. Dolls listed are
complete and in excellent condition.
Value can double or more for NRFB.

Ben-Obi-Wan Kenobi
12"..$75 - 95

BobaFett
13"....................................$155 - 175
16"....................................$175 - 200

C-3PO
12"......................................$90 - 100

Chewbacca
12"..$85 - 90

Darth Vader
12"....................................$205 - 220

Han Solo
12"....................................$500 - 700

IG-88
15"....................................$450 - 550

Jawa
8½" ....$80 - 100

Leia Organa
11½" ....$225 - 275

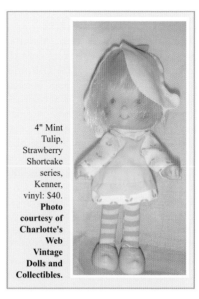

4" Mint Tulip, Strawberry Shortcake series, Kenner, vinyl: $40. **Photo courtesy of Charlotte's Web Vintage Dolls and Collectibles.**

Luke Skywalker
12"....................................$225 - 275

R2-D2, robot
7½"....................................$65 -75

Stormtrooper
12"....................................$200 - 235

Steve Scout, 1974,
9"..$15 - 18

Bob Scout, Steve's black friend
9"..$17 - 20

Strawberry Shortcake, circa 1980 -
1986, and friends
5"..$35 - 50

Baby Strawberry Shortcake,
blows kisses
15"..$30 - 35

Sweet Cookie, 1972
18"..$25 - 30

The Terminator, 1991, talks,
based on character played by
Arnold Schwarzenegger in movie
of the same name
13½" ....$20 - 25

Upsy Baby, circa 1985, battery-
operated, stands up from crawling
position, rooted hair, painted eyes
14"..$10 - 20

J.D. KESTNER

1805 - 1938, Waltershausen, Thüringia, Germany. Kestner was making dolls by the 1820s and was one of the first firms to make dressed dolls. Besides wooden dolls, papier-mâché, wax over composition, and Frozen Charlottes, Kestner made bisque dolls with leather or composition bodies, chinas, all-bisque and celluloid dolls. Supplied bisque heads to Catterfelder Puppenfabrik. Borgfeldt, Butler Bros., Century Doll Co., Horsman, R.H. Macy, Sears, Siegel Cooper, F.A.O. Schwarz and others were distributors for Kestner. Early bisque heads with closed mouths are marked "X or" XI," turned shoulder head, and swivel heads on shoulder plates are thought to be Kestners. Dolls made after 1892 are marked "made in Germany" with mold numbers.

Bisque heads with early mold numbers are stamped "Excelsior DRP No. 70 685," heads of 100 number series are marked "dep." Some early characters are unmarked or only marked with the mold number. It is believed that all dolls made after the "211" mold number was used are marked "JDK" or "JDK, Jr." Registered the "Crown Doll" (KronenPuppe) in 1915, used crown on label on bodies and dolls.

16" Kestner, Bru-look, bisque: $4,500. Photo courtesy of Richard Withington, Inc.

The Kestner Alphabet was registered in 1897 as a design patent. It is possible to identify the sizes of doll heads by this key. Letter and number always go together: B/6, C/7, D/8, E/9, F/10, G/11, H/12, H ¾ /12 ¾, J/13, J ¾ /13 ¾, K/14, K ½ /14 ½, L/15, L ½ /15 ½, M/16, N/17.

Dolls listed are in good condition with original clothes or appropriately dressed. Exceptional dolls may bring more.

Early Socket-head Child, bisque socket head, 1880 on. Closed or open/closed mouth, plaster pate, stationary or sleep glass eyes, composition ball-jointed body, sometimes with straight wrists, appropriate wig and dress in good condition, allow more for original clothes, may be marked with size numbers only
Mold 128, 169, or no mold number, closed mouth, round or long-face styles

    10" - 12" ....$2,500 - 2,900
    14" - 16"...................$3,000 - 4,300
    19" - 21"...................$2,200 - 2,800
    24" - 25" ....$2,600 - 3,200
Square face, closed mouth, some with white space between lips, no mold number
    14" - 16".....................$2,300 - 2,700

16" mold 128, Kestner, bisque, socket head, closed mouth: $4,300. Photo courtesy of Morphy Auctions.

J.D. Kestner

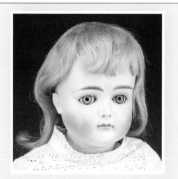

16" mold XI, Kestner, bisque: $4,000. **Photo courtesy of James D. Julia, Auctioneers.**

19" - 21".........................$2,900 - 3,200
24" - 25" ....$3,300 - 3,400
A.T. *look*, closed mouth, glass eyes, marked only with size number, for example: "15" for 24"
12" - 15" ....$7,000 - 8,000
21" ....$10,000 - 12,000
26"..........................$13,000 - 14,000
Bru look, closed mouth with space between lips, glass eyes, resembles circle dot Bru
19" - 22" ....$5,000 - 6,500
Mold X
15"............................$3,500 - 3,900
Mold XI
16"............................$3,800 - 4,000
Mold XII
17".............................$4,200 - 4,400
Mold 102, open mouth, square-cut teeth
9"...............................$2,200 - 2,400
12" - 14".....................$2,200 - 2,600
16" - 18".....................$2,800 - 3,000
24" - 25" ....$3,400 - 3,500
Mold 103, pouty closed mouth
20" ....$2,200 - 2,500
23" ....$3,300 - 3,400
31"............................$3,800 - 4,000
Pouty, no mold mark, closed mouth
18" -20" ....$3,000 - 3,500
22" - 24" ....$3,500 - 4,000
Early Shoulder-Head Child, 1880 on, bisque shoulder head, glass eyes, plaster pate, wig, kid body, bisque lower arms, marked with size numbers or letter only
Closed mouth
12".....................................$600 - 675
14" - 16"...........................$850 - 950
20" - 22" ....$800 - 900
25" - 26" ....$1,000 - 1,200
33" - 36" ....$1,600 - 1,800
AT look, closed mouth
11"..............................$2,300 - 2,700
21" - 25" ....$7,000 - 7,500
Open mouth
16" - 18"...........................$350 - 400
22" - 24" ....$500 - 550
Turned shoulder head, closed mouth
16" - 18"...........................$450 - 550
22" - 25" ....$600 - 700
28" ....$900 - 1,000
Shoulder-Head Child, 1892 on, bisque shoulder head with sleep eyes, open mouth, plaster pate, wigged, kid body
Molds 145, 147, 148, 154, 166, 195
10" - 14"...........................$200 - 300
15" - 18" ....$300 - 400
20" - 22" ....$400 - 500
26" - 29" ....$500 - 600
Bisque Socket-Head Child, open mouth, glass eyes, Kestner ball-jointed body
Mold 142, 144, 146, 164, 167, 171, 214

16" Kestner, bisque, closed mouth: $950. **Photo courtesy of Richard Withington, Inc.**

J.D. Kestner

21" Kestner, bisque, turned shoulder head, marked "K": $500. **Photo courtesy of Richard Withington, Inc.**

24" mold 154, Kestner, bisque, shoulder head: $500. **Photo courtesy of McMasters Harris Apple Tree Doll Auctions.**

8" - 12" ....$600 - 700
14" - 16"............................$600 - 700
18" - 22" ....$700 - 800
24" - 26" ....$900 - 1,100
28" - 32" ....$900 - 1,100
Mold 171, 18" size only, called Daisy
18" ....$2,100 - 2,400
Mold 129, 130, 149, 152, 160, 161, 168, 173, 174
10" - 12" ....$900 - 1,100
14" - 16".............................$600 - 700
18" - 22" ....$700 - 800
24" - 26" ....$800 - 900
28"..................................$900 -1,200
Mold 155, open mouth, glass eyes, five-piece or fully jointed body
8" - 11"..............................$700 - 850

Molds 196, 215
18" - 20" ....$550 - 650
26" - 28" ....$700 - 750
32"..................................$800 - 900
Character Baby, 1910 on, socket head, wig or solid dome with painted hair, glass eyes, open mouth, bent-leg baby body, allow more for toddler body
Marked "JDK," solid-dome bisque socket head, glass sleep eyes, molded and/or painted hair, composition bent-leg baby body, allow more for body with crown label and/or original clothes
12" - 14"............................$300 - 500
16" - 18"............................$600 - 750
21" - 25" ....$900 - 1,000
Baby Jean (so called), solid dome, fat

24" mold 171, Kestner, bisque: $900. **Photo courtesy of Morphy Auctions.**

8" mold 155, Kestner, bisque, socket head: $700. **Photo courtesy of Morphy Auctions.**

J.D. Kestner

cheeks, marked: "JDK"

12" - 13" ....$1,000 - 1,100
15" - 18".......................$1,300 - 1,600
22" - 24" ....$1,800 - 2,000

Molds 211, 226, 236, 257, 260, allow 25 percent more for toddler body or flocked hair

8" - 13" ....$400 - 600
16" - 18"............................$600 - 700
20" - 22" ....$800 - 900
24" - 26" ....$900 - 1,000

Molds 210, 234, 235, 238, shoulder head, solid dome, sleep eyes, open/closed mouth or open mouth

12" - 14"............................$750 - 900

Mold 220, sleep eyes, open/closed mouth

14"............................$3,800 - 4,200
Toddler

19" - 20" ....$5,000 - 5,500
26½" ....$8,000 - 9,000

Hilda, molds 237, 245, 1070, bald solid dome, sleep eyes, open mouth

11" - 13" ....$2,200 - 2,600
16" - 18".....................$3,000 - 3,500
20" - 22" ....$3,600 - 4,000
25" - 26"................... $4,200 - 4,500

Mold 243, Oriental baby, sleep eyes, open mouth

13" - 14" ....$5,000 - 5,500
16" - 18".....................$6,000 - 6,500

Mold 247, sockethead, sleep eyes, open mouth

14" - 16".....................$1,700 - 2,000

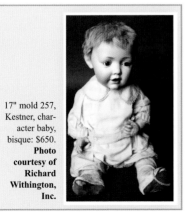

J.D. Kestner

11" mold 143, Kestner, bisque: $1,000. **Photo courtesy of Sweetbriar Auctions.**

14" mold 189, Kestner, bisque, glass eyes: $4,200. **Photo courtesy of Richard Withington, Inc.**

Toddler
    16" - 21".....................$2,000 - 3,000
Mold 255, solid-dome flange neck, glass eyes, large open/closed screamer mouth, cloth body,marked: "O.I.C. made in Germany"
    11" - 13".....................$1,800 - 2,200
Character Child, 1910 on, socket head, wig, glass eyes, composition-and-wood jointed body
Mold 143 (1897 on, precursor to character dolls), glass eyes,open mouth, jointed body
    8" - 10"..........................$900 - 1,000
    12" - 14".....................$1,000 - 1,100
    16" - 20".....................$1,300 - 1,700
Mold 178, 179, 180, 181, 182, 184, 185, 186, 187, 189, 190, 191
Painted eyes
    9" - 12" ....$2,000 - 2,800
    15"..............................$2,800 - 3,500
    18"..............................$5,000 - 6,000
Glass eyes
    12"..............................$3,200 - 3,500
    15"..............................$4,400 - 4,800
    18"..............................$5,200 - 5,400
Mold 206, fat cheeks, glass eyes, closed mouth, child or toddler

    12" - 15"....................$9,000 - 11,000
    19"...........................$22,000 - 25,000
Too few in database for a reliable range
Mold 208, for all bisque, see All-Bisque section.
Painted eyes
    12"............................$9,500 - 10,500
Glass eyes
    16".............................$6,750 - 9,000
Too few in database for reliable range
Mold 212, fat cheeks, small eye cuts, glass eyes, closed mouth
    17"...........................$10,000 - 13,000
Mold 239, socket head, sleep eyes, open mouth,
Toddler, also made as baby
    15" - 17".....................$3,600 - 4,000
Mold 241, socket head, sleep eyes, open mouth
    17" - 18".....................$4,500 - 5,000
    21" - 22" ....$5,000 - 5,500
    25" ....$6,000 - 7,000
    28" - 30" ....$8,000 - 9,000
Other Character Dolls
Mold 279 socket head, molded-bob hairstyle, glass eyes, open mouth, composition body
    15" ....$500 - 600

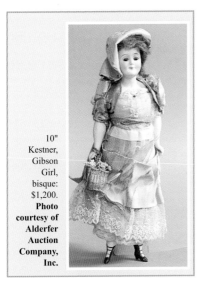

10"
Kestner,
Gibson
Girl,
bisque:
$1,200.
**Photo
courtesy of
Alderfer
Auction
Company,
Inc.**

Max & Moritz, socket head,
composition body
13" ....each $6,700 - 7,200
Lady Doll, 1898 on, bisque socket head,
glass eyes, open mouth, composition
body, slender waist, molded breasts
Mold 162
   16" - 22" ....$1,500 - 2,000
"Gibson Girl" Mold 172, shoulder head,
glass eyes, closed mouth, kid body,
bisque forearms
   10" - 13"....................$1,200 - 1,300
   15"............................$1,400 - 1,500
   18" - 21"....................$2,200 - 2,500
Wunderkind, set includes doll body,
four interchangeable heads, some with
extra apparel
With heads 174, 178, 184, and 185
   11"............................$9,000 - 9,500
With heads, 171, 179, 182, and 183
   14½" $12,650
Too few in database for reliable range
Celluloid Shoulder-Head doll,
sleep eyes, kid body, wigged
Molds 200, 201
   16" - 20" ....$225 - 350

KEWPIES

1913 on, designed by Rose O'Neill. Manufactured by Borgfeldt, later Joseph Kallus,
and then Jesco in 1984, and various companies with special license, as well as unlicensed companies. They were made of all
bisque, celluloid, cloth, composition,
rubber, vinyl, zylonite and other materials.
Kewpie figurines (action Kewpies) have
mold numbers 4843 through 4883.
Kewpies are also marked with a round
paper sticker on back that reads: "KEW-
PIES DES. PAT. III, R. 1913; Germany;
REG. US. PAT. OFF." On the front is a
heart-shaped sticker that reads: "KEW-
PIE//REG. US.// PAT. OFF." May also
be incised on the soles of the feet:
"O'Neill." Dolls listed are in good condition, add more for label, accessories, original box or exceptional doll.
All Bisque
Immobiles, standing, legs together,
immobile, no joints, blue wings,
molded and painted hair, painted
side-glancing eyes
   2" -3½ " ....$100 - 125
   4" - 5"..............................$125 - 160
   6"......................................$200 - 225
Jointed shoulders
   2" - 2½"..............................$75 - 100
   3" - 4"..............................$125 - 150
   5" -6"..............................$150 - 200
   7" - 8" ....$250 - 300
   10" - 12" ....$400 - 600
Jointed hips and shoulders
   4"......................................$600 - 650
   5" - 6" ....$700 - 850
   7" - 8" ....$950 - 1,050
   10" ....$1,150 - 1,250
   12½" ....$1,300 - 1,350
*Jointed shoulders with any article of
molded clothing*
   2½" - 4½" ....$400 - 700
   5" - 6" ....$800 - 900
   8" ....$1,000 - 1,100

Kewpies

5" standing Kewpie & 2" action Kewpie holding a rose, all bisque: $150 (5") & $100 (2"). **Photo courtesy of Richard Withington, Inc.**

With Mary Jane shoes
4½" ....$175 - 200
6½" ....$325 - 400
Bisque Action Figures
Arms folded
6"......................................$525 - 600
Aviator
8½" ....$775 - 850
Back, laying down, kicking one foot
4"......................................$250 - 300
Basket and ladybug, Kewpie seated
4"..............................$1,400 - 1,700
"Blunderboo," Kewpie falling down
4½" ....$400 - 425
Bottle, green beverage, Kewpie standing, kicking out
2½" ....$525 - 575
Bottle stopper
2".......................................$100 - 150
Box, heart shaped, with Kewpie kicker atop
4"......................................$650 - 750
Bride and Groom
3½" ....$300 - 350
5"......................................$400 - 450
Boutonnière
1½" ....$85 - 110
2" ....$110 - 130
Bunny, in lap of seated Kewpie
2"......................................$425 - 475

Candy container
4"......................................$400 - 500
Carpenter, wearing tool apron
8½" ....$975 - 1,100
Cat, on lap of seated Kewpie
3" - 3½" ....$525 - 575
Chick, with seated Kewpie
2"......................................$525 - 575
Christmas Ornament, molded bisque clip on back
2"......................................$500 - 550
Cowboy
10"....................................$700 - 800
Dog, with Red Cross Kewpie
4"......................................$250 - 300
Doodle Dog, alone
1½" ....$700 - 800
3"..............................$1,000 - 1,200
Doodle Dog, with Kewpie
2½" ....$1,000 - 1,500
Drum on brown stool, with Kewpie
3½" ....$2,000 - 2,200
Farmer
6½" ....$800 - 900
Flowers, Kewpie with bouquet in right hand
5"......................................$825 - 925
Gardener
4"......................................$300 - 350
Governor
2½" ....$325 - 375
3¼" ....$400 - 475
Guitar, standing Kewpie playing
3½" ....$300 - 350
Hatbox (turquoise), held by seated Kewpie
3"..............................$1,500 - 1,600
Hottentot, black Kewpie
3½" ....$425 - 500
5"......................................$625 - 675
9"......................................$925 - 975
Huggers
2½" ....$100 - 125
3½" ....$150 - 275
4½" ....$300 - 325
Inkwell, with writer Kewpie
4½" ....$475 - 525

Kewpies

Jack-O-Lantern between legs of
Kewpie
2".....................................$450 - 500
Jester, wearing white hat
4½" ....$500 - 575
Kneeling
4"....................................$475 - 550
Lying on Back
4"long ....$325 - 375
Lying on Tummy
3¼"long ....$275 - 325
Mailing label in hand
2¼" ....$550 - 650
Mandolin, green basket and seated
Kewpie
2"....................................$300 - 350
Mandolin, with Kewpie on place-card
holder
23/4" long...................... $150 - 200
Mayor, seated Kewpie in green wicker
chair
4"....................................$375 - 425
Minister
5"....................................$200 - 250
Policeman
4½" $1,100
Reader Kewpie seated with book
2"....................................$200 - 250
3½" ....$275 - 325
4" ....$450 - 500
2¾" long on place-card
holder ....$150 - 175
Reader Kewpie in green armchair,
seated with book
51/2" $1,350
Rose in hand, Kewpie on place card holder
2"....................................$60 - 75
Salt Shaker
2"....................................$150 - 175
Seated on bench, feeding bottle to
doodledog
3½" long ....sold at auction
for $1,700
Sailor
5"....................................$2,900
Soldier, Confederate
4"....................................$225 - 250

Soldier, Confederate, lying on stomach
aiming rifle
3"....................................$450 - 500
Soldier in Prussian helmet
5½" ....$800 - 850
Soldier in Prussian helmet with rifle
and saber
3¾" ....$900 - 1,000
Soldier lying on stomach aiming rifle
3"....................................$400 - 450
Soldier vase, vase looks like tree
6½" .... $850 -800
Soldier
2¾" ....$450 - 500
4½" ....$500 - 550
Stomach, Kewpie laying flat, arms and
legs out
4" ....$375 - 450
Sweeper with dust bin by leg
3½" - 4"...........................$300 - 400
Teddy Bear held in arm of Kewpie
3¾" ....$625 - 650
Thinker
4" - 5" ....$200 - 300
6"....................................$300 - 350
Traveler with dog and umbrella
3½" ....$1,300 - 1,550
Traveler with umbrella and bag
4"....................................$350 - 400
5"....................................$500 - 550
Vase Kewpie Gardener standing to side
of vase
6½" ....$900 - 1,000

3" Kewpie
inkwell, all
bisque:
$450.
**Photo
courtesy of
Morphy
Auctions.**

Kewpies

11" Kuddle Kewpie pair, R. Krueger, cloth mask face: pair $650. **Photo courtesy of Richard Withington, Inc.**

13" Kewpie, composition: $225. **Photo courtesy of McMasters Harris Apple Tree Doll Auctions.**

Vase, with huggers
    3¾" ....$575 - 650
Writer, seated Kewpie with pen in hand
    2"......................................$425 - 475
    4"......................................$500 - 550
Writer, seated Kewpie with pen in hand on bisque tray with note written on it
    2½" x 4½".......................$175 - 225
Carnival chalk, Kewpie with jointed shoulders
    13"....................................$75 - 125
Bisque socket head, made by Kestner, glass eyes, composition body
    12"...........................$1,600 - 2,000
Bisque flange-neck head, painted eyes, cloth body, bisque hands
    11" ....sold at auction for $3,500
Bisque shoulder head, cloth body
Painted eyes
    7" ....$875 - 1,000
Glass eyes
    12".............................$2,500 - 2,800
Celluloid
Bride and Groom
    4"..$15 - 40
Jointed arms, heart label on chest
    5"...$80 - 100

    8" ....$165 - 185
    12".....................................$275 - 325
China
Perfume holder, one-piece with opening at back of head
    4½" ....$550 - 1,100
Salt shaker
    1¼" ....$85 - 165
Hatpin holder, Blue Jasperware with Kewpie figures
    4½" ....$225 - 300
Dishes
Service for 4............................$850 - 900
German jasperware creamer .... $70 - 80
German jasperware hatpin holder,
    4½" ....$275 - 300
Cloth
Richard Krueger Kuddle Kewpie, silk-screened face, stockinette or sateen body, tagged
    8" - 10" ....$250 - 300
    13" - 14"...........................$325 - 375
    18" - 23"...........................$575 - 650
Plush, stockinette face, tagged
    8"....................................$195 - 225
Composition, made by Cameo Doll Co., Mutual Doll Co., and

Rex Doll Co.

Hottentot, all composition, heart decal on chest, jointed arms, red wings, circa 1946

11" - 13".............................$400 - 450

All composition, jointed body, blue wings

8"......................................$125 - 150

11" - 13".............................$145 - 225

Composition head, cloth body, flange neck, composition forearms, tagged floral dress

11"....................................$250 - 300

Talcum container

One-piece composition talcum shaker, heart label on chest

11"....................................$200 - 225

Hard Plastic

Original box, 1950s, Kewpie design

8½" ....$140 - 210

Sleep eyes, five-piece body, starfish hands

14"....................................$300 - 350

Metal

Figurine, cast steel on square base, excellent condition

5½" ....$40 - 55

Sitting on a stamp box

4"......................................$300 - 400

Soap

Kewpie soap figure with cotton batting, colored label with rhyme, marked: "R.O. Wilson, 1917"

4" ....$90 - 110

Vinyl

Knickerbocker, late 1950s on, vinyl mask face, plush body

8" - 12" seated ....$40 - 60

Bunny Kuddles, Kewpie mask-faced bunny wearing vinyl hat

11" seated ....$30 - 35

Cameo Dolls, 1960s, in very good condition with original clothing

10" - 12"..............................$35 - 45

14" - 16"..............................$60 - 70

27" ....$100 - 125

Jesco Dolls, 1980s, mint, all-original condition

8"..$20 - 35

12"......................................$40 - 50

18"......................................$60 - 70

24" - 27"..............................$75 - 100

R. John Wright, 1999 on, molded felt, jointed shoulders, values listed are for secondary-market dolls, dolls also available at retail

6"......................................$400 - 500

KLEY & HAHN

1902 - 1930s, Ohrdruf, Thüringia, Germany. Bisque heads, jointed composition or leather bodies, composition- and celluloid-headed dolls. Assembler and exporter; bought heads from Bähr & Pröschild, Kestner (Walkure), Hertel Schwab & Co, and RheinischeGummi. Dolls listed are in good condition, appropriately dressed.

Character Baby, bisque socket head, bent-limb composition body, molds such as 133, 135, 138, 158, 160, 161, 167, 176, 525, 571, 680 and others

11" - 13" ....$500 -550

14" mold 525 baby, Kley & Hahn, bisque: $550. **Photo courtesy of Richard Withington, Inc.**

191

Kley & Hahn

28" Walkure mold, Kley & Hahn, bisque: $700.
Photo courtesy of Richard Withington, Inc.

16" - 18"............................$550 - 650
20" - 22" ....$750 - 850
24" - 26"........................$1,000 - 1,100
Toddler body
14" - 16".......................$1,000 - 1,300
18" - 21".......................$1,500 - 1,800
26" ....$2,000 - 2,100
Mold 567 (made by Bähr & Pröschild)
character multi-face, laughing face, glass
eyes, open mouth, crying face, painted
eyes, open/closed mouth
11"...............................$1,000 - 1,400
15"...............................$1,950 - 2,100
17"...............................$2,200 - 2,400
19"...............................$2,400 - 2,600
Child, 1920, dolly face, sleep eyes,
open mouth, molds 250, 282 or
Walkure
12" - 13" ....$200 - 300
16" - 18"............................$400 - 500
22" - 24" ....$600 - 700
28" - 30" ....$700 - 800
33" - 34" ....$800 - 900
Mold 325, open mouth, marked:
"Dollar Princess"
18" - 20" ....$425 - 475

23" - 25" ....$400 - 450
Character Child, 1912, bisque socket
head, jointed composition body
Mold numbers 154, 166, 169
Closed mouth
14" - 16" ....$1,700 - 2,100
19" - 20" ....$2,400 - 2,700
27".............................$3,000 - 3,300
Open mouth
17" - 20".....................$1,000 - 1,200
Painted-eye character, molds 520, 525,
526, 531
14" - 16".....................$2,600 - 3,000
17" - 19".....................$3,200 - 3,800
20 - 23" ....$4,000 - 4,500
Mold 336, intaglio eyes, open/closed
mouth,
11" - 16".....................$4,000 - 5,000
Mold 546, 549, circa 1912, character face
12" - 14"....................$3,500 - 4,000
15" - 16" ....$4,500 - 5,000
18" - 21"....................$5,500 - 6,000
19" mold 549.......................sold at
auction for $11,500
Mold 554, 568, circa 1912, character face
21" $1,400
Too few in database for reliable range
Mold 567 two-faced character baby,
protruding ears, smiling, scowling
10" ....$800 - 1,000

C.F. KLING & COMPANY

1834 - 1940s, Ohrdruf, Thüringia, Germany.
Porcelain factory began making doll
heads in 1879, made china, bisque and
all-bisque dolls and snow babies. Often
mold number marks are followed by size
number. Dolls listed are in good condition, appropriately dressed; allow more
for exceptional doll with elaborate molded hair or bodice.
Bisque Shoulder Head, 1880 on
Painted eyes, molded hair, cloth or kid
body, molds such as 123, 124, 131, 167,
178, 182, 186, 189 and others
7" - 8"................................$25 - 275

18" Kling, bisque, shoulder head: $625. **Photo courtesy of Morphy Auctions.**

12" - 14"............................$300 - 400
15" - 16"............................$475 - 550
18" - 20" ....$625 - 700
23" - 25" ....$800 - 900
Glass eyes, molded hair, cloth or kid body, molds such as 190, 203, 204, 214, 217, 247, 254 and others
15" - 16"............................$600 - 700
22" - 23" ....$850 - 950
Bisque Lady, molded bodices, fancy hair, molds such as 135,144, 170 and others
15" - 17" ....$900 - 1,000
19" - 21".....................$1,200 - 1,600
China Shoulder Head, 1880 on, molded hair, painted eyes, closed mouth, molds such as 131, 188, 189, 202, 220, 285 and others
13" - 15" ....$200 - 250
18" - 20" ....$350 - 450
24" - 25" ....$550 - 650
Mold 188, glass eyes
18" - 20" ....$450 - 500
Bisque Socket Head, 1900 on, sleep eyes, open mouth,jointed body, molds such as 182, 370, 372, 373, 377

13" - 15" ....$225 - 350
17" - 22"............................$375 - 500
All-Bisque: See All-Bisque section.

KLUMPE

1952 - 1970s, Barcelona, Spain. Caricature figures made of felt over wire armature with painted mask faces. Figures represent professionals, hobbyists, Spanish dancers, historical characters and contemporary males and females performing a wide variety of tasks. Of the 200 or more different figures, the most common are Spanish dancers, bull fighters and doctors. Some Klumpes were imported by Effanbee in the early 1950s. Originally the figures had two sewn-on identifying cardboard tags. Dolls listed are in good condition.
Average figure
10½" ....$75 - 150
Elaborate figure, with tags & accessories
10½" ....$150 - 225

8" Klumpe, matador, cloth: $75. **Photo courtesy of Cybermogul Dolls.**

KNICKERBOCKER DOLL & TOY COMPANY

1927 - 1980s, New York, New York. Made dolls of cloth, composition, hard plastic and vinyl.

Cloth

Clown
17" ....$18 - 25

Disney characters
Donald Duck, Mickey Mouse, etc.,
all cloth
10½" - 12" ....$675 - 800
Little Lulu
12"....................................$225 - 250
Matador from Ferdinand the Bull
picture book, all cloth
23" ....sold at online auction for $1,250
Mickey Mouse, circa 1930s, oilcloth eyes
10" - 12".....................$1,500 - 2,000
Cowboy Mickey
12" - 17".....................$2,500 - 3,000
Pinocchio, cloth and plush
13"....................................$200 - 250
Seven Dwarfs, 1939 on, mask face,
mohair beard, up-turned toes
14"...........................each $125 - 175
Snow White, all cloth, mask face
16"....................................$300 - 325

Flintstones
6" ....$8 - 10
6½" ....$12 - 16

12" Little Lulu, Knickerbocker, cloth mask face: $250.
Photo courtesy of Morphy Auctions.

Holly Hobbie, 1970s, cloth, later vinyl
Cloth
7" - 9"..................................$15 - 20
14" - 16"..............................$25 - 35
26" - 28" ....$40 - 45
Vinyl
6" .... $8 - 10
11" ....$15 - 20
Baby Holly Hobbie, vinyl and cloth
15" ....$30 - 35
Levi's Big E Jeans dolls, 1973
10" - 16"..............................$30 - 35
Little Orphan Annie, 1977
16" ....$25 - 30

Composition

Blondie comic-strip characters,
composition, painted features, hair
Alexander Bumstead, molded hair
9"......................................$325 - 375
Blondie Bumstead, mohair wig
11"....................................$425 - 500
Dagwood Bumstead, molded hair
14"....................................$425 - 500
Child, 1938 on, mohair wig, sleep eyes
15"....................................$220 - 265
18"....................................$275 - 300
Disney, 1930s - 1940s
Mickey Mouse, composition, cloth body
18" ....$900 - 1,100
Jiminy Cricket, all composition
10"....................................$400 - 450
Pinocchio, all composition
14" - 17"..........................$225 - 350
Seven Dwarfs, 1939 on
9" ....each $200 - 250
Sleeping Beauty, 1939 on, bent right arm
15"....................................$325 - 375
18"....................................$400 - 450
Snow White, 1937 on, all composition,
bent right arm, black wig
15"....................................$395 - 425
20"....................................$450 - 500
Molded hair and ribbon, marked:
"WALT DISNEY//1937//KNICKER-
BOCKER"
13"....................................$200 - 225
15"....................................$225 - 275

Knickerbocker Doll & Toy Company

9" seven dwarfs,
Knickerbocker,
composition:
set $2,000.
**Photo courtesy of
Sweetbriar Auctions.**

Plastic and Vinyl Mask Face Dolls,
1950s - 1960s
Plush Body
Pinocchio
13"...$40 - 60
Baby Santa Claus, 1955 on
7" seated ....$30 - 35
Sleepy Head
23"...$30 - 35
Cloth Body
Knick the Clown
19"...$35 - 45
Lovely Lori
15"...$65 - 75
Vinyl head, cloth body
Soupy Sales
13"...$50 - 55
Quickdraw MacGraw
16 1/2 "...............................$40 - 55
Winnie Witch
13"...$45 - 50
Hard Plastic and Vinyl
Betsy Clark, 1974, all vinyl
6"..$20 - 25
Bozo Clown
14" ....$18 - 25
17" - 24"...............................$40 - 60
28" - 30" ....$60 - 80
Cinderella, two faces, one sad, one with tiara
16" ....$15 - 20
Flintstones
17"...$30 - 35

Kewpies: See Kewpies section.
Little House on the Prairie, 1978
12"..$20 - 25
Little Orphan Annie comic-strip
characters, 1982
Little Orphan Annie, vinyl
6" ....$14 - 20
11"..$20 - 25
Daddy Warbucks
7"..$9 - 12
Punjab
7" ....$9 - 12
Miss Hannigan
7"..$8 - 12
Molly
5½" ....$8 - 12
Rattle Dolls, hard plastic, jointed
shoulders, painted side-glancing eyes
6"..$15 - 20
Snoopy or Belle, Charles Schultz
character, 1965
8"...$20 - 22
Outfits MOC ....$10 - 30
Two-faced dolls, 1960s, vinyl face masks,
one crying, one smiling
12" ....$14 - 18
Dolly Pops, 1979 on, molded vinyl,
synthetic hair, molded changeable
vinyl clothing
2½" ....$15 - 20
Dolly Pops Poptown playset
1982 ....$40 - 50

GEBRÜDER KNOCH

1887 - 1919, Neustadt, Thüringia, Germany. Porcelain factory that made bisque doll heads with cloth or kid bodies.

Shoulder Head

Dolly face

9" - 15" ....$125 - 195

20" - 22" ....$400 - 500

Mold 203, 205, circa 1910

Mold 203, character face, painted eyes, closed mouth, stuffed cloth body

Mold 205, character face, intaglio eyes, open/closed mouth, molded tongue, marked: "GKN"

12" - 13" ....$500 - 600

14" - 15" ....$675 - 725

Too few in database for reliable range

Socket Head

Mold 179, 181, 190, 192, 193, 201, circa 1900, mold 201 also came as black, dolly face, glass eyes, open mouth, ball-jointed composition body

7" - 8" five-piece body ....$100 - 150

10" - 13" ....$175 - 250

18" - 25" ....$400 - 600

Mold 204, 205, circa 1910, character face

15" ....$865 - 1,150

Mold 216, circa 1912, solid dome, intaglio eyes, laughing, open/closed mouth, marked: "GKN"

11" - 13" ....$300 - 350

Too few in database for reliable range

Mold 229: See All-Bisque section.

Mold 230, circa 1912, molded bonnet, character shoulder head, painted eyes, open/closed mouth laughing,

mold 232, circa 1912, molded bonnet, character shoulder head, laughing

13" ....$675 - 900

15" ....$1,200 - 1,600

KÖNIG & WERNICKE GMBH

1912 - 1930s, Waltershausen, Germany. Doll factory made bisque and celluloid dolls with composition bodies, later dolls with hard-rubber heads. Bought bisque heads from Bähr & Pröschild, Hertel & Schwab and Armand Marseille. Made "My Playmate" for Borgfeldt. Dolls listed are in good condition, appropriately dressed.

Bisque Baby

Mold 98, 99, circa 1910, *Mold 1070,* circa 1915, made by Hertel Schwab & Co., character, socket head, sleep eyes, open mouth, teeth, tremble tongue, wigged, composition bent-leg baby body, marked: "made in Germany"

9" - 12" ....$250 - 300

15" - 16" ....$350 - 450

18" - 22" ....$550 - 700

9" dolly face, Gebrüder Knoch, bisque: $150.
Photo courtesy of Emmie's Antique Doll Castle.

14" mold 1070, König & Wernicke, bisque: $300.
Photo courtesy of Minton's Doll and Curiosity Shop.

24" - 27"............................$800 - 900
Toddler
11" -13" ....$850 - 900
15" - 17" ....$900 - 1,000
19" - 20" ....$1,100 - 1,500
Child, socket head, composition body
Dolly face
15" .... $375 - 425
26" - 29" ....$700 - 800
36"....................................$800 - 900
Mold 1070, character child, sleep eyes
15" ....$1,100 - 1,300
20"..............................$1,700 - 1,900
30" ....$2,500 - 2,600
Painted bisque child, regional dress
18" ....$125 - 175
Composition Child, composition
head, five-piece or fully jointed
body,sleep eyes, add more for flirty
eyes, open mouth
14"..................................$225 - 300
16"..................................$350 - 450
Celluloid Child, mold 777, celluloid
socket head, glass eyes, wigged
13" - 15"...........................$125 - 150
17" - 21" ....$175 - 200

RICHARD KRUEGER
1907 - 1950s, New York City. Made cloth-
mask-faced dolls.
Child, 1930 on
Cloth body
10"......................................$55 - 65
12"......................................$65 - 95
16" ....$115 - 125
20"..................................$150 - 200
Oilcloth body
10"......................................$45 - 60
14" - 16" ....$75 - 90
Walt Disney and other characters
Dwarf, plush beard
12½" ....$125 - 175
Snow White
18"..................................$300 - 350
Three Little Pigs
7" ....each $60 - 75

18" & 12½" Snow White & the Seven Dwarfs,
Krueger, cloth mask face: set $1,800. **Photo
courtesy of McMasters Harris Apple Tree
Doll Auctions.**

Pinocchio
16"....................................$500 - 600
Kuddle Kewpie: See Kewpies section.
Scootles, 1935, designed by Rose
O'Neill, yarn hair
10"....................................$750 - 800
18"....................................$825 - 875

KÄTHE KRUSE
1910 to present, Prussia, after W.W.II,
Bavaria, Germany. Made cloth dolls with
molded stockinette heads and waterproof
muslin bodies; heads, hair and hands are
oil painted. Early dolls are stuffed with
deer hair. Early thumbs are part of the
hand; after 1914 they are attached separately, later they're again part of the
hand. Marked on the bottom of the left
foot with number and name: "Käthe
Kruse," in black, red or purple ink. After
1929, most dolls had wigs, but some still
had painted hair. Later dolls have plastic
and vinyl heads. Original doll modeled
after bust sculpture "Fiamingo" by
Francois Duquesnois. Dolls listed are in
good condition, appropriately dressed;
allow significantly less for dirty or faded
examples.
Cloth
Doll I Series, 1910 - 1929, all cloth,
jointed shoulders, wide hips, painted

Käthe Kruse

18"
Hampelchen,
Käthe Kruse,
cloth: $3,500.
**Photo courtesy
of Richard
Withington,
Inc.**

eyes and hair, three vertical seams in
back of head, marked on left foot
16".............................$6,000 - 6,500
Ball-jointed knees, 1911 variant
produced by Kämmer& Reinhardt
17"..........................$12,000 - 14,000
Later model, 1929 on, slim hips
17".............................$4,000 - 5,500
Doll IH Series, wigged version, 1930 on
17".............................$3,200 - 3,500
Bambino, a doll for a doll,
circa 1915 - 1925
8" $500
Too few in database for reliable range
Doll II Series, Schlenkerchen, circa
1922 - 1936, smiling baby, open/closed
mouth, stockinette-covered body and
limbs, one-seam head
13"..............................$8,500 - 9,500
Doll V, VI, Sandbabies Series, 1920s on,
Traumerchen (closed eyes) and Du Mein
(open eyes), cloth, weighted with sand
or unweighted, with or without belly
buttons, in 19⅝" and 23⅝" sizes,
one- or three-seam heads or cloth over
cardboard,painted hair, later heads
were made in the 1930s from a heavy
composition called magnesit
19⅝" - 23½".............$6,000 - 7,000
Magnesit head, circa 1930s on
20"..............................$1,500 - 1,600

Doll VII Series, circa 1927 - 1952,
two versions
Smaller 14" Du Mein open-eye baby,
painted hair or wigged, three-seam head,
wide hips, sewn-on thumbs, 1927 - 1930
14".............................$3,500 - 4,000
Doll I version, wide hips, separately
sewn-on thumbs, painted hair or wigged,
after 1930 - 1950s slimmer
hips, painted hair, thumbs formed
with hand
14".............................$2,200 - 2,500
Doll VIII Series
Deutsche Kind, The German Child,
1929 on, modeled after Kruse's son,
Friedebald, hollow head, swivels, one
vertical seam in back of head, wigged,
disk-jointed legs, later made in plastic
during the 1950s
20" ....$2,500 - 3,000
Doll IX Series
The Little German Child, 1929 on,
wigged, one-seam head, smaller version
of Doll VIII
14".............................$1,400 - 1,600
Doll X Series, 1935 on, smaller Doll I
with one-seam head that turns
14".............................$2,500 - 2,800
Doll XII Series, 1930s, Hampelchen with
loose legs, three vertical seams on back
of head, painted hair, button and band
on back to make legs stand. The 14"

14" Käthe
Kruse, hard-
plastic head:
$150.
**Photo
courtesy of
Alderfer
Auction
Company,
Inc.**

variation has head of Doll I; the 16"
variation also has the head of Doll I,
and is known after 1940s as
Hempelschatz, Doll XIIB

    14".............................$2,500 - 3,500
    18".............................$4,000 - 5,000

Hard Plastic, 1948 - 1975, celluloid and other synthetics
US Zone mark

    14" - 19"...........................$600 - 900

Turtle Mark Dolls, 1955 - 1961,
synthetic bodies

    14".....................................$225 - 275
    16".....................................$300 - 350
    18".....................................$400 - 450

1975 to present, marked with size
number in centimeters and letter for
style as follows: "B" for baby, "H" for
hair, "G" for painted hair

    10".....................................$100 - 125
    13" - 15"...........................$125 - 175
    17" - 19"...........................$100 - 225

GEBRÜDER KUHNLENZ

1884 - 1935, Kronach, Bavaria, Germany.
Porcelain factory made dolls, doll heads,
movable children and swimmers. Butler
Bros. and Marshall Field distributed
their dolls.

Closed-Mouth Child
Mold 22, bisque solid-dome socket head,
glass eyes, closed mouth, pierced ears,
wig, wood-and-composition jointed body

    10" - 12"...........................$525 - 575

Mold 28, 31, 32, 39, circa 1890, bisque
socket head, glass eyes, closed mouth,
pierced ears, wig, wood-and-composition
jointed body

    8" - 10" ....$800 - 1,000
    15" - 16"......................$1,500 - 1,700
    21" - 23" ....$2,200 - 2,500

Mold 34, Bru type, paperweight eyes,
closed mouth, pierced ears, composition
jointed body

    12½" - 15" ....$2,900 - 4,000

15" Gebrüder
Kuhnlenz,
solid-dome
head: $650.
**Photo courtesy of
Sweetbriar
Auctions.**

    18" - 20" ....$4,500 - 6,300

Mold 38, solid-dome turned shoulder
head, closed mouth, pierced ears,
kid body

    12" - 15" ....$450 - 525
    17" - 20"...........................$700 - 800

Open-Mouth Child
Mold 41, 44, socket head, glass eyes,
open mouth, composition body

    6" - 8"...............................$175 - 200
    9" - 10" ....$275 - 325
    15" - 19" ....$425 - 500
    24" - 26" ....$650 - 750
    30" - 31" ....$900 - 1,000

Mold 165, circa 1900, socket head,
sleep eyes, open mouth, teeth

    16" - 18".........................$200 - 275
    22" - 24" ....$350 - 450
    30" - 33" ....$550 - 700

Mold 47, 61, 170, shoulder head

    14" - 16" ....$175 - 250
    18" - 20" ....$225 - 300

Character Dolls
Mold 205, shoulder head, intaglio
eyes, open/closed mouth, molded
painted hair

    20"....................................$500 - 550

No mold #, glass eyes, open/closed
laughing mouth

    15"..............................$1,000 - 1,200

Small Dolls, mold 44, socket head,

Gebrüder Kuhnlenz

glass eyes, open mouth, five-piece composition body, marked: "Gbr. K" in sunburst

7" - 8" ....$250 - 325

All Bisque, swivel neck, molds 31, 41, 44, 56, others, glass eyes

5" - 7" ....$650 - 1,000

A. LANTERNIER & CIE.

1915 - 1924, Limoges, France. Porcelain factory made dolls and heads. Lady dolls were dressed in French provincial costumes, bodies by Ortyz; dolls were produced for Association to Aid War Widows.

Adult, circa 1915

Marked: "Caprice," "Lorraine," "Favorite" bisque socket head, open/closed mouth with teeth, composition adult body

13" ....$400 - 500

16" - 18" ....$600 - 700

22" ....$800 - 900

Painted eyes

12½" ....$900 - 1,100

Child, dolly face bisque socket head, open mouth with teeth, wig, compo-

28" Lanternier, bisque, open mouth: $1,000.
Photo courtesy of Richard Withington, Inc.

sition jointed body, no mold name or marked: "Cherie," "Favorite," "La Georgienne"

12" - 14" ....$300 - 375

16" - 20" ....$425 - 500

22" - 24" ....$550 - 600

25" - 26" ....$700 - 800

Character Child, marked: "Toto"

15" - 18" ....$800 - 1,000

LAWTON DOLL COMPANY

1979 to present, Turlock, California. Founded by Wendy Lawton. Porcelain head dolls. Dolls listed are MIB; allow less for dolls missing accessories or with flaws.

Connoisseur Collections

Best Friends

Bianca & Bratwurst, 2003 ....$250 - 300

Gigi & Gigot, 2003 ....$350 - 375

Cherished Customs

The Blessing, 1990

13½" ....$165 - 195

Childhood Classics

Bobbsey Twins, 1991 ......each $135 - 175

Hans Brinker, 1985

14" ....$300 - 350

Heidi, 1984

14" ....$150 - 200

Marcella & Raggedy Ann, 1988

....$350 - 400

Pollyanna, 1986

14" ....$350 - 400

Childhood Classics II

Peter & the Wolf, 1992 ....$100 - 125

Christmas Collection

Christmas Angel, 1990 ....$100 - 150

Yuletide Carole, 1991 ....$150 - 200

Victorian Christmas, 1997 ....$175 - 200

Music of Christmas, 2001 ......$215 - 265

Childhood Classics

Nutcracker, 1995

13" ....$90 - 125

Classic Playthings II

Henrietta and her Hilda, 1996

16" ....$125 - 150
Children's Literature
Mirette, LE 750, 1998, porcelain
and wood
14" ....$250 - 300
Daughters of Faith
Ransom's Mark, 2003 ....$350 - 400
Hallelujah Lass, 2004 ....$350 - 400
Gentle Puruits, thirteen-piece jointed
wooden body
Eugenia's Literary Salon - 1995
16" ....$275 - 350
Library Collection
Secret Garden, 2000
9" ....$450 - 500
Alice in Wonderland, 2002
9" ....$425 - 450
Rebecca of Sunnybrook Farm, 2004
9" ....$250 - 300
Gallery Editions
Storybook Collection
Polly Put the Kettle on, cloth body,
porcelain hands and lower legs
14" ....$25 - 30
Toy's N' Treasures Collection
Sarah's Sock Monkey, cloth body,
porcelain hands and lower legs
12" ....$55 - 65
Ashton Drake Collection
Lawton's Nursery Rhymes
Little Bo Peep, Miss Muffet, Mary Mary,
Mary Had A little Lamb ....$25 - 35
Little Women Collection,
1994 ....each $35 - 50
Walt Disney Collection
Main Street, 1989 (250) ....$125 - 175
Liberty Square, 1990 (250) ......$200 - 300
Tish, 1991 (250) ....$250 - 350
Melissa & Her Mickey,
1994 (100) ....$450 - 600
Passionate Pusuits
The Bookworm, 2002
9" ....$350 - 375
Guild Doll Collection
Ba Ba Black Sheep, 1989, cloth body,
porcelain hands and lower legs
14" ....$200 - 300

16" Eugenia, Gentle Pursuits Collection,
Wendy Lawton, bisque: $275. **Photo courtesy
of Richard Withington, Inc.**

Lavender Blue, 1990 ....$300 - 400
Travel Doll, 1997, with trunk and
accessories ....$900 - 1,000
Haute Couture, 2002
14" ....$275 - 300
Bon Voyage, 2003 ....$350 - 400
Exclusive Editions Collection
Convention/Event dolls
1st WL Convention,
Lotta Crabtree, 1992 ....$1,300
Too few in database for a reliable range
Beatrice Louise, UFDC,
1998 Luncheon ....$890 - 975
Josephine, UFDC Regional, 1995
12" ....$700 - 750
Katrena, UFDC Convention, 2002
9½" ....$60 - 70
Store Specials
Little Colonel, exclusive for Dolly Dears,
Birmingham, Alabama ....$375 - 425

LEATHER

Leather was an available resource for
Native Americans to use for making doll
heads, bodies or entire dolls. It was also
used by American dollmakers such as
Darrow, and by French and Moroccan

10" Todhunter, elf, leather: $120.
Photo courtesy of The Museum Doll Shop.

dollmakers, as well as others. Some examples of Gussie Decker's dolls were advertised as "impossible for child to hurt itself," and leather was fine for teething babies.

Darrow, American, molded rawhide. These dolls are almost always found with very little original paint remaining, value listed reflects this condition
12"....................................$250 - 300
18" - 22" ....$400 - 450
22" in exceptional
condition......sold at auction for $6,500
French all-leather baby, molded head, jointed body, painted eyes
4" - 4½".......................$2,300 - 2,500
French boudoir-type doll, 1960s, appliqued mouth, fur eye lashes
23"...$75 - 85
Moroccan leather dolls, 1900 - 1940s, souvenir-type dolls depicting regional characters
9" - 11"...............................$25 - 45
Native American Dolls
Plains tribes, various, 1900 on
5" - 8" ....$130 - 225

13" - 15" ....$400 - 650
23".....................................$700 - 850
Eskimo, circa 1940
10"..$110
12" $125
Todhunter, M. 1926 on, England, leather-over-molded-clay face, wire-armature body wrapped with suede
10" - 12"..........................$120 - 150

LENCI

1919 - 2003, Turino, Italy. Lenci was the trademark and name of firm started by Enrico and Elena di Scavini that made felt dolls with pressed faces, also made composition-headed dolls, wooden dolls, porcelain figurines and dolls. Early Lenci dolls have tiny metal buttons and hang tags that read: "Lenci//Torino//Made in Italy." Ribbon strips marked "Lenci//Made in Italy" are found in the clothes circa 1925 - 1950. Some, but not all dolls, are marked "Lenci" in purple or black ink on the sole of the foot. Some with original paper tags may be marked with a model number in pencil. Dolls have felt swivel heads, oil-painted features, often side-glancing eyes, jointed shoulders and hips, third and fourth fingers are often sewn together, sewn-on double felt ears, often dressed in felt and organdy original clothes, excellent condition. May have scalloped socks.

The most sought after are the well-constructed early dolls from the 1920s and early 1930s, when Elena Scavini had control of the design. They were more elaborate with fanciful, well-made accessories: animals of wood or felt, baskets, felt vegetables, purses or bouquets of felt flowers. Dolls made during this era have eye shadow, dots in corner of eyes, two-tone lips with lower lip highlighted and, depending on condition, will command higher prices.

In 1936 the Garella Brothers became

Lenci

the sole owners of the company. The later dolls of the 1940s and 1950s have hard cardboard-like felt faces, with less intricate details: less elaborate appliqués, fewer accessories. Other fabrics were used, such as taffeta, cotton and rayon, all showing a decline in quality, and should not be priced as earlier dolls. The later dolls may have fabric-covered cardboard torsos. Model numbers changed over the years, so an early model number could later became another letter or number.

Lenci characteristics include double-layer ears and scalloped cotton socks. Early dolls may have rooted mohair wigs; 1930s dolls may have "frizzed" played-with wigs. Dolls listed are in clean condition and wearing original clothing. Soiled, faded examples will bring significantly less. Allow more for tags, boxes or accessories. Exceptional dolls and rare examples may bring even more.

Baby
13" - 15"......................$1,700 - 1,900
18" - 22" ....$2,700 - 3,000
1930s, Bambino, felt-over-metal baby
16" ....$5,000 - 6,500
Too few in database for a reliable range
Child
1920s - 1930s, softer face, more elaborate costume, face model numbers 300, 109, 149, 159, 110, 111
12" - 14".....................$1,000 - 1,200
16" - 22" ....$1,500 - 2,200
Model 1500, scowling face
17" - 19".....................$2,200 - 2,700
Model 400
14" - 16"......................$2,200 - 2,400
Model 500
21"............................$1,600 - 1,800
1940s - 1950s on, hard face, less intricate costume
13"...............................$300 - 400
15"...............................$400 - 500
17"...............................$500 - 600
Small Dolls

Mascottes and Miniatures, 9"
Regional costume ....$200 - 400
Child ....$300 - 475
More Elaborate Character......$600 - 900
Long-Limbed Lady Dolls, adult face, flapper or boudoir body, long slim limbs
17" - 20" ....$2,900 - 3,200
24" - 28" ....$3,500 - 4,500
32" ....$5,200 - 6,200
Rarities
Celebrities
Josephine Baker
18" ....sold at auction for $18,000
Jackie Coogan
21"..............................$3,500 - 3,600
Dorothy Gish (long-limbed lady)
31" ....sold at auction for $4,250
Mozart
11".............................$2,300 - 2,400
14".............................$3,000 - 3,200
Pastorelle
14" ....$2,900 - 3,100
Shirley Temple (series 950)
28" ....$3,400 - 3,500
Characters
Aladdin
14".............................$7,000 - 7,750

22" Lenci, baby, felt: $3,000. **Photo courtesy of Morphy Auctions.**

Lenci

13" 450 series, Lenci, felt, original box, circa 1926-1932: $1,200. **Photo courtesy of American Beauty Dolls.**

18" Lenci, lady, felt: $3,000. **Photo courtesy of Dollsantique.**

Aviator, girl with felt helmet
    18".............................$2,900 - 3,200
Becassine
    11" ....$925 - 975
    20" glass eyes ....$2,900 - 3,100
Benedetta
    19"............................$2,000 - 2,400
Black Child, wearing native garb
    15"............................$3,200 - 4,000
Cowboy
    14" ....$1,000 - 1,100
Cupid
    17"............................$4,900 - 5,200
Elf, circa 1926, black
    7" ....sold at auction for $3,000
Fascist Boy, rare
    14" ....$1,300 - 1,600
Flower Girl, circa 1930
    20".............................$1,200 - 1,400
Henriette
    26".............................$1,800 - 2,100
Indian
    17".............................$3,200 - 3,600
Laura
    16" ....$950 - 1,100

Pierrot
    21" ....$2,100 - 2,900
Pinocchio
    11," MIB $1,100
Smoker
    Painted eyes
    28" ....$2,500 - 3,000
    Glass eyes
    24"............................$4,000 - 4,200
Snake Charmer, seated, light-brown
felt
    17"..............................$8,000 - 8,500
Sport Series
    16" - 18" ....$3,000 - 6,000
Polo player
    16" - 17"....................$9,000 - 12,000
Val Gardena
    19"....................................$800 - 900
Winking Boy
    11" ....$950 - 1,050
Ethnic or Regional Costume
Asian, boy with lantern
    25" ....$4,500 - 5,000
Black Girl
    18"............................$2,500 - 3,000

Dutch boy

18".............................$4,750 - 6,000

Madame Butterfly, circa 1926

17".............................$3,000 - 3,200

25" ....$4,300 - 4,800

Marenka, Russian girl, circa 1930

19".............................$3,000 - 3,200

Sarda, Italian girl, circa 1930

19"...................................$800 - 900

Spanish girl, circa 1930

14".............................$1,200 - 1,400

19".............................$2,500 - 3,000

Tyrol boy or girl, circa 1935

18".............................$4,500 - 5,000

Eye Variations

Glass eyes

16".............................$1,400 - 1,600

22" ....$2,800 - 3,000

Flirty glass eyes

15"..............................$2,000 - 2,200

20" ....$2,600 - 2,800

Surprised eyes, widow, "O"- shaped eyes and mouth

19" - 20" ....$2,800 - 3,200

Modern, 1979 on

12" - 14"............................$90 - 150

21" - 26"...........................$100 - 300

Pinocchio, 1981

18" ....$100 - 120

Accessories

Lenci Dog ....$100 - 150

Purse ....$175 - 225

LENCI-TYPE

1920 - 1950. These were made by many English, French or Italian firms like Anili, Gre-Poir and Raynal from felt with painted features, mohair wigs. These must have original clothes and be in very good condition, tagged or unmarked. Usually Lenci-types have single-layer felt ears or no ears.

Child

Low quality

15" - 17" ....$145 - 165

High quality

11" - 15" ....$400 - 500

17" - 20"............................$500 - 575

7½" La Nicette, felt: $200. **Photo courtesy of Morphy Auctions.**

Regional costume, makers such as Alma, Vecchiotti and others

8" - 9" ....$45 - 75

11" - 15"............................$100 - 150

Smoker

16".....................................$350 - 400

Alma, elastic-strung heads

Child

11" ....$200 - 225

15" - 17".............................$400 - 600

Anili, founded by the daughter of Elena Di Scavini, molded-felt dolls

Child

16" - 21" ....$90 - 110

Gre-Poir, France, New York City, 1927 - 1930s, Eugenie Poir made felt or cloth mask face dolls, unmarked bodies, no ears, white socks with three stripes, hang tags

16" - 18"

Cloth face ....$375 - 425

Felt face ....$800 - 900

Messina-Vat, 1923 on, Turin, Italy

20" ....$300 - 375

10"& under Coronation set, Liberty of London, cloth: set $1,600.
Photo courtesy of Morphy Auctions.

LIBERTY OF LONDON

1906 - 1950s, London, England. Liberty of London was founded in 1873. In 1920 they registered the name "Liberty" for their line of needle-sculpted cloth art dolls made by the Peat sisters.

British Characters and Historical Figures, such as Shakespeare, John Bull, Queen Victoria and others

9" - 10"..............................$150 - 250

Beefeater ....$100 - 150

Coronation dolls

9" - 10" ....$200 - 250

Princess Elizabeth or Margaret

7" ....$300 - 350

A.G. LIMBACH

1772 - 1927 on, Limbach, Thüringia, Germany. This porcelain factory made bisque-headed dolls, china dolls, bathing dolls and all-bisque dolls beginning in 1872. Usually marked with three-leaf clover.

All Bisque

Child, small doll, molded hair or wigged, painted eyes, molded and painted shoes and socks, may be marked: "8661" and cloverleaf, allow more for exceptional dolls

3½" ....$55 - 65

4" - 5"................................$90 - 110

6" - 7"..............................$145 - 200

11" - 12"............................$325 - 400

Paper sticker reads: "Our Mary," all-bisque, glass sleep eyes, wigged

6" - 8"..............................$175 - 225

Baby, mold 8682, character face, bisque socket head, glass eyes, bent-leg baby body, wig, open/closed mouth, clover mark

8½" - 11" ....$275 - 350

Child

Bisque Socket Head, glass eyes, wig, open mouth, clover mark, may have name such as "Norma," "Rita," "Wally," above mold mark

18" - 20" ....$400 - 500

22" - 24"...........................$600 - 675

13" socket head, Limbach, bisque, closed mouth: $500.
Photo courtesy of Sweetbriar Auctions.

Bisque Shoulder Head, glass eyes, open mouth, kid body

10" - 11" ....$80 - 110

Lady

"The Irish Queen": See **Parian-type and Untinted Bisque** sections.

MAROTTES

1860 on and earlier. Doll's head on wooden or ivory stick, sometimes with whistle, when twirled some play music. Bisque head on stick made by various French and German companies.

Bisque

German head, open-mouth dolly-face mold, various German makers such as Armand Marseille, Gebrüder Heubach, etc.

9" - 14"...............................$425 - 650

16" - 18"...............................$700 - 900

Character mold

9" - 14" ....$900 - 1,500

French head

14" - 16" ....$1,000 - 1,400

Celluloid

11" - 15"...............................$200 - 350

ARMAND MARSEILLE

1884 - 1950s, Sonneberg, Köppelsdorf, Thüringia, Germany. One of the largest suppliers of bisque doll heads, circa 1900 - 1930, to such companies as Amberg, Arranbee, Bergmann, Borgfeldt, Butler Bros., Dressel, Montgomery Ward, Sears, Steiner, Wiegand, Louis Wolfe and others. Made some doll heads with no mold numbers, only names such as: Alma, Baby Betty, Baby Gloria, Baby Florence, Baby Phyllis, Beauty, Columbia, Duchess, Ellar, Florodora, Jubilee, Mabel, Majestic, Melitta, My Playmate, Nobbi Kid, Our Pet, Princess, Queen Louise, Rosebud, Superb, Sunshine and Tiny Tot. Some Indian dolls had no mold numbers. Often used Superb kid bodies with bisque hands. After WWII and into the 1950s the East German government continued to produce dolls marked "AM." Dolls listed are in good condition, appropriately dressed.

Child Doll, 1890 on, no mold number, or marked only: "A.M.," and molds 390, Floradora, 1894, bisque socket head,

12" marotte, Schoenau & Hoffmeister head, bisque: $500.
Photo courtesy of Morphy Auctions.

22" mold 1894, Armand Marseille, bisque, socket head: $325.
Photo courtesy of Morphy Auctions.

Armand Marseille

24" Queen Louise, Armand Marseille, bisque: $300. **Photo courtesy of Alderfer Auction Company, Inc.**

18" Floradora, Armand Marseille, bisque, shoulder head: $300. **Doll courtesy of Robin Burgess.**

open mouth, glass eyes, wig, fully jointed composition body. Dolls listed are in good condition, appropriately dressed, allow more for flirty eyes.

Composition Body
9" - 10"..............................$100 - 125
12" - 14".............................$150 - 200
16" - 18".............................$250 - 300
20" - 24" ....$300 - 350
28" - 30" ....$375 - 400
32" - 36" ....$500 - 600
40" - 42" ....$700 - 800
Five-piece flapper body, high quality
6" - 7" ....$250 - 350
10" - 13" ....$350 - 400
Five-piece body, low quality
10" - 12"............................$125 - 135
14" - 16" ....$150 - 175
Molds marked: "Queen Louise," "Rosebud"
12" - 13" ....$200 - 225
15" - 17"............................$225 - 275
22" - 24" ....$300 - 325
26" - 28" ....$350 - 400
31" - 34"............................$500 - 650
Mold marked:"Baby Betty"
14" - 16"............................$300 - 350
18" - 20" ....$350 - 400
Kid Body
Shoulder head, mold 370, 1894, 3200, or marked: "Alma," "Beauty," "Floradora," "Lily," "Mabel," "My Playmate,"

"Princess," "Rosebud"
10" - 12"............................$125 - 150
14" - 16".............................$200 - 250
18" - 20" ....$300 - 350
22" - 24" ....$350 - 400
Molds 1890, 1892, 1895, 1897, 1899, 1901, 1902, 1903, 1909
10" - 12" ....$175 - 225
14" - 16".............................$275 - 300
18" - 20" ....$325 - 400
22" - 24" ....$425 - 450
Character Baby
Baby Betty, usually found on child composition body, some on bent-leg baby body
16" $500
Too few in database for reliable range
Molds Kiddiejoy, 256, 259, 326, 327, 328, 329, 360a, 750, 790, 900, 927, 970, 971, 975, 990, 991, 992 Our Pet, 995, 996, 1330, bisque solid-dome or wigged socket head, glass eyes, open mouth, composition bent-leg baby body, allow more for toddler body or flirty eyes or exceptional doll
8" - 10" ....$250 - 300
12" - 15"............................$300 - 375
17" - 21"............................$400 - 425
24" - 26" ....$450 - 500
Mold 233
8"......................................$425 - 475
12" - 13" ....$500 - 600

Armand Marseille

14" mold 985 character babies, Armand Marseille, bisque: each $375. **Photo courtesy of Alderfer Auction Company, Inc.**

9½" Just Me, Armand Marseille, fired bisque: $1,400. **Photo courtesy of Ann Lloyd Antique Dolls.**

15".................$600 - 650
Mold 250, intaglio eyes, open/closed mouth with two lower teeth, molded hair
   9"...................$275 - 325
Mold 251/248
Open/closed mouth
   10" - 12"..................$500 - 600
Closed mouth
   12"...................$425 - 450
Mold 410, two rows of retractable teeth
   12"................$900 - 1,100
Mold 500, intaglio eyes, bent-limb composition body
   13" - 15"..................$575 - 700
Mold 518
   16" - 18"..................$400 - 600
Mold 560A
   8" - 9"................$150 - 225
   12" - 16"..................$400 - 500
Mold 580, 590
   15" - 16"..................$750 - 900
   19"...............$1,000 - 1,100
Mold 920
   21"................$650
Too few in database for reliable range
Melitta, toddler
   16"...................$800 - 900
Character Child
No mold #, bisque socket head, intaglio eyes, closed mouth, wigged, composition jointed body, marked: "A (size #) M"

20" - 25"...............$20,000 - 30,000
   34"........sold at auction for $40,000
Too few in database for reliable range
Mold 225, circa 1920, bisque socket head, glass eyes, open mouth, two rows of teeth, composition jointed body
   14"..................$3,000 - 3,600
   19"..................$4,000 - 4,650
Fany, circa 1912, may be child, toddler or baby
230, molded hair
   15" - 16"...................$7,000 - 8,000
   17" - 18"...................$9,000 - 10,000
231, wigged
   13" - 14"...................$3,800 - 4,000
   16"..................$5,000 - 5,200
Mold 250, circa 1912, domed
   9" - 13"..................$575 - 600
   15"...................$600 - 650
   18"...................$750 - 875
Mold 251, circa 1912, socket head, open/closed mouth
   10" - 13"..................$1,000 - 1,250
   17" - 18"..................$1,800 - 2,000
Mold 253: See Googlies section.
Mold 310, Just Me, circa 1929, bisque socket head, wig, flirty eyes, closed mouth, composition body
   7½" - 8"..................$1,000 - 1,200
   9" - 10"..................$1,200 - 1,500
   11"..................$1,700 - 1,900
   13"..................$2,000 - 2,400

Armand Marseille

19" mold 590, Armand Marseille, bisque, ball-jointed child body: $900. **Photo courtesy of Sweetbriar Auctions.**

Painted bisque, with outfits labeled: "Vogue"

7" - 8" ....$1,000 - 1,200
10" ....$1,500 - 1,800

Mold 345, pouty
Painted intaglio eyes

10" - 11".....................$6,500 - 7,000

Too few in database for reliable range
Glass eyes

10" ....$825 - 900

Mold 350, circa 1926, glass eyes, closed mouth

16" ....$1,950 - 2,250
20" ....$2,500 - 2,850

Mold 360a, circa 1913, open mouth

12" ....$350 - 400

Mold 400, 401, circa 1926, glass eyes, closed mouth

13" - 15"......................$1,500 - 1,600
20" - 24" ....$1,800 - $1,900

Mold 449, circa 1930, painted eyes, closed mouth

13" ....$575 - 625
18" ....$900 - 1,000

Painted bisque

11"...................................$200 - 250
15"...................................$375 - 450

Mold 450, glass eyes, closed mouth

14" ....$575 - 700

Mold 500, 600, circa 1910, domed shoulder head, molded/painted hair, painted intaglio eyes, closed mouth

10" - 12" ....$800 - 850
17" ....$800 - 950

Painted bisque

21" ....$175 - 200

Mold 520, circa 1910, domed head, glass eyes, open mouth
Composition body

12"....................................$675 - 750
19"..............................$1,800 - 2,000

Kid body

16" ....$800 - 900
20".............................$1,200 - 1,400

Mold 550, circa 1926, domed head, glass eyes, closed mouth

14" - 15"......................$1,600 - 1,900

Mold 560, circa 1910, character, domed head, painted eyes, open/closed mouth or 560A, circa 1926, wigged, glass eyes, open mouth

14"....................................$850 - 900
22"..............................$1,200 - 1,300

Mold 570, circa 1910, domed head, closed mouth

12"..............................$1,600 - 1,750

Mold 590, circa 1926, sleep eyes, open/closed mouth

11½" mold 500, Armand Marseille, bisque, solid-dome head: $500. **Photo courtesy of Richard Withington, Inc.**

Armand Marseille

9" ....$450 - 500
16" ....$900 - 1,000
18" - 20" ....$1,000 - 1,100
Mold 600, shoulder head, solid dome
with molded hair, intaglio eyes, closed
mouth
12" - 15" ....$450 - 600
Mold 690, socket head, open mouth
18" ....$800 - 850
Mold 700, circa 1920, closed mouth
Painted eyes
12½" ....$1,800 - 2,000
Glass eyes
14" ....$3,800 - 4,200
Mold 701, 711, circa 1920, socket or
shoulder head, sleep eyes, closed mouth
16" ....$2,000 - 2,250
Mold 800, circa 1910, socket head, 840
shoulder head
18" ....$2,000 - 2,200
Lady, 1910 on, bisque head, wigged,
sleep eyes, open or closed mouth, com-
position lady body
Molds 400, 401, 14"
Open mouth ....$1,100 - 1,300
Closed mouth ....$2,000 - 2,200
Painted bisque ....$900 - 1,000
Newborn Baby, 1924 on, newborn,
bisque solid-dome socket head or flange

13" Fany, Armand Marseille, bisque, circa 1912: $6,000. **Photo courtesy of Gloria's Antique Dolls.**

15" Melitta, toddler, Armand Marseille, bisque, pierced "breather" nostrils: $800. **Photo courtesy of Glenda Antique Dolls & Collectables.**

neck, may have wig, glass eyes, closed
mouth, cloth body,celluloid or
composition hands
Mold 341, My Dream Baby, 351, 345, 352,
Rock-A-Bye Baby, marked: "AM"
8" ....$100 - 125
10" - 12" ....$150 - 175
14" - 16" ....$175 - 200
22" - 24" ....$250 - 300
Bent-limb composition body
11" - 12" ....$250 - 300
16" ....$325 - 350
Toddler body
28" ....$600 - 800
Pillow puppet
10" ....$175 - 200
Baby Gloria, solid dome, open mouth,
painted hair
12" ....$300 - 325
15" ....$350 - 400
Baby Phyllis, solid dome, closed, mouth,
painted hair
9" - 10" ....$200 - 225
13" - 15" ....$250 - 275
Composition Child, 1940s - 1950s,
mold 2966 and others, sleep eyes, synthetic wig, five-piece composition body
(very thin cardboard-like composition)
22" ....$165 - 175

MARX TOY CORPORATION

1919 to present, Sebring, Ohio. Founded in 1919 as Louis Marx & Co. in New York City. Dolls listed are in perfect condition with original clothing.

Archie and Friends, characters from comics, vinyl, molded hair or wigged, painted eyes, in package

Archie, Betty, Jughead, Veronica
8½" ....$8 - 15

Freddy Krueger, 1989, vinyl, pull-string talker, based on character played by Robert England in horror movie *Nightmare on Elm Street*
10" ....$10 - 15

Johnny West Family of Action Figures, 1965 - 1976, adventure or Best of the West Series, rigid vinyl, articulated figures, molded clothes, came in box with vinyl accessories and extra clothes, horses, dogs and other accessories were available, dolls listed are complete with all accessories, allow more if NRFB or special sets

Bill Buck, brown molded-on clothing, 13 accessories, coonskin cap
11½" ....$175 - 250

Captain Tom Maddox, blue molded-on clothing, brown hair, 23 accessories
11½" ....$30 - 40

Chief Cherokee, tan or light-colored molded-on clothing, 37 accessories
11½" ....$28 - 35

Daniel Boone, tan molded-on clothing, coonskin cap
11½" ....$125 - 150

Dangerous Dan, blue figure, flocked hair and beard
11½" ....$225 - 250

Fighting Eagle, tan molded-on clothes, Mohawk hair, 37 accessories
11½" ....$50 - 70

General Custer, dark blue molded-on clothing, yellow hair, 23 accessories
11½" ....$25 - 30

Geronimo, light-colored molded-on clothing
11½" ....$28 - 40
Orange body
11½" ....$90 - 110

Jamie West, dark hair, tan molded-on clothing, 13 accessories
9" ....$30 - 35

Jane West, blond hair, turquoise molded-on clothing, 37 accessories
11½" ....$32 - 45

Janice West, dark hair, turquoise molded-on clothing, 14 accessories
9" ....$30 - 40

Jay West, blond hair, tan molded-on clothing, 13 accessories, later brighter body colors
9" ....$35 - 45

Jed Gibson, c. 1973, black figure, green molded-on clothing
12" ....$100 - 125

Johnny West, brown hair, brown molded-on clothing, 25 accessories
12" ....$60 - 75

Johnny West, with quick draw arm, blue molded-on clothing
12" ....$90 - 115

Josie West, blond, turquoise molded-on clothing, later bright-green body
9" ....$20 - 25

Princess Wildflower, off-white molded-on clothing, with papoose in vinyl cradle, 22 accessories
11½" ....$60 - 80

Sam Cobra, outlaw, 26 accessories
11½" ....$30 - 40

Sheriff Pat Garrett (Sheriff Goode in Canada), blue molded-on clothing, 25 accessories
11½" ....$28 - 35

Zeb Zachary, dark hair, blue molded-on clothing, 23 accessories
11½" ....$40 - 60

Mike Hazard Double Agent, 1967, vinyl, trench coat, 25 accessories
12" ....$60 - 80

Knight and Viking Series, circa 1960s,

Mattel

action figures with accessories
Gordon, the Gold Knight, gold molded-on clothing, brown hair, beard, mustache
11½" ....$100 - 125
Sir Brandon, blue molded-on clothing, gray hair, mustache
11½" ....$20 - 25
Sir Stuart, Silver Knight,silver molded-on clothing, black hair, mustache, goatee
11½" ....$30 - 35
Brave Erik, Viking with horse, circa 1967, green molded-on clothing, blond hair, blue eyes
11½" ....$25 - 40
Odin, the Viking, circa 1967, brown molded-on clothing, brown eyes, brown hair, beard
11½" ....$30 - 40
Miss Seventeen, 1961, hard plastic, high-heeled fashion-type, modeled like the German Bild Lilli (Barbie doll's predecessor), black swimsuit, black box, fashion brochure picturing 12 costumes, advertised as "A Beauty Queen"
18" ....$100 - 120
Miss Marlene, hard plastic, high-heeled, Barbie-type, circa 1960s, blond rooted wig
11" ....$80 - 100
Miss Toddler, also known as Miss Marx, vinyl, molded hair, ribbons, battery-operated walker, molded clothing
18" ....$65 - 75
PeeWee Herman, 1987 TV character, vinyl and cloth, ventriloquist doll wearing gray suit, red bow tie
18" ....$18 - 25
Pull-string talker, 18" ....$20 - 30
Sindy, circa 1963 on, in England by Pedigree, fashion-type, rooted hair, painted eyes, wires in limbs allow her to pose, distributed in U.S. by Marx c. 1978 - 1982
11" ....$20 - 30
Pedigree ....$50 - 75
Gayle, Sindy's friend, black vinyl

11½" Jane West, Marx, vinyl: $90. **Photo courtesy of Charlotte's Web Vintage Dolls and Collectibles.**

11".............................$50 - 75
Outfits............................$75 - 95
Soldiers, circa 1960s, articulated action figures with accessories
Buddy Charlie, Montgomery Ward exclusive, GI Joe buddy, molded-on military uniform, brown hair
11½" ....$80 - 100
Stony "Stonewall" Smith, molded-on Army fatigues, blond hair, 36 accessories
11½" ....$60 - 75
Twinkie, vinyl clothing, wigs
4½" ....$40 - 60

MATTEL

1959 to present, founded by Ruth and Elliot Handler. Many dolls of the 1960s and 1970s designed by Martha Armstrong Hand. Dolls listed are in excellent condition with all original clothing and accessories. Value can double for MIB.
Baby Beans, 1971 - 1975, vinyl head, bean bag dolls, terrycloth or tricot bodies filled with plastic and foam
12"............................$25 - 35
Talking
12"............................$60 - 70
Baby Come Back, 1976, battery-operated walker, rooted hair,
16" ....$25 - 30

Mattel

Baby First Step, 1965 - 1967, battery-operated walker, rooted hair, sleep eyes, pink dress
18"...$40 - 50
Talking
18"...$60 - 70
Longer hair, pink outfit ....
$65 - 90
Baby Go Bye-Bye and Her Bumpety Buggy, 1970, doll sits in car, battery-operated, 12 manueuvers
11"................................$75 - 140
Baby Pattaburp, 1964 - 1966, vinyl, drinks milk, burps when patted, pink jacket, lace trim
16"...$50 - 65
Baby Play-A-Lot, 1972 - 1973, posable arms, fingers can hold things, moves arm to brush teeth, moves head, no batteries, pull string and switch, 20 toys
16"....................................$18 - 22
Baby That-A-Way, 1974, crawls
15"....................................$50 - 70
Baby Say 'N See, 1967 - 1968, eyes and lips move while talking, white dress, pink yoke
17"....................................$50 - 75
Baby Skates, 1982, vinyl face and hands, rooted blonde hair, battery-operated roller-skating doll
15"....................................$40 - 45

Baby Secret, 1966 - 1967, vinyl face and hands, stuffed body, limbs, red hair, blue eyes, moves lips, whispers eleven phrases
18"....................................$30 - 65
Baby Small Talk, 1968 - 1969, infant voice, says eight phrases, additional outfits available
10¾"..................................$25 - 30
Black
10¾"..................................$40 - 50
Nursery Rhyme outfit
10¾"..................................$45 - 55
Baby Tender Love, 1970 - 1973, baby doll, realistic skin, wets, can be bathed
Newborn
13"....................................$55 - 65
Talking
16"....................................$20 - 35
Baby Magic, 1978
14" .... $20 - 25
Molded hairpiece, 1972
11½"............................... $20 - 25
Brother, sexed
11½" ....$40 - 50
Baby Walk 'n Play, 1968
11"...$8 - 12
Baby Walk 'n See
18" ....$12 - 18
Barbie: See Barbie section.
Big Jim Series, vinyl action figures, many boxed accessory sets available

24" Charmin' Chatty, Mattel, vinyl, Happy Birthday outfit: $150.
Photo courtesy of The Museum Doll Shop.

Tiny Chatty Baby, Mattel, vinyl: $100. **Photo courtesy of Charlotte's Web Vintage Dolls and Collectibles.**

Mattel

Big Jim, black hair, muscular torso
9½" .... $20 - 30
Big Jim with Talking Field Radio
9½" .... $40 - 55
Big Jack, African American
9½" .... $30 - 35
Big Josh, dark hair, beard
9½" .... $20 - 30
Dr. Steele, bald head, silver tips on right hand
9½" .... $25 - 30
Sports Camper set .... $60 - 75
Beanie, 1962, based on character from *Beanie & Cecile* TV show, vinyl head, hands, feet, cloth body, pull-string talker
18" .... $50 - 60
Bozo, 1964
18" .... $40 - 60
Buffy and Mrs. Beasley, 1967 & 1974, based on characters from *Family Affair* TV show
Buffy, vinyl, rooted hair, painted features, holds small Mrs. Beasley, vinyl head, cloth body
6½" .... $35 - 50
Talking Buffy, vinyl, 1969 - 1971, holds 6" rag Mrs. Beasley
10¾" .... $40 - 50
Mrs. Beasley
1965, vinyl head, cloth body
16" .... $160 - 200
1973, non-talker
15½" .... $115 - 130
Captain Kangaroo, 1967, cloth, Sears exclusive, talking character based on host of *Captain Kangaroo* TV show
19" .... $40 - 50
Captain Laser, 1967, vinyl, painted features, blue uniform, silver accessories, battery-operated laser gun, light-up eyes
12" .... $75 - 100
Casper, the Friendly Ghost
1964
16" .... $75 - 100
1971
5" .... $25 - 35

2½" Surfy Skiddle, Mattel, vinyl: $65. **Photo courtesy of Pieces of Old.**

Chatty Cathy Series
Chatty Cathy, 1960 - 1963, vinyl head, hard-plastic body, pull-string-activated voice, wearing pink-and-white checked or blue party dress, 1963 - 1965, says 18 phrases, red-velvet and white-lace dress, extra outfits available
Blond
20" .... $175 - 225
Black
20" .... $500 - 550
Canadian version .... $450 - 550
1995 Re-issue doll .... $75 - 100
Charmin' Chatty, 1963 - 1964, pull-string talking doll, soft vinyl head, closed smiling mouth, hard-vinyl body, long rooted hair, long legs, five records in left-side slot, one outfit with a navy skirt, white middy blouse, red sailor collar, red socks, saddle shoes, glasses, extra outfits and 14 more records available
24" .... $150 - 200
Chatty Baby, 1962 - 1964, pull-string talker, red pinafore over rompers
18" .... $80 - 100
Tiny Chatty Baby, 1963 - 1964, smaller version of Chatty Baby, blue rompers, blue-and-white striped panties, bib with name, other outfits available
15½" .... $75 - 100
Black
15½" .... $100 - 125

Mattel

2½" Sweet Pea Kiddle Kologne, Mattel, vinyl: $35. **Photo courtesy of Pieces of Old.**

Tiny Chatty Brother, 1963 - 1964, boy version of Tiny Chatty Baby, blue-and-white suit and cap, hair parted on side
15½" ....$55 - 65
Cheerful Tearful, 1966 - 1967, vinyl, blond hair, face changes from smile to pout as arm is lowered, wets when bottle-fed, cries wet tears
13" ....$60 -70
Tiny Cheerful Tearful
7"..$60 - 70
Dancerella, 1978 battery operated
19".......................................$75 - 85
Dancerina, 1969 - 1971, battery operated, posable arms, legs, turns, turning knob on head makes doll dance, pink ballet outfit
24"....................................$130 - 150
Baby Dancerina, 1970, smaller version, no batteries, turning knob on head makes doll dance, white ballet outfit
16"......................................$85 - 95
Black
16" .... $125 - 150
Teeny Dancerina
12".....................................$25 - 35
Debbie Boone, 1978

11½" ....$45 - 55
Dick Van Dyke, 1969, based on character of Mr. Potts in *Chitty Chitty Bang Bang* movie, all cloth, flat features, talks in actor's voice, cloth tag marked: "© Mattel 1969"
24" ....$100 - 120
Drowsy, 1965 - 1974, vinyl head, stuffed body, sleepers, pull-string talker
15½" ....$125 - 175
Reissue, 2001
15".....................................$30 - 40
Dr. Doolittle, 1968, based on character played by Rex Harrison in *Dr. Doolittle* movie, talker, vinyl, cloth body
24"......................................$25 - 30
All vinyl
6"......................................$15 - 20
Gramma Doll, 1970 - 1973, Sears exclusive, cloth, painted face, gray yarn hair, foam-filled cotton body, says ten phrases
11".....................................$15 - 20
Grizzly Adams, 1971
10".....................................$35 - 45
Guardian Goddesses, 1979
11½" ....$40 - 45
Herman Munster, 1965, talking cloth doll, based on character from *The Munsters* TV show
21" ....$225 - 275
Liddle Kiddles, 1966 on, vinyl-over-wire frame, posable, painted features, rooted hair, bright costumes and accessories, packaged on 8½" x 9½" cards, back marked: "1965//Mattel Inc.//Japan," dolls listed are in excellent condition with all accessories, value can double for mint in package (or on card) and NRFP, allow less for worn dolls with missing accessories
1966, First Series
3501 Bunson Bernie
3"......................................$50 - 60
3502 Howard "Biff" Boodle
3½" ....$95 - 105
3503 Liddle Diddle
2¾" ....$120 - 130

Mattel

3504 Lola Liddle
3½" ....$75 - 80
3505 Babe Biddle
3½" ....$45 - 60
3506 Calamity Jiddle
3" ....$45 - 55
3507 Florence Niddle
2¾" ....$85 - 95
3508 Greta Griddle
3" ....$55 - 75
3509 Millie Middle
2¾" ....$100 - 120
3510 Beat A Diddle
3½" ....$85 - 95
1967, Second Series
3513 Sizzly Friddle
3" ....$80 - 100
3514 Windy Fiddle
2½" ....$75 -100
3515 Trikey Triddle
2¾" ....$90 - 100
3516 Freezy Sliddle
3½" ....$70 - 90
3517 Surfy Skiddle
3" ....$70 - 80
3518 Soapy Siddle
3½" ....$75 - 90

3519 Rolly Twiddle
3½" ....$90 - 100
3548 Beddy Bye Biddle
(with robe) ....$70 - 90
3549 Pretty Priddle
3½" ....$75 - 100
1968, Third Series
3587 Baby Liddle
2¾" ....$100 - 120
3551 Telly Viddle
3½" ....$80 - 110
3552 Lemon Stiddle
3½" ....$60 - 75
3553 Kampy Kiddle
3½" ....$80 - 100
3554 Slipsy Sliddle
3½" ....$75 - 100
Storybook Kiddles, 1967 - 1968
....$75 - 150
Skediddle Kiddles, 1968 - 1970
4" ....$30 - 45
Kiddles 'N Kars, 1969 - 1970
2¾" ....$50 - 75
Tea Party Kiddles, 1970 - 1971
3½" ....$40 - 50
Lucky Locket Kiddles, 1967 - 1970
2" ....$20 - 30

16"
Shrinkin'
Violette,
Mattel,
cloth, with
box:$350.
**Photo
courtesy of
Charlotte's
Web
Vintage
Dolls and
Collectibles.**

Mattel

Kiddle Kolognes, 1968 - 1970
2"...$25 - 35
Kiddle Kones, 1968 - 1969
2"...$60 - 75
Kola Kiddles, 1968 - 1969
2"...$20 - 40
Kosmic Kiddle, 1968 - 1969
2½"..$100 - 130
Sweet Treat Kiddles, 1969 - 1970
2"...$75 - 90
Liddle Kiddle Playhouses, 1966 - 1968
....$55 - 65
Matty Mattel
16"..$45 - 55
Mork & Mindy, 1979
9"..each $18 - 20
My Child, 1986, cloth-over-vinyl head, cloth body, synthetic wig
13"..$75 - 100
Osmond Family
Donny or Marie Osmond, 1978
12"..$25 - 35
Jimmy Osmond, 1979
10"..$40 - 50
Rainbow Brite, 1983 vinyl head, cloth

body, orange yarn hair
18½" ....$60 - 70
Rock Flowers, 1970, vinyl mod dolls
6"..$10 - 15
Scooba Doo, 1964, vinyl head, rooted hair, cloth body, talks in Beatnik phrases, blond or black hair, striped dress
23"..$85 - 110
Shogun Warrior, all plastic, battery operated
23½" ....$100 - 225
Shrinkin' Violette, 1964 - 1965, cloth, yarn hair, pull-string talker, eyes close, mouth moves
16"..$200 - 250
Sister Belle, 1961 - 1963, vinyl, pull-string talker, cloth body
16"..$45 - 55
Sister Small Talk, 1967, talker, painted eyes
10"..$30 - 40
Star Spangled dolls, set uses Sunshine Family adult dolls in special costumes, marked: "1973"

10" Sister Small Talk, Mattel, vinyl, MIB: $90.
Photo courtesy of Memories of Things Past Antiques.

Pioneer Daughter ....$30 - 40
Sunshine Family, vinyl, posable, with
Idea Book, Father, Mother, Baby
Family of 3 ....$45 - 55
Steve
   9" ....$10 - 15
Stephie
   7½" ....$10 - 15
Swingy, 1968, mechanical dancing doll
   18"..$30 - 45
Tatters, 1965 - 1967, talking cloth doll,
rag clothes
   19" ....$65 -90
Teachy Keen, 1966 - 1970, Sears
exclusive, vinyl head, cloth body,
ponytail, talker, tells child to use
accessories included, buttons,
zippers, comb
   16"..$30 - 40
Timey Tell 1969, talks
   17" ....$25 - 30
Tippee Toes, 1968 - 1970, battery
operated, legs move, rides accessory
horse, tricycle, knit sweater, pants
   17" ....$40 - 50
Truly Scrumptious, based on character
from Chitty Chitty Bang Bang movie
   11½" ....$200 - 250
Talking ....$350 - 400
Welcome Back Kotter, 1973,based on
characters from Welcome Back Kotter
TV show: Gabe Kotter (Gabe Kaplan),
Vinnie Barbarino (John Travolta),
Freddie "Boom Boom" Washington
(Lawrence Hilton-Jacobs), Arnold
Hoshack (Ron Palillo)
Freddie "Boom Boom" Washington, Arnold
Horshack
   9"..$30 - 40
Vinnie Barbarino
   9" ....$30 - 35
Gabe Kotter
   9" ....$15 - 25
Zython, 1977, glow-in-the-dark head,
based on character from Enemy in Space
TV show ....$80 - 90

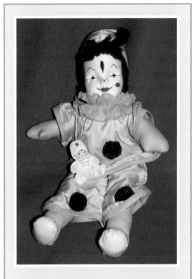

12" Mawaphil, clown, cloth mask face: $100.
Doll courtesy of private collection.

MAWAPHIL

1920 - 1942, Atlanta, Georgia. Dolls
designed by Mary Waterman Philips,
manufactured by the Rushton Co.
Stockinette crib dolls and cloth mask face
dolls.
Crib doll, all cloth, stockinette or velveteen
   8" - 12".................................$60 - 90
Cloth mask face doll, cloth body, appropriately dressed
   12" - 15".............................$100 - 200

MEGO CORPORATION

1954 to 1982. Made many vinyl "action
figure" dolls during the 1970s. Prices
shown are for excellent-condition dolls
with all appropriate clothes and accessories, value can double for MIB..
Action Jackson, 1971 - 1972, vinyl head,
plastic body, molded hair, painted black
eyes, action figure, many accessory outfits, marked: "©Mego Corp//Reg. U.S.

Mego Corporation

Pat. Off.//Pat. Pend.//Hong
Kong//MCMLXXI"
8".........................$25 - 32
Black
8".........................$55 - 65
Dinah-mite, Black ....$30 - 35
Baby Sez So, 1976
16".........................$25 - 30
Bubble Yum Baby, 1978, blows up
"gum"
14".........................$20 - 25
Candy, 1979, fashion doll
11 1/2" ....$10 - 12
18"...........................$18 - 25
Captain and Tennille, 1977, based
on recording and TV personalities
Daryl Dragon and Toni Tennille,
Toni Tennille doll has no molded
ears
12½" ....each $20 - 30
Charlie's Angels, 1977,based on
characters from TV show of the same
name: Jill Munroe (Farrah Fawcett),
Kelly Garrett (Jaclyn Smith), Sabrina
Duncan (Kate Jackson), Kris Munroe
(Cheryl Ladd), vinyl, rooted hair
9".........................$10 - 15
12½" ....$40 - 55
Cher, 1976, based on TV and
recording personalities Cher and her
husband Sonny Bono, all vinyl, fully
jointed, rooted long black hair, also
made as grow-hair doll
Cher
12".........................$35 - 45
Growing Hair Cher, 1976
12".........................$65 - 75
Sonny Bono
12".........................$25 - 35
CHiPs, 1977, based on characters of TV
show of the same name: Jon Baker
(Larry Wilcox), Frank "Ponch"
Poncherello (Erik Estrada)
8".........................$30 - 35
Diana Ross, 1977, based on recording
and movie personality, all vinyl, fully

jointed, rooted black hair, long lashes
12½" ....$55 - 75
Dukes of Hazzard, 1982, based on char-
acters from TV show of the same name:
Bo Duke (John Schneider), Luke Duke
(Tom Wopat), Boss Hogg (Sorrell
Booke), Cletus (Rick Hurst), Rosco
(James Best)
8" - 9" ....$20 - 30
Flash Gordon Series, circa 1976, vinyl
head, hard-plastic articulated body
Dale Arden
9".........................$35 - 45
Dr. Zarkov
9½" ....$35 - 35
Flash Gordon
9½" ....$60 - 70
Ming, the Merciless
9½" ....$25 - 35
Happy Days, 1976, based on characters
from TV show of the same name:
Fonzie (Henry Winkler), Richie (Ronnie
Howard), Potsie (Anson Williams),
Ralph Malph (Donny Most)
Fonzie
8".........................$30 - 45
Richie, Potsie, Ralph
8".........................each $20 - 35
Joe Namath, 1970, based on the football player and actor, soft-vinyl head,
rigid-vinyl body, painted hair and features
12".........................$100 - 135
Outfit, MIP $35
KISS, 1978, based on members of rock
group: Gene Simmons, Ace Frehley,
Peter Cris, Paul Stanley, all vinyl, fully
jointed, rooted hair, painted features
and makeup
12½" ....each $35 - 50
Kristy McNichol, 1978, based on actress
in *Family* TV show, all vinyl, rooted
brown hair, painted eyes, head marked:
"©MEGO CORP.//MADE IN HONG
KONG," back marked: "©1977 MEGO
CORP.//MADE IN HONG KONG"

9" ....$15 - 20

Laverne and Shirley, 1977, based on characters from *Laverne and Shirley* TV show: Laverne (Penny Marshall), Shirley (Cindy Williams), Squiggy (David Lander), Lenny (Michael McKean), all vinyl, rooted hair, painted eyes

11½" ....$20 - 30 each

Marvel Super Heros, 1974 on, vinyl head, rooted black hair, painted eyes, plastic body

8"

Aquaman	$70 - 190
Batgirl	$100 - 125
Batman	$100 - 150
Catwoman	$80 - 100
Falcon	$40 - 45
Flash	$50 - 75
Green Arrow	$50 - 60
Ironman	$55 - 65
Joker	$55 - 85
Mr. Fantastic	$50 - 75
Mr. Mxyzptlk	$75 - 90
Riddler	$150 - 200
Robin	$70 - 80
Spiderman	$40 - 60
Superman	$50 - 75
Supergirl	$100 -125
Wonderwoman	$90 - 100

Our Gang, 1975, based on characters from *Our Gang* movie shorts that replayed on TV, including Alfalpha, Buckwheat, Darla, Mickey, Porky, Spanky

6" ....$15 - 25

Planet of the Apes

Planet of the Apes Movie Series, circa 1970s

Astronaut

8" ....$40 - 45

Cornelius

8" ....$50 - 70

Dr. Zaius

8" ....$40 - 45

Zira

8" ....$40 -50

8" Spiderman, Mego, vinyl, circa 1977, MOC: $120. **Photo courtesy of Morphy Auctions.**

Planet of the Apes TV Series, circa 1974

Alan Verdon

8" ....$45 - 50

Galen

8," Palitoy ....$60 - 70

General Urko

8" ....$60 - 70

General Ursus

8" ....$80 - 100

Peter Burke

8" ....$40 - 50

Forbidden Zone Playset ....$125 - 150

Star Trek

Star TV Series, circa 1973 - 1975

Captain Kirk

8" ....$25 - 35

Dr. McCoy

8" ....$25 - 35

Klingon

8" ....$45 - 60

Lt. Uhura

8" ....$30 - 50

Mr. Scott

8" ....$35 - 45

8" Glinda
the Good
Witch,
Mego, vinyl:
$30.
**Doll
courtesy
of private
collection.**

Mr. Spock
    8".....................................$25 - 35
Star Trek Aliens, circa 1975 - 1976
Andorian
    8".......................................$110 - 130
Cheron
    8"......................................$35 - 45
Neptunian
    8"......................................$50 - 75
Mugato
    8"......................................$140 - 160
Talos
    8"......................................$40 - 65
The Gorn
    8"......................................$40 - 55
The Romulan
    8"......................................$100 - 125
Star Trek Movie Series, circa 1979, 12½"
dolls
Acturian ....$80 - 100
Captain Kirk ....$45 - 60
Commander Decker ....$30 - 50
Ilia ....$30 - 40
Klingon ....$65 - 75
Mr. Spock..................................$80 - 100
Starsky and Hutch, 1976, based on
characters in TV show of the same
name, Starsky (Paul Michael Glaser),

Hutch (David Soul), Captain Dobey
(Bernie Hamilton), Huggy Bear
(Antonio Fargas), also made a villain-
named Chopper, all vinyl, jointed waists
    7½" ....$25 - 35
Suzanne Somers, 1978, based on the
actress and TV personality who
played Chrissy in *Three's Company*
TV show, all vinyl, fully jointed,
rooted blond hair, painted blue eyes,
long lashes
    12½" ....$30 - 35
The Waltons, 1975, based on characters
from TV show of the same name, set of
two 8" dolls per package, all vinyl
John Boy and Mary Ellen set ....$15 - 20
Mom and Pop set..........................$15 - 20
Grandma and Grandpa set ....$25 - 30
The Wizard of Oz, 1974
*Dorothy, Glinda, Cowardly Lion, Scarecrow,
Tin Man* ....$25 - 30
Munchkins...................................$50 - 60
Wonder Woman Series, circa 1976 -
1977, vinyl head, rooted black hair,
painted eyes, plastic body
Lt. Diana Prince
    12½" ....$50 - 75
Nubia
    12½" ....$75 - 100
Nurse
    12½" ....$30 - 40
Queen Hippolyte
    12½" ....$75 - 100
Steve Trevor
    12½" ....$45 - 65
Wonder Woman
    12½" ....$90 - 125

METAL HEADS

1850 - 1930 on. Made in Germany,
Britain and America, by various manu-
factures, including Buschow & Beck
(Minerva), Alfred Heller (Diana), Karl
Standfuss (Juno), and Art Metal Works.
Various metals used included aluminum,
brass and others, and they might be

24" metal head, Minerva, painted eyes: $100. **Photo courtesy of Decades of Dolls.**

marked with just a size and country of origin, or unmarked. Dolls listed are in good condition with original or appropriate dolls. Allow significantly less for dolls with chipped paint.

Metal shoulder head, cloth or kid body, molded and painted hair, glass eyes, allow more for wigged

12" - 14"	$125 - 150
16" - 18"	$150 - 200
20" - 22"	$225 - 250

Painted eyes

12" -14"	$75 - 100
20" - 22"	$125 - 150

All metal or with composition body, metal limbs

Baby

11" - 15"	$100 - 125
16" - 20"	$150 - 175

20" tin head, composition limbs, cloth body, all original: $200. **Photo courtesy of Decades of Dolls.**

Child

15"	$300 - 350
20" - 22"	$450 - 500

Mama doll, metal shoulder head, cloth body

18"	$200 - 250

Swiss: See Bucherer section.

MISSIONARY RAG BABY (BEECHER BABY)

1893 - 1910, Elmira, New York. Julia Jones Beecher, wife of Congregational Church pastor Thomas K. Beecher, sister-in-law of Harriet Beecher Stowe, made Missionary Rag babies with the help of the sewing circle of her church. The dolls were made from old silk or cotton jersey underwear, with hand-painted and needle-sculpted features. All proceeds were used for missionary work. Sizes 16" to 23" and larger. Dolls listed are in good condition, appropriately dressed. Allow more for exceptional examples.

16"	$3,500 - 4,000
21" - 23"	$5,000 - 6,000

Black Beecher, same construction and appearance as the white babies but from brown fabric with black yarn hair. This is not the black stockinette doll often erroneously referred to as "a black Beecher," which is quite different in construction from a true Black Beecher.

21" - 23"	$6,000 - 6,500

21" Missionary Rag Baby, Beecher, cloth: $6,000. **Photo courtesy of Richard Withington, Inc.**

MOLLY-'ES

1920 to 1970s, Philadelphia, Pennsylvania. International Doll Co. was founded by Mollye Goldman. Molly-'es made cloth-mask-faced dolls, doll clothing, Raggedy Ann (briefly), as well as composition and vinyl dolls. The mask-faced dolls had yarn or mohair hair, painted features and sewn joints at the shoulders and hips.

Cloth, fine painted lashes, pouty mouth

Child

    12" baby ....$50 - 75

    15"....................................$75 - 90

    18" ....$90 - 110

    24".................................$125 - 150

    29"..................................$200 - 225

Internationals

    11" ....$65 - 75

    15".................................$75 - 100

    27" ....$130 - 175

Lady

    16" ....$125 - 150

    21" ....$175 - 225

Princess, Thief of Baghdad

Prince, cloth

    23"...............................$550 - 650

Princess

    Composition

    15"...............................$500 - 575

    Cloth

    18" ....$550 - 600

Sabu, composition

    15" ....$500 - 550

Sultan, cloth

    19" ....$600 - 650

Composition

Baby

    15" ....$140 - 190

    21" ....$210 - 225

Cloth body

    18" ....$90 - 110

Toddler

    15"...............................$170 - 200

    21"...............................$200 - 250

Child

    15"...............................$125 - 150

15" Sabu, the Thief of Baghdad, Molly-'es, composition: $500. **Photo courtesy of Richard Withington, Inc.**

    19" ....$175 - 200

Lady, allow more for ball gown

    16"...............................$225 - 275

    21"...............................$325 - 400

Hard Plastic

Baby

    14"...............................$65 - 85

    20"...............................$100 - 135

Cloth body

    17"...............................$55 - 75

    25"...............................$100 - 125

Child

    14"...............................$150 - 175

    18"...............................$325 - 375

    25"...............................$400 - 425

Lady

    17"...............................$250 - 300

    20"...............................$325 - 375

    25"...............................$375 - 425

Vinyl

Baby

    8½" ....$12 - 20

    12" ....$18 - 25

    15"...............................$28 - 40

Child

    8"...............................$12 - 20

    10"...............................$18 - 25

    15"...............................$28 - 40

Little Women

    9"...............................$45 - 55

MONICA DOLLS

1941 - 1951. Monica Dolls from Hollywood, designed by Mrs. Hansi Share. Made composition and later hard plastic with long face and painted or sleep eyes, eye shadow; unique feature is very durable rooted human hair, do not have high-heeled feet and are unmarked, but wear paper wrist tag that reads: "Monica Doll, Hollywood." Composition dolls often have pronounced widow's peak in center of forehead.

Composition, 1941 - 1949, painted eyes, Veronica, Jean and Rosalind were names of 17" dolls produced in 1942

15"	$375 - 450
17"	$575 - 700
20"	$725 - 900

17" wearing formal, excellent condition ....sold at online auction for $1,200

Hard plastic, 1949 - 1951, sleep eyes, Elizabeth, Marion or Linda

14"	$400 - 500
18"	$500 - 600

17" Monica, rooted hair, composition: $250.
Photo courtesy of McMasters Harris Apple Tree Doll Auctions.

MORAVIAN

1872 to present, Bethlehem, Pennsylvania. Cloth dolls made by the Ladies Sewing Society of the Moravian Church Guild as fundraiser to support church work. Flat-faced rag doll with sewn joints at shoulders, elbows, hips and knees, hand-painted faces, dressed in pink or blue gingham with apron and double bonnet, 18".

1800s - early 1900s ....$6,000 - 7,000
1920s - 1950s ....$2,000 - 3,000
1960s to present ....$300 - 500

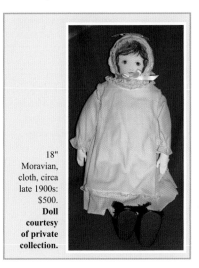

18" Moravian, cloth, circa late 1900s: $500. **Doll courtesy of private collection.**

MULTI-FACE, MULTI-HEAD DOLLS

1866 - 1930 on. Various firms made dolls with two or more faces, or more than one head.

Bisque
French
Bru, Surprise poupée, awake/asleep faces
       12" ....sold at auction for $14,500
Jumeau, crying/laughing faces, cap hides knob
       18" ....$15,500 - 16,500
Too few in database for reliable range

225

Multi-Face, Multi-Head Dolls

8" Bru, bisque, two-faced, on swaddling-baby-style candy container: $7,000. **Photo courtesy of Richard Withington, Inc.**

German
Bartenstein, bisque socket head, papier-mâché hood and molded blouse shoulder plate, cloth-over-carton body, composition limbs, awake face, glass eyes, open mouth, crying face, glass eyes, open/closed mouth
20"...$2,750
Bergner, Carl, bisque socket head, two or three faces, sleeping, laughing, crying, molded tears, glass eyes, composition jointed body, may have molded bonnet or hood, marked: "C.B." or "Designed by Carl Bergner"
12"..............................$1,200 - 1,400
15"..............................$1,300 - 1,600
Black face/white face doll
13"..$3,650
Too few in database for reliable range
Kestner, J. D., circa 1900 on, Wunderkind bisque doll with set of several different mold number heads that could be attached to body, set of one doll and body with additional three heads and wardrobe
With heads *174, 178, 184 & 185*
11"..........................$9,000 - 10,000
With heads *171, 179, 182 & 183*
14½" $12,650
Too few in database for reliable range

Kley & Hahn, solid-dome bisque socket head, painted hair, smiling baby and frowning baby, glass eyes, closed mouth, tongue, baby body
13"..............................$1,500 - 1,700
Simon & Halbig, smiling, sleeping, crying, turn ring at top of head to change faces, glass/painted eyes, closed mouth
14½" ....$3,000 - 3,200
Hermann Steiner, topsy-turvy baby
8"................................$500 - 600
Cloth
Topsy-Turvy: one black, one white head
Painted face
13"....................................$800 - 900
Lithographed face
13"....................................$650 - 700
Bruckner
13"....................................$500 - 600
China
Youth & Age of Woman, German, 1800s
13" ....$1,000 - 1,100
TopsyTurvy, white head and black head, mid-1800s
12"..............................$1,200 - 1,600
Too few in database for reliable range
Composition
Berwick Doll Co., Famlee Dolls, 1926 on, composition head and limbs, cloth body with crier, neck with screw joint allows different heads to be screwed into the body, painted features, mohair wigs and/or molded and painted hair, came in sets of two to twelve heads, different costumes for each head
Four-head set
16"....................................$400 - 500
Seven-head set
16"....................................$500 - 600
Effanbee, Johnny Tu Face
16" ....$275 - 325
Too few in database for reliable range
Ideal, 1923, Soozie Smiles, composition, sleep or painted eyes on happy face,

15" Famlee Doll, Berwick, composition, six-head set: $600. **Photo courtesy of Morphy Auctions.**

two faces, smiling, crying, cloth body, composition hands, cloth legs, original romper and hat
15½" ....$400 - 450
Three-in-One Doll Corp., 1946 on, Trudy, composition head with turning knob on top, cloth body and limbs, three faces~Sleepy, Weepy, Smiley~dressed in felt or fleece snowsuit, or sheer dresses, allow more for exceptional doll
15½" ....$150 - 175
Papier-mâché
Smiling/crying faces, glass eyes, cloth body, composition lower limbs
19".................................$650 - 700
Wax
Bartenstein, glass eyes, carton body, crier Black face, white face
12" ....$1,100 - 1,200
Smiling/crying faces
15"................................$750 - 800

MUNICH ART DOLLS

1908 - 1920s. Marion Kaulitz hand painted heads designed by Marc-Schnur, Vogelsanger and Wackerle, dressed in German or French regional costumes. Usually composition heads and bodies, distributed by Cuno & Otto Dressel and Arnold Doll Co.
Composition, painted features, wig, composition body, unmarked
14" ....$12,000 - 14,000
17" - 18" ....$16,000 - 21,000

NANCY ANN STORYBOOK DOLLS

1936 on, San Francisco, California. Started by Nancy Ann Abbott. Made small painted bisque and hard-plastic dolls with elaborate costumes. Also made 8" toddler to compete with Vogue's Ginny, 10" fashion dolls and larger size "style show" dolls. Painted bisque, mohair wig, painted eyes, head molded to torso, jointed limbs, either sticker on outfit or hang tag, in box, later made in hard plastic.

Dolls listed are in good condition with original clothing and wrist tags. Allow more for MIB; allow 30 percent or more for black dolls.
Painted Bisque
1936 - 1937, pink/blue mottled or sunburst box with gold label, gold foil sticker on clothes reads: "Nancy Ann Dressed Dolls," marked: "87," "88" or "93," "Made in Japan," no brochure
Baby
3½" - 4½" ....$500 - 600
Child
5"..............................$1,200 - 1,300
1938, early, marked: "America" (baby marked: "87," "88" or "93," "Made in Japan"), colored box, sunburst pattern with gold label, gold foil sticker on clothe reads: "Judy Ann," no brochure

Nancy Ann Storybook Dolls

5" A January Merry Maid for New Year, Nancy Ann Storybook, bisque, jointed legs: $250. **Photo courtesy of Gloria's Antique Dolls.**

Baby

3½" - 4½" ....$475 - 525

Child

5" ....$800 - 1,000

1938, late, marked: "Judy Ann USA" and "Story Book USA" (baby marked: "Made in USA" and "88, 89 and 93 Made in Japan"), colored box, sunburst pattern with gold or silver label, gold foil sticker on clothes reads : "Storybook Dolls," no brochure

Judy Ann mold...................$900 - 1,200

Storybook mold....................$550 - 750

1939, child, Story Book Doll USA, molded socks, molded bangs, (baby has star-shaped hands), colored box with small silver dots, silver label, gold foil sticker on clothes reads: "Storybook Dolls," no brochure

Baby

3½" - 4½" ....$200 - 225

Child

5".......................................$450 - 550

1940, child has molded socks only, (baby has star-shaped bisque hands), colored box with white polka dots, silver label, gold foil sticker on clothes reads: "Storybook Dolls," brochure

Baby

3½" - 4½" ....$90 - 115

Child

5".......................................$225 - 325

1941 - 1942, child has pudgy tummy or slim tummy, (baby has star-shaped hands or fist), white box with colored polka dots, silver label, gold foil bracelet with name of doll, brochure

Baby

3½" - 4½" ....$100 - 125

Child

5".......................................$200 - 250

1943 - 1947, child has one-piece head, body and "stiff" legs, (baby has fist hands), white box with colored polka dots, silver label, ribbon tie or pin fastener, gold foil bracelet with name of doll, brochure

Baby

3½" - 4½" ....$50 - 65

Child

5"...$50 - 75

Hard Plastic

1947 - 1949, child has hard-plastic body, painted eyes, (baby has bisque body, plastic arms and legs), white box with colored polka dots with "Nancy Ann Storybook Dolls" between dots, silver label, brass snap, gold foil bracelet with name of doll, brochure, allow more for special outfits

Baby

3½" - 4½" ....$55 - 70

Child

5½" ....$80 - 100

1949 on, hard plastic, black sleep eyes, white box with colored polka dots and "Nancy Ann Storybook Dolls" between dots, silver label, brass or painted snaps, gold foil bracelet with name of doll, brochure

Baby

3½" - 4½" ....$40 - 55

Child

5"...$40 - 50

Nancy Ann Storybook Dolls

Special Dolls
Mammy and Baby, marked: "Japan 1146"
or America mold
    5".................$1,000 - 1,200
Storybook USA
    5"......................$400 - 500
Topsy, bisque black doll, jointed leg
All-bisque ....$450 - 500
Plastic arms ....$150 - 200
All-plastic, painted or
sleep eyes ....$125 - 150
    With molded painted white boots,
bisque jointed-leg dolls ....$175 - 200
Series Dolls, depending on mold mark
All-Bisque
American Girl Series
    Jointed legs ....$175 - 250
    Stiff legs ....$45 - 65
Around the World Series ....$600 - 1,000
Masquerade Series
    Ballet Dancer, Cowboy,
    Pirate...............................$750 - 900
Sports Series ....$1,000 - 1,300
Margie Ann Series
    Margie Ann ....$150 - 250
Powder & Crinoline Series ......$75 - 100
Bisque or Plastic
Operetta or Hit Parade Series ..$140 - 175
Hard Plastic
Big and Little Sister Series, or
Commencement Series
(except baby) ....$75 - 100
Bridal, Dolls of the Day, Dolls of the
Month, Fairytale, Mother Goose,
Nursery Rhyme, Religious, and Seasons
Series, painted or sleep eye ....$60 - 75
Other Dolls
Audrey Ann, toddler, marked "Nancy
Ann Storybook 12"
    6"......................$900 - 975
Nancy Ann Style Show, circa 1954
Hard plastic, sleep eyes, long dress,
unmarked
    18"...............$1,000 - 1,600
Vinyl head, plastic body, all original,
complete
    18"......................$400 - 500

5" Nancy Ann Storybook, pirate, Masquerade
Series, bisque: $750. **Photo courtesy of Gloria's
Antique Dolls.**

Muffie
1953, hard plastic, wig, sleep eyes,
strung straight leg, non-walker, painted
lashes
    8"......................$300 - 350
1954, hard-plastic walker, molded
eyelashes, brows
    8"......................$175 - 200
1955 - 1956, vinyl head, molded or
painted upper lashes, rooted saran wig,
walker or bent-knee walker
    8"......................$100 - 150
1968 on, reissued, hard plastic
    8"......................$90 - 105
Lori Ann
Vinyl
    7½" ....$75 - 100
Tagged Lori Ann outfit ....$50 - 70
Debbie
Hard plastic wearing school dress,
name on wrist tag/box
    10" ....$175 - 200
Vinyl head, hard-plastic body
    10" ....$75 - 100
Hard-plastic walker
    10½" ....$125 - 150
Vinyl head, hard-plastic walker

8" Little Miss Nancy Ann, Nancy Ann Storybook, vinyl, circa 1958: $100.
Photo courtesy of American Beauty Dolls.

10" mold 22 character baby, Gebrüder Olhaver, bisque: $200.
Photo courtesy of McMasters Harris Apple Tree Doll Auctions.

10½" ....$65 - 75
Little Miss Nancy Ann, 1959, high-heeled fashion doll
8½" ....$100 - 150
Miss Nancy Ann, 1959, vinyl head, rooted hair, rigid vinyl body, high-heeled feet, wearing undergarments or day dress, marked: "Nancy Ann"
10½" ....$150 - 175
Baby Sue Sue, 1960s, vinyl
Doll only ....$100 - 125

NESBIT

House of Nesbit, 1956 on, England. Historical costume and character dolls designed by Peggy Nesbit. Hard-plastic heads on vinyl bodies.
7" - 10"
Simple costumes ....$25 - 35
Elaborate costumes ....$50 - 100

GEBRÜDER OHLHAVER

1913 - 1930, Sonneberg, Germany. Had Revalo (Ohlhaver spelled backwards omitting the two H's) line; made bisque socket and shoulder head and composition dolls. Bought heads from Ernst Heubach, Gebrüder Heubach, and others. Dolls listed are in good condition with original or appropriate clothing.

Baby or Toddler, character face, bisque socket head, glass eyes, open mouth, teeth, wig, composition-and-wood ball-jointed body (bent-leg for baby)
Baby
15" - 17" ....$300 - 375
19" - 21" ....$475 - 550
Toddler
14" ....$550 - 650
22" ....$750 - 850
Child, Mold 150, or no mold number, bisque socket head, sleep eyes, open mouth, composition body
14" - 16" ....$350 - 425
18" - 20" ....$500 - 600
24" - 28" ....$700 - 800
Shoulder head, kid body
18" - 20" ....$350 - 400
Character, bisque solid dome with molded and painted hair, intaglio eyes, composition body
Molded bob, intaglio eyes, open/closed mouth, five-piece body
12" ....$750 -900
Too few in database for reliable range
Coquette-type, molded hair ribbon with bows
High-quality bisque
12" - 13" ....$700 - 800
Low-quality bisque
11" - 12" ....$375 - 450

OLD COTTAGE DOLLS

Late 1948 on, England. Dolls were designed by Greta and Susi Fleischmann. Made with hard-rubber or plastic heads, felt body, some with wire armature, oval hang tag has trademark: "Old Cottage Dolls," may allow more for special characters.

8" - 9"..................................$60 - 100
12" - 13"............................$150 - 225

ORIENTAL DOLLS

1850 to present. Dolls depicting Asian peoples. Made by companies in Germany, America, Japan and others.

All Bisque
Heubach, Gebrüder, Chin-Chin
4"....................................$275 - 300
Kestner
6"................................$1,100 - 1,500
7½"...........................$1,800 - 1,900
8"................................$1,900 - 2,000
Simon & Halbig, mold 852, circa 1880, all-bisque, oriental, swivel head, yellow-tint bisque, glass eyes, closed mouth, wig, painted socks, curled pointed-toe shoes
4½"..................................$650 - 700
5½ " - 6 ½ "..................$875 - 950
7"..................................$975 - 1,025
Unmarked or unknown maker, presumed German or French
6"......................................$450 - 550
European Bisque
Bisque head, jointed body
Barrois Poupée, swivel neck, glass eyes, kid body ....
15"....................................$10,000
Too few in database for reliable range
Belton-type, mold 193, 206
10"..............................$1,900 - 2,075
14"..............................$2,500 - 2,700
Bru, pressed bisque swivel head, glass eyes, closed mouth
18" - 20" BruJne ....$46,000 - 56,000

Kestner, J. D., 1899 - 1930 on, mold 243, bisque socket head, open mouth, wig, bent-leg baby body, allow more for original clothing
13" - 14" ....$4,000 - 4,500
16" - 18".....................$5,000 - 6,000
Solid dome, painted hair
15"..............................$4,500 - 5,000
König & Wernicke, mold 155, glass eyes, open mouth
18"..............................$1,700 - 1,800
Armand Marseille, 1925, mold 353, solid-dome bisque socket head, glass eyes, closed mouth
Baby body
7½"..........................$1,000 - 1,100
9" - 12".........................$900 - 1,000
14" - 16".....................$1,200 - 1,500
Toddler
16"..............................$1,200 - 1,500
Painted bisque
7" $350
Too few in database for reliable range
Schmidt, Bruno, mold 500, circa 1905, glass eyes, open mouth, marked: "BSW"
13" - 14".....................$1,600 - 2,000
Schoenau & Hoffmeister, mold 4900, bisque socket head, glass eyes, open mouth, tinted composition-and-wood jointed body
8" - 10" ....$700 - 800
Simon & Halbig, mold 1079, 1099,

6" oriental, Simon & Halbig, all bisque: $775.
Photo courtesy of Morphy Auctions.

Oriental Dolls

13" mold 243 oriental, Kestner, bisque, socket head: $4,000. **Photo courtesy of McMasters Harris Apple Tree Doll Auctions.**

8½" & 15" mold 353 oriental, Armand Marseille, bisque: $1,100 (8½") & $1,500 (15"). **Photo courtesy of Sweetbriar Auctions.**

1129, 1159, 1199,1329, bisque socket head, glass eyes, open mouth, pierced ears, composition-and-wood jointed body

8" - 10"	$1,200 - 1,400
12" - 13"	$1,400 - 1,600
16" - 18"	$1,800 - 2,200
20" - 24"	$3,000 - 4,000

Unknown maker, socket head, jointed body, glass eyes, closed mouth

4½"	$550 - 650
8" - 10"	$700 - 900
12" - 14"	$1,000 - 1,200
20"	$2,600 - 2,800

Cloth

Ada Lum dolls, 1940s on, Shanghai, cloth dolls depicting Chinese people, embroidered features, black yarn hair

8" - 10"	$70 - 85
14" - 18"	$125 - 150

Shoasing Idustrial Mission, Chekang Province, China, cloth dolls depicting Chinese people, painted features

1½" - 3"	$20 - 40

Composition

Amusco, 1925, composition

17"	$1,000 - 1,200

Effanbee

Butin-nose, in basket with wardrobe, painted oriental features including black bobbed hair, bangs, side-glancing eyes, excellent color and condition

8"	$400 - 500

Patsy, painted oriental features including black bangs straight across the forehead, brown side-glancing eyes, wearing silk Chinese pajamas and matching shoes, excellent condition

14"	$700 - 800

Horsman

Molded-Turban-Head child, 1910 on, composition head and lower arms, cloth body, molded turban, painted eyes

11"	$375 - 425

Jap Rose Kids, 1911 on, composition head, arms, cloth body, molded painted hair, painted eyes, made as an advertising tie-in to Jap Rose soap

13" boy or 14" girl

	$350 - 375

Baby Butterfly, 1914 on, composition head, hands, cloth body, painted hair, features

13"	$250 - 300
15"	$350 - 400

Quan-Quan Co., California, Ming Ming Baby, all-composition jointed baby, painted features, original costume, yarn queue, painted shoes

9"	$75 - 100
11"	$100 - 150

Traditional Chinese

Man or woman, composition-type head, cloth-wound bodies, may have carved

Papier-Mâché

17" milliner's model (so called), all original, papier-mâché: $2,200. **Photo courtesy of Richard Withington, Inc.**

23" papier-mâché, glass eyes, applied hair: $4,500. **Photo courtesy of Richard Withington, Inc.**

Center part, sausage curls
11" - 14" ....$900 - 1,000
Coiled braids over ears, braided bun
9" - 11" ....$1,000 - 1,100
20" - 21" ....$2,100 - 2,300
Covered Wagon or Flat Top
6" - 10" ....$400 - 600
14" - 16" ....$800 - 900
Empire style, short curls
8" ....$750 - 850
14" - 20" ....$1,200 - 1,700
Long curls on shoulders
7" - 14" ....$1,200 - 2,000
22" $3,000
Man, molded hat, mustache, beard or other feature
6" - 10" ....$1,200 - 1,500
14" - 18" ....$3,000 - 5,000
Molded comb, side curls, braided coronet
20" - 25" ....$3,200 - 3,800
Too few in database for reliable range
Early Type Shoulder Head, German,

1840s - 1860s, cloth body, wooden limbs, topknot, bun, puff curls or braids, dressed in original clothing or excellent copy, may have some wear, allow more for painted pate, elaborate hairstyle or exceptional quality
Painted eyes
9" - 14" ....$900 - 1,400
16" - 18" ....$1,800 - 2,400
21" - 24" ....$2,200 - 2,800
26" - 30" ....$2,800 - 3,000
Glass eyes
16" - 18" ....$1,800 - 2,200
20" - 24" ....$2,500 - 3,500
27" $5,000
Long curls
14" ....$1,100 - 1,500
16" ....$2,000 - 2,200
24" ....$3,200 - 3,500
Pre-Greiner Type, 1850s, German- or American-made shoulder head, molded painted black hair, black glass eyes, cloth

Papier-Mâché

20" papier-mâché, glass eyes, German: $1,200.
Photo courtesy of Richard Withington, Inc.

body

16" - 18"	$1,200 - 2,000
20" - 25"	$1,600 - 2,200
29" - 31"	$3,000 - 4,000

French Type, 1835 - 1850, made by German companies for the French trade, painted black hair, brush marks, solid-dome, shoulder head, some have nailed-on wigs, open mouth, bamboo teeth, kid or leather body, appropriately dressed

Glass eyes

13" - 14"	$1,000 - 1,400
18" - 20"	$1,800 - 2,000
22" - 24"	$2,200 - 2,500
28" - 34"	$3,400 - 3,800

Painted eyes

8" - 12"	$600 - 800
14" - 16"	$1,100 - 1,400
17" - 20"	$1,500 - 2,500

Papier-mâché, American, Greiner 1858 - 1883: See Greiner section.

Poupard, French and German, all papier-mâché, represent swaddled baby

12"	$300 - 400

SonnebergTaufling (so-called Motschmann): See Sonneberg Taufling section.

Patent Washable, 1879 - 1910s, made by companies such as F. M. Schilling and others, shoulder head, mohair wig, glass eyes, open or closed mouth, cloth body, composition limbs

Better quality

12" - 15"	$450 - 500
18"	$575 - 625
22" - 24"	$675 -750

Lesser quality

10" - 12"	$100 - 125
14" - 16"	$175 - 200
23" - 25"	$250 - 300

Sonneberg Type, 1880 - 1910, made by Muller & Strasburger, Cuno & Otto Dressel and others, shoulder head, blond molded hair, painted blue or brown eyes, cloth body, kid or leather arms and boots, marked: "M & S Superior"

13" - 15"	$350 - 400

32" papier-mâché, Voit, flirty eyes: $6,000.
Photo courtesy of Richard Withington, Inc.

18" - 20" ....$450 - 525
24" - 29" ....$575 - 650
Glass eyes
  12"....................................$400 - 450
  16" - 18"............................$550 - 600
Wigged
  18" - 25" ....$600 - 700
Papier-mâché Child, 1920 on, head has brighter coloring, wigged, child often wearing ethnic costume, stuffed cloth body and limbs, or papier-mâché arms
French
  9" - 13"............................$100 - 125
  13" - 15"............................$200 - 275
German
  10"...$70 - 80
  15".....................................$150 - 165
Unknown maker
  8"..$50 - 60
  12" ....$90 - 115
  16" ....$150 - 175
Clowns, papier-mâché head, painted clown features, open or closed mouth, molded hair or wigged, cloth body, composition or papier-mâché arms, or five-

14" papier-mâché, patent washable type, circa 1880-1910: $500. **Photo courtesy of Cybermogul Dolls.**

piece jointed body
High-quality child body
  16" ....$800 - 1,000
  20"..........................$1,200 - 1,300
Lower-quality crude body type
  8".....................................$200 - 235
  14"...................................$450 - 485

17" papier-mâché, French type: $1,700. **Photo courtesy of Morphy Auctions.**

31" papier-mâché, Sonneberg type, painted eyes: $700. **Photo courtesy of Richard Withington, Inc.**

PARIAN-TYPE, UNTINTED BISQUE

1850 - 1900 on, Germany. The term "parian" as used in doll collecting refers to dolls of untinted bisque; in other words, the doll's skin tone is white rather than tinted. These dolls were at the height of their popularity from 1860 through the 1870s.They are often found with molded blond hair, some with fancy hair arrangements and ornaments or bonnets, can have glass or painted eyes, pierced ears, may have molded jewelry or clothing, occasionally solid dome with wig, cloth bodies, nicely dressed in good condition. Dolls listed are in good condition, appropriately dressed. May allow much more for exceptional examples.

Lady

Common hair style

Painted eyes

    Undecorated, simple molded hair

    8" - 12" ....$200 - 350

    14" - 16"...........................$400 - 450

    18" - 25" ....$500 - 600

    Molded bodice, fancy trim

14" parian (so called), molded shirt and tie: $550.
Photo courtesy of Morphy Auctions.

    8".......................................$225 - 300

    17" - 23".............................$600 - 900

    Wigged, bald head with period wig

    10" - 12"......................$1,400 - 1,600

    Glass eyes

    10".....................................$800 - 900

13" parian (so called), elaborate molded hair ornaments and earrings: $1,200. **Photo courtesy of Richard Withington, Inc.**

Parian-Type, Untinted Bisque

12" - 14" ....$1,300 - 1,600
16" - 18" ....$1,800 - 2,000
Fancy hair style, molded combs,
ribbons, flowers, bands or snoods,
cloth body, untinted bisque limbs,
allow more for very elaborate hairstyle
Painted eyes, pierced ears
  7" - 10" ....$850 - 1,200
  14" - 16" ....$1,200 - 1,400
  18" - 22" ....$1,600 - 1,800
  24" - 30" ....$1,800 - 2,000
Decorated shoulder plate
  Simple bodice or tie
  8½" ....$275 - 300
  13" - 15" ....$450 - 600
  20" - 23" ....$650 - 750
  More elaborate bodice and hair
  12" - 16" ....$2,000 - 2,400
  17" - 21" ....$3,000 - 3,400
Glass eyes, pierced ears
  12" - 15" ....$1,600 - 2,000
  18" - 20" ....$2,200 - 2,600
  Swivel neck
  14" - 15" ....$2,100 - 2,400
Named Hairstyles, painted eyes unless
otherwise noted (These are names
applied by contemporary collectors to
describe style.)
Alice in Wonderland, molded
head band or comb
  14" - 16" ....$775 - 900
  19" - 21" ....$1,000 - 1,200
Countess Dagmar, no mark, head
band, cluster curls on forehead
  12" -15" ....$750 - 900
  18" - 21" ....$1,100 - 1,600
Currier & Ives, no mark, headband,
wavy hair falling on shoulders
  7" ....$1,500 - 2,000
Dolly Madison, no mark, short
curls with molded ribbon tied
with bow
  18" - 22" ....$750 - 1,200
Empress Eugenie, headpiece snood
  12" - 15" ....$1,500 - 1,700
  25" ....$1,200 - 1,500

17" parian (so called), glass eyes: $1,000. **Photo courtesy of Richard Withington, Inc.**

Irish Queen, Limbach, marked
with clover mark and number 8552,
curls on forehead, bow above
bangs, double chignon in back
and molded bodice with high collar
  14" - 16" ....$600 - 700
Molded hat: See Bonnet-Heads section.
Necklace, jewels, or standing ruffles
  17" - 20" ....$1,800 - 2,800
Kaiserin Augusta Victoria, molded
hairstyle with beaded band, shoulder
plate with molded cross necklace,
glass eyes
  13" - 15" ....$1,100 - 1,300
  22" ....$1,000 - $1,400
Men or Boys, center or side-part
hair style, cloth body, decorated
shirt and tie
Painted eyes
  13" ....$700 - 800
  16" - 17" ....$900 - 1,100
Glass eyes
  16" ....$2,400 - 2,825

8" Ronnaug Pettersen, angel, cloth: $150. **Photo courtesy of Memories of Things Past Antiques.**

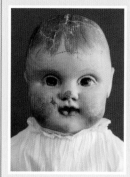

21" Philadelphia Baby, cloth: $2,000. **Photo courtesy of the Museum Doll Shop.**

RONNAUG PETTERSEN

1901 - 1980, Norway. Made cloth dolls, pressed felt heads, usually painted side-glancing eyes, cloth bodies, intricate costumes, paper tags

7" - 8"..............................$100 - 150

14½" ....$500 - 600

Nissa, gnome

11"..................................$300 - 350

DORA PETZOLD

Germany, 1919 - 1930 on. Made and dressed dolls, molded composition heads, painted features, wigs, stockinette-sawdust-filled bodies, short torsos, free-formed thumbs, stitched fingers, shaped legs.

18"..............................$1,800 - 2,500

20" - 22" ....$3,000 - 4,000

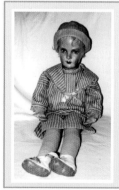

18" Dora Petzold, composition: $2,000. **Photo courtesy Jean Grout.**

PHILADELPHIA BABY (SHEPPARD BABY)

1900, Philadelphia, Pennsylvania. Rag baby sold by the J.B. Sheppard & Co. store. Molded stockinette, painted features, sewn joints at shoulders, hips, and knees. Dolls listed are in good condition, appropriately dressed. Allow more for exceptional condition.

18" - 22" ....$4,000 - 5,000

Doll in somewhat-worn condition

18" - 22" ....$1,200 - 2,200

PLEASANT COMPANY

1985 on. Middleton, Wisconsin, Founded by Pleasant T. Rowland, in 1998 the company was purchased by Mattel,

18" Samantha, American Girl, Pleasant Company, vinyl, retired: $125. **Photo courtesy of Morphy Auctions.**

Inc. Values listed are for secondary-market dolls in appropriate clothing and in good condition; many dolls are still available at retail as well.

American Girl®, vinyl doll with wig

18" ....$70 - 95
Retired dolls ....$125 - 150

POLISH RELIEF DOLLS

1914 on, Paris, France. Polish Relief dolls were created in the workshop of Madame Lazarski during and shortly after World War I. This project provided work for war refugees and the money raised from the sale of the dolls aided Polish widows and orphans. Cloth dolls with embroidered features and floss hair.

Adult

19" ....$500 -600

Child

11" - 17" ....$350 - 450

20" & 18" Polish Relief, France, cloth: $500 (20") & 400 (18"). **Photo courtesy of Richard Withington, Inc.**

17" Presbyterian rag, cloth, circa 1950s-1960s: $450. **Photo courtesy of The Museum Doll Shop.**

PRESBYTERIAN RAG DOLL

1885 on, Bucyrus, Ohio. Made by The First Presbyterian Church as fundraisers: cloth dolls with "pie-shaped gusseted" piece across top of head, flat face, painted hair and features, mitten hands, 17".

1880s - 1930s ....$4,500 - 5,000
1950s - 1980s ....400 - 450

RABERY & DELPHIEU

1856 - 1930 and later, Paris. Became part of S.F.B.J. in 1899. Some heads pressed (pre-1890) and some poured, purchased some heads from François Gaultier. Dolls listed are in good condition, appropriately dressed. May allow more for exceptional dolls.

Child

Closed mouth, bisque socket head, paperweight eyes, pierced ears, mohair wig, cork pate, French composition-and-wood jointed body

9" - 10" ....$2,400 - 2,600
12" girl in entrennes box with
trousseaux ....sold at auction
for $10,000
13" - 15" ....$3,000 - 4,000
20" - 24" ....$4,500 - 5,500
28" ....$6,500 - 7,500

241

19" Rabery & Delphieu, bébé, bisque: $4,500.
Photo courtesy of Richard Withington, Inc.

Open mouth, row of upper teeth
18" - 21" ....$1,400 - 1,600
24" - 26" ....$1,700 - 2,000

RAGGEDY ANN & ANDY

1915 to present. Rag doll designed by Johnny Gruelle in 1915, made by various companies. Ann wears dress with apron; Andy wears shirt and pants with matching hat.

P.J. Volland, 1918 - 1934, early dolls marked: "Patented Sept. 7, 1915," all-cloth, tin or wooden button eyes, painted features, some have sewn knee or arm joints, sparse brown or auburn yarn hair, oversize hands, feet turned outward. Dolls listed are in clean un-faded condition, appropriately dressed.

Raggedy Ann and Andy, 15" - 18"
Painted face ....$1,200 - 2,000
Printed face.........................$900 - 1,500
Beloved Belindy, 1926 - 1930 painted face, 1931 - 1934 print face
15".............................$1,600 - 2,500
Pirate Chieftain and other characters
18"..............................$3,000 - 4,000
Exposition, 1935
Raggedy Ann, no eyelashes, no eyebrows,

outline nose, no heart, satin label on hem of dress
18"..............................$5,800 - 7,000
Too few in database for reliable range
Mollye Goldman, 1935 - 1937, chest marked: "Raggedy Ann and Andy Dolls Manufactured by Molly'es Doll Outfitters," nose outlined in black, red heart on chest, reddish-orange hair, multi-colored legs, blue feet, some have oilcloth faces
15"...................................$750 - 850
17" - 21" ....$900 - 1,100
Baby Ann
14"...................................$750 - 850
Georgene Novelties, 1938 - 1962, Ann has orange hair and a top knot, six different mouth styles, early ones had tin eyes, later ones had plastic, six different noses, seams in middle of legs and arms to represent knees and elbows, feet turn forward, red-and-white striped legs, all have hearts printed on chest reading: "I love you," tag sewn to left side seam, several variations, all read: "Georgene Novelties, Inc."
Raggedy Ann or Andy, 1930s - 1960s
Nose outlined with black, 1938 - 1944
15" - 17"............................$300 - 350
19" - 21"............................$400 - 550
Awake/Asleep, 1940s
Nose outlined black
14"...................................$400 - 500

36" Raggedy Andy, Volland, cloth: $2,500. **Photo courtesy of James D. Julia, Auctioneers.**

Raggedy Ann & Andy

20" Raggedy Ann, Exposition, cloth: $7,000.
Photo courtesy of James D. Julia, Auctioneers.

Long nose face, 1944 - 1946
    19"....................................$500 - 700
Curved nose edges, 1946 on
    15" - 19"...........................$175 - 200
    20" - 23" ....$250 - 300
    32"..................................$300 - $350
Beloved Belindy, 1940 - 1944
    14" - 18" ....$1,700 - 2,100
Knickerbocker, 1962 - 1982, printed
features, hair color change from

orange to red, five mouth and five
eyelash variations, tags are on clothing
back or pants seam
Raggedy Ann or Andy
1964, cloud box
    15".....................................$200 - 275
Later examples
    6"...$20 - 30
    15".......................................$65 - 80
    19" ....$90 - 120
    30" - 36"...........................$100 - 125
Musical Ann
    15" ....$75 - 100
Raggedy Ann Talking, 1972
    19" ....$90 - 125
Beloved Belindy, circa 1965
    15" ....$900 - 1,000
Camel with Wrinkled Knees
    15"....................................$275 - 350
Nasco/Bobbs-Merrill, 1972, cloth head,
hard-plastic body, printed features,
apron marked: "Raggedy Ann"
    24" ....$125 - 150
Bobbs-Merrill Co., 1974, ventriloquist
dummy, hard-plastic head, hands,
foam body, printed face
    30" ....$125 - 175
Applause Toy Company, 1981 - present,

19" Raggedy Ann
& Raggedy Andy,
Georgene
Novelties, cloth,
outlined noses:
pair $800.
**Photo courtesy of
Morphy Auctions.**

8" Raggedy Ann & Raggedy Andy, Knickerbocker, cloth: pair $40. **Dolls courtesy of private collection.**

owned by Hasbro, which also markets Raggedy Ann through Playskool line

8"	$10 - 15
17"	$30 - 35
48"	$100 - 125

Limited Editions, marketed by Applause as part of Dakin line

75th anniversary Ann or Andy, 1992

19" ....$45 - 65

Molly-E Raggedy Ann, 1993

18" ....$40 - 50

Georgene reissues, 1996

15" ....$30 - 40

Ann or Andy, 1994

13" ....$70 - 80

US Patent Ann, 1995

17" ....$65 - 85

Stamp Ann, 1997

17" ....$45 - 55

Exposition Ann or Andy, 1998

17" ....$25 - 35

R. John Wright, 2004 on, molded-felt doll, secondary-market values, dolls still available at retail

Ann or Andy

17" ....$650 - $900

Three-piece set of *Ann, Andy and the Camel with the Wrinkled Knees* ....$1,800 - 2,000

Brass Key Productions, 1993 on, porcelain

7" ....$8 - 15

JESSIE MCCUTCHEON RALEIGH

1916 - 1920, Chicago, Illinois. McCutcheon was a businesswoman who developed a line of cloth and composition dolls that

15" toddler, Jessie McCutcheon Raleigh, composition: $400. **Photo courtesy of Morphy Auctions.**

were distributed by Butler Brothers and perhaps others.

Shoebutton Sue, flat face, painted spit curls, mitten hands, sewn-on red shoes, shown in 1921 Sears catalog

15"..$1,900

Too few in database for reliable range

Baby, composition head and body

10" - 12"............................$300 - 450

18"......................................$475 - 600

Child

Composition head and body, wigged

11"......................................$350 - 450

13"......................................$450 - 500

18"......................................$650 - 725

Molded hair

11" - 13".............................$500 - 700

18" ....$1,100 - 1,400

Composition head, cloth body, composition lower arms and legs

22" - 24" ....$325 - 400

RAYNAL

1922 - 1930 on, Paris. Edouard Raynal made dolls of felt, cloth or with celluloid heads with widely spaced eyebrows. Dressed, some resemble Lenci, except fingers were together or their hands were of celluloid, marked: "Raynal" on soles of shoes and/or pendant.

Cloth, 1922, molded head, cloth body, sometimes celluloid hands

14" - 16"............................$500 - 700

17" - 22".....................$1,400 - 2,000

Baby Shirley type

18"............................$1,400 - 1,800

Pressed-felt child

14" - 19".....................$2,000 - 2,500

Celluloid, 1936, then Rhodoid

Baby

18" - 24"............................$525 - 575

Child, flirty eyes

18" - 24"............................$400 - 500

Vinyl, 1960s - 1970s

Margaret

14" ....$50 - 60

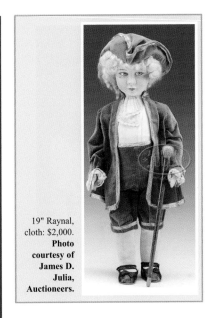

19" Raynal, cloth: $2,000. **Photo courtesy of James D. Julia, Auctioneers.**

THEODOR RECKNAGEL

1886 - 1930, Alexandrienthal, Coburg, Germany. Made bisque and composition doll heads of varying quality, incised or raised mark, wigged or molded hair, glass or painted eyes, open or closed mouth, flange neck or socket head. Dolls listed are in good condition, appropriately dressed.

Baby

Solid-dome infant, 1924, solid-dome flange-neck head, cloth body, glass eyes

6" - 8"..............................$125 - 175

Mold 121, 126, 127, 1924, bent-limb baby body, painted or glass eyes

6" - 8"..............................$150 - 175

9" - 12" ....$200 - 250

Bonnet-head baby, Mold 22, 23, 28, 44: See Bonnet-Heads section.

Child

Dolly face, 1890s - 1914

Mold 1907, 1909, 1914, glass eyes, open mouth

7" - 9"..................................$90 - 12

8" Recknagel, bisque, elaborate molded hair bow: $850. **Photo courtesy of Richard Withington, Inc.**

became popular about 1875 and continue to be made today. May allow more for a well-made beautiful doll with accessories or wardrobe.

Bisque, German
6" - 9" ....$200 - 300
10" - 13" .... $300 - 400
French Fisherfolk, bisque heads
8" - 12" ....$300 - 600
Painted bisque
4"...$45 - 65
10" ....$95 - 130
Celluloid
8"...$40 - 50
15" ....$100 - 125
Cloth
8"..$100 - 155
13" ....$125 - 175
Russian, 1920 on, all cloth, molded and painted stockinette head and hands
7"...$55 - 70
15"......................................$125 - 150
18" ....$160 - 180
Composition Child
8"..$150 - 185
13" - 16"............................$200 - 250
Walker in Dutch costume, post-World-War-II era
22" ....$100 - 125

10" - 12".............................$120 - 150
15" - 18".............................$175 - 250
22" - 24" ....$275 - 300
Character face, circa 1910 on, may have crossed hammer mark
7" - 8"...............................$350 - 375
12" - 14"............................$700 - 775
Mold 57, open/closed mouth with teeth, molded hair
9" - 10"..............................$875 - 975
Mold 58, open/closed mouth with teeth, molded hair with molded ribbon and three flowers
7".......................................$300 - 325
Mold 31, 32, Max and Moritz
8" ....each $600 - 700
12" ....each $1,200 - 1,500
Googly molds 43, 45, 46, 50, no mold number: See Googlies section.

REGIONAL-DRESS DOLLS

This category describes dolls costumed in regional dress to show different nationalities, facial characteristics or cultural background. Examples are dolls in regional costumes that are commonly sold as souvenirs to tourists. These dolls

17" Kling, bisque, shoulder head, Swedish costume, Germany: $650. **Doll courtesy of private collection.**

Jay Dolls, Dublin, Ireland, molded heads, cloth-wrapped bodies
　　5"...$35 - 40
　　7 1/2" ....$50 - 60
　　11"...$55 - 65
Native American Indian, cloth, leather, natural fibers, 1800s and early 1900s
　　5" - 8" ....$130 - 225
　　13" - 15" ....$400 - 650
　　23"......................................$700 - 850
Seminole, woven fiber
　　4½" - 6" ....$28 - 35
Skookum, 1913 on, designed by Mary McAboy, painted features, side-glancing eyes, mohair wigs, cloth figure wrapped in Indian blanket, with folds representing arms, wooden feet, later plastic, label on bottom of foot, box marked: "Skookum Bully Good"
　　4½" papoose on mailer
　　card ....$25 - 35
　　6" - 9"...................................$65 - 100
　　10 - 12" ....$200 - 300
　　14" - 16"...........................$325 - 425
　　18" - 20" ....$550 - 700
　　27" - 33".....................$1,000 - 1,350
Hard Plastic, unmarked or unknown maker
　　7"...$8 - 15

5" Connemara Woman, Jay Dolls, composition: $40. **Photo courtesy of The Museum Doll Shop.**

　　12"...$20 - 30
Baitz, Austria, 1970s, painted hard plastic, painted side-glancing eyes, open "o" mouth, excellent quality, tagged
　　8½" - 9½" ....$45 - 55
Vinyl
　　6"...$20 - 25
　　12".......................................$40 - 45
Wood
Polish, painted features, 1930s on
　　7"..$4 - 6

10"-10½" Skookums, composition: each $200-$225. **Photo courtesy of Alderfer Auction Company, Inc.**

RELIABLE TOY COMPANY

1920 on, Toronto, Canada. Made composition, hard-plastic and vinyl dolls. Composition, all-composition or composition shoulder head and arms, cloth body, some with composition legs. Dolls listed are in good condition, appropriately dressed.

Baby, 1930s
20".....................................$175 - 225
Baby Precious, 1947, Mama-style, sleep eyes, mohair wig
20"....................................$150 - 200
Barbara Scott Ice Skating Doll
15" ....$300 - 400
Her Highness
15"....................................$275 - 300
Hiawatha or Indian child
10½" ....$45 - 55
13".................................$90 - 110
16"................................$125 - 145
Military man
14" ....$125 - 175
Mountie
17"...................................$300 - 350
Nurse, painted eyes, mohair wig
18"....................................$200 - 250
Scottish child
14" ....$75 - 100
17" ....$150 - 165
Shirley Temple
18" - 22"......................$1,000 - 1,200
Toddler
13"..................................$150 - 200
Hard Plastic
Baby, 1958, sleep eyes, open mouth
8"...$40 - 50
Indian child, all hard plastic
8"...$20 - 30
Toni, P-90
14".....................................$300 - 350
Vinyl
Cindy Lou, 1961, vinyl head, rooted ponytail, sleep eyes
14" ....$20 - 30

18" Scottish child, Reliable Toy Co., composition: $125. **Photo courtesy of Morphy Auctions.**

Eaton Beauties, 1965, all vinyl, rooted hair, sleep eyes
14" ....$45 - 65
Majorette, 1960s, vinyl head, rooted hair, sleep eyes
16" ....$60 - 75
Mitzi, 1961-1962, vinyl head, rooted hair, Barbie-type
11½" ....$75 - 85
Suzy Steps, walker, 1950, Canadian version of Ideal's Saucy Walker
35"....................................$200 - 300
Tammy, Canadian version of Ideal's Tammy
12"...................................$75 - 100

REMCO INDUSTRIES

1959 - 1974, Harrison, New Jersey. One of the first companies to market with television ads. Dolls listed are in good condition with original clothing and accessories, allow more for MIB.

Addams Family, 1964
Lurch
5½" ....$95 - 130
Morticia
4¾" ....$100 - 128
Uncle Fester
4½" ....$60 - 75
Baby Crawl-Along, 1967
20"......................................$15 - 20

Baby Glad 'N Sad, 1967, vinyl and hard plastic, rooted blond hair, painted blue eyes
14" ....$12 - 18

Baby Grow a Tooth, 1968, vinyl and hard plastic, rooted hair, blue sleep eyes, open/closed mouth, one tooth, grows own tooth, battery operated
15" ....$18 - 22
Black
14" ....$20 - 25

Baby Know It All, 1969
17" ....$15 - 20

Baby Laugh A Lot, 1970, rooted long hair, painted eyes, open/closed mouth, teeth, vinyl head, hands, plush body, push button, laughs, battery operated
16" ....$55 - 75

Baby Look N'Love, 1978, vinyl, painted eyes, rooted hair, nods and turns head when squeezed.
14" ....$35 - 45

Beatles, 1964, vinyl and plastic, based on musicians Paul McCartney, Ringo Starr, George Harrison, John Lennon, Paul 4⅞," all others 4½" with guitars bearing their names,
Set of 4 ....$500 - 700
Individual Beatles .... $110 - 140

Daniel Boone, 1964, based on character played by Fess Parker on TV show of the same name
4½" ....$125 - 150

Dave Clark Five, 1964, set of five based on members of musical group, vinyl heads, rigid plastic bodies
Set ....$60 - 65
Dave Clark
5" ....$10 - 15
Other band members, name attached to leg
3" ....$6 - 10

Finger Dings, 1969 on, finger puppets, vinyl head
6" ....$25 - 35

The Monkees, based on members of musical group .... each $20 - 30

Growing Sally, 1968, doll "grows" ¾" extra clothes, additional wig
6" ....$20 - 30
Black ....$30 - 40

Heidi and friends, 1967, in plastic case, rooted hair, painted side-glancing eyes, open/closed mouth, all vinyl, press button and dolls wave
Heidi
5½" ....$30 - 35
Jan, Asian
5½" ....$25 - 30
Pip
5½" ....$35 - 45
Spunky
4½" ....$55 - 65
Winking Heidi, 1968
5½" ....$20 - 30
Hildy
4½" ....$55 - 65
Heidi's Jeep set, pink jeep ....$35 - 40

Hello Dolly, 1978, talks on phone
13" ....$12 - 16

6" Flower Finger Ding, Remco, vinyl: $35.
Photo courtesy Fourty Fifty Sixty.

Hug A Bug, 1971
4".........................$130 - 150
I Dream of Jeannie, based on character played by Barbara Eden in TV show of the same name
6".........................$45 - 55
Plastic Bottle Playset, 6," Jeannie doll, accessories ....$100 - 115
Jumpsy, 1970, vinyl and hard plastic, jumps rope, rooted blond hair, painted blue eyes, closed mouth, molded-on shoes and socks
14".........................$35 - 40
Black
14".........................$40 - 45
Kitty Karry All, 1969, featured on *The Brady Bunch* TV show as Cindy's doll
20".........................$150 - 200
Laurie Partridge, 1973, based on character played by Susan Dey on the TV show *The Partridge Family*
19".........................$125 - 150
Littlechap Family, 1963 on, vinyl head, arms, jointed hips, shoulders, neck, black molded and painted hair, black eyes, box

6" I Dream of Jeannie, Remco, vinyl, MIB: $75. **Photo courtesy of Morphy Auctions.**

Dr. John Littlechap
14½" ....$35 - 45
Judy Littlechap
12".........................$30 - 40
Libby Littlechap
10½" ....$20 - 30
Lisa Littlechap
13½" ....$20 - 30
Littlechap Accessories
Dr. John's Office ....$225 - 275
Bedroom.........................$75 - 110
Family room ....$45 - 75
Dr. John Littlechap's outfits
Golf outfit, MIP $30
Medical outfit, MIP $65
Suit, MIP.........................$50
Tuxedo, MIP.........................$70
Lisa's outfits
Evening dress, MIP.........................$90
Coat, fur trim, MIP $50
Libby's & Judy's outfits
Jeans/sweater, MIP $30
Dance dress, MIP $45
Mimi, 1973, vinyl and hard plastic, battery-operated singer, rooted long blond hair, painted blue eyes, open/closed mouth, record player in body, sings in different languages "I'd Like to Teach the World to Sing"
19".........................$65 - 75
Black
19" ....$75 - 85
Monsters, 1976, Dracula, Frankenstein, others, jointed hard vinyl
9".........................$40 - 50
Munsters, based on characters in *The Munsters* TV show
Herman, pull-string talker based on character played by Fred Gwynne
20".........................$200 - 275
Lily #1822, 1964, vinyl, one-piece body, based on character played by Yvonne DeCarlo
4¾" ....$125 - 150
Grandpa, #1821, 1964, vinyl head, one-piece plastic body, based on character

played by Al Lewis
4¾" ....$100 - 125
Herman, 1964, vinyl, one-piece body,
based on character played by
Fred Gwynne
6¾" ....$125 - 150
Orphan Annie, 1967
15" ....$95 - 120
Polly Puff, 1970, vinyl, with inflatable
furniture
12" ....$30 - 35
Ronald MacDonald, 1976, vinyl
8" ....$15 - 20
Snuggle Bun, 1969, vinyl, push button
makes headturn while doll cries
16" ....$75 - 85
Sweet April, 1971, vinyl
5½" ....$30 - 35
Black
5½" ....$45 - 50
Tippy Tumbles, 1968, vinyl, rooted red
hair, stationary blue eyes, does somer-
saults, batteries in pocketbook
16" ....$40 - 50
Tumbling Tomboy, 1969, rooted
blond braids, closed smiling mouth,

vinyl and hard plastic, battery operated
17" ....$30 - 45

RICHWOOD TOYS INCORPORATED

1950s - 1960s, Annapolis, Maryland. Produced hard-plastic dolls.
Sandra Sue, 1940s-1950s, hard plastic,
walker, head does not turn, slim body,
saran wigs, sleep eyes, some with high-
heeled feet, only marks are number
under arm or leg, all prices reflect outfits
with original socks, shoes, panties, and
accessories, 8". Dolls listed are in good
condition with appropriate clothing and
tags, naked, played-with dolls will bring
one-fourth to one-third the value listed.
Flat feet
Wearing camisole, slip, panties, shoes
and socks ....$75 - 100
Wearing school dress ....$100 - 125
Wearing party/Sunday dress ..$125 - 175
Special coat, hat and dress, limited
editions, Brides, Heidi, Little Women,
Majorette ....$175 - 225
Sport or play clothes ....$75 - 125

7½" Sandra Sue, Richwood Toys, hard plastic, flat feet, extra clothes: $250. **Photo courtesy of Alderfer Auction Company, Inc.**

High-heeled feet
Wearing camisole, slip, panties, shoes,
socks...$70 - 95
Wearing school dress................$75 - 125
Wearing party/Sunday dress ..$125 - 150
Special coat, hat and dress, limited
editions, Brides, Heidi, Little
Women, Majorette..................$150 - 175
Sport or play clothes ....$95 - 125
Sandra Sue Outfits, mint, including
all accessories
School dress................................$50 - 75
Party dress ....$60 - 85
Specials.....................................$75 - 100
Sport sets ....$75 - 85
Cindy Lou, 14," hard plastic, jointed
dolls were purchased in bulk from
New York distributor, fitted with
double-stitched wigs by Richwood
Wearing camisole, slip, panties,
shoes, socks ....$175 - 200
Wearing school dress ....$200 - 225
Wearing party dress ....$225 - 250
Wearing special outfits ....$225 - 275
Wearing sports outfits ....$200 - 250
Cindy Lou Outfits, mint, including
all accessories
School dress ....$75 - 100
Party dress ....$95 - 125
Special outfit ....$1250 - 200
Sports clothes.........................$100 - 150

GRACE CORRY ROCKWELL

1926 - 1928, USA. Artist who designed
dolls. Her bisque doll heads were made
in Germany and were distributed by
Borgfeldt. Her composition-headed dolls
were made by Averill.
Pretty Peggy, bisque socket head, open
mouth
12" - 14" ....$3,500 - 4,000
16" - 19" .... $5,200 - 6,000
Little Sister & Brother, composition,
smiling mouth, molded hair
14" .... $250 - 300

14" Grace Corry Rockwell, bisque: $4,000. **Photo courtesy of Morphy Auctions.**

ROHMER

1857 - 1880, Paris, France. Mme. Rohmer
held patents for doll bodies, made dolls
of various materials. Dolls listed are in
good condition, appropriately dressed,
may allow much more for exceptional
dolls.
Poupée (so-called fashion-type), bisque
or china glazed shoulder or swivel head

14" Rohmer, poupée peau, bisque: $6,500.
Photo courtesy of McMasters Harris Apple Tree Doll Auctions.

on shoulder plate, closed mouth, kid body with green oval stamp, bisque or wooden lower arms

Glass eyes

13" - 16" ....$6,000 - 6,500
17" - 19" ....$9,000 - 11,000
24" ....$16,000 - 17,000

Painted eyes

13" - 18" ....$3,500 - 5,800
14" with provenance and trousseau
..............sold at auction for $19,000

ROLDAN

1960s - 1970s, Barcelona. Spain. Roldan characters are similar to Klumpe figures in many respects. They are made of felt over a wire armature with painted mask faces. Like Klumpe, Roldan figures represent professionals, hobbyists, dancers, historical characters and contemporary males and females performing a variety of tasks. Some, but not all Roldans, were imported by Rosenfeld Imports and Leora Dolores of Hollywood. Figures

originally came with two sewn-on identifying cardboard tags. Characters most commonly found are doctors, Spanish dancers and bull fighters; dolls tend to have somewhat smaller heads, longer necks and more defined facial features than Klumpe. Values are for dolls in good, clean, un-faded condition; allow more for elaborate figure with many accessories.

9" - 11" ....$100 - 150

GERTRUDE F. ROLLINSON

1916 - 1929, Holyoke, Massachusetts. Designed and made cloth dolls with molded faces, painted over the cloth on head and limbs, treated to be washable. Painted hair or wigged, some closed mouth, others have open/closed mouths with painted teeth. Some dolls closely resemble the dolls of the Chase Company, while others were heavily sanded between coats of paint, giving

9½" Cataluna man, Roldan, cloth: $150. **Photo courtesy of Sidney's Second Childhood.**

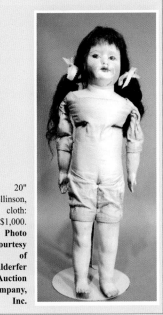

20" Rollinson, cloth: $1,000. **Photo courtesy of Alderfer Auction Company, Inc.**

253

them a look of composition. Rollinson's dolls were made by the Utley Co. (later called New England Doll Company), and distributed by G. Borgfeldt, L. Wolfe and Strobel &Wilken.

Chase-look, painted hair or wig
13" - 17".....................$1,400 - 1,800
22" - 26" ....$2,000 - 2,200
Composition-look, painted hair or wig
16" ....$900 - 1,300
22" - 24" ....$1,600 - 2,000

RUBBER

1860s on, various European and American makers produced rubber dolls.
Goodyear doll, molded shoulder head in style of china and papier-mâché dolls of the era
10" - 18".....................$1,000 - 1,500
20" - 28" ....$1,700 - 2,000
American rubber doll, 1920s on
Baby
12" - 15"...............................$65 - 75

22" rubber doll, mid-1800s: $1,000. **Photo courtesy of Richard Withington, Inc.**

SANTONS

Santons (little saints) France, 1930 on. Character figures depicting elderly peasants, also creche figures. Earthenware heads, hands and legs on wire-armature bodies. Dressed in regional or occupational costume.
7" - 8" ....$40 - 65
10" - 12" ....$75 - 100

SASHA

1945 - 2001. Sasha dolls were created by Swiss artist, Sasha Morgenthaler, who handcrafted 20" children and 13" babies in Zurich, Switzerland, from the 1940s until her death in 1975. Her handmade studio dolls have cloth or molded bodies, five different head molds, and were hand painted by herself and her assistants. To make her dolls affordable as children's playthings, she licensed Götz Puppenfabrik (1964 - 1970 and 1995 - 2001) in Germany and Frido/Trendon Ltd. (1965 - 1986) in England to manufacture 16" Sasha dolls in series. The manufactured dolls are made of rigid vinyl with painted features. Price range reflects rarity, condition and completeness of doll, outfit and packaging, and varies with geographic location. Dolls listed are in good condition, with original clothing. Allow more for MIB.
Original Studio Sasha, circa 1940s - 1974, made by Sasha Morgenthaler in Switzerland, some are signed on soles of feet, have wrist tags or wear labeled clothing
20"...........................$9,000 - 13,000
Götz Sasha, 1964 - 1970, Germany, girls or boys, two face molds, marked "Sasha Series" in circle on neck and in three-circle logo on back, three different boxes were used, identify by wrist tag and/or booklet
16" ....$700 - 900
Frido/Trendon Ltd., 1965 - 1986,

Sasha

England, body unmarked, wrist tags, current catalogs were packed with doll
Child
1965 - 1968, packaged in wide box
16".................$500 - 600
1969 - 1972, packaged in crayon tubes
16".................$550 - 700
Sexed Baby, 1970 - 1978, cradle, packaged in either a straw basket and box or a styrofoam cradle, white or black doll.................$150 - 175
Unsexed Baby, 1978 - 1986, packaged in either straw basket and box or styrofoam cradle ....$75 - 100
Child, 16"
1973 - 1975, packaged in shoebox-style box
1975 - 1980, packaged in shoebox-style box
1980 - 1986, packaged in photo box with flaps
Sasha, 101, 103, sailor...........$200 - 300
Gingham 107.......................$150 - 200
Marina ....$300 - 350
Caleb (black) ....$150 - 200
Cora (black) ....$275 - 350
Gregor ....$175 - 250
#1 Sasha Anniversary doll
16".................$175 - 225
1986, Sasha Sarimodel #117S, black hair, estimated only 400 produced before English factory closed in January 1986
16".................$700 - 800
Model # 130E Sasha Wintersport, 1986, blond hair
16".................$400 - 600
Limited Editions
Made by Frido/Trendon Ltd. in England, packaged in box with outer sleeve picturing individual doll, limited-edition Sashas marked on neck with date and number, number on certificate matches number on neck
1981 Velvet, light-brown wig ..$250 - 300
1982 Pintucks, blond wig ....$225 - 275

1983 Kiltie, red wig ....$275 - 325
1984 Harlequin, rooted blond hair ....$200 - 275
1985 Prince Gregor, light-brown wig...........................$175 - 225
1986 Princess Sasha, blond wig ....$1,000 - 1,500
Götz Dolls Inc., 1995-2001
Child, 1995 - 1996, neck marked: "Götz Sasha"; back marked: "Sasha Series" in three-circle logo, about 1,500 of the dolls produced in 1995 did not have mold mark on back, earliest dolls packaged in generic Götz box, later examples were packaged in tube, wrist tag, mini-catalog
16½" ....$175 - 300
Baby, 1996, unmarked neck, back marked "Sasha Series" in three-circle logo, first babies were packaged in generic Götz box or large tube, packaged in small Baby tube, Sasha wrist tag, Götz booklet, catalog
12" ....$125 - 150

16" Sasha Pintucks, Frido/Trendon, vinyl: $250. **Photo courtesy of Alderfer Auction Company, Inc.**

255

BRUNO SCHMIDT

1898 - 1930, Waltershausen, Germany.
Made bisque, composition and wooden-
headed dolls, after 1913 also celluloid.
Acquired Bähr & Pröschild in 1918.
Often used a heart-shaped tag. Dolls listed are in good condition, appropriately
dressed.

Character Baby, bisque socket head,
glass eyes, composition bent-leg body
*Mold 2092, 2094, 2095, 2097 circa 1920,
Mold 2097, circa 1911*

   13" - 15" ....$400 - 500
   18" - 20" ....$625 - 750
   33"....................................$750 - 850
Mold 2097, toddler
   15"....................................$750 - 800
   21" ....$1,100 - 1,300
   34"............................$1,600 - 1,700

Child, no mold numbers, bisque socket
head, jointed body, sleep eyes, open
mouth, allow additional $50 for flirty
eyes,marked: "BSW"

   14".....................................$350 - 450
   18" - 20" ....$525 - 600
   22" - 24" ....$600 - 700

Character
Oriental, mold 500, circa 1905, yellow-
tint bisque socket head, glass eyes,
open mouth, teeth, pierced ears, wig,
yellow-tint composition jointed body

16" mold
2048, Bruno
Schmidt,
bisque:
$1,000.
**Photo
courtesy of
Richard
Withington,
Inc.**

   11" - 14" ....$1,375 - 1,600
   18"..............................$1,800 - 2,000
Mold 529, circa 1912, painted eyes,
closed mouth, marked: "2052"
   20" ....$2,800 - 4,000
Mold 539, circa 1912, solid dome or
wig, painted eyes, closed mouth,
marked: "2023"
   24"..............................$3,000 - 3,200
Mold 537, Wendy (so-called),
circa 1912, sleep eyes, closed mouth,
marked: "2033"
   11" - 13"..................$14,000 - 16,000
   15" - 17".................$18,000 - 22,000
   20"...........................24,000 - 28,000
Mold 2025, closed mouth with slight
smile, intaglio eyes, wigged
   21" ....sold at auction for $10,073
Mold 2048, 2096, Tommy Tucker
(so-called), mold 2094 from 1912 on,
mold 2096, from 1920 on, solid
dome, molded and painted hair or
wig, sleep eyes, open or closed mouth,
composition jointed body
Open mouth
   12" - 14" ....$900 - 1,000
   18" - 20"....................$1,000 - 1,500
   26" - 28"....................$1,800 - 2,100
Mold 2072, circa 1920, sleep eyes,
closed mouth
   16"..............................$2,200 - 2,450
   19"..............................$2,500 - 2,900

FRANZ SCHMIDT

1890 - 1937, Georgenthal, Thüringia, Germany. Made, produced and exported
dolls with bisque, composition, wood
and celluloid heads. Used bisque heads
made by Simon &Halbig. Heads marked:
"S & C," molds 269, 293, 927, 1180,
1310. Heads marked: "F.S. & C," molds
1250, 1253, 1259, 1262, 1263, 1266,
1267, 1270, 1271, 1272, 1274, 1293,
1295, 1296, 1297, 1298, 1310. Walkers:
mold 1071, 1310. Dolls listed are in good
condition, appropriately dressed.

Baby, bisque head, solid dome or cut out for wig, bent-leg body, sleep or set eyes, open mouth, some pierced nostrils, allow more for flirty eyes

Mold 1271, 1272, 1295, 1296, 1297, 1310
10" - 12"	$300 - 400
13" - 14"	$450 - 525
18" - 20"	$600 - 700
22" - 24"	$750 - 850

Toddler
10" - 12"	$800 - 900
16" - 20"	$975 - 1,100
22" - 24"	$1,600 - 2,000

Character Face

Mold 1237, baby, glass eyes, open mouth, molded hair, breather
13"	$1,200 - 1,300

Mold 1257, baby, glass eyes open mouth with wobble tongue, molded hair, breather
13" Toddler	$900 - 1,000

Mold 1266, 1267, circa 1912, solid dome, painted eyes, closed mouth, marked: "F.S. & Co."
14"	$2,750 - 2,850
19" - 23"	$3,700 - 4,000

Mold 1270, circa 1910, solid dome, painted eyes, open/closed mouth
9"	$575 - 650
13"	$1,500 - 1,800

Child

Dolly face, five-piece body, Mold 269, circa 1890s, Mold 293, circa 1900, glass eyes, open mouth, marked: "S & C"
5" - 7"	$275 - 350
10" - 12"	$425 - 500
19" - 23"	$500 - 575
27" - 29"	$800 - 900

Character

Mold 1259, circa 1912, character, sleep eyes, pierced nostrils, open mouth, marked: "F.S. & Co."
15"	$400 - 500

Mold 1262, 1263, circa 1910, painted eyes, closed mouth, marked: "F.S. & Co."
17" - 24"	$19,000 - 22,000

27" mold 269, Franz Schmidt, bisque, socket-head, flirty eyes: $900. **Photo courtesy of Morphy Auctions.**

Mold 1272, circa 1910 solid dome or wig, sleep eyes, pierced nostrils, open mouth, marked "F.S. & Co."
9½"	$850 - 950

Mold 1286, circa 1915, molded hair, side-glancing glass eyes, marked: "F.S. & Co. 1286/40 Germany"
14" - 16"	$8,000 - 12,000

SCHMITT & FILS

1854 - 1891, Noget-sur-Marne & Paris, France. Made bisque and wax-over-bisque or wax-over-composition dolls. Heads were pressed. Used neck socket similar to later composition Patsy dolls. Dolls listed are in good condition, appropriately dressed; allow more for exceptional doll with wardrobe or other attributes.

Child, pressed bisque head, glass eyes, closed mouth, pierced ears, mohair or human-hair wig, French composition-and-wood eight-ball-jointed body, straight wrists

Early round face
12" - 14"	$17,000 - 20,000
15" - 16"	$19,000 - 22,000
18" - 24"	$24,500 - 28,000

Pear-shaped face
14" - 16"	$17,000 - 20,000

Long-face modeling
16" - 18"	$20,000 - 25,000

14" Schmitt & Fils, bisque, closed-mouth bébé: $15,000. **Photo courtesy of Richard Withington, Inc.**

13" mold 585 character baby, Schoenau & Hoffmeister, bisque: $250. **Photo courtesy of Richard Withington, Inc.**

24" - 26" ....$30,000 - 35,000

Wax over papier-mâché, swivel head, cup-and-saucer-type neck, glass eyes, closed mouth, eight-ball-jointed body

16" - 17"....................$5,000 - 6,000

SCHOENAU & HOFFMEISTER

1901 - 1939, Burggrub, Bavaria. Porcelain factory produced bisque heads for dolls, also supplied other manufacturers, including Bruckner, Dressel, Eckhardt, E. Knoch and others. Dolls listed are in good condition, appropriately dressed; allow more for exceptional dolls.

Baby, bisque solid-dome or wigged socket head, sleep eyes, teeth, composition bent-leg body, closed mouth, newborn, solid dome, painted hair, cloth body, may have celluloid hands, allow more for original outfit

Solid-dome infant

10" - 12"............................$350 - 450

13" - 15" ....$500 - 550

Mold 169, 170, 585 (also incised "PorzellanfabrikBurggrub"), bent-limb body

13" - 15" ....$225 - 250

18" - 20"............................$325 - 375

23" - 25" ....$425 - 475

Hanna, sleep eyes, open/closed mouth, bent-leg baby body, allow $100 more for

toddler body

13" - 15" ....$400 - 450

18" - 20" ....$500 - 600

22" - 24" ....$700 - 900

Princess Elizabeth, 1929, socket head, sleep eyes, smiling open mouth, chubby-leg toddler body

16" - 17"....................$2,000 - 2,200

20" - 22" ....$2,500 - 3,000

25" ....$3,500 - 4,000

Child, dolly face, bisque socket head, open mouth with teeth, sleep eyes, composition ball-jointed body

10" dolly face, Schoenau & Hoffmeister, bisque, five-piece body: $175. **Photo courtesy of Emmie's Antique Doll Castle.**

A. Schoenhut & Company

20" Princess Elizabeth, Schoenau & Hoffmeister, bisque: $2,500. **Photo courtesy of Richard Withington, Inc.**

15" Schoenhut, baby, wood: $550. **Photo courtesy of McMasters Harris Apple Tree Doll Auctions.**

Mold 1906, 1909, 2500, 4000, 4600, 4700, 5000, 5500, 5700, 5800
- 10" - 12"...........................$150 - 200
- 14" - 16"...........................$275 - 350
- 18" - 24"...........................$400 - 500
- 26" - 28" ....$600 - 700

Mold 914, circa 1925, character
- 24" - 25" ....$450 - 550
- 27" - 28" ....$650 - 700
- 31" ....$900 - 1,100

Mold 4900, circa 1905, oriental, dolly-face
- 8" - 10" ....$700 - 800

Shoulder-head dolly, open mouth with teeth, sleep eyes, kid body
Mold 1800
- 14" - 22"...........................$125 - 200

A. SCHOENHUT & COMPANY

1872 - 1930 on, Philadelphia, Pennsylvania. Made all-wood dolls, using spring joints, had holes in bottoms of feet to fit into stands. Later made elastic-strung dolls with cloth bodies. Carved or molded and painted hair or wigged, intaglio or sleep eyes, open or closed mouth. Later made composition dolls. Dolls listed are in good condition, appropriately dressed; allow more for exceptional dolls.
Babies
Graziano Infants, circa May 1911 - 1912

Schnickel-Fritz, carved hair, open/closed grinning mouth, four teeth, large ears, toddler
- 15"...............................$3,600 - 4,000

Tootsie Wootsie, carved hair, open/closed mouth, two upper teeth, large ears, child body
- 15" ....$3,800 - 4,200

Too few in database for reliable range
Model 107, 107W (walker), 108, 108W (walker), 1913 - 1926, 109W, 110W, 1921 - 1923
Baby, nature (bent) limb
- 13" - 15" ....$400 - 550
Toddler
- 11" - 14"..........................$500 - 600
- 17".................................$600 - 700
Elastic strung, 1924 - 1926
- 14" ....$675 - 750
Cloth body with crier
- 14" ....$750 - 825

Bye-Lo Baby, cloth body, sleep eyes, closed mouth, stamp reads: "Grace S. Putnam"
- 13".................................$2,400

Too few in database for reliable range
For the following dolls, values are as listed below (allow more for earlier examples and those in all-original condition)
Carved hair
- 14" - 16" ....$2,000 - 3,500
- 19" - 21" ....$2,500 - 4,000

A. Schoenhut & Company

Wigged
14" ....$800 - 900
16" ....$1,100 - 1,300
19" - 21" ....$2,000 - 2,500
Child
Graziano Period, 1911 - 1912, dolls may
have heavily carved hair or wigs,
painted intaglio eyes, outlined iris, all
have wooden spring-jointed bodies,
16" tall, marked with 16 before the
model number, for example: "16/100"
Model 100, girl, carved hair, solemn face
Model 101, girl, carved hair,
grinning, squinting eyes
Model 102, girl, carved hair, bun on top
Model 103, girl, carved hair, loose
ringlets
Model 200, boy, carved hair, short curls
Model 201, boy, carved hair, based on
K*R 114
Model 202, boy, carved hair, forelock
Model 203, boy, carved hair, grinning,
some with comb marks
Model 300, girl, long curly wig, face
of 102
Model 301, girl, bobbed wig, bangs,
face of 300
Model 302, girl, wig, based on K*R 101

15" Schoenhut, boy, wood, carved hair: $3,000. **Photo courtesy of Richard Withington, Inc.**

Model 303, girl, short bob, no bangs,
grinning, squinting eyes
Model 304, girl, wig in braids, ears
stick out
Model 305, girl, snail braids, grinning,
face of 303
Model 306, girl, wig, long curls, face
of 304
Model 307, girl, short bob, no bangs,
"dolly-type" smooth eye
Model 400, boy, short bob, K*R 101
face
Model 401, boy, side-part bob, face
of 300/301
Model 402, boy, side-part bob, grin
of 303
Model 403, boy, dimple in chin
Transition Period, 1911 - 1912, designs by
Graziano and Leslie, some models have
changed, 16" -17," may no longer have
outlined iris, now have a groove above
knee for stockings
Model 100, girl, same, no iris outline
Model 101, girl, short carved hair,
bob/bow, round eyes, smile
Model 102, girl, braids carved around
head
Model 103, girl, heavy carved hair in
front, fine braids in back
Model 104,girl, fine carved hair in
front, fine braids in back
Model 200, boy, carved hair, same,
no iris outline
Model 201, boy, carved hair, same,
iris outline, stocking groove
Model 202, boy, carved hair, same,
smoother
Model 203, boy, smiling boy, round
eyes, no iris outline
Model 204, boy, carved hair brushed
forward, serious face
Model 300, girl, long curly wig,
dimple in chin
Model 301, girl, bob wig, face of 102
Model 302, girl, wig, same like K*R 101
Model 303, girl, wig, similar to 303G,
smiling, short bob, no bangs

A. Schoenhut & Company

Model 304, girl, wig, braids, based on K*R
Model 305, girl, wig, braids, face of 303
Model 306, girl, long curly wig, same face as 304
Model 307, girl, smooth eyeballs
Model 400, boy, same like K*R 101
Model 401, boy, like K*R 114 (304)
Model 402, boy, smiling, round eyes
Model 403, boy, same as 300, side-part bob
Model 404, boy, same as 301, side-part bob
Classic Period, 1912 - 1923, some models discontinued, some sizes added, those marked with * were reissued in 1930
Model 101, girl, short carved hair bob, no iris outline
    1912 - 1923, 14"
    1911 - 1916, 16"
Model 102, girl, heavy carved hair in front, fine braids in back
    1912 - 1923, 14"
    1911 - 1923, 16"
    1912 - 1916, 19" - 21"
Model 105, girl, short carved bob, carved ribbon around head
    1912 - 1923, 14" - 16"
    1912 - 1916, 19" - 21"
Model 106, girl, carved molded bonnet, short hair
    1912 - 1916, 14," 16," 19"
Model 203, 16" boy, same as transition
Model 204, 16" boy, same as transition
Model 205, boy, carved hair, covered ears
    1912 - 1923, 14" - 16"
    1912 - 1916, 19" - 21"
Model 206, 19" boy, carved hair, covered ears
    1912 - 1916
Model 207, 14" boy, carved short curly hair ....1912 - 1916
Model 300, 16" girl, wigged, same as transition
1911 - 1923

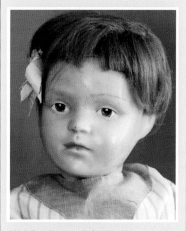

22" Schoenhut, wood: $2,500. **Photo courtesy of Richard Withington, Inc.**

Model 301, 16" girl, wigged, same as transition
    1911 - 1924
Model 303, 16" girl, wigged, same as transition 305
    1911 - 1916
Model 307, 16" girl, long curly wig, smooth eye
    1911 - 1916
Model 308, 14" girl, braided wig
    1912 - 1916
    1912 - 1924
    19," bobbed hair
    1917 - 1924
    19" - 21," bob or curls
Model 309, 16," girl, wigged, long curls, bobbed hair, two teeth
    1912 - 1913
    19" - 21"
Model 310, girl, wigged, same as 105 face, long curls
    1912 - 1916
    14" - 16"
    19" - 21"
Model 311, girl, wigged, heart-shape 106 face, bobbed wig, no bangs
    1912 - 1916
    14" - 16"

A. Schoenhut & Company

""" 1912 - 1913
19"
Model 312, 14,"girl, wigged, bobbed,
1912 - 1924, bobbed wig or curls
1917 - 1924
Model 313, girl, wigged, long curls,
smooth eyeball, receding chin
1912 - 1916
14" - 16"
19" - 21"
Model 314, 19,"girl, wigged, long curls,
wide face, smooth eyeball
1912 - 1916
19"
Model 315, 21," girl, wigged long curls,
four teeth, triangular mouth
1912 -1916
Model 403, 16," boy, wigged, same
as transition, bobbed hair, bangs
1911 - 1924
Model 404, 16," boy, wigged, same
as transition
1911 - 1916
Model 405, boy, face of 308,
bobbed wig

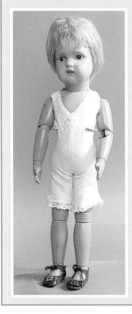

17" Miss
Dolly,
Schoenhut,
wood, decal
eyes: $425.
**Photo
courtesy of
Alderfer
Auction
Company,
Inc.**

1912 - 1924
14"&19"
Model 407, boy, wigged, face of 310 girl
1912 - 1916
19" - 21"
Miss Dolly
Model 316, 1915 - 1925, girl, wigged,
curls or bobbed wig, painted or
decal eyes, all four sizes, open mouth,
teeth
15" - 21"..........................$350 - 500
Model 317, 1921 - 1928, girl, wigged,
long curls or bob, sleep eyes, open
mouth, teeth, four sizes
15" - 21"..........................$700 - 900
Composition doll, 1924, molded
curly hair, painted eyes, closed moth
13" ....$900 - 1,000
Manikin
Model 175, 1914 - 1918, man, slim
body, ball-jointed waist
19" ....$3,000 - 3,500
Small dolls, such as circus figures,
storybook and comic characters
Circus performers, may allow much
more for rare figures
Bisque head
    Bareback Lady Rider or
Ringmaster, all original
    9"......................................$350 - 550
Wooden heads
    Clowns
    8".....................................$250 - 300
    Lion Tamer
    8½" ....$350 - 450
    Ringmaster, Acrobat Gent, Lady
    Bareback Rider
    8"....................................$250 - 325
    Animals, may allow much more
for rare animals
    Camel
    8" $200
    Giraffe
    11" $350
    Horse
    7"..$350

7½" Schoenhut, ringmasters from circus, bisque heads: $500 & $550 (with hat).
Photo courtesy of Alderfer Auction Company, Inc.

Tiger
7½" $200

Cartoon Characters

Barney Google & Sparkplug, based on comic-strip characters created by Billy De Beck
7½" & 8" ....pair $400 - 600

Maggie and Jiggs, based on cartoon strip "Bringing up Father"
7" - 9" ....pair $350 - 450

Max and Moritz, carved figures, painted hair, carved shoes
8" ....each $500 - 550

Mary and her lamb ....$650 - 750

Pinn Family, all wood, egg-shaped head, original costumes, names such as Bobby Pinn, Hattie Pinn, Ty Pinn, etc.
5" - 9" ....$95 - 125
Black Pinn dolls
9" ....$250 - 300

Rolly-Dolly figures
9" - 12" ....$350 - 850

Teddy Roosevelt
8" ....$800 - 1,600

SCHUETZMEISTER & QUENDT

1889 - 1930 on, Boilstadt, Gotha, Thüringia. Porcelain factory that made and exported bisque doll heads, all-bisque dolls and Nankeen dolls. Used initials "S & Q" incised on some models, mold 301 was sometimes incised "Jeannette." Dolls listed are in good condition, appropriately dressed.

Baby, character face, bisque socket head, sleep eyes, open mouth, bent-leg body

Mold 201, 204, 300, 301, circa 1920
10" - 12" ....$300 - 350
14" - 17" ....$375 - 450
19" - 25" ....$550 - 775

Mold 252, circa 1920, character face, black baby
15" ....$550 - 600

Child

Mold 101, 102, circa 1900, dolly face
16" - 17" ....$325 - 400
19" - 22" ....$450 - 525

Mold 1376, circa 1900, character face
19" ....$475 - 550

S.F.B.J.

Société Française de Fabrication de Bébés & Jouets, 1899 - 1930 on, Paris and Montreuil-sous-Bois. 1922 - 1930 on. After 1922 S.F.B.J. was renamed Union Nationale Inter-Syndicale and used the mark: "UNIS FRANCE." Competition with German manufacturers forced many French companies to join together, including Bouchet, Fleischmann & Bloedel, Gaultier, Rabery & Delphieu, Bru, Jumeau, Pintel & Godchaux, Remignard and Wertheimer and others. This alliance lasted until the 1950s. Fleischman owned controlling interest. 1922 - 1930 on. Dolls listed are in good condition, appropriately dressed; more for exceptional dolls.

Child, bisque head, glass eyes, open mouth, pierced ears, wig, composition jointed French body

Jumeau type, no mold number, open mouth
13" - 15"	$1,250 - 1,500
20" - 22"	$1,600 - 1,700
24" - 26"	$1,900 - 2,000
28"	$2,200 - 2,300

Mold 301
6" - 8" five-piece body
	$250 - 300
8" - 10"	$450 - 525
12" - 14"	$525 - 600
18" - 20"	$450 - 500
22" - 24"	$600 - 800
26" - 28"	$800 - 1,200

Bleuette: See Bleuette section.

Kiss Thrower
24"	$1,650 - 1,750

Mold 60
6" - 8"	$300 - 400
12" - 14"	$400 - 500
18" - 21"	$600 - 700
25" - 28"	$700 - 800

14" mold 301, S.F.B.J., bisque, all original: $600. **Photo courtesy of Richard Withington, Inc.**

21" mold 236, S.F.B.J., bisque, open/closed mouth, glass eyes: $1,800. **Photo courtesy of Morphy Auctions.**

Mold 301 or 60, papier-mâché head
8" - 10"..............................$125 - 150
13" -16" ....$175 - 200
18" - 22" ....$250 - 300
Character Faces, bisque socket head,
wigged or molded hair, set or sleep
eyes, composition body, some with
bent-limb baby, toddler or child
body, mold number 227, 235 and
236 may have flocked hair, allow
more for toddler body
Mold 226, glass eyes, closed mouth
18" - 20" ....$2,200 - 2,400
Mold 227, glass eyes, open mouth,
teeth
14"..............................$1,500 - 1,600
17"..............................$1,600 - 1,800
19" - 21"......................$2,000 - 2,500
Mold 230, glass eyes, open mouth,
teeth
12" - 14"..........................$650 - 700
20 - 23" ....$1,100 - 1,300
Mold 233, circa 1912, glass eyes,
crying mouth
14" - 16"......................$3,600 - 4,000
Mold 234
18"..............................$2,800 - 3,050
Mold 235, glass eyes, open/closed
mouth
14" - 15"......................$1,100 - 1,300
18" ....$1,500 - 1,600
Mold 236, glass eyes, laughing
open/closed mouth
Baby
12" - 13" ....$750 - 850
15" - 17" ....$900 - 1,100
20" - 22" ....$1,300 - 1,500
Toddler
13" ....$1,100 - 1,300
15" - 18"......................$1,400 - 1,500
Mold 237, glass eyes, open/closed mouth
13" - 14"......................$1,800 - 2,000
16" - 17"......................$2,000 - 2,500
Mold 238, small open mouth
14"..............................$1,000 - 1,200
18"..............................$1,800 - 2,000

27" mold 251, S.F.B.J., bisque: $2,000. **Photo courtesy of James D. Julia, Auctioneers.**

Mold 239, circa 1913, designed by
Poulbot
13"..........................$16,000 - 17,000
Mold 242, circa 1910, nursing baby
13" - 15" ....$2,900 - 3,000
Mold 247, glass eyes, open/closed mouth
Baby body
6½" ....$550 - 650
Child or toddler
13"..............................$1,300 - 1,400
16"..............................$1,500 - 1,700
20" ....$2,000 - 2,300
Mold 248, circa 1912, glass eyes, lowered
eyebrows, very pouty closed mouth
10" - 12" ....$7,500 - 8,000
Mold 250, open mouth with teeth
12" ....$3,300 trousseau box
18" - 20" ....$3,250 - 3,400
Mold 251, open/closed mouth, teeth,
tongue
10" - 12" $2,800- 3,000
15" - 18".....................$1,400 - 1,600
27"..............................$1,800 - 2,000
Mold 252, glass eyes, closed pouty
mouth,
Baby
8"...............................$2,000 - 2,200
10" ....$2,600 - 3,000
13" - 15" toddler ....$4,500 - 5,500
19"..............................$6,000 - 6,500

20" mold 252 toddler, S.F.B.J., bisque: $7,000.
Photo courtesy of Richard Withington, Inc.

Unis France, marked dolls, 1922 - 1930 on

Mold 60, 301, bisque head, fully jointed composition-and-wood body, wig, sleep eyes, open mouth

5" - 6"	$75 - 120
8" - 10"	$325 - 375
13" - 16"	$425 - 500
21" - 23"	$525 - 600

Five-piece composition body, glass eyes

5" - 8"	$250 - 300
10" - 14"	$300 - 350

Mold 247, 251, toddler body

15"	$900 - $1,050
27"	$1,200 - $1,400

SHIRLEY TEMPLE

1934 on, Ideal Novelty and Toy Company, New York. Designed by Bernard Lipfert. Dolls listed are in very good condition, all original. Allow more for exceptional dolls or special outfits like Ranger or Wee Willie Winkie.

Composition, 1934 - 1940s, composition head, jointed body, dimples in cheeks, green sleep eyes, open mouth, teeth, mohair wig, tagged original dress, center-snap shoes, prototype dolls may have paper sticker inside head and bias-trimmed wig

Shirley Temple

11"	$450 - 600
13"	$500 - 700
16"	$800 - 900
17"	$850 - 875
18"	$700 - 800
20"	$850 - 950
22"	$900 - 1,000
27"	$1,100 - 1,200

Baby Shirley

15"	$1,100 - 1,300
18"	$1,100 - 1,200
21"	$1,300 - 1,400

Hawaiian, Marama, Ideal used the composition Shirley Temple mold for this doll based on a character from the movie *Hurricane*, black yarn hair, Hawaiian costume including grass skirt

18"	$875 - 950

Accessories

Button, three types	$125
Buggy, wicker or wood	$500 - 575
Dress, tagged	$125 - 575
Satin pajamas, tagged	$670
Trunk	$175 - 225

Reliable Shirley Temple, composition, made in Canada

18" - 22"	$1,000 - 1,200

Japanese, unlicensed Shirley dolls

All bisque

6"	$195 - 225

Celluloid

5"	$100 - 125
8"	$100 - 125

Celluloid

Dutch Shirley Temple, circa 1937 on, all celluloid, open crown, metal pate, sleep eyes, dimples in cheeks, Dutch costume, head marked: "Shirley Temple," may have

additional marks

13".....................................$295 - 320

15".....................................$295 - 320

Cloth

Wacker Manufacturing Co. Chicago, painted features, side-glancing eyes, molded face, mohair wig

17".....................................$300 - 400

Composition, Japanese, heavily molded brown curls, painted eyes, open/closed mouth with teeth, body stamped: "Japan"

7½".....................................$200 - 225

Vinyl, dolls listed are in excellent condition, original clothes, accessories; the newer the doll the better the condition it must be to command higher prices, value can double for MIB

1957, all vinyl, sleep eyes, synthetic rooted wig, open/closed mouth, teeth, two-piece slip and undies, tagged: "Shirley Temple," gold plastic pin with script that reads: "Shirley Temple," back of head marked: "ST//12"

12".....................................$100 - 150

1958 - 1961, some have flirty ("Twinkle") eyes; allow more for flirty eyes or 1961

Cinderella, Bo Peep, Heidi or Red Riding Hood, back of head marked: "S.T.//15," "S.T.//17," or "S.T.//19"

15".....................................$150 - 225

17".....................................$175 - 250

19".....................................$325 - 375

1960, jointed wrists, marked: "ST-35-38-2"

35" - 36".....................$1,000 - 1,600

1972, Montgomery Ward reissue, plain box

17".....................................$125 - 150

1973, red-dotted "Stand Up and Cheer" outfit

16".......................................$45 - 55

1982 - 1983

8"...$15 - 40

12".......................................$15 - 40

1984, designed by Hank Garfinkle, marked: "Doll Dreams & Love"

36".......................................$55 - 75

Danbury Mint, re-issue, value can double for MIB

36".....................................$75 - 100

Porcelain

1987 on, Danbury Mint, various outfits

18".......................................$50 - 70

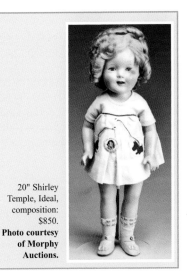

20" Shirley Temple, Ideal, composition: $850.
Photo courtesy of Morphy Auctions.

12" Shirley, Ideal, vinyl, original box: $150.
Photo courtesy of Cybermogul Dolls.

SIMON & HALBIG

1869 - 1930 on, Hildburghausen and Grafenhain, Germany. Porcelain factory that made heads for Jumeau (200 series), bathing dolls (300 series), porcelain figures (400 series), perhaps dollhouse or small dolls (500 - 600 series), bisque-headed dolls (700 series; 900 - 1000 series), bathing and small dolls (800 series). The earliest models of a series are marked with the last digit of their model number ending with an 8, socket heads end with 9, shoulder heads end with 0, and models using a shoulder plate for swivel heads end in 1. Dolls listed are in good condition, appropriately dressed. May allow more for all-original or exceptional dolls.

Molded hair lady, 1850s - 1860s, molded hair, painted or glass eyes
12" - 18"....................$1,200 - $2,000
Shoulder-head child, 1870s, molded hair, painted or glass eyes, closed mouth, cloth body, bisque lower arms, appropriately dressed, marked: "S&H," no mold number
10"............................$2,000 - 2,500
13" - 15".....................$1,500 - 1,800

14" mold 949, Simon & Halbig, bisque, shoulder head, closed mouth: $2,200. **Photo courtesy of Morphy Auctions.**

10" mold 939, Simon & Halbig, bisque, socket head, open mouth: $1,100. **Photo courtesy of Sweetbriar Auctions.**

17" - 19".....................$1,800 - 2,000
21" - 23".....................$2,100 - 2,200
Swivel neck
9" - 10" ....$2,000 - 3,400
12" ....$2,000 - 2,200
Poupée (fashion-type), 1870s, bisque socket head, bisque shoulder plate, kid or twill-over-wood body, glass eyes, closed mouth, wigged
Kid body
10" ....$1,800 - 2,000
15" - 18" ....$2,300 - 2,800
Twill-over-wood body
10" - 11"....................$6,000 - 9,000
15" - 16" ....$11,000 - 14,000
Closed-mouth child, 1879, socket head, most have composition-and-wood body, glass eyes, wigged, pierced ears, appropriately dressed
No mold #
16" - 19" ....$4,000 - 6,000
Mold 719
16" ....$5,900 - 6,100
18" - 22" ....$7,500 - 8,000
Edison phonograph mechanism in torso
23" ....$4,900 - 5,400

Simon & Halbig

14" mold 940, Simon & Halbig, bisque, socket head: $2,000. **Photo courtesy of Morphy Auctions.**

Mold 739
  15" - 20" ....$1,700 - 2,600
Mold 749
  22" ....$3,000 - 4,000
Mold 905, 908
  11" ....$1,600 - 1,800
  15" - 17" ....$2,000 - 3,300
Mold 919
  15" ....$5,300 - 7,200
  19" ....$6,000 - 8,150
Mold 929
  14" ....$1,725 - 2,300
  23" ....$2,450 - 3,400
Mold 939
  14" - 16" ....$1,800 - 2,000
  18" - 20" ....$2,200 - 2,500
  26" - 27" $2,700- 2,800
Mold 949
  10" - 12" ....$2,000 - 2,300
  14" - 16" ....$2,200 - 2,700
  21" - 23" ....$4,000 - 4,300
  31" ....$4,300 - 4,500
Mold 720, 740, 940, 950, dome
shoulder head, kid body
  8" - 10" ....$350 - 450
  14" - 18" ....$700 - 900
  20" - 22" ....$1,200 - 1,600
All-bisque child: See All-Bisque
German section.

Open-mouth child, 1889 - 1930s, socket head, composition body (sometimes French), wigged, glass eyes may be stationary or sleep, appropriately dressed
Mold 530, 540, 550, 570, *Baby Blanche*
  10" ....$350 - 400
  20" - 22"" ....$400 -600
Mold 719, 739, 749, 759, 769, 939, 979
  5½" ....$375 - 550
  9" - 13"........................$1,000 - 1,200
  15" - 17" ....$1,400 - 1,600
  20" - 22" ....$1,400 - 1,600
  26" - 30" ....$3,000 - 3,200
Mold 905, 908
  18" ....$1,750 - 2,200
  22" ....$1,425 - 2,600
Mold 929, 949
  15" - 17" ....$2,100 - 2,800
  22" - 24" ....$2,900 - 3,100
  27" - 29" ....$4,000 - 4,200
Mold 1009
  15" - 16" ....$725 - 800
  19" - 21" ....$900 - 1000
  24" - 25" ....$1,500 - 1,700
Mold 1029
  16" - 18" ....$475 - 575
  24" - 25" ....$700 - 800

22" mold 1009, Simon & Halbig, bisque, socket head: $1,000. **Photo courtesy of Richard Withington, Inc.**

Simon & Halbig

15½" mold 1279, Simon & Halbig, character, bisque: $1,600. **Photo courtesy of Morphy Auctions**

28".......................................$825 - 900
Mold 1039, 1049, 1059, 1069, 1078, 1079
Flapper body
  8" - 10" ....$400 - 500
Child body
  10" - 13" ....$775 - 900
  16" - 18"...........................$650 - 750
  21" - 25"...........................$550 - 650
  27" - 28" ....$700 - 900
  30" - 33" ....$700 - 900
  36" ....$900 - 1,000
Mold 1109
  13"................................$750 - 800
  18"..............................$1,000 - 1,000
Mold 1248, 1249, Santa
  6"................................$550 - 650
  10" - 13".........................$750 - 850
  15" - 18" ....$900 - 1,000
  20" - 24".......................$1,100 - 1,300
  26" - 28" ....$1,400 - 1,600
  38" ....$2,000 - 2,400
Open-mouth shoulder-head child, 1889

- 1930s, kid body
Mold 1009, 1039
  12" - 13" ....$400 - 500
  19"................................$500 - 600
  23"................................$700 - 800
Mold 1010, 1040, 1070, 1080
  18" ....$375 - 425
  23" - 25" ....$500 - 550
  28" - 30" ....$600 - 650
Mold 1250, 1260
  16" ....$475 - 525
  18" - 19"...........................$600 - 700
  23" - 26" ....$750 - 900
Character Face, 1909 on, bisque socket head, composition body, wig or molded hair, glass or painted eyes, open or closed mouth, appropriately dressed
Mold 111
  18" - 22"..................$16,000 - 18,000
Mold 150, circa 1912, intaglio eyes, closed mouth
  13" - 15" ....$6,000 - 10,000
Too few in database for reliable range
Mold 151, circa 1912, painted eyes, closed laughing mouth
  13" - 15" ....$7,000 - 8,000
  22" - 25" ....$12,000 - 15,000
Too few in database for reliable range
Mold 152, lady, intaglio eyes
  18" - 24"..................$16,000 - 20,000
Mold 153, circa 1912, molded hair, painted eyes, closed mouth
  16 - 17" ....$13,000 - 17,000
Too few in database for reliable range
Mold 600, circa 1912, sleep eyes, open mouth
  17" $900
Too few in database for reliable range
Mold 611, solid dome
  16"...........................$4,000 - 5,000
Mold 729, circa 1888, laughing face, glass eyes, open/closed mouth
  16"...........................$1,900 - 2,550
Mold 769, paperweight eyes, open mouth

Simon & Halbig

17".............................$2,500 - 3,000
Too few in database for reliable range
Mold 969, circa 1887, open smiling
mouth
17" - 19".......................$4,500 - 7,600
Too few in database for reliable range
Mold 1019, circa 1890, laughing,
open mouth
14"..............................$4,275 - 5,700
Too few in database for reliable range
Mold 1269, 1279, sleep eyes, open
mouth
14" ....$1,100 - 1,500
16" - 20".......................$1,600 - 1,800
22" - 25" ....$4,000 - 5,000
Mold 1299, circa 1912, marked: "S&H"
13".............................$1,200 - 1,600
1300 Series, character faces
13" man with molded
moustache ....$7,800 - 9,000
Too few in database for reliable range
22" Mold 1305 witch $14,000
Mold 1448, circa 1914, bisque socket
head, sleep eyes, closed mouth,
pierced ears, composition-and-wood
ball-jointed body
16" $17,500
20" - 24" ....$25,500 - 27,500
Too few in database for reliable range
Little Women (so-called), 1909, mold
1160, shoulder-head lady, fancy
hairdo wig, glass eyes, closed mouth,
cloth body, bisque lower limbs,
appropriately dressed
6" - 7"...........................$300 - 375
10" - 11".........................$450 - 500
14" ....$650 - 700
Baby, character face, 1910 on, molded
hair or wig, painted or glass eyes, open
or closed mouth, bent-leg baby body,
appropriately dressed, allow more for
flirty eyes or toddler body
Mold 1294, circa 1912, glass eyes, open
mouth
16"...............................$550 - 750
19" ....$800 - 1,100

Mold 1294, clockwork mechanism
moves eyes
26" - 31"......................$1,800 - 2,600
Mold 1428, circa 1914, glass eyes,
open/closed mouth
13" - 16".......................$1,100 - 1,300
Toddler
12"............................$2,000 - 2,100
16"............................$2,100 - 2,300
Mold 1488, circa 1920, glass eyes,
open/closed or open mouth
12"............................$3,000 - 3,200
19" - 20"......................$4,600 - 5,100
Mold 1489, circa 1925, glass eyes, open
mouth, tongue, incised: "Erika"
20" - 23" ....$4,200 - 6,000
Mold 1498, circa 1920, solid dome,
painted or sleep eyes, open/closed
mouth
24"..$3,700
Too few in database for reliable range
Lady, 1910 on, bisque socket head,

9½" mold 1488 character, Simon & Halbig,
bisque, glass eyes: $9,000. **Photo courtesy of
Gloria's Antique Dolls.**

Simon & Halbig

20" mold 1294 character baby, Simon & Halbig, bisque: $1,800. **Photo courtesy of Richard Withington, Inc.**

24" mold 1154, Simon & Halbig, bisque, lady body: $2,300. **Photo courtesy of Sweetbriar Auctions.**

composition lady body, sleep eyes, wigged, appropriately dressed
Mold 1079, glass eyes, open mouth
24".......................$1,500 - 2,000
Mold 1159, circa1894, glass eyes, open mouth, Gibson Girl (so-called)
Flapper body
12" - 15" ....$1,600 - 1,900
Lady body
18" - 20" .... $1,500 - 2,000
22" - 24" ....$2,000 - 2,300
28" ....$2,600 - 3,000
Jumeau lady body
20" - 25" ....$2,800 - 3,200
Mold 1199, open mouth
34".........................$17,500 - 18,000
Too few in database for reliable range
Mold 1303, circa 1902, lady face, glass eyes, closed mouth
14" $5,815
Mold 1305, circa 1902, old woman, glass eyes, open/closed laughing mouth
18" $10,035
Too few in database for reliable range
Mold 1308, circa 1902, old man,

molded mustache, dirty face, may be solid dome
18".............................$4,200 - 5,600
Too few in database for reliable range
Mold 1329, Asian
14" - 15".......................$1,500 - 2,200
Too few in database for reliable range
Mold 1468, 1469, circa 1920, flapper, glass eyes, closed mouth
14" - 15" ....$2,800 - 3,500

SNOW BABIES

1901 - 1930 on. All-bisque dolls covered with ground porcelain slip to resemble snow, made by Bähr & Pröschild, Hertwig, C.F. Kling, Kley & Hahn, and others. Germany. Mostly unjointed, some jointed at shoulders and hips. The name comes from the story of the Eskimos naming explorer Admiral Robert Peary's daughter Marie, born in 1893, Snow Baby; her mother published a book in which she called her daughter Snow Baby and showed a picture of the little girl in white snowsuit. These little

Snow Babies

figures have painted features and come in various poses. Figures listed are in good condition; allow more for exceptional figures. Snow Babies continue to be made today. Department 56 makes a line of larger-scale figures (see below) and reproductions of earlier Snow Babies are being produced by German companies and by individual artisans.

Single Snow Baby, standing or sitting
1½" ....$60 - 75
3" - 4"................................120 - 150
Snow Baby child, wire-jointed limbs
3½" .... $125 - 150
Action Babies
Baby with umbrella
2¾" ....$75 - 125
Bear on sled
3"............................$175 - 200
Child on skis
4½" ....$350 - 375
Riding on bear ....$300 - 350
Riding on sled
2"......................................$75 - 100
Riding on reindeer
2½" ....$300 - 325
With broom
4½" ....$500 - 550
Melting snowman
1½" ....$75 - 95
Pushing carriage holding two babies
2½" ....$200 - 225
Polar Bear
1½" ....$80 - 100
Santa on igloo with baby inside
3½" ....$110 - 140
Santa riding camel, elephant or polar bear
2 ½" ....$330 - 375
Throwing snowballs
2½" ....$125 - 175
Two Snow Babies, molded together
1½" ....$110 - 135
3" ....$175 - 200
Three Snow Babies, molded together
3"............................$300 - 350

10" Snow Baby, bisque, shoulder head: $400. **Photo courtesy of Morphy Auctions.**

Three on sled
2½" ....$200 - 250
Skiing down a hill, two babies
2½" ....$200 - 250
Snow Baby doll, jointed hips, shoulders
3" - 4"................................$275 - 350
5"......................................$400 - 500
Snow Baby shoulder-head doll, circa 1910, German, cloth body
10"......................................$450 - 500
New Snow Babies, contemporary commercial reproductions by Department 56 are larger and the coloring is cream-colored. Values listed are for secondary-market pieces, which must be mint to command higher prices; many are still available at retail.
Snow Baby winged clip ornament
1986 ....$35 - 50
Snow Baby Adrift
1987 ....$40 - 55
Polar Express
1988 ....$30 - 50
All Fall Down, set of four
1989 .... $30 - 40
Penguin Parade
1989 ....$35 - 45
1990 on, pieces, various..............$15 - 50
Disney pieces, various ....$65 - 85
Eloise on the Polar Express
2002 ....$30 - 35

SONNEBERG TAUFLING

1851 - 1900 on, Sonneberg, Germany. Various companies made infant dolls that had special separated bodies with bellows and voice mechanisms. Motschmann is erroneously credited with the body style, but he did patent the voice mechanism. Some bodies stamped "Motschmann" refer to the voice mechanism. The Sonneberg Taufling was made with head, shoulder plate, pelvis, lower arms and lower legs of papier-mâché/composition, wax over papier-mâché, china, and bisque. Body parts are put together with twill cloth in what are called "floating" joints. Dolls have glass eyes, closed or open mouth, painted hair or wigs. Dolls listed are in good condition.

Bisque: See also Jules Steiner section.

7" - 12"	$2,700 - 4,500
14" - 19"	$5,500 - 6,500

China

6" - 7"	$4,500 - 5,500
10" - 12"	$3,200 - 3,400
14" - 16"	$3,700 - 4,000

Papier-mâché/composition or wax over papier-mâché

8" - 12"	$900 - 1,200
13" - 15"	$1,400 - 1,600
18" - 20"	$1,800 - 2,300
22" - 24"	$2,400 - 2,800

Wood

Bébé tout en Bois, carved-wooden socket head, closed mouth, painted hair, glass eyes, twill-and-wood torso, nude

9"	$1,100

Too few in database for reliable range

MARGARETE STEIFF

1877 to present, Giengen, Wurtemburg, Germany. Known for their plush stuffed animals, Steiff also made clothes for children, dolls with mask faces in 1889, clown dolls by 1898. Most Steiff dolls of felt, velvet or plush have seam down the center of the face, but not all. Registered trademark button in ear in 1905. Button-type eyes, painted features, sewn-on ears, big feet/shoes enable them to stand alone, all in excellent condition. For soiled, ragged or worn dolls, allow 35 percent of prices listed.

19" Sonneberg Taufling, wax over papier-mâché: $2,250. **Photo courtesy of Dolls and Lace.**

20" Steiff, character men, felt: each $3,000. **Photo courtesy of James D. Julia, auctioneers.**

12" Vera, Steiff, molded felt face: $775. **Photo courtesy of Morphy Auctions.**

16" Steiff, tennis lady & gentleman in morning coat, felt, limited editions, 1986 - 1987: each $90. **Photo courtesy of Alderfer Auction Company, Inc.**

Adults

    14½" - 18" ....$2,000 - 2,800

Characters, center-seam face, military men in uniform, conductors, firemen, English bobbies, bellhops and others

    10½" - 15" ....$2,900 - 5,000

    18" - 22" ....$8,000 - 10,000

Children

Center-seam face

    12" - 14" ....$1,500 - 1,700

    16" - 18" ....$1,800 - 2,000

Molded-felt face

    12" - 13" ....$775 - 1,000

Made in U.S. Zone Germany, 1947 - 1953, glass eyes

    12" ....$500 - 600

Rubber-head doll, cloth body

    12" - 13" ....$125 - 150

Vinyl characters, wire armature in body

Max or Moritz

    4" .... $125 - 175

Limited Editions, 1986 - 1987, felt, characters such as Tennis Lady,

Gentleman in Morning Coat, Peasant Lady, Peasant Jorg

    MIB ....$80 - 100

HERMANN STEINER

1909 - 1930 on, near Coburg, Germany. Porcelain and doll factory first made plush animals, then made bisque, composition and celluloid-headed dolls. Patented the Steiner eye with moving pupils.

Baby

Mold 240, circa 1925, newborn, solid dome, sleep eyes, closed mouth

    6" - 8½" ....$95 - 125

    12" - 16"............................$300 - 350

Molds 245, 246, circa 1926, character, solid dome, glass eyes, open/closed mouth, laughing baby, teeth, cloth or composition body

    13" -15" ....$475 - 600

Topsy-Turvy baby doll

    8" ....$500 - 600

Child

Dolly face, no mold number, glass eyes,

Hermann Steiner

14" Hermann Steiner, baby, bisque: $325.
Photo courtesy of Morphy Auctions.

open mouth, jointed composition body
  6" - 10" ....$100 - 175
  6" flapper body................$225 - 250
  14" - 16"...........................$250 - 350
  18" - 20" ....$350 - 400
Shoulder-head child, no mold number,
glass eyes, open mouth, kid body
  18" ....$150 - 175
Living Steiner-eye doll, character, molded
hair, Steiner patented eye
  9' - 10" ....$400 - 650
Mold 128, character, bisque socket head,
sleep eyes, open mouth, teeth, wig, composition-and-wood jointed body
  8" - 9" ....$250 - 300
  14"....................................$400 - 500
Mold 401, shoulder head, solid dome,
painted eyes, open/closed laughing
mouth, teeth, molded tongue
  15" ....$350 - 475

JULES STEINER

1855 - 1891 on, Paris. Made dolls with
pressed heads, wigs, glass eyes, pierced
ears, jointed composition bodies.
Advertised talking, mechanical jointed
dolls and bébés. Some sleep eyes were
operated by a wire behind the ear,
marked: "J. Steiner." May also be marked:
"Bourgoin." Dolls listed are in good condition, appropriately dressed. Allow
more for original clothes or rare mold
numbers.
Baby with Taufling (Motschmann-type)
body, solid-dome bisque shoulder
head, hips, lower arms and legs, twill
body, glass eyes, closed mouth, wig
  12" - 14" ....$13,000 - 15,000
  20" - 22" ....$10,000 - 12,500
Gigoteur, crying, kicking child,
key-wound mechanism, solid-dome
head, glass eyes, open mouth, two
rows tiny teeth, pierced ears, mohair
wig, papier-mâché torso
Earlier, paler doll head
  17" - 20" ....$3,500 - 4,500
Later, more highly colored head
  17" - 20"......................$1,900 - 2,500
Round-face Bébé, 1870s, early
unmarked, pale pressed bisque socket
head, rounded face, pierced ears,
bulgy paperweight eyes, open mouth,
two rows teeth, wig, composition-and-
wood jointed body

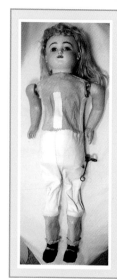

22" Gigoteur,
Steiner, bisque:
$2,800.
**Photo courtesy of
Joan & Lynette
Antique Dolls
and Accessories.**

Hermann Steiner

16" - 18"....................$5,500 - 6,800
Closed mouth, round face, dimples in chin

16" - 18"................$10,000 - $11,500
Bébé with Series marks, 1880 on, red ink stamped mark "Bourgoin," stamp on body reads: "Caduceus," pressed bisque socket head, cardboard pate, wig, pierced ears, glass paperweight eyes, closed mouth, French composition-and-papier-mâché (purple) body, straight wrists or bisque hands, Series C and A more common, marked with series mark: "Sie" and letter and number, may allow much more for rare Series B, E, F, and G models

Series A or C
8" - 10" ....$9,000 - 10,000
14" - 16" ....$10,000 - 11,000
21" - 23" ....$11,000 - 14,000
27" - 28" ....$15,000 - 18,000
38" ....$18,000 - 21,000
Series E
12" - 15" ....$15,000 - $20,000
Series F
10½"......sold at auction for $25,875

16" Steiner, bisque, Fre A mark: $9,000. **Photo courtesy of Morphy Auctions.**

10½" F series Steiner, bisque: sold at auction for $25,875. **Photo courtesy of James D. Julia, auctioneers.**

Series G
29" ....sold at auction for $25,000
Bébé with figure marks, 1887 on, bisque socket head, pierced ears, glass eyes, closed mouth, wig, composition-and-wood jointed French body, may use body marked: "Le Parisien" or "Le Petit Parisien," head marked: "Fre" and letter and number, and "J. Steiner," figure marks included A, B, C, D, E, A and C are the most often found

Closed mouth
A or C
8" - 10" ....$6,000 - 7,000
12" - 16" ....$7,500 - 9,000
18" - 24" ....$10,000 - 11,000
28" - 29"................$11,000 - 12,000
Open mouth
Figure A
18" - 23" ....$3,600 - 4,500
Figure B
19" - 25" ....$7,000 - 8,500
Figure E
24" - 26"................$29,000 - 31,000
Phénix Baby, 1899 on, registered by Jules Mettais, successor of Jules Nicholas Steiner, bisque socket head, closed mouth, composition body
17" - 22" ....$5,000 - 7,000

SUN RUBBER

1919 - 1950s, Barberton, Ohio. Made rubber and, later, vinyl dolls. Dolls listed are in excellent condition, allow less for faded, cracked dolls or missing paint, value can double for MIB.

Psyllium, 1937, molded painted hard rubber, moving head, blue pants, white suspenders, black shoes and hat
   10" ....$12 - 18

One-piece Squeeze dolls, 1940s, designed by Ruth E. Newton, molded clothes, squeaker, names such as Bonnie Bear, Happy Kappy, Rompy and others
   8" ....$15 - 20

So-Wee, 1941, molded hair, painted or sleep eyes
   10" - 12" ....$20 - 40
   Black ....$45 - 55

Sunbabe, 1950, drink-and-wet baby, painted eyes, molded hair
   8" - 13" ....$30 - 35
   Black ....$35 - 45

Betty Bows, 1953, drink-and-wet baby, molded hair with loop for ribbon, jointed body
   11" ....$65 - 95

Constance Bannister Baby, 1954, drink-and-wet baby, molded hair, sleep eyes
   18" ....$65 - 100

Tod-L-Dee, 1950s, all-vinyl, soft, stuffed one-piece body, molded underclothes and shoes, molded painted hair, sleep eyes, open mouth, also Tod-L-Tee &Tod-L-Tim
   10" ....$30 - 40

Peter Pan, 1950s, all-vinyl, soft, stuffed one-piece body, molded outfit, molded painted hair, sleep eyes
   10" ....$25 - 30

Amosandra: See Black or Brown Dolls section.

Gerber Baby: See Advertising Dolls section.

SWAINE & COMPANY

1910 - 1927, Huttensteinach, Thüringia, Germany. Made porcelain doll heads marked: "S & Co.," with green stamp. May also be incised: "DIP" or "Lori."

10" So-Wee baby, Sun Rubber: $25. **Doll courtesy of private collection.**

15" Swaine & Co, bisque, open/closed mouth, intaglio eyes, marked "BP": sold at auction for $2,070. **Courtesy of James D. Julia, auctioneers.**

Baby

Baby Lori, solid dome, open/closed-mouth, molded hair, sleep eyes, marked: "Lori"

16" - 18".....................$1,200 - 1,400
23"..............................$1,600 - 2,000

Mold 232, Lori variation, open mouth

12" - 14" ....$800 - 1,000
20" - 23" ....$1,400 - 1,600

DI, solid dome, intaglio eyes, closed mouth

11" - 13"...........................$650 - 700
17" ....$1,100 - 1,300

DV, solid dome, sleep eyes, closed mouth

13" ....$900 - 1,100
15"..............................$1,200 - 1,300

FP, S&C, socket head, sleep eyes, closed mouth

8".......................................$750 - 850

Too few in database for reliable range

Child

BP, socket head, painted eyes, open/closed smiling mouth, teeth

14½ - 17"....................$4,000 - 5,750

Too few in database for reliable range

DIP, S&C, socket head, sleep eyes, closed mouth

8" - 10" ....$600 - 700
12" - 14".........................$850 - 950

Toddler body

8"..............................$1,000 - 1,300
13" - 14" ....$1,100 - 1,400

TERRI LEE

1946 - 1962, Lincoln, Nebraska, and Apple Valley, California. Founded by Violet Lee Gradwohl, the company went out of business in 1962. In 1997, Fritz Duda, Violet's nephew, was instrumental in founding Terri Lee Associates, which now produces Terri Lee dolls. First dolls were composition, then hard plastic and vinyl; dolls are now being made from a newer type of hard plastic. Closed pouty mouth, hand-painted features, wigged, jointed body. Values listed are for dolls in good condition and wearing original clothing. Allow significantly less for undressed, played-with dolls. Allow more for dolls in mint condition, with fancy costume or additional wardrobe.

Terri Lee

Composition, 1946 - 1947

16"....................................$850 - 900

Painted hard plastic, 1947 - 1949

16" ....$800 - 1,000

Flesh-colored hard plastic, 1949 - 1952

16"....................................$750 - 800

Hard plastic, 1952 - 1962

16"....................................$325 - 450

Vinyl, 1950 - 1951, allow less if sticky

16"....................................$200 - 300

Talking

16"....................................$250 - 300

Hard plastic, 1997 - 2005, secondary-market values listed, dolls are available at retail as well

16" ....$50 - 100

Benji, painted plastic, brown, 1946 - 1962, black lamb's wool wig

16"..............................$1,800 - 2,000

16" Jerri Lee, hard plastic: $450. **Photo courtesy of Richard Withington, Inc.**

10" Tiny Terri Lee, hard plastic: $200. **Photo courtesy of McMasters Harris Apple Tree Doll Auctions.**

Connie Lynn, 1955, hard plastic, sleep eyes, fur wig, bent-limb baby body
    19".....................................$350 - 400
Gene Autry, 1949 - 1950, painted plastic
    16"...........................$1,600 - 1,800
Jerri Lee, hard plastic, caracul wig
    16"....................................$400 - 550
Vinyl, 16".............................$1,000 - 1,100
Linda Lee, 1950 - 1951, vinyl
    12"...$60 - 75
1952 - 1958, vinyl baby
    10" ....$80 - 110
Mary Jane, Terri Lee look-alike, hard-plastic walker
    16"....................................$200 - 225
Patty Jo, 1947 - 1949
    16"..............................1,200 - 1,500
Bonnie Lou, black
    16"..............................$1,000 - 1,200
Tiny Terri Lee, 1955 - 1958
    10"....................................$150 - 200
Accessories
Terri Lee Outfits
Girl Scout/Brownie uniform $50
School dress $150
Shoes..$35
Tiny Terri Lee dresses ....$20 - 50

A. THUILLIER

1875 - 1893, Paris. Made bisque-headed dolls with composition, kid or wooden bodies. Some of the heads were reported to have been made by François Gaultier. Bisque socket head or swivel on shoulder plate, glass eyes, pierced ears, cork pate, wig, nicely dressed, in good condition. Dolls listed are in good condition, appropriately dressed. May allow more for exceptionally beautiful dolls.
Early child, closed mouth with white space
    12" - 13" ....$55,000 - 70,000
    15" - 22" ....$64,000 - 70,000
Later child, open mouth with molded teeth
    20" - 27" ....$25,000 - 28,000

TONNER DOLL COMPANY

1991 to present, Kingston, New York. Robert Tonner is a fashion designer and sculptor who has created numerous dolls in porcelain and vinyl. Tonner Doll Company also owns Effanbee Dolls. Values listed are for secondary-market dolls complete and in good condition; value may double for MIB. Some dolls are available at retail as well.
American Models, 1993 on, vinyl, basic dolls at low end of value, dolls in elaborate costume at high end of value
    16".....................................$75 - 100
    19".....................................$200 - 300
    22".....................................$150 - 300
Ann Estelle, 1999, character based on artwork of Mary Engelbreit, hard plastic, blond wig, glasses, basic dolls at low end of value, dolls in elaborate costume at high end of value
    10" ....$45 - 100
Sophie, 10"................................$55 - 100
Ann Estelle, 8" version on Tiny Betsy

body ....$38 - 42
Betsy McCall: see Betsy McCall section.
Kripplebush Kids, 1997, hard plastic,
Marni, Eliza, Hannah
8" ....$30 - 40
Baby Blue Margaret O'Brien
centerpiece from 2000 Tonner
convention ....sold at online auction
for $78
Kitty Collier, 2000
18" ....$45 - 55
Miss America of the 1960s,
Limited edition of 500 ....sold at
online auction for $199
Tiny Kitty Collier, vinyl, basic dolls
at low end of value, dolls in elaborate
costume at high end of value
10" ....$45 - 100
Tyler Wentworth, 1999, fashion-type,
long, straight, brunette, blond, or
red hair, allow more for special
costumes
16" ....$40 - 70
Twightlight Series
Jacob Black (based on character
played by Taylor Lautner), 2010
17½" ....$65 - 75

TROLLS

Trolls portray supernatural beings from Scandinavian folklore. They have been manufactured by various companies including Helena and Martii Kuuslkoski who made Fauni Trolls, circa 1952 on, (sawdust-filled cloth dolls), Thomas Dam, 1960 on, Scandia House (later Norfin®), Uneeda Doll and Toy Wishniks®, Russ Berrie, Ace Novelty, Treasure Trolls, Applause Toys, Magical Trolls and many other companies who made vinyl look-alikes of lesser quality, mostly unmarked, to take advantage of the fad. Most are all vinyl or vinyl with stuffed-cloth bodies.

Troll Figures
1960s
2½" ....$45 - 75
5" ....$65 - 75
7" ....$70 - 100
Bank, 8" ....$22 - 28
10" ....$45 - 55
12" ....$50 - 75
15" ....$75 - 95
1977
3" ....$12 - 18
9" ....$30 - 40
12" ....$35 - 45
Thumb sucker, 18" $55
Too few in database for reliable range
Wishnik trolls, Uneeda
3" ....$15 - 25
7" ....$35 - 50
1990s re-release
6" ....$12 - 18
Troll Animals, Thomas Dam, 1964
Cow
6" ....$75 - 125
Elephant
2½" ....$50 - 65
Giraffe
12" ....$60 - 75
Horse
6" ....$100 - 110

10" Tiny Kitty, Summer, Tonner Doll Company exclusive for The Toy Shoppe, vinyl, MIB: $100. **Photo courtesy of McMasters Harris Apple Tree Doll Auctions.**

UNEEDA

1917 on, New York City. Made composition-headed dolls, including Mama dolls, then made transition to plastics and vinyl.

Composition

Lucky Lindy, 1927, composition head and lower arms, cloth body, cardboard tag, oilcloth aviator suit, marked: "Uneeda"

17".....................................$200 - 225

Rita Hayworth, as Carmen, 1939, in *The Loves of Carmen* movie, all composition, red mohair wig, unmarked, cardboard tag

14".....................................$350 - 400

Baby doll, 1930s, composition head, arms and legs, cloth body

14".....................................$50 - $75

Hard Plastic and Vinyl

Baby Dollikins, 1960, vinyl head, hard-plastic jointed body with jointed elbows, wrists and knees, drinks and wets

21".....................................$150 - 200

Baby Trix, 1965

19".....................................$18 - 25

11½" Miss Dollikin, Uneeda, vinyl: $50. **Photo courtesy of Pieces of Old.**

31" Pollyanna, Uneeda, vinyl, MIB: $300. **Photo courtesy of Charlotte's Web Vintage Dolls and Collectibles.**

Bareskin Baby, 1968

12½".....................................$15 - 20

Blabby, 1962 on

14".....................................$50 - 75

Chubby, 1976, vinyl, rooted hair, sleep eyes

18".....................................$15 - 25

Debteen, 1967, all vinyl, rooted hair, side-glancing stationery eyes

19".....................................$35 - 40

Dollikin, 1957 on, multi-joints, allow more for special costumes or outstanding condition, marked: "Uneeda//2S"

19".....................................$150 - 250

21".....................................$300 - 375

Dolly Walker, 1967

36".....................................$50 - $75

Fairy Princess, 1961

32".....................................$75 - 100

Freckles, 1960, vinyl head, rigid-plastic body, head marked: "22"

32".....................................$75 - 100

1973, ventriloquist doll, vinyl head, hands, rooted hair, cotton-stuffed cloth body

30".....................................$45 - 60

Vinyl

Granny & Me, 1978
11½" & 5½" ....$28 - 32 set
Jennifer, 1973, rooted side-parted
hair, painted features, teen body,
mod clothing
18" ....$15 - 20
Little Sophisticates, 1967, large
mod-style head, closed eyes, painted
smile, rooted hair
8 ½ " ....$35 - $55
Magic Meg, w/Hair That Grows,
vinyl and plastic, rooted hair,
sleep eyes
16" ....$30 - 45
Miss Dollikin, also called Action Girl,
1957 on, fashion-type
11½" ....$24 - 30
Pee Wees, 1965 on, rooted hair,
painted eyes
3 ½" ....$8 - $12
Petal People, 1968, vinyl, rooted hair,
seated inside a vinyl flower in a
pot (measured 12½")
2 ½ " ....$20 - $30
Pir-thilla, 1958, blows up balloons,
vinyl, rooted hair, sleep eyes
12½" ....$10 - 15
Priscilla, 1960s
12½" ....$15 - 18
Purty, 1973, long rooted hair, vinyl,
plastic, painted features
11" ....$20 - $25
Pollyanna, 1960, for Disney
11" ....$25 - 35
17" ....$50 - 70
31" ....$125 - 175
Saranade, 1962, vinyl head, hard-plastic
body, rooted blond hair, blue sleep
eyes, red-and-white dress, speaker in
tummy, battery-operated phonograph
and records
21" ....$75 - 100
Suzette (resembles Ideal's Carol
Brent doll)
12" ....$40 -55
Tiny Teen, 1957 - 1959, vinyl head,

rooted hair, pierced ears, six-piece
hard-plastic body, high-heeled feet,
made to compete with Little Miss
Revlon, wrist tag
10½" ....$35 - 55
Bob 11" ....$40 - 50
Tinyteens, 1968 on, vinyl, rooted hair,
posable body, rooted lashes, 12 dolls
in series
5" ....$35 - 55
Wendy, 1960s Barbie®-type, rooted hair,
painted eyes
11½" ....$25 - $35

VINYL

1950s on. By the mid-1950s, vinyl
(polyvinylchloride) was being used for
dolls. Vinyl became a desirable material
because it was soft to the touch and
allowed hair to be rooted; the market was
soon deluged with dolls manufactured
from this product. Many dolls of this
period are by little-known manufacturers,
unmarked or marked only with a number. With little history, these dolls need
to be mint-in-box and complete to warrant
top prices. May allow more for special
accessories or wardrobes.

14"
Roberta
Ann,
Roberta
Doll
Co.,
vinyl, all
original:
$300.
**Photo
courtesy
of
Pieces
of Old.**

Vinyl

Unknown Maker
Baby, vinyl head, painted or sleep eyes, molded hair or wig, bent legs, cloth or vinyl body
    12"..$8 - 10
    16".......................................$10 - 12
    20".......................................$16 - 20
Child, vinyl head, jointed body, painted or sleep eyes, molded hair or wig, straight legs
    14".......................................$10 - 14
    22".......................................$18 - 25
Adult, vinyl head, painted or sleep eyes, jointed body, molded hair or wig, smaller waist with male or female modeling for torso
    8"..$20 - 25
    18".......................................$55 - 75
Susie Sad Eyes, vinyl, made in Hong Kong, large painted "sad" eyes, mod clothing
    8"..$45 - 65
Baby Barry Toy Co., New York City, 1950s
Alfred E. Newman
    20"......................................$250 - 300
Captain Kangaroo
    16".......................................$100 - 130
    19" - 24".............................$15 - 190

13" Buddy Palooka, Personality Doll Corp, vinyl: $300. **Photo courtesy of Morphy Auctions.**

Christopher Robin
    18"..................................$100 - 135
Daisy Mae
    14"..................................$125 - 175
Emmett Kelly (Willie the Clown)
    15"....................................$85 - 100
    21"..................................$110 - 130
Li'lAbner
    14"..................................$120 - 160
    21"..................................$150 - 200
Mammy Yokum, 1957
    Molded hair
    14"....................................$40 - 65
    21"....................................$50 - 75
    Yarn hair
    14"..................................$125 - 150
    21"..................................$200 - 250
    Nose lights up
    23"..................................$275 - 325
Pappy Yokum, 1957
    14"....................................$40 - 65
    21"....................................$50 - 75
    Nose lights up
    23"..................................$275 - 325
Belle Doll & Toy Co, Brooklyn, New York, 1950s
Ballerina or Miss-Revlon-type
    18"....................................$20 - 40
Little Miss Margie, 1955- 1957, Miss-Revlon-type
    10 ½" ....$26 - 40
Dee & Cee, Canada
Calypso Bill, 1961, black, vinyl, marked: "DEE CEE"
    16"..............................each $35 - 50
Sweet Sue Teen Aged Doll, Cissy-type
    17"....................................$35 - 50
Willy, vinyl toddler, molded hair, sleep eyes
    16"....................................$35 - 45
Flagg and Co., Brookline, Massachusetts, 1947 on, produced vinyl dolls with wire armatures
    8"......................................$30 - 40
Furga, Italy

Vinyl

Alta Moda Series, 1965 on, Simonna, Sylvie, Sussannah, vinyl doll, rooted hair, inset angled eye-lashes

17".....................................$400 - 600

Simonna outfit

1967, MIB.......................$300 - 330

Glad Toy/BrookGlad

Poor Pitiful Pearl, 1955, vinyl, some with stuffed one-piece vinyl bodies, others jointed

13" ....$75 - 125

17" ....$175 - 225

Juro Novelty Co

Dick Clark, 1958, vinyl head, hands, feet, cloth body

26"................................$125 - 150

Libby

I Dream of Jeannie, 1966

20"................................$125 - 150

Playmates, 1985 on, made animated talking dolls with battery-powered tape player in torso, extra costumes, tapes and accessories were available, allow more for black versions, value may double for MIB

Amazing Amy, 1998, vinyl, cloth body, interactive

20"..................................$25 - 35

Cricket, 1986 on

25".......................................$40 - 55

Corky, 1987 on

25".......................................$40 - 50

Jill, 1987, hard-plastic jointed body

33"...................................$125 - 200

Royal Doll Co.

Lonely Lisa, 1964, designed by Keane, large sad eyes

19" .... $50 - 70

1965

11½" ....$40 - 50

Mod Joy, 1965, vinyl, painted eyes, rooted hair

12" .... $30 - 35

Sayco, 1907 - 1950s, New York City, first made composition dolls, then hard plastic and vinyl Miss America Pageant, 1950s

11" - 14".............................$80 - 125

20"..................................$200 - 225

Pouty girl, soft-vinyl head, rooted hair, sleep eyes, soft, stuffed vinyl body

22"....................................$40 - 45

Walker, costumed as a bride

28".......................................$65 - 75

Shindana, 1968 - 1983, Operation Bootstrap, Los Angeles, ethnic features

14" ....$40 - 65

5" and under, dollhouse dolls, Flagg, vinyl, MIB: $100. **Photo courtesy of Alderfer Auction Company, Inc.**

Talking Tamu, black, ethnic features

16" ....$145 - 180

Tomy

Kimberly, 1981 - 1985, closed mouth, allow more for black version

17" ....$35 - 45

Getting Fancy Kimberly, 1984, open mouth with teeth

17" ....$30 - 40

Tristar

Poor Pitiful Pearl, circa 1955 on, vinyl jointed doll, extra party dress

11" ....$60 - 75

Unique

Ellie Mae Clampett, 1964

11½" ....$30 - 35

Worlds of Wonder, circa 1985 - 1987 on, Fremont, California, made battery-powered talking dolls and Teddy Ruxpin, extra accessories, voice cards

Pamela, The Living Doll, 1986 on

21" ....$75 - 100

Julie, 1987 on

24" ....$75 - 100

Extra costume ....$20 - 30

Teddy Ruxpin, 1985 on, animated talking bear

20" ....$75 - 100

VOGUE DOLL COMPANY

1930s on, Medford, Massachusetts. Jennie Graves started the company and dressed "Just Me" and Arranbee dolls in the early years before Bernard Lipfert designed Ginny. After several changes of ownership, Vogue was purchased in 1995 by Linda and Jim Smith.

Composition dolls

Dora Lee, sleep eyes, closed mouth

11" ....$400 - 475

Jennie, 1940s, sleep eyes, open mouth, mohair wig, five-piece composition body

13" ....$300 - 350

19" ....$375 - 425

Cynthia, 1940s, sleep eyes, open mouth,

mohair wig, five-piece composition body

13" ....$300 - 350

W.A.A.C. doll, wearing Women's Army Auxiliary Corps uniform

13" ....$600 - 700

Ginny Family

Toddles, composition, 1937 - 1948, name stamped in ink on bottom of shoe, some early dolls which have been identified as "Toodles" (spelled with two o's) are blank dolls from various companies used by Vogue, painted eyes, mohair wig, jointed body, some have gold foil labels that read: "Vogue." Dolls listed are in good condition with original clothes,allow more for fancy outfits such as Red Riding Hood or Cowboy/Cowgirl, or with accessories

7½" - 8" ....$400 - 500

Painted-Eye Ginny, 1948 - 1949, hard plastic, strung joints, painted eyes, molded hair with mohair wig, head marked: "Vogue," body marked: "Vogue Doll,"clothing tagged: "Vogue Dolls" or "Vogue Dolls, Inc. Medford Mass.," inkspot tag on white with blue letters

8" ....$500 - 600

11" Dora Lee, Vogue, composition: $475. **Photo courtesy of American Beauty Dolls.**

Vogue Doll Company

Crib Crowd, 1950, baby, curved legs, sleep eyes, poodle cut (caracul) wig
8".......................................$600 - 750
Strung Ginny, 1950 - 1953, hard plastic, sleep eyes, strung joints, painted eyes, molded hair with mohair wig, head marked: "Vogue," body marked: "Vogue Doll," clothing tagged: "Vogue Dolls" or "Vogue Dolls, Inc. Medford Mass.," inkspot tag on white with blue letters
8".......................................$300 - 500
Painted Lash Walker Ginny, 1954, sleep eyes, strung, dynel wigs, back marked: "GINNY//VOGUE DOLLS//INC.//PAT PEND.//MADE IN U.S.A."
8".......................................$200 - 350
Black Ginny, 1953 - 1954
8".......................................$500 - 600
Molded Lash Walker Ginny, 1955 - 1957, hard plastic, seven-piece body, sleep eyes, Dynel or saran wigs, head marked: "VOGUE," back marked: "GINNY//VOGUE DOLLS//INC.//PAT. NO. 2687594//MADE IN U.S.A."
8".......................................$175 - 225
Bent-knee Molded Lash Walker Ginny, 1957 - 1962, hard plastic, jointed knees, sleep eyes, dynel or saran wigs, head marked: "VOGUE," back marked: "GINNY//VOGUE DOLLS//INC.// PAT.NO.2687594//MADE IN U.S.A."
8".......................................$150 - 225
Ginny, 1960, walker carried 8" identically dressed doll, unmarked
36" $350
Too few in database for reliable range
Vinyl Walker Ginny, 1963 - 1965, soft-vinyl head, hard-plastic walker body, sleep eyes, molded lashes, rooted hair, head marked: "GINNY," back marked: "GINNY//VOGUE DOLLS, Inc.//PAT. NO.2687594//MADE IN U.S.A."
8".......................................$30 - 45

8" Toddles, Vogue, composition: $425. **Photo courtesy of Richard Withington, Inc.**

Ginny, 1965 - 1972, all vinyl, straight legs, non-walker, rooted hair, sleep eyes, molded lashes, head marked:"Ginny." back marked: "Ginny//VOGUE DOLLS, INC."
8".......................................$30 - 45
Ginny, 1972 - 1977, all vinyl, non-walker, sleep eyes, molded lashes, rooted hair, some with painted lashes, head marked: "GINNY," back marked: "VOGUE DOLLS©1972//MADE IN HONG KONG//3," made in Hong Kong by Tonka
8".......................................$25 - 40
Ginny, 1977 - 1979, "Ginny From Far-Away Lands," made in Hong Kong by Lesney, all vinyl, sleep eyes, jointed, non-walker, rooted hair, chubby body, generally same as Tonka doll, head marked: "GINNY," back marked: "VOGUE DOLLS 1972//MADE IN HONG KONG//3," painted eyes, 1980 - 1981, head marked: "VOGUE DOLLS//©GINNYTIM//1977," back marked: "VOGUE DOLLS©1977// MADE IN HONG KONG"
8".......................................$20 - 30

Vogue Doll Company

8" strung Ginny, Coronation Queen, Vogue, hard plastic: $600. **Photo courtesy of Richard Withington, Inc.**

Sasson Ginny, 1981 - 1982, made in Hong Kong by Lesney, all-vinyl, fully jointed, bendable knees, rooted Dynel hair, sleep eyes in 1981, painted eyes in 1982, slimmer body, head marked "GINNY," back marked: "1978 VOGUE DOLLS INC//MOONACHIE N.J.//MADE IN HONG KONG"
8" ....$18 - 25

Ginny, 1984 - 1986, made by Meritus® in Hong Kong, vinyl, resembles Vogue's 1963 - 1971 Ginny, head marked "GINNY®," back marked: "VOGUE DOLLS//(a star logo)//M.I.I. 1984//Hong Kong," porcelain, head marked: "GW//SCD//5184," back marked: "GINNNY//®VOGUE DOLLS//INC//(a star logo) MII 1984//MADE IN TAIWAN"
8" ....$35 - 55

Ginny, 1986 - 1995, vinyl, by Dakin, soft vinyl, back marked: "VOGUE®DOLLS//©1984 R. DAKIN INC.//MADE IN CHINA, hard vinyl, back marked "VOGUE//®//DOLLS//©1986 R. DAKIN and Co.//MADE IN CHINA"
8" ....$15 - 20

Ginny Baby, 1959 - 1982, vinyl, jointed, sleep eyes, rooted or molded hair, drinks and wets, some marked: "GINNY BABY//VOGUE DOLLS INC."
12" ....$40 - 45
18" ....$50 - 60

Ginny outfits
Talon Zipper MIB $250
Vinyl shoes MIB $30

Ginnette
1955 - 1969, 1985 - 1986, vinyl, jointed, open mouth, 1955 - 1956, painted eyes, 1956 - 1969, sleep eyes, marked: "VOGUE DOLLS INC"
8" ....$100 - 125
1962 - 1963, rooted-hair Ginnette
8" ....$75 - 100

Jan, 1958 - 1960, 1963 - 1964, Jill's friend, called Loveable Jan in 1963 and Sweetheart Jan in 1964, vinyl head, six-piece rigid-vinyl body, straight leg, swivel waist, rooted hair, marked: "VOGUE"
10½" ....$75 - 100

Jeff, 1958 - 1960, vinyl head, five-piece rigid vinyl body, molded and painted hair, marked: "VOGUE DOLLS"
11" ....$75 - 100

Jill, 1957 - 1960, 1962 - 1963, 1965, seven-piece hard-plastic teenage body, bent-knee walker, high-heeled doll, big sister to Ginny (made in vinyl in 1965), extra wardrobe, marked: "JILL//VOGUE DOLLS//MADEI NU.S.A.//©1957"
10½"
Wearing leotard ....$75 - 100
Wearing street dres ....$125 - 175
Wearing formal ....$225 - 300

Jimmy, 1958, Ginny's baby brother, all vinyl, painted eyes, open mouth, Ginnette, marked: "VOGUE DOLLS/INC."
8" ....$65 - 100`

Little Miss Ginny, 1965 - 1971, all vinyl, promoted as a pre-teen, one-piece hard-plastic body and legs, soft-vinyl head and

arms, sleep eyes, head marked:
"VOGUE DOLL//19©67" or
"©VOGUE DOLL//1968," back
marked: "VOGUE DOLL"
12".......................................$30 - 40
Miss Ginny, 1962 - 1964, soft-vinyl
head could be tilted, jointed vinyl arms,
two-piece hard-plastic body, swivel waist,
flat feet, 1965 - 1980, vinyl head and
arms, one-piece plastic body
15" - 16"...............................$35 - 45

Hard Plastic and Vinyl
Baby Dear, 1959 - 1964, 18" vinyl baby
designed by Eloise Wilkin, vinyl limbs,
cloth body, rooted topknot or rooted
hair, white tag on body reads: "Vogue
Dolls, Inc.," left leg stamped:
"1960/E.Wilkins," 12" size made in 1961
12".....................................$90 - 130
18"....................................$175 - 200
Baby Dear One, 1962, one-year-old
toddler version of Baby Dear, sleep
eyes, two teeth, neck marked:
"C//1961//E.Wilkin//Vogue
Dolls//Inc.," tag on body
25"....................................$80 - 125
Baby Dear Musical, 1962 - 1963,
12" metal, 18" wooden shaft winds,
plays tune, doll wiggles
12".....................................$100 - 150
18"....................................$200 - 250
Baby Too Dear, 1963 - 1965, two-year-old
toddler version of Baby Dear, all vinyl,
open mouth, two teeth
17"....................................$150 - 200
23"....................................$250 - 300
Brikette, 1959 - 1961, 1979 - 1980,
swivel-waist joint, green flirty eyes in
22" size only, freckles, rooted straight
orange hair, head marked: "VOGUE
INC.//19©60," paper hang tag reads
"I'm//Brikette//the//red headed//imp"
22"....................................$125 - 175
1960, sleep eyes only, platinum,
brunette or orange hair
16"....................................$75 - 100
1980, no swivel waist, curly pink, red,

8" Ginny, PLW Kinder Crowd, Vogue, hard
plastic, MIB: $475. **Photo courtesy of Richard
Withington, Inc.**

purple or blond hair
16"......................................$45 - 60
Li'l Imp, 1959 - 1960, Brikette's little
sister, vinyl head, bent-knee walker,
green sleep eyes, orange hair, freckles,
head marked: "R and B//44,"back
marked: "R and B Doll Co."
10½" ....$65 - 90
Wee Imp, 1960, hard-plastic body,
orange saran wig, green eyes, freckles,
marked: "GINNY//VOGUE
DOLS//INC.//PAT.No.
2687594//MADE IN U.S.A."
8" ....$150 - 175
Littlest Angel, 1961 - 1963; 1967 - 1980
1961 - 1963, also called Saucy Littlest
Angel, vinyl head, hard-plastic bent-
knee walker, sleep eyes, same doll as
Arranbee Littlest Angel, rooted hair,
marked: "R & B"
10½" ....$100 - 125
1967 - 1980, all vinyl, jointed limbs,
rooted red, blond or brunette hair,
looks older
11"......................................$65 - 85
14"......................................$75 - 100
Love Me Linda (Pretty as a Picture),
1965, vinyl, large painted eyes, rooted
long straight hair, came with portrait,
advertised as "Pretty as a Picture" in
Sears and Montgomery Ward catalogs,

marked: "VOGUE DOLLS/©1965"
15"...$45 - 65
Welcome Home Baby, 1978 - 1980,
newborn, designed by Eloise Wilkin,
vinyl head and arms, painted eyes,
molded hair, cloth body, crier,
marked: "Lesney"
18"...$40 - 60
Welcome Home Baby Turns Two, 1980,
toddler, designed by Eloise Wilkin,
vinyl head, arms and legs, cloth body,
sleep eyes, rooted hair, marked:
"42260 Lesney Prod.
Corp.//1979//Vogue Doll"
22"...$90 - 125

IZANNAH WALKER

1840s - 1888, Central Falls, Rhode Island.
Made cloth stockinette dolls with pressed
mask faces, oil-painted features, applied
ears, brush-stroked or corkscrew curls,
stitched hands and feet, some with painted boots. All in good condition with
appropriate clothing.
Very good condition
17" - 19" ....$17,000 - 22,000
Fair condition
17" - 19"...................$8,000 - 12,000

WAX

1850 - 1930. Made by English, German,
French and other firms, reaching heights
of popularity circa 1875. Seldom marked,
wax dolls were poured, sometimes reinforced with plaster, and less expensive,
but more durable, than wax-over-papier-
mâché or composition dolls. English makers included Montanari, Pierotti and
Peck. German makers included Heinrich
Stier. Dolls listed are in good condition
with original clothes, or appropriately
dressed. Allow more for exceptional dolls;
much less for dolls in poor condition.
Slit-head wax, English, 1830 - 1860s,
wax-over-composition shoulder head,
hair inserted into slit on center top of
head, glass eyes may use wire closure
11" - 14"............................$525 - 650
16" - 19"............................$700 - 900
23" - 25".....................$1,100 - 1,300
Poured Wax, 1850s - 1900s
Baby, shoulder head, painted features,
glass eyes, English Montanari-type,
closed mouth, cloth body, wig or hair
inserted into wax
10" - 13" ....$925 - 1,200
18" - 25" ....$1,600 - 2,000

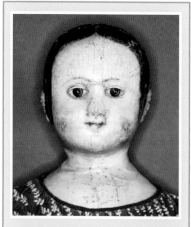

19" Izannah Walker, cloth: $18,000. **Photo courtesy of Richard Withington, Inc.**

14½" wax, slithead, English: $650. **Photo courtesy of Richard Withington, Inc.**

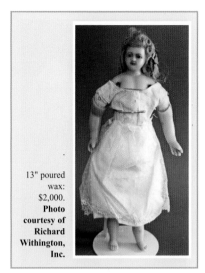

13" poured wax: $2,000. **Photo courtesy of Richard Withington, Inc.**

18" reinforced wax: $1,000. **Photo courtesy of McMasters Harris Apple Tree Doll Auctions.**

Child, shoulder head, inserted hair, glass eyes, wax limbs, cloth body

13" - 15" ....$900 - 1,100
18" - 22" ....$1,700 - 2,200
25" - 27" ....$3,000 - 4,000

Adult

Lady, elaborate costume brings high end of price range

11" - 15".....................$1,800 - 3,500
23" - 27" ....$2,200 - 4,500

15" Princess Victoria portrait doll by Pierotti, circa 1902 ....sold at auction for $3,000

Wax over Composition or Reinforced, 1860s - 1890s

Child

circa 1860 - 1890, early poured-wax shoulder head, reinforced with plaster, inserted hair, glass eyes, cloth body

10" - 12"...........................$700 - 800
14" - 16"...........................$850 - 900
20" - 22".......................$1,000 - 1,100
25" - 29" ....$1,200 - 1,400

25" socket head, glass eyes

16" - 18"......................$1,500 - 1,800

Later wax-over-composition shoulder head, open or closed mouth, glass eyes, wig, cloth body

10" - 12"..........................$250 - 300
15" - 17"..........................$350 - 400
21" - 23"..........................$525 - 675

Molded hair, wax over composition, shoulder head, glass eyes, cloth body, wooden limbs, molded shoes

13" - 15" ....$200 - 400
19" - 23" ....$450 -500

Alice in Wonderland style, molded

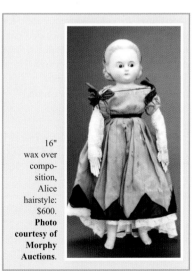

16" wax over composition, Alice hairstyle: $600. **Photo courtesy of Morphy Auctions**.

headband
16".............................$600 - 650
Lady
Wigged
12" - 15" ....$700 - 800
22" - 25" ....$900 - 1,200
Molded hair and gloves
15" - 22" ....$1,000 - 3,000
Bonnet Heads: See Bonnet-Heads
section.
Wax crèche figure, 1880 - 1910,
poured-wax Christ Child, inset hair,
glass eyes
6" ....$100 - 125
13" - 23" ....$450 - 700
Wax fashion, 1910 - 1920, wax head,
wire-armature body, by makers such as
Lafitte et Desirat and others, usually
on wooden base
11" - 14" ....$500 - 600

NORAH WELLINGS

1926 - 1960, Wellington, Shropshire, England. The Victoria Toy Works was founded by Norah Wellings and her brother Leonard. Norah had previously worked as chief designer for Chad Valley. They made cloth dolls with molded heads and bodies of velvet, velveteen, plush and felt, specializing in sailor souvenir dolls for steamship lines. The line included children, adults, blacks, ethnic and fantasy dolls.

Baby, molded face, oil-painted features, some papier-mâché covered by stockinette, stitched hip and shoulder joints
10" ....$275 - 375
15"....................................$425 - 600
22"....................................$775 - 900
Child
Painted eyes
12" - 14"...........................$400 - 475
16" - 18"...........................$500 - 550
22" - 23" ....$575 - 625
26" - 28" ....$650 - 700

9" Little Pixie People, Norah Wellings, cloth: each $100. **Photo courtesy of Richard Withington, Inc.**

Glass eyes
15" -18" ....$800 - 1,100
22" - 26" ....$1,300 - 2,000
Characters in uniform, regional dress, Pixie People, floppy limbs, painted eyes, Mounties, Sailors, Policemen, Scots, others
8" - 10"...............................$75 - 125
13" - 14".............................$175 - 225
Black or Asian
8" - 13" ....$150 - 200
16" - 18"...........................$160 - 240
Black Islander, glass eyes
13"....................................$180 - 250
16"....................................$300 - 325
Jolly Toddlers
11"....................................$150 - 220

WOODEN

Wooden dolls have been made from the earliest recorded times. During the 1600s and 1700s they became the luxury play dolls of the era. They were made commercially in England, Germany, Switzerland, Russia, United States and other countries. By the late 1700s and early 1800s, inexpensive German wooden dolls were the affordable doll of the masses and were exported worldwide.

English

William & Mary Period, 1690s - 1700, carved-wooden head, tiny multi-stroke eyebrow and eyelashes, colored cheeks, human-hair or flax wig, wooden body, fork-like carved-wooden hands, jointed wooden legs, cloth upper arms, medium to fair condition

    18" - 22" ....$30,000 - 36,000
    28", circa 1690 ....sold at
                auction for $35,112

Too few in database for reliable range
Queen Anne Period, early 1700s, dotted eyebrows, eyelashes, painted or glass eyes, no pupils, carved oval-shaped head, flat wooden back and

hips, nicely dressed, good condition

    14"..........................$15,000 - 25,000
Too few in database for reliable range
    18"..........................$30,000 - 45,000
Too few in database for reliable range
    25"..........................$36,000 - 51,000
Too few in database for reliable range
Georgian Period, 1750s - 1800, round wooden head, gesso coated, inset glass eyes, dotted eyelashes and eyebrows, human-hair or flax wig, jointed wooden body, pointed torso, medium to fair condition

    9"................................$2,500 - 3,500
    13" - 16" ....$6,000 - 9,000
    18" - 24" ....$10,000 - 11,000
1745 example, unusual style, all original, with provenance ....sold at
                auction for $91,836

1800 - 1840, gesso-coated wooden head, painted eyes, human-hair or

9" wooden, English: $3,000. **Photo courtesy of Richard Withington, Inc.**

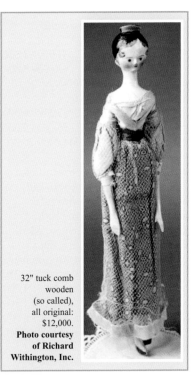

32" tuck comb wooden (so called), all original: $12,000.
Photo courtesy of Richard Withington, Inc.

Wooden

17" tuck comb wooden (so called): $3,500. **Photo courtesy of Richard Withington, Inc.**

flax wig, original clothing comes down below wooden legs

12" - 15"	$1,500 - 3,000
18" - 22"	$2,800 - 3,800

Continental European, 1700s, early 1800s, very fine details

5" - 6"	$5,000 - 6,000
12" - 14"	$6,000 - 9,000
25" - 32"	$14,000 - 20,000

German

1810 - 1850s, delicately carved painted hair style, spit curls, some with hair decorations such as so-called tuck comb, all-wooden head and body, pegged or ball-jointed limbs, wooden earrings, sideburn man, etc., allow more for exceptional original costume

4½"	$650 - 750
7" - 9"	$800 - 1,200
12" - 13"	$1,200 - 1,500
17" - 18"	$3,500 - 4,000
21"	$6,000 - 6,500

1850s - 1900

All wood with painted plain hair style, may have spit curls

1"	$100 - 125
4" - 5"	$450 - 550
6" - 8"	$600 - 800
14" - 17"	$950 - 1,500
23"	$2,000 - 2,700

Wooden shoulder head, fancy carved hair style, wooden limbs, cloth body

12"	$800 - 900
23"	$1,700 - 2,000

Bohemian, red painted torso

8" - 10"	$375 - 500
14" - 16"	$650 - 800

1900 on, turned wooden head, carved nose, painted hair, lower legs with black shoes, peg jointed

11"	$60 - 80

Bébé Tout en Bois, 1900 - 1914, all-wooden doll made by German firms such as Rudolf Schneider, Schilling and others for the French trade, child or baby, fully jointed body, glass eyes or painted, open mouth, glass eyes bring higher end of price range

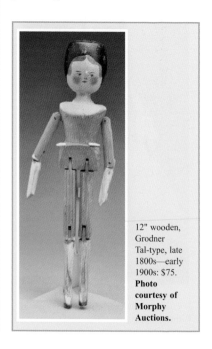

12" wooden, Grodner Tal-type, late 1800s—early 1900s: $75. **Photo courtesy of Morphy Auctions.**

Wooden

9" - 12" ....$450 - 550
15" ....$650 - 775
18" ....$775 - 875
23" ....$1,100 - 1,400

Kokeshi, 1900 on, Japan, traditional simple turned wooden dolls made for native and foreign tourist trade, allow more for unusual design or known artist

1850s - 1900
7" - 14" ....$900 - 1,000
1900 - 1930
7" - 9" ....$200 - 400
1950 to present
7" - 9" ....$35 - 90

Matryoshka, Russian nesting dolls, 1900 on, set of wooden canisters that separate in the middle, brightly painted with a glossy finish to represent adults, children, storybook or fairytale characters and animals. These come in sets usually of five or more related characters, each doll opens to reveal a smaller doll nesting inside, allow much more for unusual design or known artist.

12" Jointed Doll Co., Springfield, Vermont, wood: $1,000. **Photo courtesy of Morphy Auctions.**

Pre-1930s set
4" ....$70 - 100
7" ....$115 - 150
9" ....$175 - 230
New set
5" ....$12 - 20
7" ....$18 - 30
Political set: Gorbachev, Yeltsin
5" ....$20 - 35
7" ....$50 - 60

Swiss, 1900 on, carved-wooden dolls with dowel-jointed bodies, jointed at elbow, hips, knees, examples with elaborate hair bring higher end of values

8" - 10" ....$300 - 600
12" - 16" ....$525 - 800
18" ....$900 - 1,100

Springfield, Vermont
Cooperative Manufacturing Co., 1873 - 1874, Joel Ellis manufactured wooden dolls with pressed heads and mortise and double tenon joints, with metal hands and feet painted black or blue, painted black molded hair sometimes

8" wooden, Swiss: $550. **Photo courtesy of Richard Withington, Inc.**

5½" Peggity, Tynietoy, wood: $600. **Photo courtesy of Richard Withington, Inc.**

blond; similar-type wooden dolls were made by Jointed Doll Co. under patents by Martin, Sanders, Johnson, Mason & Taylor; a variety of head and jointing styles were used on these dolls.

Ellis, Joel (Cooperative Manufacturing Co.)
12" ....$1,100 - 1,500
15"..............................$1,700 - 2,000
Jointed Doll Co.
11½" ....$700 - 1,000
Tynietoy, 1917 on, Providence, Rhode Island, sold peg-wooden types called Peggity dolls
5"....................................$500 - 600
Ramp Walker dolls, early to mid-1900s, such as Wilson Walkies, wooden-body characters that walk down an incline
4½" ....$30 - 45
Santa, Easter bunny ....$60 - 80
Scary Ann, 1928, push lever raises hair ....sold at auction for $315
Krahmer Dolls, 1947 on, Germany, wooden heads, cloth bodies
1947 - 1960s
10" - 13"............................$200 - 450
1970 - 1980s
10" - 13"............................$100 - 150
Schoenhut: See Schoenhut section.

22" Milwaukee WPA doll, cloth: $1,200. **Photo courtesy of Morphy Auctions.**

WPA, VARIOUS PROJECTS

1935 - 1943, Federal Works Progress Administration project provided work for artisans and home workers. Some states also ran dollmaking projects under the WPA.
Milwaukee, Wisconsin project
Molded stockinette doll, cloth body, cotton-yarn hair, painted features, tab-hinged joints and hips
22" ....$900 - 1,200
Black ....$2,200 - 3,000
Flat-face cloth doll, embroidered features, cotton-yarn hair
11".................................$400 - 425
14"..................................$450 - 500
16"..................................$625 - 700
New York City project, cloth mask face
14" $250
Too few in database for reliable range
Project unknown, papier-mâché doll, wearing regional or historic costume
12" - 16" ....$200 - 300

BIBLIOGRAPHY

Anderton, Johana Gast. *Twentieth Century Dolls*. Des Moines, Illinois: Wallace Homestead Book Co., 1971.

___. *More Twentieth Century Dolls*, Volumes I & II. Des Moines, Illinois: Wallace Homestead Book Co., 1974.

___. *The Collector's Encyclopedia of Cloth Dolls*. Lombard, Illinois: Wallace Homestead Book Co., 1984.

Angione, Genevieve and Judith Whorton. *All Dolls Are Collectible*. New York: Crown Publishers, Inc., 1977.

Bullard, Helen. *Crafts and Craftsmen of the Tennessee Mountains*. Falls Church,Virginia: The Summit Press Ltd., 1976.

___. *The American Doll Artist*. Boston, Massachusetts: Charles T. Branford Co., 1965.

___. *The American Doll Artist*. Kansas City, Missouri: Athens Publishing Co., 1975.

Cieslik, Jurgen and Marianne. *German Doll Encyclopedia*. Cumberland, Maryland: Hobby House Press, 1985.

Coleman, Dorothy S., Elizabeth A. and Evelyn J. *The Collector's Encyclopedia of Dolls, Volumes I & II*. NewYork: Crown Publishers, Inc., 1968, 1986.

___. *The Collector's Book of Dolls' Clothes*. New York: Crown Publishers, Inc., 1975.

DeMillar, Suzanne and Dennis Brevik. *Arranbee Dolls*. Paducah, Kentucky: Collector Books, 2004.

Edward, Linda. *Cloth Dolls From Ancient to Modern*. Atglen, Pennsylvania: Schiffer Publishing, 1997.

Fawcett, Clara Hallard. *Dolls: A Guide for Collectors*. New York: H.L. Lindquist Publications, 1947.

___. *Dolls: A New Guide for Collectors*. Boston, Massachusetts: Charles T Branford Co., 1964.

Foulke, Jan. *Blue Book of Dolls and Values, Volumes 2-14*. Cumberland, Maryland: Hobby House Press,1976, 1978, 1980, 1982, 1984, 1986, 1987, 1989, 1991, 1993, 1995, 1997, 1999.

Gräfnitz, Christiane. *German Paper-Mache Dolls 1760 - 1860*. Germany: Verlag Puppen & Spielzeug, 1994.

Izen, Judith. *American Character Dolls*. Paducah, Kentucky: Collector Books, 2004.

___. *Collector's Guide to Ideal Dolls*. Paducah, Kentucky: Collector Books, 2005.

___ and Carol Stover. *Collector's Encyclopedia of Vogue Dolls*. Paducah, Kentucky: Collector Books, 2005.

Jacobs, Flora Gill. *Dolls' Houses in America*. New York: Charles Scribner's Sons, 1974.

___. *A History of Dolls' Houses*. New York: Charles Scribner's Sons, 1953.

Jensen, Don. *Collector's Guide to Horsman Dolls*. Paducah, Kentucky: Collector Books, 2002.

Johl, Janet Pagter. *The Fascinating Story of Dolls* (republished). Watkins Glen, New York: Century House, 1970.

___. *More About Dolls*. New York: H. L. Lundquist Publications, 1946.

___. *Still More About Dolls*. New York: H. L. Lundquist Publications, 1950.

___. *Your Dolls and Mine*. New York: H. L. Lundquist Publications, 1952.

Judd, Polly. *Cloth Dolls*. Cumberland, Maryland: Hobby House Press,1990.

___. and Pam. *Americas, Australia & Pacific Islands Costumed Dolls*. Grantsville, Maryland: Hobby House Press, 1997.

King, Constance Eileen. *The Collector's History of Dolls*. New York: Bonanza Books, 1981.

Bibliography

Lavitt, Wendy. *American Folk Dolls*. New York: Alfred A. Knopf, Inc., 1982.

Lechler, Doris Anderson. *Bleuette - Her Gautier-Languereau Ads and Catalogues of Fashion 1905 - 1960*. Self published.

___. *Bleuette - Her Faces, Fashions and Family*. Self published.

McFadden, Sybill. *Fawn Zeller's Porcelain Dollmaking Techniques*. Cumberland, Maryland: Hobby House Press, 1984.

McGonagle, Dorothy. *A Celebration of American Dolls*. Grantsville, Maryland: Hobby House Press, 1997.

Merrill, Madeline Osborne. *The Art of Dolls*. Cumberland, Maryland: Hobby House Press, 1985.

Mertz, Ursula. *Collector's Encyclopedia of Composition Dolls*. Paducah, Kentucky: Collector Books, 1999.

___. *Collector's Encyclopedia of Composition Dolls Vol. II*. Paducah, Kentucky: Collector Books, 2004.

Mills, Winifred and Louise Dunn. *The Story of Old Dolls and How to Make New Ones*. New York: Doubleday, Doran & Co., Inc., 1940.

Patino, Estelle. *American Rag Dolls*. Paducah, Kentucky: Collector Books, 1988.

Pardee, Elaine and Jackie Robertson. *Encyclopedia of Bisque Nancy Ann Storybook Dolls*. Paducah, Kentucky: Collector Books, 2003.

Robertson, Julie Pelletier. *Celluloid Dolls, Toys & Playthings*. Paducah, Kentucky: Collector Books, 2006.

Revi, Albert Christian. *Spinning Wheel's Complete Book of Dolls*. New York: Galahad Books, 1975.

Richter, Lydia. *Treasury of German Dolls*. Tucson, Arizona: HP Books, 1984.

___. *The Beloved Käthe Kruse Dolls*. Cumberland, Maryland: Hobby House Press, 1983.

Schiffer, Nancy. *Indian Dolls*. Atglen, Pennsylvania: Schiffer Publishing Ltd., 1997.

Singleton, Esther. *Dolls*. New York: Payson & Clark Ltd., 1927.

St. George, Eleanor. *The Dolls of Yesterday*. New York and London: Charles Scribner's Sons, 1948.

___. *Dolls of Three Centuries*. New York and London: Charles Scribner's Sons, 1951.

Smith, Patricia. *Antique Collector's Dolls Vol. 2*. Paducah, Kentucky: Collector Books, 1976.

Sorenson, Lewis. *Lewis Sorensen's Doll Scrapbook*. Alhambra, California: Thor Publications, 1976.

Sutton, Sydney Ann. *Scouting Dolls Through the Years*. Paducah, Kentucky: Collector Books, 2003.

Theirault, Florence. *Catalog Reprint Series*. Annapolis, Maryland: Gold Horse Publishing, 1998.

Trotter, Gillian. *Norah Wellings Cloth Dolls and Soft Toys*. Grantsville, Maryland: Hobby House Press, 2003.

Van Patton, Joan and Linda Lau. *Nippon Dolls & Playthings*. Paducah, Kentucky: Collector Books, 2001.

Whitton, Blair. *Bliss Toys and Dollhouses*. New York: Dover Publications.

COLLECTOR'S RESOURCES

Antique Doll Dealers

Ann Lloyd Antique Dolls
5632 S. Deer Run Rd.
Doylestown, PA 18902
215-794-8164
Website: www.rubylane.com/shops/anntiquedolls

American Beauty Dolls
Nancy Stronczek
26 Bouker St.
Greenfield, MA 01301
413-774-3260
E-mail: njs@crocker.com
Website: www.rubylane.com/shops/americanbeautydolls

Aunt Mary's Antique Dolls
P.O. Box 198
Hawleyville, CT 06440
203-426-9557
E-mail: mfurse@earthlink.net
Website: www.rubylane.com/shops/auntmarysantiquedolls

Charlotte's Web Vintage Dolls and Collectibles
Charlotte Adams-Scott
Bardstown, KY 40004
502-489-4581
Website: http://www.rubylane.com/shop/charlottewebcollectible

Connectibles
Maida Webster
47 Buttery Rd.
New Canaan, CT 06840
203-253-1162
Websites: www.connectibles.net, www.buyconnectibles.com

Cybermogul Dolls
Marie Witherill
Statesville, NC 28677
E-mail: cybermogul@Rd.runner.com
Website: www.rubylane.com/shops/cybermogul

Decades of Dolls
Rae-Ellen Koenig
848 Dunkels Church Rd.
Kutztown, PA 19530-8821
610- 894-9882
Website:
http://www.rubylane.com/ni/shop/decadesofdolls

Dollsantique
Patricia Vaillancourt
201 Colorado Ave. #3
Stuart, FL 34994
561-512-7193
Website:www.dollsantique.com

Dolls and Lace
P.O. Box 743
Lehi, UT 84043 USA
E-mail: dollsandlace@hotmail.com
Website: www.dollsandlace.com

Dollyology Vintage Dolls
Kate Eaton
15516 Sunken Bridge Rd.
Grass Valley, CA 95949
E-mail:dollyology@gmail.com
Website:www.rubylane.com/shops/dollyologyvintagedolls

Emmie's Antique Doll Castle
Robbin Wilson
400 W. 32nd Ct.
Sand Springs, OK 74063
918-241-0269
Website: www.rubylane.com/shops/emmiesgirl

Fourty Fifty Sixty
Ben Cassara/Joe Bucchi
Rutherford, NJ 07070
Websites: www.fourtyfiftysixty.com, www.rubylane.com/shops/fourtyfiftysixty

Glenda Antique Dolls & Collectables
Gray's Antique Market,1-7 Davies Mews
London W1K 5AB, England
020 8367 2441(Mobile telephone)07970 722750
E-mail: glenda@glenda-antiquedolls.co.uk
Website: www.glenda-antiquedolls.co.uk

Gloria's Antique Dolls
Gloria & Mike Duddlesten
E-mail: dollstx@cableone.net
Website: www.rubylane.com/shop/dollstx

Hatton's Gallery of Dolls
E-mail:info@hattonsgallery.com
Website: www.hattonsgallery.com

Joan & Lynette Antique Dolls and Accessories
6551 Carrollton Ave.
Indianapolis, IN 46220
Website:www.rubylane.com/shops/joan-lynetteantiquedolls

Collector's Resources

Joy's Antique Dolls
Joy Frizzell
P. O. Box 30
Westcliffe, CO 81252-0030
719-783-4500
Website: www.joysantiquedolls.com

Linda Kellermann
11013 Treyburn
Dr. Glen Allen, VA 23059
E-mail: lindas-antiques@erols.com

Doris Lechler
949 E. Cooke Rd.
Columbus, OH 43224
614-261-6659
E-mail: dorislechler@aol.com

Memories of Things Past
Elizabeth Schmahl
Website: www.rubylane.com/shops/memoriesofthingspastantiques

Minton's Doll and Curiosity Shop
Sherry Minton
4035 N. Orange Blossom Trail
Orlando, FL 32804
407-293-3164
Website: http://www.rubylane.com/shop/mintonsdollandcuriosityshop

Museum Doll Shop
104 Van Zandt Ave.
Newport, RI 02840
401-847-6866

Joy Macielle
E-mail: joy@qualityvintagedollpatterns.com
Website: qualityvintagedollpatterns.com

My Dear Dolly
P.O. Box 303
Sparta, NJ 07871
E-mail: mydeardollypat@yahoo.com
Website: mydeardolly.com

My Dolly Dearest
P.O. Box 909
8 S Village Circle
Adamstown, PA 19501
717-484-1137
E-mail: sidneyjeffrey@mydollydearest.com

N.A.D.D.A.
National Antique Doll Dealers Association
Website: www.nadda.org

Never Enough Dollars
Jean Grout
1070 Laurel Rd. E. #298
Nokomis, FL 34275
Website: http://www.rubylane.com/shop/neverenoughdollers

Sharing My Dolls & Stuff
Helen Welsh
799 Bent Creek Dr.
Lititz, PA 17543
E-mail: helen1005@aol.com
Website: www.rubylane.com/shops/sharingmydollsnstuff

Sidney's Second Childhood
Sidney Bennett
1116 Mistletoe Circle
Hermitage, TN 37076
615- 883-3637
Website:http://www.rubylane.com/shop/sidneyssecondchildhood

Trish's Treasures Antique Dolls
Website: www.rubylane.com/shops/antiquedolls

The Doll Works
Judith Armitstead
P.O. Box 195
Lynnfield, MA 01940
Website: www.TheDollWorks.net

Turn of the Century Antiques
1475 South Broadway
Denver, CO 80210
303-702-8700
Website: www.turnofthecenturyantiques.com

Usefulcollectibles
Marsha Anderson
Liberty, MO
816-781-5598

Auction Houses

Alderfer Auction Company, Inc.
501 Fairgrounds Rd.
Hatfield,PA 19440
215-393-3000
Fax: 215-368-9055
Website: www.alderferauction.com

eBayAuction Site
Website: www.ebay.com

Collector's Resources

James D. Julia, Inc.
203 Skowhegan Rd
Fairfield, ME 04937
207-453-7125
Website:www.jamesjuliaauctions.com

McMasters Harris Apple Tree Doll Auctions
Ohio & Kansas City
800-842-3526
E-mail: mark@mcmastersharris.com
Website:www.mcmastersharris.com

Morphy Auctions
2000 N. Reading Rd.
Denver, PA 17517
717-335-3435
Website: 111.morphyauctions.com

Skinner, Inc.
274 Cedar Hill St.
Marlborough, MA 01752
508-970-3232
Website: www.skinnerinc.com

Sweetbriar Auctions
P.O. Box 37
Earleville, MD 21919
410-275-2094
E-mail: sweetbriar@live.com
Website: www.sweetbriarauctions.com

Withington Auctions Inc.
17 Atwood Rd.
Hillsborough, NH 03244
603-478-3232
E-mail:withington@conknet.com
Website: www.withingtonauction.com

Doll Manufacturers

Adora Original Doll®
300 Columbus Circle
Edison, NJ 08837
800-779-5335
E-mail: info@charismabrands.com
Website: www.adoradoll.com

Alexander Doll Company, Inc.
615 West 131stSt.
New York, NY 10027
Gale Jarvis, President
212-283-5900
Fax: 212-283-4901
E-mail: ma@alexdoll.com
website: www.madamealexander.com

American Girl
8400 Fairway Place
Or
P. O. Box 620497
Middleton, WI 53562-0497
800-360-1861 US & Canada
800-831-5210 outside US & Canada
Website: www.americangirl.com

Bella! Productions
Christina Bougas, Artistic Director
Bella! Studios
16295 Highway 175
Cobb, CA 95426
Mailing address: P.O. Box 1166
Cobb, CA 95426-1166
626-359-9097
E-mail: info@cleabella.com
Website: www.cleabella.com

Berdine Creedy Originals, Inc.
5015 NW 71 Place
Gainesville, FL 32653
352-336-2510
Fax: 352-336-7282
E-mail: berdine@berdinecreedy.com
Website: www.berdinecreedy.com

Charisma Brands, LLC
23482 Peralta Dr., Ste. A
Laguna Hills, CA 92653
949-587-9400; 800-779-5335
Fax: 949-587-9300
Website: www.charismabrands.com

D.A.E. Originals
David Escobedo & Brian Schafer
835 N. 94th Place
Mesa, AZ 85207-5280
480-380-3119
E-mail: dae@daeoriginals.com
Website: www.daeoriginals.com

Heidi Plusczok Puppen Design
Heidi Plusczok
Erlenweg 5
D-61130 Nidderau, Germany
+49-6187-23222
Fax: +49-6187-24608
E-mail: plusdolls@aol.com
Website: www.heidiplusczok.com

Horsman Ltd.
Kenneth Young
3 Park Place, Ste. 1-118
Glen Head, NY 11545
516-504-0387

Collector's Resources

Fax: 516-504-0397
E-mail: info@horsmanltd.com
Website: www.horsmanltd.com

Kish & Company
Helen & Tamas Kish
1800 West 33rd Ave.
Denver, CO 80211
303-972-0053
Fax: 303-932-2405
Website: www.kishandcompany.com

Käthe Kruse Puppen GmbH
Andrea-Kathrin Christenson, CEO
86609 Donauwörth
Alte Augsburger Str. 9, Germany
011-49-09-06-7-06-78-0
Fax: 011-49-09-06-78-70
E-mail: familie@kaethe-kruse.de
Website: www.kaethekrusepuppe.de

The Lawton Doll Company
Wendy & Keith Lawton
P.O. Box 1227
Hillmar, CA 95324
209-632-3655
Fax: 209-632-6788
E-mail: info@lawtondolls.com
Website: www.lawtondolls.com

Middleton Doll Company, Inc.
615 West 131st St.
New York, NY 10027
800-242-8450; 301-895-4793
Website: www.leemiddleton.com; www.mycollection.middleton-doll.com

Nancy Ann Storybook Dolls, Inc.
Claudette Buehler and Delene Budd
P. O. Box 5072
El Dorado Hills, CA 95762
916-934-0726
Website:www.nancyannstorybookdolls.com

Terri Lee Associates
212 Kinzie #5
Chicago, IL 60654
888-837-7450; 312-222-0704
E-mail: info@terrilee.com
Website: www.terrilee.com

Tonner Doll Company
Robert Tonner, CEO
P.O. Box 4410
Kingston, NY 12402
845-339-9537

Fax: 845-339-1259
Website: www.tonnerdoll.com

Vogue Doll Company, Inc.
Linda Smith, President
P.O. Box 756
Oakdale, CA 95361-0756
209-848-0300
Fax: 209-848-4423
E-mail: info@voguedoll.com
Website: www.voguedolls.com

Artist Organizations

NIADA (National Institute of American Doll Artists)
Website: www.niada.org

ODACA (Original Doll Artist Council of America)
Website: www.odaca.org

O.P.D.A.G.(The Original Paper Doll Artists Guild)
Jenny Taliadoros
P. O. Box 14
Kingfield, ME 04947
207-265-2500; 800-290-2928
Website:www.opdag.com

Collector Clubs & Newsletters

The Review (official publication of the Madame Alexander Doll Club)
Manhattan Station
P. O. Box 2739
New York, NY 10027-9998
212-368-1047
E-mail: info@madc.org
Website: www.madc.org
Quarterly newsletter

Chérie Amies de Bleuette Revue
Linda Justice, Editor
4143 Mercier
Kansas City, MO 64111
E-mail: lindasruffles@yahoo.com
Quarterly publication

Chatty Cathy Collectors Club
Melissa Gilkey Mince, Editor
E-mail: ChattynMe@aol.com
Website: www.ttinet.com/chattycathy/

Doll Collecting
Denise Van Patten
E-mail: denise@dollymaker.com
http://collectdolls.about.com
Weekly newsletter

Collector's Resources

Doll Costumer's Guild™
Pat Gosh, Editor
P O Box 247
New Harmony, IN 47631
812-682-3802
Fax: 812-682-3815
E-mail: patgosh@aol.com
Website: www.dollcostumersguild.com
Quarterly publication

Dionne Quintuplet Collectors Too Newsletter
Leonard Belsher & Dee Dee Backus, Editors
P. O. Box 468
Shawville, Quebec J0X 2Y0 Canada
819-647-1965
E-mail: quintly2000@yahoo.ca
Quarterly newsletter

Greetings
Louise Leek
10158 Land Catherine
Streetsboro, OH 44141
Semi-annual, covers paper dolls

Friends of Hitty Newsletter
Virginia Ann Heyerdahl, Editor
2704 Belleview Ave.
Cheverly, MD 20785-3006
301-772-1555
Fax: 301-772-6241
E-mail:heronconsults@aol.com
Four issues per subscription; irregular frequency

*T.H.E.L.M.A (The Hoyer Enthusiastic Ladies Mail
Association*--a by-mail doll group celebrating past
and present Mary Hoyer dolls via newsletter
format)
Thelma R. Bernard, Founder, Editor & Publisher
P. O. Box 42604
Las Vegas, NV 89114-0604
E-mail: starrlady@webtv.net
Quarterly newsletter

Ideal Collectors' Newsletter
Judith Izen, Editor
P.O. Box 623
Lexington, MA 02173
E-mail: Jizen@rcn.com
Website: www.dollsofourchildhood.com
Quarterly newsletter

Kish Collectors Society
Bi-annual or tri-annual newsletter
See Doll Manufacturers: Kish & Company

*Doll One: The Newsletter for the Käthe Kruse
Family*
Tri-annual newsletter
See Doll Manufacturers: Käthe Kruse Puppen
GmbH

*Modern Doll, Inc. (Modern Doll Collectors
Convention)*
Patsy Moyer, President
P. O. Box 311
Deming, NM 88031-0311
763-634-2614
E-mail: moddoll@yahoo.com
Website:www. moderndollcollectors.com
registrar@moderndollcollectors.com

Now & Then
Arlene Del Fava
67-40 Yellowstone Blvd.
Forest Hills, NY 11375
Tri-annual, covers paper dolls

The Paper Doll Circle
Lorna Currie Thomopolous
28 Ferndown Gardens
Cobham, KT11 2BH
Surrey, England
E-mail: Forever19@live.co.uk
Website: www.paperdollcircle.webs.com/
Triannual newsletter

Sasha Friends
Sharon Sams, Editor & Publisher
304 12th Ave. NW
Altoona, IA 500097
Chris Kading, Editor & Publisher
P.O. Box 104
Ames, IA 50010
E-mail: Sharon_sams_2000@yahoo.com;kad-
ing@att.net
Quarterly newsletter

Australian Shirley Temple Collectors News
Victoria Horne, Editor
55 Botanic Dr.
Glen Waverly
Victoria, 3150, Australia
03 9561 0238
Quarterly newsletter

Shirley Temple Collectors by the Sea
P.O. Box 6203
Oxnard, CA 93031
317-300-1339
E-mail: info@shirleytempledollclub.com
Monthly newsletter

Collector's Resources

Tonner Doll Collectors Club
Quarterly newsletter
See Doll Manufacturers: Tonner Doll Company

United Federation of Doll Clubs, Inc.
10900 North Pomona Ave.
Kansas City, MO 64153
816-891-7040
Fax: 816-891-8360
E-mail: ufdcinfo@ufdc.org
Website: www.ufdc.org

Publications

Antique Doll Collector
Keith Kaonis, Advertising & Creative Director
Donna Kaonis, Editor-in-Chief
Puffin Company, LLC
P.O. Box 239
Northport, NY 11768
888-800-2588
631-261-4100
Fax: 631-261-9684
E-mail: Antiquedoll@gmail.com
Website: www.antiquedollcollector.com
Monthly magazine

Collectors United
Gary Green, Publisher
P.O. Box 1160
Chatsworth, GA 30705
706-695-8242
Fax: 706-695-0770
E-mail: diang@collectorsunited.com
Website: www.collectorsunited.com
Monthly newspaper

Contemporary Doll Collector
Ruth Keessen, Publisher & Editor
2145 W. Sherman Blvd
Muskegon, MI 49441
231-755-2000
Subscription information: 800-458-8237
Fax: 231-755-1003
Website:www.scottpublications.com; www.contemporarydollcollector.com
Bi-monthly magazine

Doll Castle News
Barry Mueller, Publisher
Dorita M. Mortensen, Editor
P.O. Box 601
Broadway, NJ 08808
908-689-4236; 800-572-6607
E-mail:editor@dollcastlemagazine.com
E-mail :info@dollcastlemagazine.com

Website: www.dollcastlemagazine.com
Bi-monthly magazine

Doll News (official publication of the United Federation of Doll Clubs, Inc.)
See Collector Clubs and Newsletters:
United Federation of Doll Clubs
Quarterly magazine

Dolls
Carrie Ferg, Publisher
Jones Publishing, Inc.
N7528 Aanstad Rd, P. O. Box 5000
Iola, WI 54945-5000
715-445-5000; 800-331-0038
Fax: 715-445-4053
E-mail: jonespub@jonespublishing.com
Website: www.jonespublishing.com
Monthly magazine

Fashion Doll Quarterly
Pat Henry, Publisher
299 Eastern Parkway
Germantown, NY 12526
E-mail: fdqmag@mac.com
Website: www.fashiondollquarterly.net
212-961-0662
Quarterly magazine

Paper Doll Review
Jenny Taliadoros
P. O. Box 14
Kingfield, ME 04947
Website: www.paperdollreview.com
Quarterly publication

Paper Doll Pal
Jim Faraone
19109 Silcott Springs Rd.
Purcellville, VA 20132
540-338-3621
E-mail: jimfaraone@erols.com
Website:www.erols.com/jimfaraone
Quarterly publication

Museums

Arizona

Arizona Doll and Toy Museum
Inez McCrary, Director & Curator
602 E Adams St., Phoenix, AZ
602-253-9337
Website: www.artcom.com/museums/nv/af/85004-23.htm
Hours: Tue. - Sat.: 10 - 4; Sun.: 12 - 4.

Collector's Resources

Colorado

Denver Museum of Miniatures, Dolls & Toys
Wendy Littlepage, Director
1880 Gaylord St.
Denver, CO 80206
303-322-1053
Fax: 303-322-3407
E-mail: comments@dmmdt.org
Website: www.dmmdt.org
Hours: Wed. - Sat.: 10 - 4; Sun.: 1 - 4.
Closed holidays

Louisiana

The Enchanted Mansion, A Doll Museum
190 Lee Dr.
Baton Rouge, LA 70808-4953
Mailing address: 172 Lee Dr., Ste.3
Baton Rouge, LA 70808
225-769-0005
Fax: 225-766-6822
E-mail: temansion@tem.brcoxmail.com
Website: www.Enchantedmansion.org
Hours: Mon., Wed. - Sat.: 10 - 5.

The Lois Loftin Doll Museum
120 South Washington Ave.
DeRidder, LA 70634
337-463-6217
E-mail: w1bg@beau.org
Website: www.library.beau.org/museum/doll.html-beau.lib.la.us/doll
Hours: Tues.- Sat.: 10 - 4.

Missouri

U.F.D.C.
10900 N. Pomona Avenue
Kansas City, MO 64153
816-891-7040
Fax: 816-891-8360
Website: www.ufdc.org
Hours: 10 - 4; Closed holidays

New York

Museum of the City of New York
1220 Fifth Avenue @ 103rd St.
New York, NY 10029
212-534-1672
Fax: 212-423-0758
E-mail: info@mcny.org
Website: www.mcny.org
Hours: Open daily:10 - 6

Margaret Woodbury Strong Museum
1 Manhattan Square
Rochester, NY 14607
585-263-2700
Websites: thestrong.org; museumofplay.org
Hours: Mon.-Thurs.:10-5; Fri.-Sat.: 10-8; Sun.: 12-5

New Jersey

Princeton Doll and Toy Museum
8 Somerset St.
Hopewell, NJ 08525
609-333-8600
Website: www.princetondollandtoy.org
Hours: Mon., Fri. & Sat.:10 - 5

Ohio

Mid Ohio Historical Museum Doll & Toy Museum
700 Winchester Pike
Canal Winchester, OH
Website: www.dollmuseumohio.org
614-837-5573
Hours: April-Dec., Wed. - Sat.: 11 - 4:30

The Children's Toy & Doll Museum:
206 Gilman St.
Marietta, OH 4575
740-373-5900
E-mails: info@toyanddollmuseum.com
djdekern@suddenlink.net
Website: www.toyanddollmuseum.com
Hours: May-Oct., Sat. Sun.: 1 - 4 (or by appointment)

Pennsylvania

The Philadelphia Doll Museum
Barbara Whiteman, Director
2253 North Broad St.
Philadelphia, PA 19132
215-787 - 0220 Fax: 215-787-0226
E-mail: bwhiteman@philadollmuseum.com
Website: philadollmuseum.com/
Hours: Thurs. - Sat.: 10 - 4: Sun.:12 - 4

Texas

Museum of American Architecture & Decorative Arts
Houston Baptist University
7502 Fronden Rd.
Houston, TX 77074
281-649-3000
Website: www.hbu.edu/hbu/MAADA_Dolls_in_
Ancient_Times.asp?SnID=1408308141

Collector's Resources

Vermont

Shelburne Museum
6000 Shelburne Rd., P.O. Box 10
Shelburne, VT 05482
802-985-3346
Fax: 802-985-2331
E-mail: info@Shelburnemuseum.org
Website: www.shelburnemuseum.org
Hours: May 13-Oct.28, Mon. - Sat.: 10-5; Sun.: 12-5
(Additional summer hours)

Wisconsin

La Crosse Doll Museum
1213 1/2 Caledonia St.
La Crosse, WI 54603-2514
Website:rivverRd.s.com/states/wisc/wi10/attractions
608-785-0020
Hours: Mon. - Sat.: 10 - 5;Sun.: 11 - 4:30

The Fennimore Doll & Toy Museum and Gift Shoppe
1135 6th St.
Fennimore, WI 53809
608-822-4100
Website:www.dollandtoymuseum.com; www.fen-
nimore.com
Hours: May - Oct,Mon.- Sat.:10-4

SYMBOL INDEX

LETTER INDEX

308

MOLD INDEX

Mold Index

310

Mold Index

311

Mold Index

Mold Index

Mold Index

Mold Index

Mold Index

MARKS INDEX

Alabama Baby

Albama Indestructible Dolls Marks:
"MRS. S.S. SMITH//MANUFACTURER AND
DEALER IN//THE ALABAMA
INDESTRUCTIBLE DOLL//ROANOKE, ALA.//
PATENTED//SEPT. 26, 1905."

Henri Alexandre

Alt, Beck, & Gottschalck

Arranbee Doll Company

ARRANBEE//DOLL
Co. or R & B

Max Oscar Arnold

Art Fabric Mills

Art Fabric Mills Marks:
'ART FABRIC MILLS, NY,
PAT. FEB. 13TH, 1900" on
shoe or bottom of foot

Georgene Averill

Tag on original outfit reads:
"BONNIE BABE COPYRIGHTED
BY GEORGENE AVERILL MADE
BY K AND K TOY CO."

COPR GEORGENE AVERILL
1005/3652 GERMANY

Bä hr & Pröschild

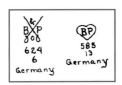

Marks Index

Barbie®

1659 - 1962
BARBIE™
PATS. PEND.
©MCMLVIII
BY//MATTEL, INC.

1963 - 1968
MIDGE™©1962
Barbie®/©1958
BY//MATTEL, INC.

1964 - 1966
©1958//MATTEL, IN.
U.S. PATENTED
U.S. PAT. PEND.

1966 - 1969
©1966//MATTEL, INC.
U.S. PATENTED//
U.S. PAT. PEND//
MADE IN JAPAN

E. Barrois

E 3 B
E. 8 DEPOSE B.

C.M. Bergmann

```
C.M.B
SIMON & HALBIG
Eleonore
```

Bru

Fashion-Type Mark:
Marked "A" through "M," "11" to "28," indicating size numbers only

Bru Jne Marks:
"BRU JNE," with size number on head, kid over wood body marked with rectangular paper label.

Bru Jne R. Marks:
"BRU JNE FL" with size number on head, body stamped in red, "Bébé Bru," and size number.

Bebe Brevete Marks:
"Bébé Breveté"
Head marked with size number only; kid body may have paper Bébé Breveté label.

Bye-Lo Baby

```
© 1923 by
Grace S. Putnam
MADE IN GERMANY
7372 145
```

Catterfelder Puppenfabrik

C. P.
208/34 S
Deponiert

1100
Catterfelder Puppenfabrik
2

Century Doll Company

CENTURY DOLL C°.
Kestner Germany

Chuckles mark on back:
'CHUCKLES//A
CENTURY DOLL"

Chase Doll Company

"CHASE STOCKINET DOLL"
on left leg or under left arm.
Paper label, if there, reads
"CHASE//HOSPITAL DOLL//
TRADE MARK//PAWTUCKET,
RI//MADE IN U.S.A."

M. J. C.
Stockinet Doll
Patent Applied For

Chase doll mark,
1889 - 1894

PAWTUCKET, R.I.

Chase doll mark,
1908 - 1945

Columbian

"COLUMBIAN DOLL,
EMMA E. ADAMS,
OSWEGO, NY"

Marks Index

Danel & Cie

E. (Size number) D. on head,
Eiffel Tower "PARIS BEBE"
on body; shoes with "PARIS
BEBE" in star.

Cuno & Otto Dressel

Heubach•Köppelsdorf
Jutta-Baby
Dressel
Germany
1922
10

E.D.

EDEN BEBE
PARIS

Eegee

Trademark, EEGEE,
or circle with the words,
'TRADEMARK//EEGEE//
Dolls//MADE IN USE'

Later changed to just
initials, E.G.

Effanbee

Some marked on shoulder
plate, "EFFANBEE//BABY
DAINTY"
or "EFFANBEE//DOLLS//
WALK, TALK, SLEEP"
in oval

Fulper Pottery Company

Marks Index

Gans & Seyfarth Puppenbabrik

François Gaultier

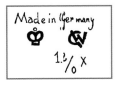

Gesland

E. GESLAND
B^{TE} S. G. D. G.
PARIS

Ruth Gibbs

RG on back shoulder blade
Box Labeled:
"GODEY LITTLE LADY DOLLS"

Gladdie

Wm. and F. & W. Goebel

Ludwig Greiner

**GREINER'S
PATENT HEADS.
No. 0.
Pat. March 30th, '58.**

Marks Index

Gund

"A Gund Product, A Toy of Quality and Distinction."

From World War II on: Stylized "G" with rabbit ears and whiskers.

Mid 1960s - 1987: Bear's head above the letter "U."

From 1987 on: "GUND."

Heinrich Handwerck

HANDWERCK
5
Germany

Max Handwerck

Max Handwerk
Bebe Elite
286/3
Germany

283/28.5
MAJC.
HANDWERCK
GERMANY.
2 1/4

Carl Hartman

Globe Baby
DEP
Germany
C 3 H

Marks Index

Karl Hartman

Hasbro

1964 - 1965
*Marked on right
lower back:*
*G.I. Joe TM//COPYRIGHT 1964//
BY HASBRO //PATENT PENDING//
MADE IN U.S.A.//GIJoe"*

1967
Slight change in marking:
*COPYRIGHT 1964//BY HASBRO
*//PATENT PENDING//MADE IN
U.S.A.//GIJoe"*
*This mark appears on all four
armed service branches, excluding
the black action figures.*

Hertel, Schwab & Company

Ernst Heubach

Gebrüder Heubach

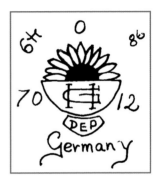

E.I. Horsman

"E.I.H.//CO."
and "CAN'T
BREAK'EM"

Marks Index

Mary Hoyer Doll Manufacturing Company

"THE MARY HOYER
DOLL" or
'ORIGINAL MARY
HOYER DOLL"

Adolph Hülss

Ideal Novelty and Toy Company

"IDEAL" (in a diamond), "US
of A: IDEAL NOVELTY," and
"TOY CO. BROOKLYN, NEW
YORK," and others

Jumeau

E.J. Bébé
1881 - 86
6
E.J.

Jumeau, early EJ mark
1881 - 1883

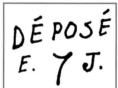

Jumeau, EJ Déposé mark
1883 - 1886

DÉPOSÉ
TETE JUMEAU
B^{TE}   SGDG
6

Jumeau, mark used on body
after 1887

JUMEAU
MEDAILLE D'OR
PARIS

Tété Jumeau mark

Marks Index

Kamkins

Heart-shaped sticker:
'KAMKINS//ADOLLY MADE
TO LOVE//
PATENTED//FROMT//L.R.
KAMPES//STUDIOS//
ATLANTIC CITY//N.I."

Kämmer & Reinhardt

J.D. Kestner

Kewpie

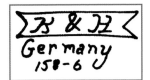

Kley & Hahn

C.F. Kling & Company

Marks Index

Gebrüder Knoch

Lanternier

König & Wernicke

Lenci

Richard Krueger

"KRUEGER NY//REG. U.S.
PAT. OFF/
/MADE IN U.S.A." on body
or clothing seam

A.G. Limbach

Käthe Kruse

Gebrüder Kuhnlenz

Marks Index

Armand Marseille

Armand Marseille
Germany
390
A. 4. M.

Queen Louise
Germany
7.

Made in Germany
Florodora
A 5 M

May Freres Cie

On head:
MASCOTTE
On body:
Bebe Mascotte Paris
Child marked:
Mascotte on head

Morimura Brothers

Mark for Morimura Brothers,
Japan 1915 on

Gebrüder Ohlhaver

Petite et Dumontier

P 3 D

Rabery & Delphieu

Mark: R. 3. D

Theodor Recknagel

Marks Index

Rohmer

Bruno Schmidt

Franz Schmidt

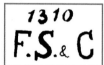

Schmitt & Fils

Shield on back: "SCH" in
shield on bottom of
flat-cut derriere

Schoenau & Hoffmeister

A. Schoenhut & Company

Marks Index

Schuetzmeister & Quendt

S.F.B.J.

Shirley Temple

Shirley Temple//
IDEAL Nov. & TOY on
back of head and
SHIRLEY TEMPLE on
body. Some marked
only on head and
with a size.

Simon & Halbig

1079
HALBIG
S&H
Germany

S&H. 1249
DEP
Germany
SANTA

Germany
S'H 13-1010 DEP.

Margarete Steiff

Button in ear

Hermann Steiner

Made in
Germany
HermSteiner
$\frac{18}{0}$

Marks Index

Swaine & Company

A. Thuillier

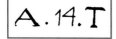

Unis France

Unis France mark

Unis France diamond
mark

Louis Wolfe & Company

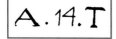

INDEX

Index

Index

Index

Index

Index

Index

Index

Index

Index

Index

Index

Index

Index

Index

Index

Index

Index

Index

Index

Index

About the Author

Linda Edward has been collecting and dealing in antique, vintage and contemporary dolls since 1976. From 1987 through 2005, she exhibited a collection of more than 1,800 dolls at The Doll Museum in Newport, Rhode Island, where she lives with her husband, Al. She has also mounted doll exhibits throughout Rhode Island, and loaned dolls to the Rhode Island Historical Society for their 1989 exhibit on Martha Chase.

A lover of doll research, she has contributed dozens of articles to publications including *Doll News, Antique Doll Collector, Doll Reader, Contemporary Doll Collector* and *Dolls* and served as editor of *Doll News*, the official magazine of the United Federation of Doll Clubs (UFDC). An active member of the Ida Lewis Doll Club in Region 14, she is also a past director of Region 14 and has been a certified UFDC competitive-exhibit judge since 1998. In 2006 she received the UFDC Award of Excellence for Educational Endeavors Through Dolls and in 2009 she received the UFDC Award of Excellence for Contributions to *Doll News*. She is a past president of Doll Collectors of America and is currently serving as 1st Vice-President of UFDC.

Author of *Cloth Dolls: Ancient to Modern*, Ms. Edward took over the authorship of *Doll Values* with the ninth edition, which was published in 2007.

The History of *Doll Values*

Reverie Publishing Company is pleased to become the publisher of this long-standing price guide, now in its twelfth edition. Originally titled *Doll Values: Antique to Modern*, it was published by Collector Books from 1997 until 2011. The first seven editions of the book were authored by Patsy Moyer and published annually; Carol Stover and Barbara DeFeo collaborated on the eighth edition. Linda Edward has been the author of all subsequent editions.